# The world universities' response to COVID-19: remote online language teaching

Edited by Nebojša Radić, Anastasia Atabekova, Maria Freddi, and Josef Schmied

Published by Research-publishing.net, a not-for-profit association
Contact: info@research-publishing.net

© 2021 by Editors (collective work)
© 2021 by Authors (individual work)

The world universities' response to COVID-19: remote online language teaching
Edited by Nebojša Radić, Anastasia Atabekova, Maria Freddi, and Josef Schmied

**Publication date**: 2021/05/24

**Rights**: the whole volume is published under the Attribution-NonCommercial-NoDerivatives International (CC BY-NC-ND) licence; **individual articles may have a different licence**. Under the CC BY-NC-ND licence, the volume is freely available online (https://doi.org/10.14705/rpnet.2021.52.9782490057924) for anybody to read, download, copy, and redistribute provided that the author(s), editorial team, and publisher are properly cited. Commercial use and derivative works are, however, not permitted.

**Disclaimer**: Research-publishing.net does not take any responsibility for the content of the pages written by the authors of this book. The authors have recognised that the work described was not published before, or that it was not under consideration for publication elsewhere. While the information in this book is believed to be true and accurate on the date of its going to press, neither the editorial team nor the publisher can accept any legal responsibility for any errors or omissions. The publisher makes no warranty, expressed or implied, with respect to the material contained herein. While Research-publishing.net is committed to publishing works of integrity, the words are the authors' alone.

**Trademark notice**: product or corporate names may be trademarks or registered trademarks, and are used only for identification and explanation without intent to infringe.

**Copyrighted material**: every effort has been made by the editorial team to trace copyright holders and to obtain their permission for the use of copyrighted material in this book. In the event of errors or omissions, please notify the publisher of any corrections that will need to be incorporated in future editions of this book.

Typeset by Research-publishing.net

Cover illustration by © 2021 University Of Cambridge Language Centre (designed by John Wilcox and reproduced with kind permissions from copyright owner)
Cover layout by © 2021 Raphaël Savina (raphael@savina.net)

ISBN13: 978-2-490057-92-4 (Ebook, PDF, colour)
ISBN13: 978-2-490057-93-1 (Ebook, EPUB, colour)
ISBN13: 978-2-490057-91-7 (Paperback - Print on demand, black and white)
Print on demand technology is a high-quality, innovative and ecological printing method; with which the book is never 'out of stock' or 'out of print'.

British Library Cataloguing-in-Publication Data.
A cataloguing record for this book is available from the British Library.

**Legal deposit, France**: Bibliothèque Nationale de France - Dépôt légal: mai 2021.

# Table of contents

vi  Notes on contributors

xx  Acknowledgements

xxi Foreword
*Sabina Schaffner*

1   Introduction to The world universities' response to COVID-19: remote online language teaching
*Nebojša Radić, Anastasia Atabekova, Maria Freddi, and Josef Schmied*

## Section 1. AFRICA

33  Teaching Arabic during the pandemic: the remote online classroom
*Yasser Kashef*

49  Going virtual, staying face-to-face: trajectory of ELT classes during the pandemic
*Daniel A. Nkemleke*

63  Online remote language teaching during and beyond the pandemic: echoes from the Anchor University in Lagos
*Tunde Ope-Davies*

79  An immersive Arabic language course in Cairo moves online
*Heba Salem*

95  The University of Rwanda response to COVID-19
*Valentin Uwizeyimana*

## Section 2. AMERICAS

111 COVID-19-driven sudden shift to remote teaching: the case of the Languages for the Community Program at the Universidad Nacional del Litoral
*María del Valle Gastaldi and Elsa Grimaldi*

Table of contents

125 Remote language teaching in the pandemic context at the University of São Paulo, Brazil
*Mônica Ferreira Mayrink, Heloísa Albuquerque-Costa, and Daniel Ferraz*

139 Creating communities of practice: The Harvard Language Center's role in supporting language instruction during the pandemic
*Andrew F. Ross and Sarah Luehrman Axelrod*

## Section 3. ASIA

155 Sudden shift to online learning during the COVID-19 pandemic: the case of Arabic at Qatar University
*Abeer Heider*

167 The response of the University of Isfahan to COVID-19: remote online language teaching
*Adel Rafiei and Zahra Amirian*

179 A blended learning model supported by MOOC/SPOC, Zoom, and Canvas in a project-based academic writing course
*Li Zhang and Yunjie Chen*

199 Online training of prospective language teachers: exploring a new model
*Hang Zheng and Lianyue Zhang*

## Section 4. EUROPE

217 Tracks for Russian university students' multilingual development within remote education during the pandemic
*Anastasia Atabekova, Alexander Belousov, and Oleg Yastrebov*

235 Teaching online in translation studies: a teacher-researcher's feedback from France
*Geneviève Bordet*

249   Braving remote instruction at Vilnius University: response to the COVID-19 pandemic
*Loreta Chodzkienė, Julija Korostenskienė, and Olga Medvedeva*

265   Stumble or fall? Responses to moving language learning online at Durham University during the 2020 pandemic
*Mark Critchley*

279   Reflection on digital language teaching, learning, and assessment in times of crisis: a view from Italy
*Maria Freddi*

295   University of Cambridge Asian, Middle Eastern and Persian studies during the pandemic
*Mahbod Ghaffari*

307   University of Cambridge Modern and Medieval Languages: response to COVID-19
*Silke Mentchen*

321   COVID-19 and the Autonomous University of Barcelona: current trends on language teaching and learning strategies
*Sonia Oliver del Olmo*

337   COVID-19 emergency teaching: from CULP to remote CULP
*Nebojša Radić*

353   Remote online teaching in modern languages in Germany: responses according to audiences and teaching objectives
*Josef Schmied*

## Section 5. OCEANIA

371   "Stay home, be safe, and be kind": University of Auckland's Italian course goes online in a week
*Barbara Martelli*

384   Author index

# Notes on contributors

## Editors

**Nebojša Radić** is the Director of the Cambridge University Language Programme (CULP), the university-wide world languages provision. His research interest focuses on the methodology of computer-mediated teaching, the remote/online delivery of language provision, teacher training, programme management, as well as creative and translingual writing, world literature, and literary self-translation. Nebojša has published academic works and fiction in Serbian, Italian, and English.

**Anastasia Atabekova**, Full Professor, DSc in comparative linguistics, RUDN University Rectorate's Counselor for multilingual development, Head of the RUDN Academic Council Commission on Foreign Languages, Head of the RUDN Law Institute department of foreign languages, author of over 350 publications including monographs and research articles, indexed in international databases (Scopus h=10, WoS h=3), her research interests focus on language rights, policy, management, interdisciplinary discourse studies, and specialized translation and interpreting (legal settings) issues; she is also a certified translator and interpreter (English/Spanish – Russian).

**Maria Freddi** is Associate Professor of English language and linguistics at the University of Pavia, Italy, where she teaches English for academic purposes courses (English for science and technology, academic and popular writing), corpus linguistics methodology, descriptive grammar, and text analysis. From 2011 to 2013 she was Director of the Language Centre of her university. In recent years she has been involved in two EU-funded research projects, namely COST Action 15221-WeReLaTe on developing synergies between teaching/learning and research and writing, and, as of September 2019, in the Becoming a Digital Global Engineer (BADGE) project aimed at developing language materials for students of engineering in the global digital world.

**Josef Schmied** has just retired as Professor of English language and linguistics after teaching at Chemnitz University of Technology since April 1993, concentrating on his research projects. His main research interests are in *language and culture* (sociolinguistics, English in Africa and China), *language and computers* (corpus linguistics, Internet English, non-native digital agents in hybrid societies), and *language and cognition* (elearning, academic writing). He likes to work with international students, also in summer schools and as a guest professor, e.g. in Guangzhou/China in 2015 and in Modena/Italy in 2019 – and hopes to be able to do that again soon.

## Invited author

**Sabina Schaffner** has been the Director of the University of Zurich and ETH Zurich Language Centre since 2005. She holds a teaching diploma for French and Russian in high school education, a doctorate in Russian literature from Freiburg/Fribourg University, and a Master's degree in coaching and organisational development form Northwestern University of Applied Sciences, Switzerland). From 2008 until 2018, Sabina was Co-president of the Association of Language Centres at Swiss Higher Education Institutions (SSH-CHES), and she has been President of the European Confederation of Language Centres in Higher Education (CercleS) since September 2019.

## Authors

**Heloísa Albuquerque-Costa** is Professor of the Department of Modern Languages and the Postgraduate Program in Foreign Languages and Translation (French as a foreign language) of the University of São Paulo. She is a member of the research groups Linguagem, Educação e Virtualidade (LEV), and Grupo de Pesquisa sobre Políticas Linguísticas e de Internacionalização no Ensino Superior (GPLIES). Email: heloisaalbuqcosta@usp.br

**Zahra Amirian** is Associate Professor in TEFL, University of Isfahan, Iran. She has taught English to EFL learners for more than 15 years. Her main research interests are task-based language teaching, genre studies, intercultural communicative competence, and translation studies. Email: z.amirian@fgn.ui.ac.ir

Notes on contributors

**Anastasia Atabekova**, see Editors' list

**Sarah Luehrman Axelrod** is an online language pedagogy specialist, writer, and editor. She has worked as the interim Assistant Director of the Language Center and holds a PhD in Italian literature from Harvard University.

**Alexander Belousov**, Full Professor, DSc in history, PhD in economics, RUDN Law Institute Deputy Director for part-time studies, and author of over 100 publications, his research interests embrace a wide range of issues relating to the state regulation of the economy, public administration, higher education policy, and management; Prof Belousov has been leading the RUDN University trade union organization for over 30 years and has a comprehensive experience in bridging the interests and aspirations of diverse university stakeholders within diverse professional and multicultural settings; he is also a certified translator (French – Russian).

**Geneviève Bordet** is an associate lecturer in the Department of Applied Linguistics of the University of Paris, France. Her first research focus is on devices used to build an 'academic voice' in PhD abstracts such as the determiner 'this' and labelling nouns. She has also published research on information retrieval, corpus studies, and decision-making in translation.

**Yunjie Chen** is an undergraduate student at Shanghai JiaoTong University majoring in English and a major member of the Innovative Practice Program for College Students under the guidance of Professor Li Zhang, focusing on the effectiveness and acceptance of online teaching and learning.

**Loreta Chodzkienė** graduated from Vilnius University in English philology, did her internship at the University of Kent (UK), obtained a CELTA diploma at SIH, defended her PhD "EU Pedagogues' Intercultural Communicative Competence and Its Developmental Socio-educational Factors" (social sciences). Currently she has been running the courses on communication across cultures, academic research writing, and intercultural internships for the students of the Faculty of Philology, Vilnius University.

## Notes on contributors

**Mark Critchley** is Director of the Centre for Foreign Language Study at Durham University. Mark is also currently Chair of the Association for University Language Communities in the UK and Ireland (2019 to date), and a member of the Coordinating Committee of CercleS, the confederation of language centres in higher education in Europe.

**Daniel Ferraz** is Professor of the Department of Modern Languages and the Graduate Program of Linguistics and Literacy Studies of the University of São Paulo. He is the coordinator of the Grupo de Estudos sobre Educação Linguística em Línguas Estrangeiras (GEELLE). Email: danielfe@usp.br.

**Maria Freddi**, see Editors' list

**María del Valle Gastaldi** is a teacher of English. She has a degree in English linguistics and is currently finishing an education Master's program. Professor and Researcher at UNL, she is Head of the Extension and Professional Development Area, UNL's Language Center, and co-author of several articles on methodology and linguistics.

**Mahbod Ghaffari** has a PhD in linguistics and a certificate in leadership in higher education. He has taught Persian language and culture, linguistics, methodology, and Iranian cinema at universities in the UK and Iran since 1998 and joined the department of Middle Eastern Studies, University of Cambridge in 2013. Mahbod has published many books and articles in linguistics and teaching Persian.

**Elsa Grimaldi** is a teacher of English. She has a Master's degree in English, area of applied linguistics, and is Scientific English Editor at Argentina's National Research Council, Professor and Researcher at UNL, former Area Coordinator at the Language Center, UNL, and Author of several publications in the field of genre pedagogy.

**Abeer Heider** has a MA in teaching Arabic as a second language from the American University in Cairo. She then became a lecturer in AUC, in the

## Notes on contributors

department of Arabic for non-natives; ALI and CASA program during 2007 until 2013. Later on, she moved to Qatar and worked as a lecturer in the national university; Qatar University from 2013 until present, teaching Arabic as a second language too. During that time, she took her PhD in using technology and educational games involving technology in Arabic classes, from the Islamic University in Minnesota in 2019.

**Yasser Kashef** is a lecturer of Arabic as a foreign language at TAFL Centre, Alexandria University. Additionally, he is an ESL instructor at AMIDEAST, a member of the academic committee of the Erasmus+ international project XCELING and an assessment specialist at a few international educational bodies. Mr Kashef holds degrees in applied linguistics that are mainly concerned with translation and teaching foreign languages.

**Julija Korostenskienė** is an experienced linguist and language educator with teaching experience both in Europe and the United States of America. After her graduation with a PhD in linguistics from Purdue University (Indiana, USA), she has taught a broad range of EAP and ESP courses offered by the Institute of Foreign Languages, Faculty of Philology, Vilnius University. She has also developed a methodology for teaching English for science to Vilnius University staff and is author of an innovative course: Language in Leadership.

**Barbara Martelli** is professional Teaching Fellow in Italian at the University of Auckland, New Zealand, where she completed her PhD in Italian studies. She holds an MA in cultural anthropology and ethnology from the University of Bologna and a BA in communication sudies from the University of Milan. Her fields of interest include crime fiction, medical anthropology, and language teaching.

**Mônica Ferreira Mayrink** is Professor of the Department of Modern Languages and the Postgraduate Program in Spanish Language and Spanish and Hispanic American Literature of the University of São Paulo. She is the coordinator of the research groups Linguagem, Educação e Virtualidade (LEV) and Recursos

## Notes on contributors

Didáticos para a Aula de Espanhol como Língua Estrangeira (ReDiPAELE). Email: momayrink@usp.br.

**Olga Medvedeva** is an experienced teacher and teacher trainer (EUROLTA master teacher trainer since 2012); she worked as a project manager with over 20 international projects. Her professional research interests include foreign language didactics, applied linguistics, international/intercultural communication, teacher training, ICT in language learning/teaching, and teaching languages for specific purposes. Project-relevant publication: ODLAC Tutors Guide: Open Development of Language Competencies (ODLAC)-225219-CP-1-AT-MINERVA-MPP, 2008, ISBN 978-9955-568-73-5 (co-author).

**Silke Mentchen** has been teaching German as a foreign language at all levels in tertiary education since 1994. At Cambridge University, she is the Senior Language Teaching Officer in the German and Dutch section and responsible for the language programme of the section. She is also Fellow and Director of Studies at Magdalene College. She has been the Faculty's Director of Outreach and School Liaison, works as coordinator for various WP projects (she is the Faculty's adviser for the Prince's Teaching Institute), and is the section's coordinator for HE+, the University's Widening Participation project.

**Daniel A. Nkemleke** is professor in linguistics at the Ecole Normale Supérieure, University of Yaoundé I. He has received several scholarship awards including Humboldt (2006-2008 and beyond), Fulbright (2010-2011), Humboldt Alumni Prize for Innovative Research Initiative (2014), and a European Research Council Consolidator grant (2016-2021) in collaboration with peers in four other universities (with PI in University of Warsaw, Poland).

**Sonia Oliver del Olmo** has a degree in Anglo-German philology (University of Barcelona,1992) and a PhD in translation and interpretation (University Pompeu Fabra, 2004). She is Lecturer in the Department of English and German philology in the Autonomous University of Barcelona, where she teaches English for academic purposes and advanced academic abilities in the Masters' programme.

Notes on contributors

**Tunde Ope-Davies** (Opeibi) is Professor of English, digital cultures, and discourse studies at the University of Lagos, Nigeria. He is the founder and director of the Centre for Digital Humanities, University of Lagos (CEDHUL). He is a fellow of the Commonwealth Scholarship Commission, and Alexander von Humboldt Foundation, Germany. He is the convener of the Lagos Summer School in Digital Humanities (LSSDH).

**Nebojša Radić**, see Editors' list

**Adel Rafiei** is an assistant professor in linguistics at the University of Isfahan-Iran. He has been teaching linguistic morphology, lexicography, and Persian to non-Persian speakers since 2008. His main research interests Persian morphology and task-based teaching of Persian.

**Andrew F. Ross** is Director of the Language Center at Harvard University. He also serves as the current president of the International Association for Language Learning Technology (IALLT), and is Deputy Director of Education Support Services for the Faculty of Arts and Sciences at Harvard.

**Heba Salem** is Senior Arabic Language Instructor at AUC and is currently the executive director for the Center of Arabic Study Abroad. She completed her MA in TAFL from AUC, where she taught various levels of Egyptian and modern standard Arabic. She has taught in the US at the University of Texas at Austin, the University of Maryland, and Middlebury. She co-authored Umm al-Dunya, the advanced Egyptian colloquial textbook, printed by AUC Press 2012.

**Josef Schmied**, see Editors' list

**Valentin Uwizeyimana**, PhD, is Lecturer at the University of Rwanda in Rwanda, and a Research Fellow at Technische Universität Chemnitz in Germany, the University of South Africa, and Stellenbosch University in South Africa. His research interests include applied linguistics, technology for language teaching and learning, and the use of emerging technologies in education.

Notes on contributors

**Oleg Yastrebov**, DSc in laws, DSc in economics, PhD in laws, Full Professor; since 2020 Oleg has been serving as RUDN University Rector, head of the RUDN Law Institute Department of Administrative and Financial Law, Deputy Chairman of Russian Higher Attestation Commission on Research Degree Awards (VAK) on Jurisprudence, Vice-President of the Association of Legal Education of the RF, member of the Russian Higher Qualification Board of Judges, author of over 200 research works, and a certified translator (Spanish – Russian).

**Li Zhang** is Professor at the School of Foreign Languages in Shanghai Jiao Tong University. She is interested in research about teaching methodology, especially computer assisted language teaching. She has obtained the Excellent Professor Award, Excellent Teaching Award, Excellent Course Award, Best Research Award, and First Prize Research Paper Award from the university and other academic communities in China.

**Lianyue Zhang** is an associate professor in the College of International Education at Qingdao University in China. Her main research interests are pedagogical research on teaching Chinese as a second language, and second language acquisition, with a particular focus on native language influence.

**Hang Zheng** is a postdoctoral researcher in the Department of Chinese at the Sun Yat-Sen University at Zhuhai China. She received her PhD in East Asian languages and cultures from the University of Illinois at Urbana-Champaign in the US. Her main research interests are instructed second language acquisition and psycholinguistics.

## Reviewers

**Irina E. Abramova** is DSc in language theory, associate professor. She is Head of the Department of Foreign Languages for Humanities at Petrozavodsk State University (Russia), and leads the university-wide shared resources center for language teaching. She has also shaped and enhanced the sociolinguistic concept of speech behavior of bilinguals as applied to the Russian contexts.

## Notes on contributors

**Heloísa Albuquerque-Costa**, see Authors' list

**Sarah Luehrman Axelrod**, see Authors' list

**Geneviève Bordet**, see Authors' list

**Steve Buckledee** worked as an EFL teacher in Portugal, Spain, and Italy before taking up an academic post in 2004. His research interests include second language acquisition, stylistics, and critical discourse analysis. His main publications are *The Language of Brexit* (2018, Bloomsbury Academic) and *Tabloiding the Truth* (2020, Palgrave Macmillan).

**Marcela Cazzoli** is Associate Professor in Hispanic studies at Durham University. Her research interests cover the acquisition and teaching of second languages and the sociolinguistic outcomes of language contact. At present, she is working on developing a transnational approach to language teaching in higher education and is leading an outreach project on (socio) linguistic awareness in secondary schools.

**Chenguang Chang** is Professor of linguistics in the School of International Studies, Sun Yat-sen University. His research interests include systemic functional linguistics, discourse analysis, translation studies, and English education. His most recent publications include *Linguistic Sustainability* (co-edited with Yu Changsen, 2020) and *Working with Discourses: Corpus and Systemic Functional Perspectives* (co-edited with Josef Schmied and Matthias Hofmann, 2020).

**Loreta Chodzkienė**, see Authors' list

**Mark Critchley**, see Authors' list

**Olga Dontcheva-Navratilova** is Associate Professor of English linguistics at the Faculty of Education, Masaryk University, Czech Republic. Her research interests include English for academic and specific purposes and political discourse. She has published the books Analysing Genre: The Colony Text of UNESCO Resolutions (2009), Coherence in Political Speeches (2011), and co-authored Persuasion in Specialised Discourse (2020).

**Daniel Ferraz**, see Authors' list

**Maria Freddi**, see Editors' list

**Daniel K. Gakunga** graduated from the University of Nairobi where he earned his PhD in comparative and contemporary issues in education in 2013. He is Senior Lecturer in comparative and international education, Educational Consultant, and Researcher. He is also Member of the Special Projects Committee World Council of Comparative Education Societies (WCCES).

**María del Valle Gastaldi**, see Authors' list

**Mahbod Ghaffari**, see Authors' list

**Elsa Grimaldi**, see Authors' list

**Lana Habib** is the Executive Director of the TAFL Centre at Alexandria University since April 2011. She is a lecturer of Francophone Literature and Modern and Contemporary Poetry in the Department of French Language and Literature – Faculty of Arts – Alexandria University. She is also a TOT trainer in the program of the strategies of the communicative approach in teaching Arabic as a foreign language. Dr Habib works on developing intercultural competence in foreign language classes

**Abeer Heider**, see Authors' list

**Yasser Kashef**, see Authors' list

**Julija Korostenskienė**, see Authors' list

Notes on contributors

**Elena I. Kovaleva** is Associate Professor of English language and literature with a PhD in linguistics and an MA in German and English language teaching (Academic Credentialing Commission Chicago, USA), head of the Department of Theory and Practice of Translation and Communication at Moscow Pedagogical State University (Russia), and author of over 70 publications, including monographs, research papers, and teaching toolkits on academic discourse and rhetoric.

**Natalie Kübler** is Full Professor at University of Paris. Her main research interests explore languages for specific purposes, specialized phraseology, terminology, corpus-based translation studies, and learner corpora. She was one of the first to introduce corpus linguistics into translation training in France 20 years ago and was the promoter of the MeLLANGE project. She is in charge of the CLILLAC-ARP research lab and has created the PERL in 2015, in which an inter-university team of 15 people creating blended online languages courses and doing research in applied linguistics.

**Anna A. Lebedeva** is DSc in comparative linguistics, Full Professor, holds the position of the Head of the Department of Foreign Languages at the All-Russian State University of Justice (Russian Academy of Justice under the Ministry of Justice of the Russian Federation), author of over 50 publications including monographs, textbooks of the English language for lawyers-to-be, and papers indexed in the international databases, and her research interests embrace a wide range of topics related to teaching LSP, exploring cognitive and cultural aspects of translation, formation, and development of legal terminology.

**Xinghua (Kevin) Liu** is Associate Professor of Applied Linguistics at Shanghai Jiao Tong University, China. He serves as the Chief Editor for International Journal of TESOL Studies and the Co-editor for International Journal of Chinese Language Teaching.

**Mpine Makoe** is the Commonwealth of Learning Chair in Open Education Practices/ Resources at the University of South Africa (UNISA). She is also a National Research Foundation (NRF) rated research professor in Open Distance eLearning (ODeL). She is an OER ambassador for the International Council of Distance Education (ICDE) and a director of African Council for Distance Education (ACDE).

**Franco Manai** holds a Laurea in Languages (Pisa University) and a PhD (Brown University). He taught Italian in schools, colleges and universities in Italy, France, the USA, Canada, New Zealand, and China, including Liceo Classico of Oristano, Brown University, Vassar, Wellesley, and Smith Colleges, The Universities of British Columbia, Bordeaux, Auckland and Shanghai. He also taught Italian at a distance and blended.

**Barbara Martelli**, see Authors' list

**Mônica Ferreira Mayrink**, see Authors' list

**Silke Mentchen**, see Authors' list

**Manuel Moreira da Silva** is a senior lecturer at Porto Accounting and Business School (ISCAP – IPP) and Vice-dean for Research and Internationalization. He holds an MD from Porto University in terminology and translation and a PhD from New University of Lisbon in linguistics. He is the Coordinator of the Research Unit in Languages, Communication, and Education at CEOS.PP and a member of the Executive Committee of the Portuguese Language Centres Association (ReCLes.pt).

**Daniel Nkemleke**, see Authors' list

**Sonia Oliver del Olmo**, see Authors' list

**Paul Ayodele Onanuga** teaches at the Department of English and Literary Studies, Federal University Oye-Ekiti, Nigeria. He is a recipient of the Georg Forster Fellowship (Alexander von Humboldt Foundation), spent at the Technische Universität Chemnitz, Germany. His research interests revolve around Nigerian hip-hop studies, computer-mediated discourse analysis, and presently, queer sexualities on digital media. He has published in reputable journals.

**Tunde Ope-Davies**, see Authors' list

**Tatyana G. Popova** is Doctor of Science (DSc, PhD) in Linguistics. She is Full Professor of the Department of Foreign Languages at the Military University (Moscow, Russia), author of over 700 publications that include monographs and research papers on communicative strategies, cross cultural communication, discourse studies, and translation, Supervisor and Reviewer of many PhD dissertations on the mentioned topics, and Academician of the Russian Academy of Natural Sciences.

**Nebojša Radić**, see Editors' list

**Andrew F. Ross**, see Authors' list

**Heba Salem**, see Authors' list

**Sabina Schaffner**, see Invited author's list

**Josef Schmied**, see Editors' list

**Marc Silver** is Professor of English language and linguistics at the University of Modena and Reggio Emilia, Italy. He has published in the field of argumentation, on the relationship between language and culture, and about the metadiscoursal and epistemological consequences of language choice. His most recent works on academic discourse focus on cross-disciplinary variation both in a corpus and in a discourse perspective.

**Valentin Uwizeyimana**, see Authors' list

**Elena G. Vyushkina** is a PhD holder in pedagogy, an associate professor of the Foreign Languages Department at Saratov State Law Academy (Saratov,

Russia), a Russian national representative at the International Negotiation Competition, an international law student competition on disputes resolution, and author of research papers and textbooks on legal English. She teaches legal English, trains law-students for international competitions, and runs optional original CLIL courses on *client consultation* and *mediation*.

**Li Zhang**, see Authors' list

# Acknowledgements

The Editors wish to thank the University of Cambridge Language Centre and RUDN University, Moscow, without whose generous financial support this publication would not have been possible.

Nebojša Radić, Anastasia Atabekova, Maria Freddi, Josef Schmied

# Foreword

## Sabina Schaffner[1]

I was very happy to accept the request to write a foreword to this publication. This collection of case studies is special for several reasons. Firstly, because of the geographical and institutional diversity of the authors, bringing together experiences of teaching under COVID-19 restrictions in the university language classroom from 18 countries and five continents. Secondly, the publication is interesting because of the variety of case studies that testify to different strategies and emphases in dealing with pandemic-related challenges. Finally, the case studies collected strikingly demonstrate the **creative** responses of language teachers in a variety of contexts to meet the challenges of the pandemic crisis.

The case studies make it clear that overcoming a crisis – also in the field of education – does not primarily work with prefabricated strategies and plans. Coping has more to do with successful improvisation. Improvisation can produce the unexpected. In the article *Blühende Fantasie* (Flourishing imagination) in die ZEIT of 29/30 December 2020[2], Sebastian Kempkens reflected on the story of the successful landing of the 13 crew after an accident damaged their oxygen supply as an example of successful improvisation. After their oxygen supply was compromised due to an explosion, the astronauts, in cooperation with their NASA colleagues, had to build an emergency filter that allowed them the necessary supply of oxygen until the emergency landing, and ensured their own survival. What is interesting for Kempkens is that improvisation does not necessarily have to result in innovation: the tinkered air filter was not later put into production as a successful invention,

---

1. University of Zurich, Zürich, Switzerland; sabina.schaffner@sprachen.uzh.ch; https://orcid.org/0000-0002-4929-0171

2. https://www.zeit.de/2021/01/improvisation-corona-krisenpolitik-2020-apollo-13-mission-ronald-reagan/komplettansicht

How to cite: Schaffner, S. (2021). Foreword. In N. Radić, A. Atabekova, M. Freddi & J. Schmied (Eds), *The world universities' response to COVID-19: remote online language teaching* (pp. xxi-xxii). Research-publishing.net. https://doi.org/10.14705/rpnet.2021.52.1260

## Foreword

> "but perhaps that is not so important. Something else seems important to me. [...] What stuck with me was understanding that our salvation does not lie in any plans we may have made at some point. It is we ourselves. We can find solutions even if we haven't already written them down somewhere. Improvisation means not knowing what's coming – and still being sure of reaching the goal"[3].

I can only congratulate the editorial team, Nebojša Radić from the University of Cambridge, Anastasia Atabekova from RUDN University, Moscow, Maria Freddi from the University of Pavia, and Josef Schmied from Technische Universität Chemnitz on the idea of this extraordinary publication project. They have provided a platform for language teachers around the world. Many colleagues will find a similar experience to their own in the testimonies of the authors. These testimonials encourage us to use and appreciate improvisation and to learn from its results as a community. The next challenges will certainly not be long in coming. Then, too, we will have to count on our courage and our ability to improvise.

I wish you a stimulating reading experience!

---

3. "Aber vielleicht kommt es darauf gar nicht so sehr an. Wichtiger scheint mir etwas anderes. [...] Was hängen blieb, war die Erkenntnis: Nicht irgendwelche Pläne, die wir irgendwann mal gemacht haben, sind unsere Rettung. Wir selbst sind es. Wir können auch dann Lösungen finden, wenn wir sie nicht schon irgendwo notiert haben. Improvisieren, das heißt: nicht wissen, was kommt – und trotzdem sicher sein, ans Ziel zu gelangen".

# Introduction to The world universities' response to COVID-19: remote online language teaching

### Nebojša Radić[1], Anastasia Atabekova[2], Maria Freddi[3], and Josef Schmied[4]

## 1. Project rationale

March 2020 saw the advent of a pandemic that is having a profound impact on all facets of our lives with special reference, in our case, to language education. Universities worldwide found themselves in an emergency predicament and we had to suddenly abandon traditional forms of classroom and/or blended learning and move to a completely remote online delivery of courses. The imperative to continue teaching in these new circumstances did not come, as very often is the case, from the relevant institutional administrations in a top-down manner, but from our own, inner pedagogical and human instincts. The usual lines of communication with our students and colleagues were cut off and we had to find and resort to new ways of communicating and teaching. We had no precedents to refer to and found ourselves in the situation to search for innovative solutions using the already existing technology, skills, resources, and methodological approaches. This situation was challenging in the extreme.

---

1. University of Cambridge, Cambridge, United Kingdom; nr236@cam.ac.uk; https://orcid.org/0000-0001-6859-5774

2. RUDN University Law Institute, Moscow, Russia; atabekova-aa@rudn.ru; https://orcid.org/0000-0003-2252-9354

3. University of Pavia, Pavia, Italy; maria.freddi@unipv.it; https://orcid.org/0000-0003-2893-1790

4. Chemnitz University of Technology, Chemnitz, Germany; josef.schmied@phil.tu-chemnitz.de; https://orcid.org/0000-0001-8499-3158

**How to cite:** Radić, N., Atabekova, A., Freddi, M., & Schmied, J. (2021). Introduction to The world universities' response to COVID-19: remote online language teaching. In N. Radić, A. Atabekova, M. Freddi & J. Schmied (Eds), *The world universities' response to COVID-19: remote online language teaching* (pp. 1-30). Research-publishing.net. https://doi.org/10.14705/rpnet.2021.52.1261

Introduction

Searching for solutions and support, our language learning community developed, in many ways, new lines of communication. It was then, in June 2020 that we had the idea of writing a case study each to be published together in one volume, to make some of the informal conversations that had happened during the lockdown formally available to the whole community. We come from different countries, different institutions with distinct academic, linguistic, cultural, and professional backgrounds and yet we all found ourselves in the position to have to solve a major puzzle – a pandemic-caused lockdown that fragmented our established practices.

We realised very quickly, however, that the potential pool of candidates interested in joining our effort was much larger. As the number of contributors increased we decided to cover a large proportion of the world. After reaching out to fellow language practitioners from around the world, we are proud to be able to announce that this collection of case studies brings together colleagues from 18 countries, five continents, and a very diverse range of higher education institutions. This project brings together colleagues from Argentina, Brazil, Cameroon, China, Egypt, France, Germany, Iran, Italy, Lithuania, New Zealand, Nigeria, Qatar, Russia, Rwanda, Spain, UK, and USA.

Thus, an essential feature of this survey is its global perspective. Although we accept that globalisation may challenge some local traditions, we are convinced that global networking can support language practitioners and critical discussion as well as provide reference to good practices. While it is true that we reacted in a hurry, our reaction was predictable from the point of view of:

- the framework of our core beliefs – pedagogical approach and philosophy; and

- the institutionally available technological expertise.

As is visible from the chapters' opening sections that describe the wider institutional, cultural, and academic context of the university where the authors work, the common objective was to carry on teaching languages in a way that could guarantee the same quality as before the pandemic crisis. At the same time, however, technology posed issues of accessibility, so that a trade-off between quality and accessibility had to be found. What we, as editors, thought would bring interest to the project was to draw common analytical lines along which to compare case studies that could be representative of individual contexts. The qualitative case study seemed the most appropriate research perspective to help understand as complex a phenomenon as education in times of crisis in that a case study "ensures that the issue is not explored through one lens, but rather a variety of lenses which allows for multiple facets of the phenomenon to be revealed and understood" (Baxter & Jack, 2008, p. 544).

By bringing together these studies, this book documents the higher education pedagogical responses to the COVID-19 emergency in 2020, focusing on language instruction worldwide. Furthermore, this project unites international language professionals around a common pedagogical platform as well as encourages active and impactful networking. Eventually, the project signposts the path to a flexible and diverse approach to language teaching and learning.

## 2. Scope of the project

Since our call for papers left the responses open to individual authors, we received very diverse contributions in terms of genre conventions and approaches. These range from narratives of how an entire language unit was reorganised because of the pandemic to reflective pieces of single teachers taking stock of their teaching and assessment practices to data-oriented, empirical analyses of students' responses to surveys. Some writers were happy with the more centralised approaches, others with individual creativities. Some were more concerned with technical details, others with suitable responses to student problems. Some of the authors are early career teachers and others are more experienced colleagues in managerial roles. We did not want to prioritise any of these perspectives, as we consider them all as worthy contributions to this global survey and the understanding of our practice. We believe that the forced migration to remote teaching offered an opportunity for everyone to expand

Introduction

their teaching and learning experience. We thus document the challenges in the national and institutional contexts, while at the same time we present these as opportunities that can serve as a new basis for international exchange and progress in digital language teaching and learning.

Each chapter should be read independently. Therefore, of the keywords in each chapter three to four are specific to the context and contents described, and the remaining ones are common to the whole book project, namely *COVID-19, online language teaching*. The table in the supplementary material link synoptically presents the scope of the project with details about the technology used, types of classes, proficiency level, and issues that we think stand out as special to each contribution.

Dissemination and networking are no less important than the process of documentation. This volume is published under the Creative Commons licence and made readily available online. The project also features a website with a link to a downloadable copy of the publication and some basic information such as the outline, the full list of participating institutions, and biographical details about the contributors. Furthermore, we planned an official launch under the auspices of CercleS (*Confédération Européenne des Centres de Langues de l'Enseignement Supérieur / European Confederation of Language Centres in Higher Education*) followed by other presentations and events. We also plan a follow-up project that will seek to continue to document ongoing changes in our practices and expect most of the current participants as well as some new ones to contribute.

## 3. Research Questions (RQs)

In putting this collection together, our research interest was to record how language practitioners, both teaching and managerial staff, engaged in the deployment of their best skills and knowledge to meet the needs of their academic communities, and thus gain insights into the ideas and processes involved. Given the very wide scope of the collection and the different contributor backgrounds, the RQs below underlie each of the case studies and indeed guide our editorial contribution. However, they are not intended as prescriptive guidelines, rather leaving everyone the freedom to express their culturally, linguistically, institutionally, and personally diverse experiences and views.

- RQ1. What was the decision-making process like in shifting to remote online teaching? Were the changes implemented in top-down or bottom-up fashion?

- RQ2. Technology, administration, or pedagogy, which was the driving force for change?

- RQ3. Predictably, responses to the emergency varied depending on the specific contexts. However, is it possible to discern some patterns emerging?

- RQ4. How have teachers managed to maintain or include interactive elements in their teaching?

- RQ5. How learner-centred was the switch to remote online teaching?

- RQ6. How were task-based approaches included in remote online teaching?

- RQ7. To what extent was the process of moving to remote online teaching able to cater for the diversity of the student body?

- RQ8. What methodological developments did we record?

## 4. Methodology

Guided by case study methodology, we collected 23 chapters written by colleagues from 18 different institutions around the world on the assumption

## Introduction

that the nature and scope of the measures taken in response to a globally critical emergency situation was contingent on the cultural background of the country, single institution, teaching staff, students body, access to technology, experience in deploying technology, funding, as well as a range of other variables.

The first draft of the articles was collected by early November 2020. Each article was refereed by two colleagues internal to the project as well as one external reviewer. The required changes were documented and the articles sent back to the authors for revision. The revised versions together with the authors' responses were collected again in early January 2021 and sent to the editorial team for further review and standardisation. The editors made further suggestions for improvement and these were completed by late February when the articles went to the publisher for similarity check (to avoid plagiarism), formatting, and proofreading. The whole process was completed by the end of April 2021.

We tried to make the articles as comparable in format as possible. To do so, we required, and mostly adhered to, a fairly standard outline and posed the overarching question to all contributors: *how did you go about moving to teach remotely during the emergency?*, in other words, *what has it been like?*, a question which we did not have time to pose back in the spring of 2020 because we were too busy doing the work. In terms of content, we asked contributors to address these points and structure:

- institutional, cultural, and academic backgrounds;
- type of course;
- usual and emergency delivery patterns;
- technology deployed;
- teacher training and support;
- student and teaching staff feedback;
- teaching/learning outcomes;
- discussion/lessons learnt;
- limitations; and
- conclusion and way forward.

In editing the final versions of the articles we tried to standardise not only the format but also the concept and style as much as possible to make the case studies comparable and meaningful as a whole. At the same time, however, since only few contributors have English as their first language, we strived to preserve the original 'accent' of the author by letting the diverse cultural traits shine through the chapters. We will read, therefore, how the University of Isfahan made telephone calls to all 15 thousand of their students to comfort them about the emergency situation, how the University of Auckland insisted on kindness, how the University of Cairo consulted their overseas students about the format of the teaching, how Italy was the first to decide to shift online, how in Chinese classes the pandemic helped to initiate new forms of native/non-native interaction, or how a Chinese model blended different platforms of pre-, in- and after-class activities, and how in Africa some universities were privileged to provide an institutional frame whereas others looked at their students' smartphone practices and adapted their teaching to students.

We thought that such valuable cultural insights were inspiring and well worth reporting and highlighting. In all, the chapters offer a positive outlook in challenging times through reflective reports, case studies, and best practices.

## 5. Key concepts

The very title of this volume introduces three key concepts in need of clarification: *remote*, *online*, and *language teaching*. We start by contextualising the notion of *remote* in relation to learning as, first of all, a continuation of the more traditional concept of *distance* learning; we use *online* to denote activities and/or learning/teaching resources that are accessible in digital format via the internet. An online activity is normally integrated into a blended learning mode of delivery, classroom *and* online teaching/learning. The term *remote*, however, denotes a situation where students do not attend the institution *in situ* at all and have no access to face-to-face, classroom-based teaching. They engage with their studies fully and completely at a distance, remotely. In terms of *language teaching* we discuss a number of relevant aspects in the following subsections.

Introduction

## 5.1. Distance learning becomes remote learning

Distance learning started in Europe with correspondence courses over 100 years ago and the term was used to describe a range of institutional and educational situations (Valentine, 2002). Correspondence stayed the main vehicle of distance learning until the middle of the 20th century and the advent of new technologies such as radio and television (Imel, 1998). This ushered an era where learning materials were delivered at a distance by postal service on audio and video tapes. Since the mid 90's the internet allowed real-time, live, video and audio enhanced communication and teaching to take place at a distance (Ostendorf, 1997).

Since the practice has been around for so long and in so many diverse settings, making use of several generations of technologies, it is not easy to give a clear, unambiguous, and all-encompassing definition of distance learning. Greenberg (1998) suggests that it is "a planned teaching/learning experience that uses a wide spectrum of technologies to reach learners at a distance and is designed to encourage learner interaction and certification" (p. 36). This definition has historical merits but also as it lays the foundation for further developments in this field and in that respect can be operationalised for the purposes of our study. Greenberg's (1998) assertion allows very wisely, we note, for further technological advancements to be instrumentalised and more importantly, for the focus of this activity to firmly rest on the educational role of technology, namely 'to reach learners' in pedagogically meaningful ways (e.g. through interaction and certification).

An offshoot of the more recent technology-enhanced forms of distance learning is *distributed learning*, a pedagogy empowered by the new media and experiences that enabled the evolution of synchronous, group, presentation-centred forms of distance education. Such new forms were able to replicate traditional teaching-by-telling across barriers of distance and time (Dede, 1996, p. 4).

These concepts were made possible thanks to technological advancements. Approaches to the design and production of teaching materials evolved accordingly as did methodological developments in classroom-based teaching and the integration of online learning activities into an effective curriculum. Teachers became increasingly aware of the role and most importantly, we would argue, of the possibilities of technology. Since the early 90's of the 20th century, Information Technology (IT) has become an increasingly important part of the practice of language teaching and started being referred to as Computer Assisted Language Learning (CALL). Originally perceived as an approach to language learning that makes use of IT in the preparation and/or delivery of the teaching, CALL evolved into an exciting scholarly field of studies described as "the search for and study of applications of the computer in language teaching and learning" (Levy, 1997, p. 1). While the role of CALL will be discussed further in the next sub-section dedicated to blended learning, let us just assert here that the CALL theoretical framework and practice opened the door to the kind of IT-enhanced remote online learning that we are witnessing today. With the advent of social networking and multimedia tools at the turn of the new millennium, IT is now an essential part of our communication patterns and the teaching of languages. Computers have become increasingly networked and the internet fully multimedia capable. Facebook, YouTube, and the full range of messaging, communication, and authoring tools have blurred the distinction between face-to-face, classroom teaching and Virtual Learning Environment (VLE) and given birth to concepts such as blended or *inverted* learning (Baker, 2000; Lage, Platt, & Treglia, 2000; Whittaker, 2013) and the *flipped classroom* (Andujar, Salaberri-Ramiro, & Cruz Martínez, 2020; Bliuc, Goodyear, & Ellis, 2007; Chandra & Fisher, 2009; Donnelly, 2010; Strayer, 2012).

As we see from this brief overview of distance and remote learning, technology, in different aspects and guises, has been part and parcel of teaching and learning much before the advent of online IT. The efforts we describe in this collection therefore, while indeed, of an urgent nature, do have a precedent in our practice.

### 5.2. Blended learning is no longer the same as hybrid learning

A useful operational definition of blended learning with special reference to language teaching is certainly the following: "'blended learning' is the term most commonly used to refer to any combination of face-to-face teaching with

## Introduction

computer technology (online and offline activities/materials)" (Whittaker, 2013, p. 12, and see also Graham, 2013). We must note, however, that this definition is very broad and encompasses classroom or laboratory-based activities as long as IT is involved in their delivery. It is also true that in the US blended learning was adopted widely and quickly and researchers began referring to it as the "new traditional" (Ross & Gage, 2006, p. 167) or the "new normal" model of course delivery (Norberg, Dziuban, & Moskal, 2011, p. 207). Dziuban et al. (2018) note that another definition put forward at the time described blended learning as "a combination of online and in-class instruction with reduced in-class seat time for students" (Parsad, Lewis, & Tice, 2008, p. 1). This second definition introduces the notion of the reduction of in-class time without loss of educational impact. The theoretical possibility of reducing class time without producing a negative educational impact, or even with an enhancement of learning opportunities, has been instrumental in the implementation of the emergency moves to remote online teaching described by the case studies in this book.

In the early days of blended learning there was another term that was used as a synonym – *hybrid learning* (see for instance Allen & Seaman, 2003; Klimova & Kacetl, 2015). It is important to clarify that today, with special reference to this study, we use the term 'hybrid' in the sense given to the term by more recent researchers in the field such as Beatty (2019) and Lederman (2020), who use the term 'hybrid-flexible' or 'HyFlex' to describe a pedagogical situation where some students are attending the class and are in a face-to-face teaching situation whereas others choose, or are compelled by, e.g. health considerations, to follow the lesson remotely, online. This brings about a further useful terminological distinction between *asynchronous* and *synchronous* communication and teaching. Asynchronous communication takes place by sending someone emails (historically, paper-based letters) and/or messages via a messaging service or an online forum. Such a teaching style requires students to attend to communications and tasks sent and set for them by the teacher. Synchronous communication, by contrast, is real-time and requires two people to engage in a communicative or teaching/learning activity at the same time. It is important to note that none of the two modes require participants that share the same physical place. Both synchronous and asynchronous teaching styles, the flipped classroom strategy, and the blended learning modes of delivery at large, enable the extension and enrichment of the classroom social environment that is beneficial for language acquisition (Loewen, 2020; Ortega, 2014; VanPatten & Benati, 2015). This is specifically true when we take into consideration other key concepts that need to be addressed in this overview – that of *participatory communication* and *collaborative* learning (Dooly, 2018; Macaro, 1997; Richards, 2006).

## 5.3. From CALL to 'pre-tasks' and resources

CALL was framed and characterised by the tools at our disposal in the 90's: floppy disks, CD/Roms and DVDs, limited bandwidth (not multimedia capable) and web pages with asynchronous discussion forums. We should emphasise that CALL theory and practice laid a solid foundation for the blended-teaching endeavours of the past 20 years as well as for solving our more recent COVID-19 emergency teaching puzzle. Such an IT-enhanced environment made possible the re-evaluation of teaching approaches and practices that lead to the formulation of the concept of the flipped classroom introduced in 5.1. When it comes to second language acquisition, however, a number of researchers assert that the concept of communicative 'pre-tasks' (Ellis, Li, & Zhu, 2019) antedates that of the flipped classroom (for a discussion see Cunningham, 2017). If so, we can argue that language teaching is at the forefront of the application of novel pedagogical approaches. Since the beginning of this millennium language teaching has made increasing use of technology to access, evaluate, design, produce, and deliver digital teaching resources online, at a distance, or to the classroom smartboards. Such materials are typically stored in an online depository and students are asked to attend to them outside of their class time. We slowly witnessed the demise of the old fashioned, pen-and-paper-based homework and the rise of self-study. As already discussed, blended learning came to language teaching as a natural extension of the changes witnessed in communication and presentation patterns in society as a whole. It can be said that CALL described and informed our practice in the last decade of the 20th century while 21st century online technical affordances made it possible for language acquisition to take place beyond classrooms, linguistic laboratories, and study centres. Learners' networked homes and student dormitories became a multimedia capable, resource-rich hub of communication and interaction that is linguistically meaningful and fully integrated with the classroom.

## 5.4. Collaborative learning at the heart of online language teaching

Kessler (2013, p. 307) suggests that by participating and communicating via social media platforms we develop a sense of ownership as well as belonging to a community and that of obligation. Indeed, CALL practice fostered a significant interactive element and enabled collaborative learning to take place (Davies, 2016). Such co-constructed participatory environments rely upon communities of users who find such a participation meaningful and rewarding. Not only do we develop a sense of community and belonging with peers in the classroom setting, we do so in a virtual, online setting too. Given that such a social environment is beneficial to our language learning aspirations, participation and communication should be encouraged by remote online teaching settings.

There are a number of tools that enable such an extension and diversification of the classroom social environment. The flipped classroom is one of them, but given its all-encompassing nature and role, the VLE is certainly the most prominent one and the one that needs to be discussed first. There are a number of commercially and open source available VLEs (e.g. Moodle, Black Board, Canvas) and their main function is to create environments akin to the classroom but technologically enhanced as to offer to the learner the opportunity to engage with the resources and in communicative tasks in a flexible and low-anxiety[5] manner (see RQ2 and RQ4).

## 5.5. Pedagogical issues in remote language teaching

Apart from challenges in terms of the mode of delivery, technology, and overall approach to remote online teaching, some key aspects relate to the field of our immediate pedagogical interest – the teaching of foreign or world languages.

---

5. For a discussion on the role of anxiety in second language acquisition see Horwitz (2010).

We mention both these terms as their usage is heavily conditioned by the geographical and cultural context of the relevant contributors and you will see them used in different chapters by different authors. Most of the contributors teach the English language for a range of purposes, but others teach Arabic, Chinese, German, and Persian. A number of contributors are managers of language programmes offering a variety of languages. These could be and are described in different settings as foreign, second, as well as world languages. This project brings together teachers and experts in the field whose standard, pre-COVID practice varies and makes any generalisation about the relevant approaches and methodologies unwise. We try, however, to offer a theoretical framework that might be able to, if not accommodate, then at least position the described teaching situations in relation to some of the main recent language teaching trends (see also RQ1).

The cornerstone pedagogical points of reference that we identified relate to *communicative* and *learner-centred* approaches where interactivity is of paramount importance (see RQ4 and RQ8). Communicative language teaching was introduced in the 70's and over time there were many different definitions and interpretations of this approach. Spada (2007) argues that these interpretations range from the emphasis on the communication of messages and meaning to a focus on the analysis and practice of language forms. The range could be so wide that a number of second language acquisition researchers argue that the term has become empty and impractical while Spada asserts that this is a matter of balance, integration, and equilibrium. Many of our world languages' syllabi are informed by a 'focus on form' task-based approach where learners' attention is attracted to linguistic functions as they engage in the performance of tasks (Long, 1985; see RQ6). This approach sits in contrast with a structure-based approach known as 'focus on forms', where linguistic features are taught directly and explicitly (Ellis, 2015, 2016; Long, 1991).

The other notion central to contemporary language pedagogy is that of learner-centred teaching (see RQ5 and RQ7). Nunan (1988) put forward the concept of a curriculum mediated and articulated through a collaboration between the teacher and the students. Indeed, the notion that a teacher should understand the academic, cultural, and linguistic backgrounds, learning styles, needs, and preferences has become, in most institutions, part and parcel of our standard teaching practice (see Benson, 2012, p. 30; Nunan, 2012). Furthermore, such a learner-centred approach leads to the notion of a learner autonomy that implies the understanding of the purpose of one's learning, the acceptance of responsibility for it, the participation in the setting of goals, the taking of initiatives in planning and executing the relevant activities, and regularly reviewing and evaluating the effectiveness of the learning process (Holec, 1981; Little, 1991).

## 6. Discussion of the RQs

### 6.1. Decision-making trends, driving forces, and patterns for change

Contemporary higher education pays consistent attention to the university governance issues, given an increasing focus on the contemporary transformations of higher education in line with societal needs. COVID-19 has highlighted the importance of the comprehensive institutional response to the advent of the pandemic. The forced migration to a completely remote online teaching/learning required that the university leadership and academic staff provide timely solutions to those challenges which emerged with regard to the educational process management. Therefore, it is logical that all the chapters consider the respective issues.

- RQ1. What was the decision-making process like in shifting to remote online teaching? Were the changes implemented in a top-down or bottom-up fashion?

Every chapter provides a particular background regarding the institutional administration actions in the face of the COVID-19. Some authors mention national (**Mentchen**; **Salem**; **Uwizeyimana**) or regional (e.g. **Oliver del Olmo**) decrees and further move to particular internal regulations. In contrast, others focus on university-wide institutional governance (e.g. **Bordet**; **Radić**; **Ross &**

Axelrod). Furthermore, there is also mention of interuniversity experience in tailoring internal institutional regulations to the tasks of 'conventional' study-abroad programmes of international students from different countries (**Kashef**), as well as interuniversity cooperation within the country national framework (**Salem**). One chapter reports on a thorough institutional survey to profile pre- and post-COVID-19 university policies in Rwanda (**Uwizeyimana**).

Most chapters reveal the dominance of the top-down trend in the university pathway to introduce changes in the organisation of the educational process (**Heider**; **Martelli**; **Mayrink et al.**; **Oliver del Olmo**; **Zheng & Zhang**). However, such an approach does not seem to affect the spirit of institutional academic freedom, as the emergency requires a coordinated response from the departments and/or language centres, namely managerial staff, teaching staff, specialists from the technical support division, and students.

- RQ2. Technology, administration or pedagogy, which was the driving force for change?

Each chapter explores the use of technology. This angle stands in line with the project rationale that focuses on remote online language teaching. What seems genuinely relevant for the contemporary landscape is that every author examines concrete tools for content delivery, students' self-study, and assessment issues, etc. Scholars also mention hardware and software issues (**Radić**), and consider the integration and specific choice of platforms and services (**Chodzkienė et al.**; **Ghaffari**) for asynchronous and online learning (**Mentchen**; **Ope-Davies**; **Zheng & Zhang**). Further, researchers specify possible options of digital tools choice for various learning formats, e.g. lectures, workshops, self-study, exams (**Critchley**; **Schmied**), and underline the importance of software compatibility across partner universities (**Kashef**).

However, the authors seem to be unanimous in prioritising the human factor and pedagogy that are considered the driving force to tailor the learning process to the remote context, to customise the technology to a diverse student body in terms of social, cultural, and academic background. As far as

Introduction

administration is concerned, the chapters reveal either explicitly or implicitly that administrative initiatives and actions coordinate the pathway to change, provide the learning/teaching process' continuity, and consistency of teachers' and students' activities.

- RQ3. Predictably, responses to the emergency varied depending on the specific contexts. However, is it possible to discern some patterns emerging?

A brief tour across chapters raises awareness to some common patterns across countries and continents. Online remote language teaching during the COVID-19 pandemic has enforced the overall university community focus on "language as a social practice" (e.g. **Mayrink et al.**). The project data confirms that institutional stakeholders' capacity and readiness to collaborate are crucial for the emergency disruptions to be tackled (e.g. **Atabekova et al.**). The chapters highlight the critical importance of the teachers' and students' human side; their interaction (e.g. **Freddi**; **Nkemleke**). Furthermore, the authors coincide in underlining the importance of content adaptation, specifics of course delivery, and implementation due to various learning activities (e.g. **Atabekova et al.**; **Bordet**; **Schmied**). The data also reveals the ongoing adaptation of formative assessment to new contexts (e.g. **Rafiei & Amirian**; **Martelli**), the increasing role of teachers and students' feedback (e.g. **Chodzkienė et al.**; **Freddi**; **Kashef**; **Radić**), and the need for academic community training and support (e.g. **Uwizeyimana**) to help both students and teachers overcome fatigue and stress (e.g. **Mentchen**). Finally, those scholars seem prophetic who argue that, following the pandemic, the digital and face-to-face modalities will co-exist (e.g. **Gastaldi & Grimaldi**), and move beyond traditional institutional curriculum boundaries (e.g. **Critchley**).

## 6.2. Communicative, interactive, and learner-centred approaches

Since many teaching approaches over the last few years have been developed under the general label of *communicative*, it is interesting to analyse to what extent such approaches have been lost or, to take a more positive and creative stance, how such approaches have been integrated into remote online teaching practices. Of course, many communicative elements seemed to be difficult or even lost during the forced migration to remote online practices, but if we look at some details in the reports we can be much more optimistic, since problems have made us aware of many things that we had taken for granted, in many cases more explicit interaction cues may be necessary, but in some cases the digital mode has even opened up new opportunities.

- RQ4. How have teachers managed to maintain or include interactive elements in their teaching?

The loss of face-to-face interaction in remote online teaching and the problem of multimodal interaction is mentioned in almost all chapters. Some contributions mention it more than ten times (e.g. **Mayrink et al.**; **Ope-Davis**; **Salem**; **Schmied**; **Zheng & Zhang**). The initial problem was usually the camera, i.e. many young, especially female, learners did not want to switch on the camera. Such users may see it as an advantage when they can choose a background in their platform (like in Zoom). No camera may be seen as acceptable as a privacy right, but it does not help teachers when they would like to rely on multimodal cues to see how their learners react to their teaching, which parts of their teaching seem to be understood easily, which students they can ask, etc. It is difficult to pick up such interactive cues when the camera is not on, especially when microphones also have to be muted in larger groups or disturbing internet technicalities.

But the interactive elements were not restricted to the normal teacher-student interaction or the even more challenging student-teacher interaction (e.g. **Zhang & Chen**). Teacher-teacher interaction is usually not mentioned explicitly, but it is clear that the exchange of experience and advice is always useful in the peer group and student-student interaction is discussed in many contributions, especially in task-based learning or activities in breakout rooms, for instance.

- RQ5. How learner-centred was the switch to remote online teaching?

Introduction

Although learner-centred approaches are extremely important in modern foreign-language teaching, they were mentioned explicitly only rarely (e.g. in **Freddi** or **Ross & Axelrod**) and more often implicitly. Thus, a lot of the group work and breakout room discussions can be included in this perspective. The problems mentioned with reference to breakout rooms, however, are not more dramatic than in similar face-to-face activities and moving from a digital breakout room to another may even be easier and more effective. The possibility to record group discussions more easily may even give teachers a chance to analyse activities afterwards and to adapt their teaching (as done in e.g. **Freddi**'s video). Of course, the recording must not be on if students need the privacy to discuss their own progress or their teachers' instructions or help openly and critically.

Another positive result of the pandemic was that it brought the learner back to the centre of the educational process through various forms of content negotiation: **Mayrink et al.** focus on forms of assessment; **Heider** and **Gastaldi and Grimaldi** are concerned about students' satisfaction; **Freddi** presents various forms of enhanced feedback and project-based learning; **Salem** and **Oliver del Olmo** both emphasise the centrality of feedback; **Atabekova et al.** argue in favour of the flipped classroom methodology and demonstrate various degrees of learner engagement depending on year and level of study.

As this can only partly compensate for the lack of informal common room or cafeteria meetings, which are not to be underestimated as learning opportunities, digital meeting places have been proposed as digital solutions (e.g. Kumospace). This may bring learning closer to language acquisition in less institutional settings – whether this is appreciated by language learners still needs to be analysed.

- RQ6. How were task-based approaches included in remote online teaching?

Task-based learning is mentioned in many contributions, as it is part of a modern curriculum (e.g. **Nkemleke**; **Ross & Axelrod**). Tasks are discussed as a central element of learning in several contributions (e.g. **Zheng & Zhang**). Of course, which tasks are possible in online teaching depends on the platform or tool used. The well-known open source platform Moodle offers a wide choice. Etherpad provides a good opportunity for brainstorming where each contribution can be allocated through different colours to individual learners. In BigBlueButton, the shared notes feature offers an opportunity for anonymous contributions of the entire class, which may be seen as a disadvantage by teachers, but as an advantage by more introverted learners. For smaller groups, breakout rooms are available on many platforms and are frequently used in teaching.

Breakout rooms are good if students are good at organising their own and their group's work, as in in-class cultures where leadership is built into the education system, e.g. course speakers like in China (**Zheng & Zhang**). It is always crucial that instructions come across clearly to the learners, since it is impossible for teachers to monitor all groups at the same time. This is why the random allocation of breakout rooms may not be chosen by teachers for pedagogical reasons: they may intend to group students according to levels and tasks or reckon that they need one better student in certain groups who can lead on the others.

## 6.3. Students diversity and other emergent methodological lessons

- RQ7. To what extent was the process of moving to remote online teaching able to cater for the diversity of the student body?

That diversity of the student body is emphasised by the online shift is apparent in all the chapters. Diverse teaching approaches were used depending on, primarily, level of study (undergraduate, graduate and post-graduate), class size (ranging from small seminar to large lecture), and course objectives, i.e. general language or language for specific purposes (e.g. translation training in **Atabekova et al.**; **Bordet**). Combined with the online mode, these traditional pedagogical distinctions brought about improved patterns of interaction, as different ways of managing interaction were experimented with, depending on level of study, class size, and course objective. In some instances the chat function of the video conferencing tool is used to facilitate question-and-answer and prompt active student engagement, when the shutoff of the video or the number of students connected do not allow for more direct spoken conversation to take place. Some chapters stress interactivity and the interpersonal dimension as a crucial feature of these new teaching/learning processes catering for student diversity. Particularly, **Oliver del Olmo**, calls language pedagogy at UAB during the pandemic "a new interactive scenario". **Ross and Axelrod** talk about the need to "foreground the use of student-centered, interactive, and task-based activities, and to help teachers find ways to minimize one-way transferral of information for students to absorb". **Atabekova et al.** compare BAs, MAs, and PhDs and observe how different years and levels of study correspond to different degrees of teacher-student and peer-to-peer interaction.

Diversity may be both an advantage and a disadvantage in online classes, intercultural aspects may be more difficult to overcome, but they may also be a realistic challenge closer to the real-life workplaces of the future that students have to be trained for (e.g. **Freddi**; **Schmied**).

- RQ8. What methodological developments did we record?

Some of the issues discussed in relation to the previous RQs already point to the methodological changes that we record through this collection of case studies. One of the major developments emerging from the chapters concerns the communicative approach: some (e.g. **Gastaldi & Grimaldi**; **Heider**; **Ross & Axelrod**) make explicit that the specific pedagogical paradigm in which they operate is still very much influenced by the communicative approach and many of the digital developments discussed reinforce that paradigm. Notably, the notion of 'scaffolding' in **Ross and Axelrod** is used as a metaphor for the kind of extra support teachers should be offering students when working remotely. Even the chapters that do not explicitly mention it refer to notions that are linked to the communicative approach. **Atabekova et al.**, for example, have the flipped classroom methodology as one crucial way of structuring remote learning.

Another evident development is what we could call the shift from *unintentionally blended* language teaching/learning to *blended by design*: all of the chapters show that the higher education system had already undergone an extensive digitalisation process long before the pandemic and that language education had already been using tools specific to teaching and learning such as Moodle to support face-to-face teaching. This existing digital base is what allowed universities to continue their first mission, i.e. teaching, during the first lockdown. However, as already stated with reference to RQ3, a more intentional blended language learning represents the way forward for many contributors (e.g. **Critchley**; **Freddi**; **Gastaldi & Grimaldi**; **Mayrink et al.**; **Oliver del Olmo**; **Radić**).

This is linked to the other major development emerging from the collection, namely that of innovation in language teaching and learning. Many chapters recognise that, if the initial response was dictated by an emergency, a sudden crisis nobody could have forecast, there is an immense potential for adapting and innovating processes and practices during times of crisis (e.g. **Freddi**; **Heider**; **Radić**). In order to implement innovation, many chapters call for centralised support that should be offered to teaching staff at a time of profound changes. This would contribute to overcoming the clash between technological and educational values and to better understanding between those in charge of the changes at the system level and the teaching staff as frontline implementers. Some others, written by those in charge of language provision within language centres (e.g. **Critchley**; **Gastaldi & Grimaldi**; **Radić**; **Ross & Axelrod**), have set up study groups to advance knowledge of technology-based language learning or provided faculty-wide support (e.g. **Ross & Axelrod**). A very detailed recount of the kind of centralised support offered by the institution is given in **Oliver del Olmo**'s chapter, where, on one hand, the university has provided its members with consistent and timely information and advanced technical support; on the other, education experts set up a series of training sessions very much focused on the pedagogical implications of the technical affordances of the various tools more than the technicalities of each tool.

The challenge for the higher education system, therefore, is whether they/we are capable of sustainable innovation, of efficient and positive changes that

Introduction

will benefit a wider students' population, in the specific case analysed here, as regards language teaching and learning.

## 7. Limitations to this study

The main limitation to our work was time pressure as we felt it was important for this collection to be published and the experiences shared as widely as possible within the briefest period of time. We therefore limited the scope of this volume to the collection of case studies and stopped short from engaging in a thorough analysis that could offer a more general overview of the state of world language teaching during the 2020 emergency period.

The special feature mentioned at the beginning, namely 'global', necessarily leads to limitations. Although we attempted to include current experiences from as many different countries as possible, our networks were limited and it is understandable that colleagues had to make a special effort to share their personal responses to a global crisis which demanded their full attention and energy. We are extremely grateful to those who managed our deadlines and accepted our continuous efforts at harmonising contributions.

However, we did neither attempt nor want to harmonise too much, because we believe that every language teacher deserves an opportunity to develop his or her own teaching identity, depending on learners and contexts. The individual contributions in this volume showcase a wide range of educational traditions from different parts of the world. This also applies to the academic writing conventions and preferences. We observed that some writers tend towards more descriptive styles, whereas others added generalisations or even theoretical perspectives; some prefer more tentative statements, others rely on quantitative statistical data. The emphasis on practical approaches to teaching in different contexts and by both native and non-native teachers and writers allows us to include local styles that may not be supported by prescriptive usage books, but show the authors' personality and identity. Although we tried to clarify technical terms, we noticed different lexical conventions that we found interesting and useful for a global state-of-the art survey. We also left author-specific idiomaticity and some grammatical special features untouched, when the general understanding was not affected.

## 8. Conclusions and way forward

The pandemic has boosted the digital technological component even in contexts that were not inclined to remote education by tradition or vocation. VLEs like Moodle or Canvas are no longer extraneous to the course setup and will gradually be perceived as such by all teaching staff across the board. Technology can now be more fully integrated into the face-to-face classroom in a more balanced way. What is yet unknown is to what extent institutions are ready to dive into the flexibility of models and curricula that characterise blended learning and this includes the deployment of and access to authentic resources. An additional dimension of this flexible model is of course the de-territorialisation of languages, students, and teachers: languages are not necessarily spoken within the boundaries of countries and/or territories while students and teachers can be located anywhere in the world.

The way forward stresses the fundamental role of the *blended learning* modes of delivery which do not exclude face-to-face, classroom teaching or, conversely, fully remote designs. Such future modes are likely to include *hybrid* deliveries to students *in situ* and in remote locations, simultaneously and in real-time. In terms of teacher training, teaching methodology, and materials design, such a hybrid mode is demanding and will require strong and multi-faceted institutional support. It might require additional teaching tools too such as the Owl (Owls Labs) that integrates a 360-degree camera, microphone, and speaker combined into one easy-to-use device[6]. The tool allows students attending the lesson remotely to view all in-class participants on the screen and to participate interactively.

---

6. https://uk-shop.owllabs.com/products/meeting-owl-pro

## Introduction

If we may be allowed to make a general statement about the contributions in this volume, we can say that all colleagues showed and documented their passion, willingness, and ability to innovate and the imagination to create, as well as their belief in the key role of education. We can assert furthermore that what clearly transpires from all the studies is a foremost focus on the student and their academic and personal characteristics and needs.

We would like to conclude by offering an observation and posing a question. In this volume we discuss the emergency period from the point of view of language teaching. However, the impact of this situation on most world societies is far greater and far-reaching. For one, our communication patterns have changed. Our social and professional interaction with family, friends, and colleagues has moved online and we have adopted different tools and developed new strategies to cope with this situation. Will we ever go back to the old normal patterns of face-to-face meetings, conferences, and lessons? That is hard to imagine.

We are very likely to take with us into the future all the new skills we learnt and approaches we developed. If the patterns of communication have changed and we are no longer confined to talking to people face-to-face, do we need to study, acquire, and learn a language in a face-to-face setting? Do we need a classroom to learn how to communicate online in a foreign tongue? If the answer is no, this represents a palpable and meaningful paradigm shift. Either way, the future of the teaching and study of world languages looks exciting and judging by our contributors and their contributions, we are in good, safe hands.

These observations assert the critical importance of training and supporting teaching staff. The COVID-19 pandemic caused in language teaching, as in other ways of life, an acceleration of developments and a confluence of modern trends such as the use of authentic resources and establishing students as autonomous learners, the de-territorialisation of language and language teaching, and learner-centred approaches and teacher empowerment – the pandemic has instigated an unprecedented range of responses that demonstrate the innovative spirit of teachers and the advantages of global networking. This survey aims at making a modest contribution in documenting that language teachers have used the opportunities to develop their profession further for the benefit of international communication in our modern digital societies.

Of course, this compilation of 'COVID-19 responses' is not the only ongoing academic discourse on language teaching during the pandemic. Many related publications are country-based because the national context usually sets the legal and conventional frame for teaching and learning. The technological basis also depends on national grids, funds, and training traditions. We have tried to include this in the framing at the beginning of our contributions. In this setting, many comparative projects chose a national background, e.g.

- Plutino and Polisca (2021) on the UK; and
- Henaku, Agbozo Edzordzi, and Nartey (forthcoming) on Ghana.

Some chose a smaller teaching perspective, focusing on English only (Wong, 2020), others took a much wider perspective, observing the entire education system, national (e.g. Traxler, Smith, Scott, & Hayes, 2020) or global (UNESCO, 2020). Many concentrated on sharing their personal experience with colleagues, some also included the student experience explicitly (Amrane-Cooper et al., 2020).

What most of these publications have in common is that they show that instead of lamenting about the forced migration, teachers demonstrated their positive outlook: they were open to adopting technology if and when they saw its pedagogical values and if they were able to adapt them to their immediate needs in the virtual classroom. They combined face-to-face conversational conventions with new technical affordances. They readjusted teaching methodologies and examination practices. And they took the opportunity to leap forward into the digital age of language teaching and learning that will equip teachers and students for their digital future.

Our collection documents the individual global perspective in language teaching and learning. We tried to include the national and institutional context as a

Introduction

baseline and the diversity of creative responses as individual choices that may be inspiring to others. It is clear that the technology choice is easy, it is the standard international tool of the international teaching community. What is not so easy is the critical digital literacy for teachers and learners: the supportive, resourceful teacher and the independent, confident learner – and this pandemic provided the necessary opportunities of practice to develop resilience and collaborative efforts for all stakeholders[7].

To conclude, this collection testifies to global language teaching efforts in higher education during the 2020 COVID-19 emergency period and will serve, we trust, as a useful point of reference. Based on the collated evidence, we are proud to conclude that our profession rose magnificently to this specific challenge and that we are confident that it will continue to thrive in many diverse educational and learning contexts. And finally, we hope to have been moderately, at least, successful in offering inspiration and encouragement to colleagues around the world.

## 9. Supplementary materials

https://research-publishing.box.com/s/ubu13w6qsph7j1c4sgjj5j6rlolk051c

---

[7]. An international comparison not directly related to teaching, but to projects can be found in a DAAD (2021) working paper. It is not representative but rather a survey of innovative international project partners (n=398 all, 238 not German) that shows results that are similar to ours: The online tools (p. 10) used have a similar variation as ours and the future expectations are also that "we continue with methodologies developed" (p. 6) in blended formats. The issues of integrating social media and inverted classroom methodologies are comparable (p. 4). The problems noticed include lack of interaction and the social divide (p.13), as illustrated in many contributions in our volume. The 'lessons learnt' partly coincide with our experience (excerpts from p. 12; translated by Josef Schmied):
- Face-to-face teaching can be reduced but not replaced by online teaching!
- In synchronous formats, interaction and exchange should always be in the foreground.
- Practice-oriented content is very difficult to convey in digital form.
- E-lectures should not be too long as it is very difficult to concentrate on longer e-lectures.
- The supervision effort is immense and places more of a burden on teachers than the occasional appointments in traditional lectures.
- Access to some tools (e.g. Zoom) is blocked in some countries. The amount of data for downloads is also capped or... there may be political obstacles to digitalisation.
- Non-verbal interaction and group dynamics are not very noticeable in online teaching and are difficult to interpret.
- [Teachers] had to fundamentally rethink and question their teaching, which was very good for the quality of the teaching.

# References

Allen, I. E., & Seaman, J. (2003). *Sizing the opportunity: the quality and extent of online education in the United States, 2002 and 2003*. The Sloan Consortium. http://files.eric.ed.gov/fulltext/ED530060.pdf

Amrane-Cooper, L. et al. (2020 August 3). *Flexible learning in uncertain times: student experience*. https://www.youtube.com/watch?v=iC86TvyTzmk&feature=youtu.be

Andujar, A., Salaberri-Ramiro, M. S., & Cruz Martínez, M. S. (2020). Integrating flipped foreign language learning through mobile devices: technology acceptance and flipped learning experience. *Sustainability, 12*(3), 1110. https://doi.org/10.3390/su12031110

Baker, J. W. (2000). The "Classroom Flip": using Web course management tools to become the guide by the side. In J. A. Chambers (Ed.), *Selected papers from the 11th International Conference on College Teaching and Learning* (pp. 9-17). http://www.classroomflip.com/files/classroom_flip_baker_2000.pdf

Baxter, P., & Jack, S. (2008). Qualitative case study methodology: study design and implementation for novice researchers. *The Qualitative Report, 13*(4), 544-559. https://doi.org/10.46743/2160-3715/2008.1573

Beatty, B. (2019), *Hybrid-Flexible course design: implementing student-directed hybrid classes*. EdTech Books. https://edtechbooks.org/hyflex

Benson, P. (2012). Learner-centered teaching. In A. Burns & J. C. Richards (Eds), *The Cambridge guide to pedagogy and practice in second language teaching* (pp. 30-37). Cambridge University Press.

Bliuc, A.-M., Goodyear, P., & Ellis, R. A. (2007). Research focus and methodological choices in studies intostudents' experiences of blended learning in higher education. Internet and Higher Education, 10(4), 231-244. https://doi.org/10.1016/j.iheduc.2007.08.001

Chandra, V., & Fisher, D. L. (2009). Students' perceptions of a blended web-based learning environment. *Learning Environments Research, 12*, 31-44. https://doi.org/10.1007/s10984-008-9051-6

Cunningham, U. (2017). Flipping the language classroom. *The New Zealand Language Teacher, 43*, 41-50.

DAAD. (2021). *Digitale Lehre im Zuge der Corona Pandemie. Ergebnisse einer Umfrage bei Dozentinnen und Dozenten geförderter DAAD-Projekte*. https://static.daad.de/media/daad_de/pdfs_nicht_barrierefrei/der-daad/analysen-studien/daad_arbeitspapier_corona_digitale_lehre.pdf

Davies, G. (2016). *CALL (computer assisted language learning)*. https://www.llas.ac.uk/resources/gpg/61#ref9

Dede, C. (1996). The evolution of distance education: emerging technologies and distributed learning. *American Journal of Distance Education, 10*(2), 4-36. https://doi.org/10.1080/08923649609526919

Donnelly, R. (2010). Harmonizing technology with interaction in blended problem-based learning. *Computers & Education, 54*(2), 350-359. https://doi.org/10.1016/j.compedu.2009.08.012

Dooly, M. (2018). Collaborative learning. In J.I. Liontas & M. DelliCarpini (Eds), *The TESOL encyclopedia of English language teaching* (pp. 1-7). John Wiley & Sons.

Dziuban, C., Graham, C. R., Moskal, P. D., Norberg, A., & Sicilia, N. (2018). Blended learning: the new normal and emerging technologies. *International Journal of Educational Technology in Higher Education, 15*(3). https://doi.org/10.1186/s41239-017-0087-5

Ellis, R. (2015). The importance of focus on form in communicative language teaching. *Eurasian Journal of Applied Linguistics, 1*(2), 1-12.

Ellis, R. (2016). Focus on form: a critical review. *Language Teaching Research, 20*(3), 405-428. https://doi.org/10.1177/1362168816628627

Ellis, R., Li, S., & Zhu, Y. (2019). The effects of pre-task explicit instruction on the performance of a focused task. *System, 80*, 38-47. https://doi.org/10.1016/j.system.2018.10.004

Graham, C. R. (2013). Emerging practice and research in blended learning. In M. G. Moore (Ed.), *Handbook of distance education* (3rd ed., pp. 333-350). Routledge.

Greenberg, G. (1998). Distance education technologies: best practices for K-12 settings. *IEEE Technology and Society Magazine, Winter*, 36-40.

Henaku, N., Agbozo Edzordzi, G., & Nartey, M. (forthcoming). (Eds.). *COVID-19 in Ghana: communicative reflections*.

Holec, H. (1981). *Autonomy and foreign language learning*. Pergamon. [First published 1979, Strasbourg: Council of Europe].

Horwitz, E. K. (2010). Foreign and second language anxiety. *Language teaching, 43*(2), 154-167.

Imel, S. (1998). *Myths and realities of distance learning*. ERIC Clearinghouse on Adult, Career, and Vocational Education (Eric Document Reproduction Service No. ED 414 446).

Kessler, G. (2013). Collaborative language learning in co-constructed participatory culture. *Calico Journal, 30*(3), 307-322.

Klimova, B. F., & Kacetl, J. (2015). Hybrid learning and its current role in the teaching of foreign languages. *Procedia-Social and Behavioral Sciences, 182*, 477-481. https://doi.org/10.1016/j.sbspro.2015.04.830

Lage, M. J., Platt, G. J., & Treglia, M. (2000). Inverting the classroom: a gateway to creating an inclusive learning environment. *The Journal of Economic Education, 31*(1), 30-43. https://doi.org/10.1080/00220480009596759

Lederman, D. (2020 May 13). The HyFlex option for instruction if campuses open this fall. *Inside Higher Ed.* https://www.insidehighered.com/digital-learning/article/2020/05/13/one-option-delivering-instruction-if-campuses-open-fall-hyflex

Levy, M. (1997). *CALL: context and conceptualisation*. Oxford University Press.

Little, D. (1991). *Learner autonomy 1: definitions, issues and problems*. Authentik.

Loewen, S. (2020). *Introduction to instructed second language acquisition*. Routledge.

Long, M. (1985). A role for instruction in second language acquisition: task-based language training. In K. Hyltenstam & M. Pienemann (Eds), *Modelling and assessing second language acquisition* (pp. 77–100). Multilingual Matters.

Long, M. (1991). Focus on form: a design feature in language teaching methodology. In K. de Bot, R. Ginsberg & C. Kramsch (Eds), *Foreign language research in cross-cultural perspective* (pp. 39-52). John Benjamins. https://doi.org/10.1075/sibil.2.07lon

Macaro, E. (1997). *Target language, collaborative learning and autonomy* (vol. 5). Multilingual matters.

Norberg, A., Dziuban, C. D., & Moskal, P. D. (2011). A time-based blended learning model. *On the Horizon, 19*(3), 207-216. https://doi.org/10.1108/10748121111163913

Nunan, D. (1988). *The learner-centred curriculum: a study in second language teaching*. Cambridge University Press.

Nunan, D. (2012). *Learner-centered English language education: the selected works of David Nunan*. Routledge. https://doi.org/10.4324/9780203096888

Ortega, L. (2014). *Understanding second language acquisition*. Routledge.

Ostendorf, V. A. (1997). Teaching by television. In T. E. Cyrs, R. J. Menges & M. D. Svinicki (Eds), *Teaching and learning at a distance: what it takes to effectively design, deliver, and evaluate programs. New directions for teaching and learning 71* (pp. 51-57). Jossey-Bass Publishers.

Parsad, B., Lewis, L., & Tice, P. (2008). *Distance education at degree-granting postsecondary institutions: 2006-2007* (pp. 90-95). National Center for Education Statistics, Institute of Education Sciences, US Department of Education.

Plutino, A., & Polisca, E. (2021). (Eds). *Languages at work, competent multilinguals and the pedagogical challenges of COVID-19*. Research-publishing.net. https://doi.org/10.14705/rpnet.2021.49.9782490057832

Richards, J. C. (2006). Preface. In S. G. McCafferty (Ed.), *Cooperative learning and second language teaching*. Cambridge University Press.

Ross, B., & Gage, K. (2006). Global perspectives on blended learning: insight from WebCT and our customers in higher education. In C. J. Bonk & C. R. Graham (Eds), *Handbook of blended learning: global perspectives, local designs* (pp. 155-168). Pfeiffer.

Spada N. (2007). Communicative language teaching. In J. Cummins & C. Davison (Eds), *International handbook of English language teaching*. Springer. https://doi.org/10.1007/978-0-387-46301-8_20

Strayer, J. F. (2012). How learning in an inverted classroom influences cooperation, innovation and task orientation. *Learning Environments Research, 15*(2), 171-193. https://doi.org/10.1007/s10984-012-9108-4

Traxler, J., Smith, M., Scott, H., & Hayes, S. (2020). Learning through the crisis: helping decision-makers around the world use digital technology to combat the educational challenges produced by the current COVID-19 pandemic. Report. *EdTech Hub*. https://docs.edtechhub.org/lib/CD9IAPFX/download/5N87EV2E/Traxler%20et%20al.%20-%202020%20-%20Learning%20through%20the%20crisis%20Helping%20decision-maker.pdf

UNESCO (2020). *Education: from disruption to recovery.* https://en.unesco.org/covid19/educationresponse

Valentine, D. (2002). Distance learning: promises, problems, and possibilities. *Online journal of distance learning administration, 5*(3).

VanPatten, B., & Benati, A. G. (2015). *Key terms in second language acquisition*. Bloomsbury Publishing.

Whittaker, C. (2013). Introduction. In B. Tomlinson & C. Whittaker (Eds), *Blended learning in English language teaching: course design and implementation*. British Council.

Wong, C. (2020). (Ed.). *Special issue: ELT in the time of the coronavirus 2020* (Part 1+2) https://www.tesolunion.org/journal/lists/folder/8MTEu4NDg5/

# Section 1.
# AFRICA

# 1. Teaching Arabic during the pandemic: the remote online classroom

## Yasser Kashef[1]

### Abstract

The chapter gives the reader insights of teaching Arabic as a foreign language during the consequences of COVID-19. It tackles the outcomes of the spring and summer semesters in 2020 among students of Ningxia, Aarhus, Copenhagen, Cambridge, and Berlin universities. It sheds light upon the challenges faced by students, teachers, and management and how they are handled. The chapter depends on the collectives of two surveys carried out by the Teaching Arabic as a Foreign Language (TAFL) team. It includes students' and instructors' feedback and the means of delivery of Arabic classes amid the pandemic. It also covers the needs of the online classroom in Arabic as a foreign language. It shares language achievements during the pandemic, and recommendations for the future.

Keywords: COVID-19, online language teaching, Arabic, higher education, training, Alexandria, Egypt.

## 1. Introduction

Amid the COVID-19 pandemic, educational institutes were on a forked road whether to postpone their semesters or turn to online classes. The TAFL centre of the Alexandria University turned most of its classes into online classes due to a number of factors that are to be discussed below. It has provided

---

1. Alexandria University, Alexandria, Egypt; yasserkashef2@gmail.com; https://orcid.org/0000-0002-9769-9553

**How to cite:** Kashef, Y. (2021). Teaching Arabic during the pandemic: the remote online classroom. In N. Radić, A. Atabekova, M. Freddi & J. Schmied (Eds), *The world universities' response to COVID-19: remote online language teaching* (pp. 33-47). Research-publishing.net. https://doi.org/10.14705/rpnet.2021.52.1262

Chapter 1

online sessions in spring 2020 for students of Aarhus University, Cambridge University, Copenhagen University, and Ningxia University. Similarly, back in 2011, the TAFL centre experienced the evacuation of the students of American programmes due to political unrest in Egypt at that time. Such experience made the TAFL instructors, 12 at that time, jobless. As a result, some of the teachers made their way to online classes via skype. Thus, the idea of moving physical classes into remote/online ones was fully grasped.

This chapter focuses on how staff and students reacted to the first wave of the pandemic.

## 2. Institutional context

Alexandria University is a public university in Alexandria, Egypt. It was established in 1938 as a satellite of Fouad University, becoming an independent entity in 1942. The TAFL centre is established in 1985 as part of Alexandria University. It receives students from various cultural and educational backgrounds worldwide, and it immerses them in the Egyptian culture where they learn Arabic interactively.

The TAFL centre has a team of experienced Arabic language teachers who come with years of commended performance, as they take learners to higher levels of language proficiency. The centre is concerned with presenting an authentic image of the cultures of Egypt and the Arab/Islamic world. Moreover, the centre aims at creating a cultural bridge between Egypt and the international community, regardless of the world of politics altogether.

The centre receives students mainly from Ningxia University and China Center for International Economic Exchanges (CCIEE) programmes (China), Cambridge and Edinburgh universities (UK), Copenhagen and Aarhus universities (Denmark), and from other parts of the world like Senghor University (African countries), and a number of students from French and American universities.

## 3. Going online

In March 2020, the 30-student programme of Ningxia University was asked to depart from Alexandria, Egypt due to the consequences of COVID-19. The Chinese administration inquired about the possibility of having Arabic classes online. Aarhus University students were obliged to go back to Denmark following the same procedures a week after. The students of the Cambridge University programme were also asked to return back to the UK and have their Arabic classes online. To accommodate the requests mentioned above, the TAFL administration encouraged instructors of Arabic who have experience in teaching online to be in charge of the required classes. During that time, the rest of the instructors would have the opportunity to develop the necessary skills to be on track to start teaching online. Some individual initiatives were taken by instructors to help their colleagues. Based on their experience teaching online classes, a team of three instructors gave a workshop on how to adapt Al Kitaab, third edition (Brustad, Al-Batal, & Al-Tonsi, 2011), to online teaching. Some chapters of the book, which integrates standard Arabic with colloquial varieties, were taught to seven students from Aarhus University totally online for six weeks in the spring semester, 2020. Another workshop was given to all TAFL instructors, numbering 17, on how to harness some websites and applications in online sessions. It was given in April 2020 to TAFL instructors via Zoom. It focused on using Kahoot! and similar applications to facilitate teaching new vocabulary in Arabic. It also offered alternative applications to Zoom to be used with Chinese students such as Zhumu[2] – a Zoom-like application that is compatible with Chinese software. The goal was achieved and all physical classes were turned into virtual ones including activities and material. This time we had the opportunity to get ourselves organised and to think about how to deal with what the coming weeks would bring along.

A report (see supplementary materials, Appendix A) was made to gather data about the training and workshops that TAFL instructors received from 2019 to 2020 that focused mainly on online language teaching and technology. It

---

2. https://www.zhumu.com/download

was carried out via Google Forms. The respondents to this survey, 15 out of 17 instructors, have provided us with the data that included the following:

- title of the training or the workshop;
- the organisation that gave this training;
- the language of the training;
- whether or not there were fees for the training; and
- whether or not a certificate of attendance was issued upon the completion of the training.

It was concluded that 90% of instructors received over four training sessions about online language teaching. 40% of the training was given by international bodies and 60% was given by national ones. 59% of the training was in the Arabic language while 41% of the training was in English. 93% of the training was for free. 54% of the training gave certifications.

The TAFL team carried out an oral survey on the phone about the teachers' online experience during the spread of COVID-19 and here are the results of that survey. The team contacted 15 instructors for 15 minutes each. 90.9% of instructors were 24-34 years old. The programmes that were frequently used in online teaching were Zhumu (100%), Zoom (90.9%), Skype (27.3%), Google Meet (9.1%), Webex, and Microsoft Teams (9.1%).

In the conventional study-abroad experience, where the number of students can be from 4 to 18 per class, students have teaching hours, office hours, language-partnering sessions, and a number of extracurricular activities. They work in groups in class to practise Arabic, and then they meet up with their Egyptian language partners to practise colloquial Arabic in cafés or on the street. Because of all these activities, typical students would pick up the Arabic language and culture naturally and gradually, directly and indirectly. For instance, students would learn new words from flyers and menus written in Arabic, or they would engage in a simple conversation with the taxi driver on their way to the cinema. All of these activities would need to be condensed into a couple of hours online during the pandemic. Hence, the decision to move fully online had its costs in terms of the immersive experience of the students. The spring semester that normally starts in February was rescheduled to begin in March. A number of challenges followed.

One of the main challenges was in supporting the Chinese students, as they use certain apps and Zoom and Google were not the best technical options to use with them as some features are blocked in their region. A good alternative was a Chinese app named Zhumu that had all what a teacher would find in Zoom. A further challenge was how to keep classes as communicative as possible, almost similar to physical classes. Having 'break-out rooms' is a good virtual option but it could not fulfil all of the functions of working in groups. The instructor would not be able to follow what happens in the separate rooms and would not, therefore, be able to correct students' mistakes and provide immediate feedback. In addition, some classes could not be replicated as an online alternative was not a viable option. For instance, Arabic pronunciation[3] sessions were omitted from the schedule. One of the activities in phonetics sessions is to use a tongue depressor for each student to refer to a certain articulator and associate it with certain sounds: such an activity could not be replicated virtually nor physically due to the pandemic. Removing such sessions was a great loss, as students quickly pick up intonation and stress patterns in these classes.

Dealing with internet connectivity and efficiency was a major challenge. In Arabic as a Foreign Language (AFL) classes instructors usually warm up using a song on YouTube or using an educational game such as Kahoot!. Due to slow internet connections however, it took too long for everyone to participate. The synchronisation of sound and images was badly affected. What is more, while

---

3. 'Pronunciation sessions' are classes that not only focus on Arabic phonetics, but also phonology; intonation and syllabic stress. These classes are taught by Arabic phoneticians who help students overcome pronunciation challenges on various levels.

scanning books was not an obstacle, uploading the accompanying audiovisual materials was. Some materials were available on clouds such as Google Drive. Other materials were sent via email or WeChat. Giving oral feedback to students was another challenge as it was frequently interrupted, as such the instructor had to write down his/her feedback again.

Finally, as some classes were taught from home, the lack of technical support was another challenge to some of the instructors. As a result, academic directors of the Arabic programmes at TAFL centre would normally meet bi-weekly to discuss students' progress and language needs. Teachers would spare some time during their coffee or lunch breaks to keep up-to-date with students' understanding of classes and activities. Amid the pandemic, all breaks became a matter of luxury. The administration and teaching staff made themselves available to students 24/7, not only to make sure that everything was clear and smooth academically, but also to double check that students were in good health and could access their classes online.

## 4. Student feedback

In the surveys (see supplementary materials, Appendix B) focusing on the academic aspects of the spring and summer semesters 2020, students praised the communicative method (Brandl, 2008) used by the instructors. The surveys were conducted via Google Forms at the end of each semester. The respondents were 30 students from Ningxia University (China), seven students from Cambridge University (UK), seven students form Aarhus University (Denmark), one student from Sciences Po Institute (France), and one student from Berlin University (Germany). They showed their gratitude to the instructors for being able to alleviate the pressure they felt at first and for leading them to impressive results. The online classes enhanced students' vocabulary mastery and they indicated that the modern standard Arabic classes were an 'excellent opportunity' to practise speaking in a natural context. No matter how satisfied students were with their learning experience, they could not stop expressing how 'stressed' they were throughout their online experience.

Students also felt stressed when they did not know the appropriate answers or when they forgot new vocabulary items, and also in the context of introductions. They suggested that they should listen to the audio/video before class at home to find out details and that they should get additional writing assignments. They also indicated that their internet service was interrupted sometimes. Here are the results of students' feedback on the online sessions presented throughout spring and summer semesters as shown in Table 1.

Table 1. Students' feedback

| Internet connection and the software used | 98.9% strongly satisfied | 1.1% agree |
|---|---|---|
| Teachers were punctual | 99.6% strongly satisfied | 0.4% agree |
| Presentations were clear and organised | 86.6% strongly satisfied | 13.4% agree |
| Instructors effectively used time during class | 90.6% strongly satisfied | 9.4% agree |
| Course content | 77% strongly satisfied | 23% agree |

As for the human aspect, the students summarised the advantages of the remote study experience as follows:

- the advantage of living with the family while studying;

- a new experiment whose success came unexpectedly;

- the flexibility of being in other cities and continuing to study. "Despite my presence in Cairo, I was able to join the classes of TAFL centre in Alexandria, and had it not been for the opportunity to teach remotely, I would not have been able to join the centre's summer programme. I have the freedom to travel and move from one city to another during the semester without this affecting my attendance. Actually, this was the perfect choice for me during the Corona pandemic. I was very pleased with the experience and I hope to repeat it in the future because technology provided all the tools that helped the instructors to provide an effective communication class", said one of the respondents who was a former student at TAFL centre before and amid the pandemic; and

- self-reliance and easier access to information. "I can prepare intensively and rely more on myself. I also feel comfortable with the ease of obtaining information with the help of the professor or via the Internet, and if I were to choose between real and virtual classrooms, I would choose the virtual one", added a respondent who is a multilingual learner.

The disadvantages they mentioned were as follows:

- difficulty communicating with colleagues after class;

- absence of a blackboard: "Even a virtual blackboard doesn't help me like a real one", a respondent said;

- lack of privacy: "My sister is playing with her friend in the room and making loud noises", mentioned one of the respondents; and

- some students prefer to study in regular classes because they feel lonely: "I feel bored and lonely", added the respondent.

TAFL centre also carried out a survey about the impact of online teaching on the students' personal lives and here are the results:

- 66.7% of the students live with their families;

- 100% of students have a space for online learning;

- 66.7% the of students think that online teaching imposed restrictions on their families, while 22.2% of them didn't face that issue;

- 66.7% of the students enjoyed their online learning experience, 16.7% of them enjoyed it partially, and 16.7% did not enjoy it;

- 33.3% of the students think that working from home paved the way for a stronger kind of bond between family members, 33.3% think the opposite, and the rest of them partially think so;

- 66.7% of the students think about repeating the experience of distance learning, even partially, if the opportunity arises; and

- 66.7% of the students think that their families became more appreciative of their learning experience.

## 5. The teacher perspective

We believe that the core of the learning process is the teacher who guides the rest of elements to help students achieve their objectives smoothly. Thus, we shed light upon the teachers' perspective to measure merits and demerits of the educational process amid the pandemic. Another oral survey of two parts, academic and human aspects, was created to gather all these insights for research purposes.

The demerits as shown by the instructors:

- 90.9% of the teachers were satisfied with the online software used for online teaching and 9.1% were strongly satisfied;

- the skills that teachers faced some challenges teaching while were: listening (54.5%) and writing (18.2%), while the rest of the teachers faced no problems (27.3%);

- the skills that teachers could not evaluate easily and successfully were: listening (36.4%), reading (9.1%), and writing (9.1%), while the rest of the teachers faced no problem (45.5%);

- the aspects of communicative teaching that teachers could not apply effectively were: working in groups (54.5%) which was reflected in the students' results in their oral exams, getting students engaged in class activities (27.3%), sharing course materials (18.2%), and dealing with individual differences (9.1%);

- the class activities that the teachers could not do effectively were: role-playing (36.4%) and presentations (9.1%), while the rest of the teachers faced no challenges in doing any class activities (54.5%); and

- the technical issues that the teachers faced were: the internet speed (72.7%), the low quality of the used computer devices used (36.4%), and the power outage (36.4%).

The merits as shown by the instructors:

- 90.9% of teachers did not face any issues in homework corrections and giving feedback;

- 90.9% of the teachers were satisfied with achieving their classes' goals; and

- 90.9% of the teachers were generally satisfied with their online teaching experience.

These results led some students to perform less well than expected. This can be clearly seen in their Oral Proficiency Interviews (OPIs) according to the ACTFL (2012) guidelines. Only 43.5% of students levelled up to one sublevel in their Arabic OPIs after taking the course online. The usual number is around 70%. General suggestions for the improvement of teaching may be summed up as follows: reducing the number of students in the classroom; requesting special support for Internet quality; and supporting the use of paid applications to avoid disconnection during the class and to get more advantages.

Regarding the human aspect, the team examined the impact of online teaching on the teachers' personal lives and here are the results:

- 90.9% of the teachers live with their families;

- 100% of the teachers have an office room for online teaching;

- 66.7% of the teachers think that online teaching has imposed restrictions on their families, while 22.2% of them did not face that issue;

- 88.9% of the teachers enjoyed their online teaching experience and 11.1% of them enjoyed it partially;

- 77.8% of the teachers think that working from home paved the way for a stronger kind of bond between family members;

- 100% of the teachers think about repeating the experience of working from home, even partially, if the opportunity arises; and

- 66.7% of the teachers think that their families became more appreciative of their work.

The short answers questions showed that (1) most of the teachers' families preferred that teachers work from home to ensure that they were protected from the dangers of mixing with others during the COVID-19 pandemic, (2) some family members felt uncomfortable as a result of imposing restrictions that hampered their comfort at home, and (3) most children expressed their happiness with this decision that mothers spend all their time with them while one child expressed her dissatisfaction with her mother having to work at all.

In general, most teachers agreed on the advantages of working from home as follows: time saving; flexibility in setting appointments; avoiding traffic jams; providing support for the family as much as possible; and strengthening family bonds.

The survey also found some disadvantages: difficulty in teaching in case of family emergencies; being bored as a result of staying at home; missing the work environment and personal professional space; lack of privacy; and imposing restrictions on the rest of family members.

## 6. Outcomes

Although the whole world undergoes a difficult time dealing with the pandemic, some aspects seem to be fruitful. The management starts to change its notion from crisis management method into setting strategies to maintain a healthy flexible work environment where teaching skills can be more innovative. Thus, the outcomes of the pandemic encounter can be found in two main parts; achievements and future requirements.

### 6.1. Achievements

- A committee of senior instructors was established to help develop educational curricula that meet the virtual needs as there is a lack of material that can be fit to online classes in AFL.

- A group of experienced examiners with different backgrounds was created to compile and create virtual assessment tools such as placement tests, evaluative exams, and proficiency-oriented exams.

- A wide range of graduation projects were collected to help in both documenting students' proficiency in the language and disseminating Arabic classes. This would be the result of replacing final exams with final projects such as videos, skits, and other creative outcomes.

- We taught 2,782 online contact hours (out of the 3,868 'normal' hours) in both spring and summer semesters 2020.

- 12 out of 17 instructors at TAFL Centre received more than five different training programmes/workshops online to enhance their digital teaching skills in the spring and summer semesters in 2020.

- Paying more attention to non-academic elements in encouraging students to achieve their desired level of proficiency in Arabic. Teaching amid the pandemic was an eyeopener to students' human side. The educational process does not only depend on curricula and students' academic achievements, but it also depends on their culture and bonds with society.

## 6.2. Future requirements

- Decrease the number of learners in classes so they can benefit more from the offered academic time and feel less stressed.

- Have a teaching assistant in virtual classes to follow the different groups in the breaking rooms to fulfil the academic objectives of each and every class.

- Have an alternative to some of the extracurricular activities where Arab culture is the goal. Virtual platforms are needed not only to enhance students' awareness of the target culture but also to let them interact with native-speakers and fully grasp that target culture. This leads us to the question of whether or not virtual cultural activities can be an alternative to the study-abroad experience.

- Agree on common issues with regard to internet connectivity as the pandemic experience has shown us that both developing and developed countries suffer from poor internet. Hence, there will be a worldwide demand to have solutions for technical support and internet improvement where advanced teaching tools can be simpler and more adequate.

- Give more space for further research with regard to humanistic theory and distance learning in teaching foreign languages. More trainings are needed in this regard for future requirements and improvements in Egyptian universities.

Chapter 1

## 7. Conclusion

It is profoundly useful to test the weaknesses and strengths of our educational body. Writing this chapter gave us the opportunity to examine what we achieved as well as what we need to do in the future. By moving online, the TAFL centre has become fully aware of the logistic and academic needs. In the transitioning phase, instructors created and compiled a number of educational materials to be used for online classes. In time of need, alternative and creative solutions are made.

We realise that we need to improve our research skills and give more time to explore new methods and approaches. Dealing with various students from totally different backgrounds has enhanced our overview of the teaching process. Besides our regular surveys at the end of each semester, the team of contributors dedicated their time to carry out oral surveys with their colleagues to tackle the challenges they face amid the first wave of the pandemic. This move was made specially for the sake of creating this chapter.

The COVID-19 experience is still an ongoing story that we really hope will have a happy end, or at least a safe one. In this chapter, we attempt to show the world how students and teachers can go through the same experience and bear the consequences of a world disaster by sharing their enthusiasm within class activities. Teachers feel urged to give not only academic feedback on assignments but also endless support to the young people they teach. Teaching Arabic as a foreign language has developed a new path where more students can be reached and more teachers be trained.

## 8. Acknowledgements

I would like to express my sincere gratitude to my colleagues at the TAFL centre, Alexandria University, for providing me with the needed data as well as sharing their personal accounts on their experience teaching amid the first wave of the pandemic. I really appreciate your support: Dr Lana Habib, director of TAFL centre, Alaa Khalil, Samar Zayed, and Shrouk Fahmy, instructors of Arabic at the TAFL centre, for contributing to this chapter by collecting data and sharing reports. I would also thank Dr Rania Abdul Meguid, lecturer at the English Department, Alexandria University, for her helpful comments in proofreading the chapter.

## 9. Supplementary materials

https://research-publishing.box.com/s/cqslfyl1udjofqek89415s18akmbbryr

## References

ACTFL. (2012). *Proficiency guidelines*. https://www.actfl.org/resources/actfl-proficiency-guidelines-2012/arabic/arabic-consensus-project/speaking

Brandl, K. (2008). *Communicative language teaching in action putting principles to work*. Perason Prentic Hall.

Brustad, K., Al-Batal, M., & Al-Tonsi, A. (2011). *Al-Kitaab fii ta'allum al-'Arabiyya* [A textbook for beginning Arabic]. Georgetown University Press.

# 2 Going virtual, staying face-to-face: trajectory of ELT classes during the pandemic

## Daniel A. Nkemleke[1]

### Abstract

COVID-19 caught everyone by surprise, and even the most advanced higher education institutions around the world probably had challenges moving from Face-to-Face (F2F) to online teaching and learning. For Cameroon, where internet connectivity is still very low, both teachers and students have had a hard time switching to virtual classrooms. This chapter discusses the challenges they have faced in navigating this trajectory in the department of English at the Ecole Normale Supérieure (ENS) of the University of Yaoundé 1 (UYI) during the period of lockdown. Based on the experience of 14 teachers who grappled with 14 online courses and F2F mode, the study concludes that due to students' inability to access the internet with ease, any online teaching/learning at ENS has to be largely complemented with F2F activities.

Keywords: COVID-19, online language teaching, Ecole Normale Supérieure Yaoundé, Cameroon.

---

1. University of Yaoundé 1, Yaoundé, Cameroon; nkemlekedan@yahoo.com; https://orcid.org/0000-0002-0048-9067

How to cite: Nkemleke, D. A. (2021). Going virtual, staying face-to-face: trajectory of ELT classes during the pandemic. In N. Radić, A. Atabekova, M. Freddi & J. Schmied (Eds), *The world universities' response to COVID-19: remote online language teaching* (pp. 49-61). Research-publishing.net. https://doi.org/10.14705/rpnet.2021.52.1263

Chapter 2

# 1. Introduction

## 1.1. Administrative riposte in the light of a health pandemic

The coronavirus disrupted academic agendas in higher education institutions across the world (Azzi-Huck & Shmis, 2020; Kathmandu, 2020; Ngogi, 2020) and African universities, which have limited technology infrastructures and seem to have suffered the most (Aborode et al., 2020; Thelma & Adeniran, 2020). According to a recent UNESCO report, 9.8 million African students experienced disruption in their studies due to the closure of higher education institutions[2]. Cameroon officially acknowledged the presence of the COVID-19 pandemic in its territory when two cases were detected at a local airport in the capital city of Yaoundé on March 6, 2020, barely a month into the second semester (Onana, 2020). On March 18, the government officially closed down schools and universities and outlined social distancing measures in public places throughout the country. This new status quo raised fear and anxiety on the part of many actors and stakeholders of society, including our university administration, whose immediate preoccupation was how to bring the academic year to a successful end while safeguarding the health of all members of the university community. Prior to the government lockdown of March 18, the rector of the UYI had anticipated the worst case scenario and had issued his first press release on March 16, in which F2F lectures in amphitheatres and other lecture halls with a capacity of more than 150 students were temporarily suspended. Also, a virtual platform was created at the University Centre for Information Technology (CUTI) for teachers to upload content online[3]. The rector's press release was reported on the official website of the state-owned radio station (CRTV) as follows[4]: "[t]here will be a change in the university's programme from March 17 to April 13, 2020, in order to avoid a crowd of students in one area and to avoid the spread of COVID-19". In another press release on March 25, the rector asked all institutions of the

---

2. https://en.unesco.org/covid19/educationresponse

3. https://www.camerounweb.com/CameroonHomePage/NewsArchive/Coronavirus-l-universit-de-Yaound-1-suspend-ses-cours-498841

4. http://www.crtv.cm/2020/03/covid19-university-of-yaounde-i-takes-preventive-measures/

university to explore the opportunities that technology offers for hybrid learning and to envisage creating online platforms to deliver content.

## 1.2. Technology-based-learning at the UYI: a review of digital experiences prior COVID-19

In the past several years, the UYI has identified the digital teaching method as a key asset to solve the problem of high student-enrolment numbers in the institution. In fact in 2007, the government had defined technology-based education as one of its key strategic development goals and had urged all sectors of society to begin a process of adaptation to this new exigency (ANTIC, 2007)[5]. Consequently, in 2008 the Alumni of the Alexander von Humboldt Foundation in Cameroon applied for and obtained German Academic Exchange Service (DAAD) funding to run four e-learning schools in the span of two years in Yaoundé (2011-2012), with the last one held in Stuttgart, Germany (Teke, 2012). These e-learning schools trained a critical mass of university teachers who were to replicate their expertise with subsequent generations of peers. Specifically, they went through the following with keen interest: (1) e-learning in higher education, concepts, and templates (July 2011); (2) content development and content organisation for e-learning (December 2011); (3) teaching and learning with different models of e-learning (April/May 2012), and (4) quality assessment and review of e-learning content and learning processes (November 2012).

The multiplier effect of this venture has been significant. Teke (2012), for example, undertook a project to digitalise a course on critical theory for postgraduate students at the UYI and assess the contribution of the project on the critical development of students in technology-based skills. The experience of Teke (2012) in running such a course online enabled him to conclude that "the dynamism of the lecturer [online] and the multiple involvements of learners militate in favour of an effective e-learning atmosphere" (p.74). This is corroborated by the experience of others working in similar situations in Cameroon, who concluded that in a multivariate e-learning platform, students

---

5. See "ICT in Education in Cameroon" (2007): www.infodev.org/en/Document.390.pdf

often learn even ahead of timed lectures (Achale, Mambeh, & Chomgwain, 2007). In the same perspective, a survey of the perception of 218 students, 57 residents, and 32 teachers in the Faculty of Medicine and Biomedical Sciences (FMBS) in the UYI by Bediang et al. (2013) reports that "most participants have fairly good experiences in accessing content online, although good practices about their use remained insufficiently known" (p. 7). On the whole, the study concludes that Information and Communication Technology (ICT) integration in the FMBS is still mostly individually-based and lacks coordination. Further, a survey by Nkemleke and Tume (2020) on the use of WhatsApp to conduct a summary writing class at the time of coronavirus at ENS reveals that students' perception of teaching and learning through technology was very positive. This positive perception was mainly due to easy accessibility of smartphones and other digital platforms by students. The Faculty of Engineering (polytechnique) of the UYI houses the most important learning management system, Moodle, of the institution. It also runs a MOOCS for course development programmes. Experts from polytechnique provide regular training programmes for online courses and management to staff in other university faculties. On an individual level, teachers in the UYI run personal online platforms with students for purposes of research. For example, I run an intra-African/German Postdoc Mentoring Online (iAG-POSMO[6]) platform for academic mentoring of junior scientists in the humanities from countries across Africa; 90% of the 51 members are in Cameroon. This platform is an affiliate of the bigger platform we have been running since 2015[7]. Initially sponsored by a grant from the Alexander von Humboldt Foundation, the Academic Writing for Africa platform mentors research students online and prepares them for the writing of grant applications.

In brief, students and teachers in the UYI in general, and ENS Yaoundé in particular, are familiar with online platforms even if not on a very general scale. Before the outbreak of COVID-19, teachers had been used to delivering lectures to groups of students via Google Classroom, video conferences via WhatsApp, Zoom, etc. In fact, the Moodle platform that ENS presently manages has been

---

6. https://iag-posmo.org/

7. http://academicwriting-network4africa.org/

in place for about a decade. Although COVID-19 had been a surprise to many in Cameroon as it had been elsewhere, our students were already familiar with online environments for educational purposes when the rector called for the intensification of online learning. This does not, however, mean that every teacher and student is positively motivated to engage with this. In fact, there are a number of digital novices among the students' and teachers' population of the university for whom the call for online classes was to be very challenging.

## 2. Objectives

Following the instructions of the university administration above, ENS, a teacher training institution of the UYI, began a series of consultations with teachers to implement instructions from the university hierarchy. This present article reports on the trajectory of our language/literature teaching courses in the department of English at ENS Yaoundé and how we grapple with teaching at this time of COVID-19, between the virtual space and F2F interaction. To attain this objective, it is important to mention the support that we received from university administration.

While the coronavirus outbreak uncovered the lack of preparation of many colleagues in the department to go online at a short notice, administrative support came readily and on time to dissipate lingering anxieties. One of the very first actions the rector took was to announce that teachers were to be paid an allowance for putting courses online. Table 1 below details the number of press communiques and circular letters signed by the rector at various moments during the lockdown to guide the conduct of activities in the different faculties and university schools.

Application of the above directives required a certain amount of preliminary work at the level of each department. Since online learning is not just a question of uploading lecture notes and videos on a virtual platform, teachers had to write their lectures in a manner that would be easy for students to understand when they access them. But this was not done without difficulty, however. Section 3 outlines a profile of what teachers uploaded and the virtual platforms they used. It is followed by a preliminary survey of students' reaction and perception of the whole exercise. Section 4 concludes this chapter.

Table 1. Decisions taken by the rector to guide the conduct of pedagogic activities during COVID-19

| Date | Content |
| --- | --- |
| March 16, 2020 (Ref. 20-321/UYI/CAB/R) | Press communique to faculty administrators, teachers, and students announcing the creation of an online platform at the CUTI |
| May 26, 2020 (Ref. 20-042/UYI/CAB/R) | Press communique to faculty administrators, teachers, and students announcing preparation for the resumption of F2F lectures in strict respect of barrier measures such as fragmentation of large classes into manageable groups |
| September 11, 2020 (Ref. 202208/UYI/CAB/R) | Circular letter to deans and directors of university faculties and schools, announcing the putting in place of virtual amphitheatres: each teacher/student is to be attributed an institutional email address |
| October 15, 2020 (Ref.202639/UYI/CAB/R) | Press communique to faculty administrators, teachers, and students announcing preparation for the resumption of F2F lectures for the first semester 2020/2021 academic year in strict respect of barrier measures such as fragmentation of large classes into manageable groups |

## 3. Discussion: our teaching experiences during COVID-19

This section is divided into three phases. The first is the planning phase, where teachers designed lecture notes which were uploaded onto a virtual platform intended for students' self-study. The second is the follow-up phase, where teachers were encouraged to engage with students in interactive platforms of their choice. The third phase is the return to a pre-COVID-19 F2F situation. This last phase had been necessary to address recurrent complaints by the students who had some difficulties understanding some of the material put online. At the same time, it was an opportunity for teachers who had been unable to hold an online class (e.g. Teacher 7 in Table 2) to meet the students and accelerate their teaching programmes.

## 3.1. The planning phase: self-study material for students uploaded on a virtual platform

In response to the communique of March 16 (Table 1), teachers got to work, each person from their own location, because communication at this time of lockdown was only by telephone, emails, WhatsApp, and SMS. Heads of departments and heads of teaching units, including coordinators of different classes, contacted students via WhatsApp messages or telephone to inform them of what was happening. Once each teacher had finished preparing their lecture notes with accompanying documents, s/he sent them to CUTI, which had the responsibility to upload them onto a platform (see Figure 1 and supplementary materials for the content of 14 English language teaching courses uploaded). Students were informed to access them using a simple internet link.

Figure 1. CUTI interface @ UYI[8]

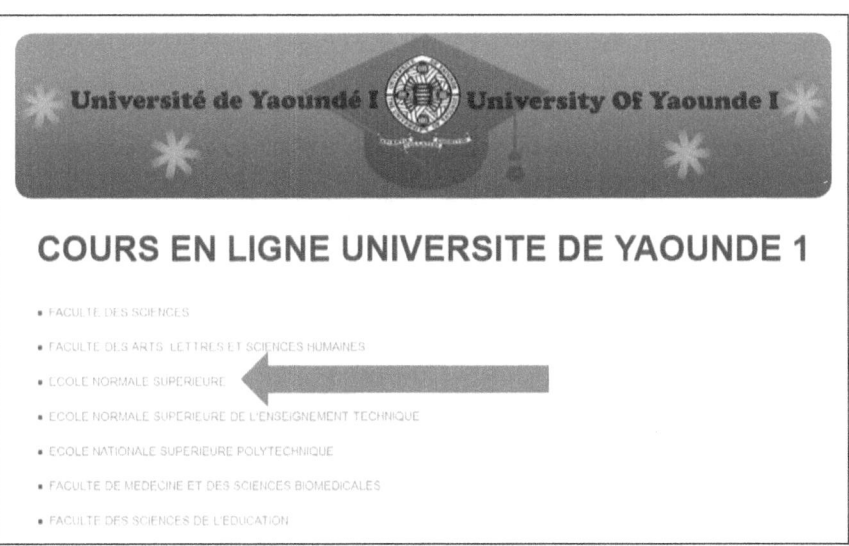

---

8. http://www.coursuy1.uninet.cm/

Obviously, asking students to download online study material was not without challenges. The department was ready at every moment to listen to the difficulties that students might encounter. To anticipate this, communication lines between the different classes and the teachers were kept open through class delegates, who would receive feedback from peers and then share the information with the teachers through personal SMS, telephone, and, in some cases, teachers' personal WhatsApps. This information would then be discussed during weekly coordination meetings at the level of the department. Up to this point, what we did not give a serious thought to, both at the level of the department and at the level of the school council, was that CUTI is only a repository of content.

Successful online learning is not guaranteed just by placing content online; rather, such material has to be accompanied by clear task-based instructions (Tuovinen, 2000; Zimmerman, 2012) and students have to be able to get instant feedback on their performances (Roussel, 2011). Students reported that they had difficulties understanding many of the materials which teachers had put online. Some reading texts had no 'how-to-do' instructions. Of course, problems with the content of these lecture notes were to be expected since the work had been done at short notice and under pressure.

Once it became clear from this preliminary feedback that some explanations of the online content would be necessary, the need for some kind of virtual interaction and eventually a return to a pre-COVID-19 F2F situation began to be contemplated.

## 3.2. The follow-up phase: teachers interact with students on virtual platforms

In one of our weekly school coordination meetings, it was recommended that teachers should engage students in some form of virtual interaction, so specific questions from students could be addressed. Such follow-up was easy to begin, at least, for most of us in the department of English, since it had been a general practice for every class to have a WhatsApp forum. Table 2 shows the different web apps that were used to organise classes after this recommendation.

Table 2. Teachers/web apps used for online interaction

| Teacher/ Apps used | WhatsApp class forum | Individual WhatsApp | Google classroom | Facebook group | Zoom | Padlet group | SMS | Tel. | Email |
|---|---|---|---|---|---|---|---|---|---|
| Teacher 1 | x | x | - | - | - | - | - | x | x |
| Teacher 2 | x | - | - | - | - | - | - | x | - |
| Teacher 3 | x | x | - | - | - | - | - | - | x |
| Teacher 4 | x | - | - | - | x | - | - | x | - |
| Teacher 5 | x | x | - | - | - | - | x | x | x |
| Teacher 6 | x | - | - | - | - | - | x | - | - |
| Teacher 7 | - | - | - | - | - | - | - | - | - |
| Teacher 8 | x | - | - | x | - | x | - | - | x |
| Teacher 9 | x | x | - | x | - | - | x | - | - |
| Teacher 10 | x | - | - | - | - | - | x | - | x |
| Teacher 11 | x | - | - | - | - | - | - | x | - |
| Teacher 12 | x | x | x | - | - | - | - | - | x |
| Teacher 13 | x | - | - | - | - | - | - | - | - |
| Teacher 14 | x | - | - | - | x | - | - | x | - |

Thirteen of the 14 teachers in the department interacted with students on WhatsApp – a very popular web app among students in ENS. Fifteen attested that they were also engaged with students through the latter's personal WhatsApp accounts (individual WhatsApp), SMS, and telephone to address specific questions that these students had posed to them through the same channels. The students reported that Padlet, Facebook, and Google classroom were not as user-friendly as WhatsApp, and this explains why those teachers who used them also used WhatsApp in the end. Three teachers used Zoom a few times. Teacher 7 was unable to use any of the applications. He could only get to the students in the F2F session. This, however, was not an isolated case. Many teachers in other departments at ENS waited to resume teaching only when F2F activities started on June 1. This present F2F session, though welcomed by the students, still posed problems to some. From the feedback received from them, only 60% (i.e. 58/98) said they were fully satisfied with the whole online project. This is a thing they had not been used to. Many cited lack of connectivity, power failure, the timing of the virtual classes, etc. as sources of problems and wished to come back to a F2F classroom situation. On the other hand, some teachers acknowledged that they had not been able to satisfactorily explain the content of their courses in this virtual classroom phase, not least because of the difficulties of having students linked up at the scheduled time to participate. These preoccupations led to the return of F2F lectures.

### 3.3. June 1, 2020: return to F2F classes

On May 26, 2020 the rector asked all deans and directors of schools of the UYI to prepare for the resumption of F2F classes beginning June 1. This resumption of teaching in lecture halls did not invalidate online activities. In fact, in the spirit of the communique, a hybrid model of learning/teaching remained the official policy of the university, and any F2F activity had to be done under strict social distancing rules which involved the fragmentation of classes into manageable groups. F2F teaching lasted for three weeks from June 1. During this time, those who had already advanced significantly with online teaching had the opportunity to revise; and those who had not been able to do anything significant online, accelerated work. At the end of the three weeks of teaching, a semester exam was successfully conducted under the same safety conditions.

## 4. Conclusion: what we have learned from remote teaching experience

Teaching and learning English at the time of COVID-19 has been challenging for both students and teachers. The decision for classes to go online was unexpected. On the whole, both teachers and students received online teaching and learning with mixed feelings. While many teachers struggled to adapt to online environments, a few, for want of hands-on experience, stayed at the fringes, preferring only minimal engagement with technology. On the other hand, students cited internet connectivity, power failure at the time of online discussions, etc. as some sources of difficulty for them. Teachers themselves were not always at the top of the technology drive. My direct experience as Chair of the department, who also had the responsibility to oversee the implementation of these virtual classes, is that the frequency with which online discussions were conducted was not enough for significant assimilation of any language content. I do not think we should just be contented with the fact that a teacher and a group of students went online. COVID-19 has taught us that the trend to technology-based learning is irreversible, either to solve the problem of safety or to solve the problem of high student-enrolment numbers that Cameroonian (and elsewhere in African) universities are currently experiencing. Consequently, we need to begin to formulate benchmarks for online teaching efficiency. The other issue to address is that of resources to access content online. UNESCO data suggests that 89% of students in sub-Saharan Africa do not have access to the internet (Aborode et al., 2020, p. 7).

The statistics for teachers is not better, either. African universities and other education stakeholders have to consider investing in the infrastructure that makes access to www cheap or free for students. Such modest attempts are already going on in countries like Rwanda and Tunisia, where universities are partnering with internet providers to provide zero-rated access to specific educational and information websites for the benefit of higher education (Aborode et al., 2020). Cameroon still has to get to this level. With a 60% (i.e. 59/98) approval by students who went through the experience of online teaching/learning during COVID-19 lockdown, a fair conclusion is that any online teaching has to be largely complemented with F2F activities.

## 5. Acknowledgements

I wish to thank all our students of the English/bilingual studies sections at ENS Yaoundé of the 2019/2020 academic year who participated in the online classes and willingly gave feedback on how they felt about the courses. I also would like to thank Dr Silke Mentchen of the Faculty of Modern and Medieval Languages and Linguistics, University of Cambridge and Dr Mahbod Ghaffari of the Department of Modern & Medieval Languages, University of Cambridge, UK, for the editorial input they made on the original manuscript.

## 6. Supplementary materials

https://research-publishing.box.com/s/a7cqxxelf67lzma9j5vhmx1pfo6fn8rf

## References

Aborode, A., Anifowoshe, O., Ifeoluwapo Ayodele, T., Rebecca Iretiayo, A., Oluwafemi David, O. (2020). Impact of COVID-19 on education in Sub-Saharan Africa. *Preprints*. https://www.preprints.org/manuscript/202007.0027/v1

Achale, T., Mambeh, C., & Chomgwain, L. (2007). The use of information and communication technology (ICT) for quality education in cameroon state universities. ERNWACA.

ANTIC. (2007). *National development strategy on information and communication technologies*. Cameroon. https://www.antic.cm/index.php/fr/info-tic/statistiques-tic.html

Azzi-Huck, K., & Shmis, T. (2020 March 18). Managing the impact of COVID-19 on education systems around the world: how countries are preparing, coping, and planning for recovery. *World Bank Blogs*. https://blogs.worldbank.org/education/managing-impact-covid-19-education-systems-around-world-how-countries-are-preparing

Bediang. G., Stoll, B., Geissbuhler, A., Klohn, A. M., Stuckelberger, A., Nko'o, S., & Chastonay, P. (2013). Computer literacy and e-learning perception in Cameroon: the case of Yaoundé Faculty of Medicine and Biomedical Sciences. *BMC Medical Education*, 1-8. https://doi.org/10.1186/1472-6920-13-57

Kathmandu, K. (2020). COVID-19 educational disruption and response: continuation of radio education for secondary level students in Nepal. UNESCO. https://en.unesco.org/news/covid-19educational-disruption-and-response-continuation-radio-education-secondary-level

Ngogi, E. M. (2020). The impact of Covid-19 pandemic on education: navigating forward the pedagogy of blended learning. *University of Pretoria, South Africa, 5*, 4-9.

Nkemleke, D., & Tume, L. (2020). WhatsApp-based learning in Ecole Normale Supérieure de Yaoundé-Cameroon at the time of coronavirus. *International Journal of TESOL Studies, 2*(3), 13-31. https://doi.org/10.46451/ijts.2020.09.15

Onana, C. (2020). Effets socio-economiques potentiels de la pandemie du covid-19 au Cameroun [white paper]. https://www.researchgate.net/publication/341993175

Roussel, S. (2011). A computer assisted method to track listening strategies in second language learning. *ReCALL, 23*(2), 98-116. https://doi.org/10.1017/s0958344011000036

Teke, C. (2012). Digitalizing learning contents in Cameroon's higher education: toward standardizing a critical theory course site in the University of Yaoundé 1. *Bhatter College Journal of Multidisciplinary Studies, 2*, 66-75.

Thelma, O., & Adeniran. A. P. (2020). *Covid-19: impending situation threatens to deeper Nigeria's education crisis.* https://www.africaportal.org/publications/covid-19-impending-situation-threatens-deepen-nigerias-education-crisis/

Tuovinen, J. E. (2000). Multimedia distance education interactions. *Educational Media International, 37*(1), 16-24. https://doi.org/10.1080/095239800361473

Zimmerman, T. D. (2012). Exploring learner to content interaction as a success factor in online courses. *International Review of Research in Open & Distance Learning, 13*(4), 152-165. https://doi.org/10.19173/irrodl.v13i4.1302

# 3. Online remote language teaching during and beyond the pandemic: echoes from the Anchor University in Lagos

## Tunde Ope-Davies[1]

### Abstract

The outbreak of the coronavirus (COVID-19) brought along with it a number of socio-political, public health, administrative, economic, and educational challenges and impacts across the world. Teaching and learning as a critical component of our social existence have been equally impacted with new technologies providing both the tools and affordances for effective virtual learning. This chapter discusses the adoption and application of digital technologies for online teaching and learning at Anchor University, Lagos (AUL), a private tertiary institution in Lagos, Nigeria. The study foregrounds its theoretical principles on Kirkwood and Price's (2014) perspective on Technology-Enhanced Learning (TEL) and Herring's (2004) Computer-Mediated Discourse Analysis (CMDA). The dataset was drawn from Google Classroom's platform deployed by AUL during the COVID-19 crisis. I used qualitative content-based analysis to discuss how the selected data reflect the reality of TEL during the pandemic. The study argues that the deployment of new technologies for teaching and learning in higher education utilised the existing framework and availability of digital tools and mobile communication networks resulting from the phenomenal development of the Information and Communication Technologies (ICT) industry in Nigeria. It confirms that the availability of a range of digital technologies and social media platforms has improved the possibilities of adapting to remote

1. University of Lagos, Lagos, Nigeria; bopeibi@unilag.edu.ng; https://orcid.org/0000-0002-1772-6356

How to cite: Ope-Davies, T. (2021). Online remote language teaching during and beyond the pandemic: echoes from the Anchor University in Lagos. In N. Radić, A. Atabekova, M. Freddi & J. Schmied (Eds), *The world universities' response to COVID-19: remote online language teaching* (pp. 63-78). Research-publishing.net. https://doi.org/10.14705/rpnet.2021.52.1264

# Chapter 3

learning during the period and beyond. It concludes by highlighting socio-educational benefits of remote teaching and learning and some challenges of teaching language-related courses in Nigeria and other similar cultural contexts.

**Keywords: COVID-19, online language teaching, virtual learning environment, Nigeria.**

## 1. Introduction and the context of the study

The outbreak of the pandemic has accelerated the development of life-changing technologies that now enable the modern world to accomplish tremendous things thought near-impossible several years ago. The deployment of these new technologies and the emergence of 'new normal phenomena' have succeeded in reconfiguring the motions, mechanics, and dynamics of our daily lives. While teaching online has been increasingly popular in western institutions as far back as the early 1990's when computers and the internet were becoming widespread, the COVID-19 crisis has accelerated its spread and growth across the world.

In this part of the world, the transition from classroom-based to remote teaching and learning represents a paradigm shift for many educational institutions in Nigeria. Prior to the COVID-19 era in March 2020, some efforts had been made to create viable online learning environments through different learning management systems, especially the popular massive open online courses. However, while online distance learning has become popular with the establishment of the National Open University Nigeria to compete with other conventional universities offering online courses, the COVID-19 public health crisis accelerated the pace of remote teaching and learning in Nigeria. The emergence of more recent software/platforms such as Google Classroom, Microsoft Teams, Zoom, Skype, Telegram, and WhatsApp accelerated the development of online learning during the pandemic.

Historically, the growth of the mobile communication system and internet services in Nigeria at the turn of the century has contributed widely to the acceleration of the digitalisation initiatives that began around the late 1990's. At the tertiary education level around the country, aggressive digitalisation and automation of administrative and aspects of academic activities began in the early 2000's. Most institutions of higher learning realised the urgency to move their administrative processes such as processing of admission documents, students' registration, examination results, and procurement of academic transcripts, etc.

On March 30th, 2020, the federal government of Nigeria announced total lockdown in some major cities following the spread of the pandemic. Consequently, schools were shut and students were forced to stay at home. Some state governments utilised traditional media platforms such as radio and television to deliver instructions on different subjects to pupils and students in public schools. Proprietors and owners of private secondary schools relied on new media technologies and digital platforms because the student populations are usually drawn from children from the upper and middle classes with stronger economic power. Such students in these categories constitute about 37.5% of the total population of students (Oyediran et al., 2020; NESG, 2020). Since their parents can afford to give their wards smartphones, laptops, or other devices with internet connectivity, it was not difficult for such private schools to switch to remote teaching. Some popular platforms deployed by some secondary schools include WhatsApp, Telegram, Skype, Jitsu, and Facebook. The use of mobile devices to teach and receive educational content suddenly became fashionable in urban areas like Lagos, Abuja, Port-Harcourt, and Kaduna where the lockdown was more pronounced. Private companies offering online lessons, applications, and tutorials also grew.

At the post-secondary educational level, most private and faith-based universities relied on web-based platforms with technical affordances for text-based and audio-visual interactions that also allowed synchronous, real-time communication such as Zoom, Google Meet, or Google Classroom, for remote teaching and learning. Despite challenges that included high cost of internet data, epileptic power supply that have been part of the daily experience of Nigerians before the public health crisis, COVID-19 provided an entirely new experience and paradigm shift in online teaching and education management services in Nigeria. It is observed however that most public universities were confronted with challenges such as lack of teaching facilities in digital format, widespread lack of experience in remote teaching among academic staff, and the lingering strike action by university teachers. On the other hand, many private universities with existing robust digital infrastructure and technologies were able to move swiftly from face-to-face, in-person teaching to virtual teaching.

Since March 2020 therefore, remote teaching has increasingly become very fashionable and moving to the level of defining the future of higher education in Nigeria. It is this new trend that constitutes the focus of this study on how new technologies are promoting virtual learning, against the backdrop of the pandemic, using a private university as a case study.

## 2. Technology, remote teaching, and online interaction

Kirkwood and Price's (2014, p. 1) description of remote teaching and learning as TEL focuses on the application of ICT to teaching and learning. As technologies are being used in other sectors of human activities to improve the mechanics and dynamics of our daily life, it is assumed that technologies have the potential to enhance learning. It is true that some challenges may impede this new mode of teaching such as the cost of financial investment made by institutions for infrastructure, equipment, and technical support staff, personal investment made by staff and students in using the technology for teaching and learning which will include the cost of alternative power supply, personal internet services/data, and laptop, desktop or smartphones. TEL however has been found to offer some benefits to learners and instructors especially during public health crises such as COVID-19.

Gillet-Swan (2017) asserts that the prevailing assumption is that "technological incorporation, learning enhancement, and student engagement are mutually and inextricably linked" (p. 21). However, Orlando and Attard (2015) argue that "teaching with technology is not a one size fits all approach as it depends on the types of technology in use at the time and also the curriculum content being taught" (p. 119). The availability of different technologies has made this argument plausible. Herring (2001) considers how synchronous and asynchronous models of Computer-Mediated Communication (CMC) influence online discourse behaviour. As mentioned elsewhere (Opeibi & Oluwasola, 2013),

> "CMC has been used as tool kits to study and explain how the new media technologies influence the strategies in which language users within a given virtual sphere engage a wide range of audience through the virtual protocols (Herring, 2001)" (p. 123).

Herring's (2004) CMDA argues that online interaction overwhelmingly takes place by means of discourse (p. 1). One of the assumptions of CMDA germane to this study is encapsulated in the view that these new technologies may shape the process and pattern of online communication in virtual learning environments especially as they promote both asynchronous and synchronous communication with its socio-technical features.

## 3. Methodology

As part of the data collection procedures adopted for the study, I used datasets extracted from the Google Classroom's platform deployed by AUL and some screenshots taken from the tutorials conducted for academic staff in preparation for online teaching during the COVID-19 crisis. Google Classroom was adopted because it was one of the best and simple-to-learn-and-operate technologies. The methodology thus involved participant-observation, manual online data harvesting from the Google Classroom platform, and selected slides from the presentations made during the training exercise for staff prior to the commencement of the virtual teaching. Additional data was extracted from an unscheduled telephone interview and interaction with another language teacher at AUL. The dataset was subjected to qualitative content analysis based on theoretical constructs discussed above.

Chapter 3

## 4. Presentation and description of data

AUL started its online classes in May 2020 after about one-week training for its staff. The use of Google Classroom as the platform of choice was based on its simple technical affordances, its integration to Google Mail Services and easy compatibility with virtually all the operating systems and mobile devices. Since Google Classroom does not mandatorily require a complex and sit-in desktop computer, most students and staff found it very convenient to use their smartphones to participate in class discussions and access online contents shared by their lecturers. Both staff and students had been trained on how to use the platform prior to the full deployment of the technology.

The first phase of the preparation for lecturers involved training programmes on how to register students on the platform, lecture schedule management, attendance management, reports submission, managing course assessment tests, and conducting examinations. The training programmes also included how to use exam.net for course assessments and examination. A few of the screenshots from the AUL website are shown in supplementary materials.

It is noteworthy that the series of training organised by the ICT unit was instrumental to the success of the near-seamless remote teaching and learning at AUL during the pandemic-driven lockdown. Both administrative and academic procedures such as class scheduling, students and teachers' attendance and online participation, submissions of reports, and examination verifications were integrated on the platform (see Figure 1 and Figure 2). The initial apprehension among members of staff especially those with minimal ICT skills was addressed with confidence-building strategies adopted during the training. AUL students were equally trained on how to use the platform hence they were able to participate actively in the virtual classes from different parts of the country. For example, one of my students in the ENG 422 (multilingualism) class lives in the north-eastern part of the country. She was able to attend the online classes and wrote the exams virtually along with others in Lagos, and other parts of the country. Thankfully, the Google Classroom platform offers near-seamless synchronous CMC that fosters wider reach and

Tunde Ope-Davies

intensive interaction between the lecturer and the students as discussed further in the next section (Figure 3).

Figure 1. Online examination in progress

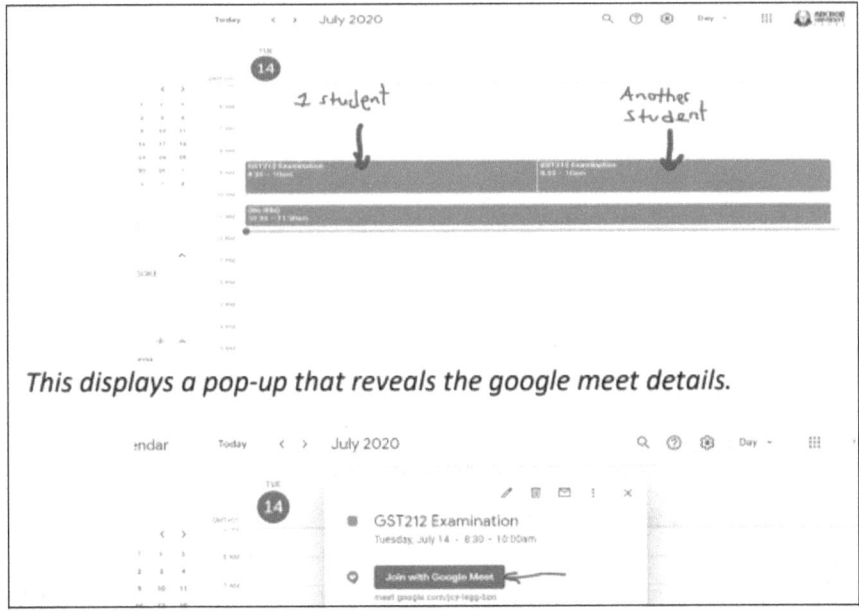

Figure 2. Students' examination verification and authentication process

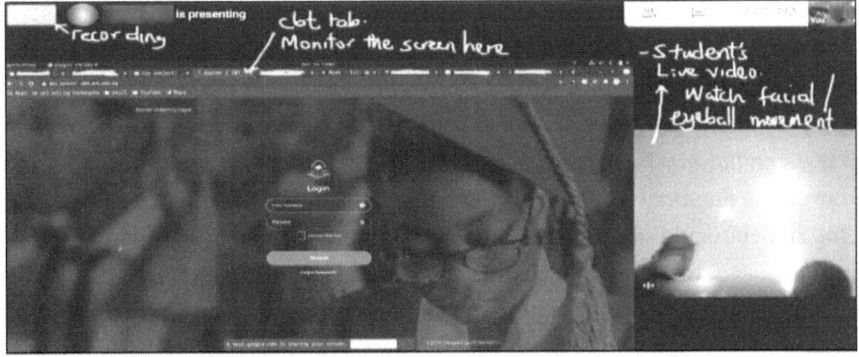

69

Figure 3. A typical synchronous interaction on Google Classroom platform

## 5. Discussion

In Zhu, Herring, and Bonk (2019), evidence shows that using CMDA can help to better understand how patterns in online communication can show "how teaching presence, social presence, and cognitive presence are manifested in an online learning environment" (p. 1). This study confirms this perspective as demonstrated in the excerpts discussed below.

In this section, I present a typical classroom interaction in one of the courses that I taught during the pandemic lockdown. The course titled 'Multilingualism' was a compulsory final year course. Out of five students that registered for the course, the number of those who were active fluctuated between three and four. One student could not join the online class due to a number of environmental, financial, and infrastructural challenges. The class started on May 4th, 2020 and ended on September 8th, 2020. It was a two-unit course and we had the class twice a week for two hours lasting up to 17 weeks.

From the screencast presented in the previous section, it is clear that the university management painstakingly created the resources and training opportunities for staff and students to maximise the resources on the platforms for a seamless online learning environment. The enhancement of the online learning environment is amplified through the deployment of new technologies, especially Google Classroom, Google Meet, exam.net, and WhatsApp that created active interactive sessions. Teachers had the option to adopt either text-based synchronous content delivery, audio-visual mode, or a hybrid method. It was however discovered most teachers and students chose the text-based mode because it was less costly and more effective due to poor internet network in most locations in Nigeria. The text-based online mode allows teachers and students to interact by simply using the keyboard functions to type their instructions and responses in real-time. Many participants found the interactions easy and exciting because the students are already familiar with the technicality of sending SMS and posting private chats on WhatsApp, Instagram, and Twitter. The experience thus shows clearly that the students transferred some socio-technical habits used in other traditional social media platforms to the online teaching environments. The advantage was that it helped them to adapt quickly and easily to the new remote learning environment especially by engaging effectively in synchronous real-time discourse practice.

In terms of style and language, the study observed a mixture of formal and informal expressions in the online academic discourse. While the formal learning environment was recognised, a number of conversational discursive features occurred in the virtual interactive space.

One important discourse feature of the technology-driven learning environment is the use of conversational tones that elicited some level of familiarity between the lecture and the students. This strategy is important to encourage the social and cognitive presence of the learners during the class. In the excerpts below extracted from the Google platform, the lecturer displays high teaching presence through the use of (phatic) expressions that promote familiar social relationship and sometimes mixed with a positive emotional tone in order to create an open communication environment for student-teacher interaction (Zhu et al.,

2019). Phatic expressions include social pleasantries that merely perform social functions indicating the willingness of the speakers and listeners to observe conventional local expectations for politeness and mutual conversation. For instance, in some of the excerpts, the lecturer announces his online presence with phatic expressions such as "Good morning class…" or "Dear students it is my pleasure to welcome you to this platform…".

In order to enhance learning, the lecturer relies on the feature of synchronous CMC on the platform. The style helped to compensate for the absence of face-to-face in-person interaction and encourage a positive feedback mechanism. The process also enabled the sustenance of interactivity through friendly questioning strategies. Examples include "we want to start in the next two mins, are we ready?". In addition, the use of the inclusive 'we' in some of the screencasts is a discourse strategy used by the lecturer to create a friendly rapport, gain the attention of the learners, and establish familiarity with the students; consider the six examples in Table 1.

Table 1. Examples of discourse between the lecturer and the students

| | | |
|---|---|---|
| 1 | Lecturer | "Dear students, I hope we are all getting along. Do you have any questions so far?" |
| | Student 1 | "None" |
| 2 | Lecturer | "Brillant! Thank you [Student 2] and [Student 5], [Student 1] I'm waiting for yours." |
| | Students | [silence] |
| | Lecturer | "What again can we say about language policy? Each of you should provide at least two sentences" |
| 3 | Lecturer | "Now before I finally release you to get ready for your exams, let me mention two or three concepts more that are associated with multilingualism. These include, diglossia, codeswitching, speech community etc. Please do read them up" |
| | Student 1 | "Okay sir" |
| 4 | Lecturer | "Now I will arrange a make-up test on Friday for those who missed the tests. Remind me on Thursday after getting clarification from your HOD" |
| | Student 2 | "Yes sir, thank you so much sir" |
| 5 | Student 3 | "Thank you sir, have a blessed day" |
| | Lecturer | "Best wishes to you all, do enjoy the rest of the week." |

| 6 | Lecturer | "If you don't have any questions, please ensure you read all the notes, materials and texts that are relevant to the course. I wish you all the best and pray that the good Lord will empower you to excel in Jesus' name. Amen. Do enjoy the rest of the week! Cheers!" |
| | Student 4 | "Thank you sir" |

From the six excerpts, it is noticed that the socio-technical affordances of the platform were used to promote social relationships in the course of the lectures which also enhanced learning possibilities. For example, the instructor attempts to establish a warm teacher-student online relationship and positive learning environment by adopting discourse strategies that close social gaps. In a phone call interview conducted with a few of the students, the feedback was very encouraging. They confirmed that the class was very interactive and the rate of assimilation of course content by the students was very high.

The excerpts also reveal other interesting discourse features. One, as a component of the online discursive practice, there are sociolinguistic cues that define the relationship between the lecturer and the students, which is a reflection of the sociocultural context where respect for teachers and lecturers plays out prominently in in-person classroom interactions. With the transference of offline behaviour to the online platform, the students' online discourse behaviour is thus highly influenced by their knowledge of the status differentiation and politeness requirements in the status-conscious society. In Nigeria, students are required to show maximum respect and deference to their lecturers in almost all matters with the use of discourse markers such as Sir and Ma'am. Some of the extracts above show the frequent use of the expressions like "yes sir", "okay sir", and "thank you so much sir" during the online lectures. This social norm reflects the strict observance and conformity to existential modes of addressing in this formal context. It also demonstrates how online environments still accommodate offline discursive practices as a system of rule-sharing where appropriateness in language use plays a key role in student-lecturer classroom discourse.

Two, we find another significant registerial feature that reflects the sociocultural context social relationship between the lecturer and the students shows forth in the use of socio-religious expressions. The religious-based expression from the students demonstrates the success of the social relationships built online over the 17-week period and a reflection of the university's approbational sociocultural context. The discourse fragment in Excerpt 4 is consistent with the policy, values, and practice at AUL as a faith-based institution owned by the Deeper Christian Life Ministry, a Christian religious organisation in Nigeria. It is very common to find frequent use of religious expressions within and outside learning environments. In fact, religious activities are a mandatory component of the extra-curricular activities in the institution. Generally speaking, religious expressions are acceptable in conventional university environments in Nigeria although the country claims to be a secular state. Both Christian and Islamic organisations have strong and flourishing educational institutions in the country that allow students and staff to practise their faiths. The mapping of the offline discourse behaviour into online learning environments enhances remote learning and supports scholars' views on the interconnectedness between offline and online discourse habits especially as the use of smartphones and social media networks continues to proliferate among young people.

Three, this COVID-19 crisis has revealed the power of digital technologies for teaching and learning in low-income and middle-income countries. This socio-technological advantage of the wide use of mobile phones in Nigeria has obviously equipped most students at AUL with the skills to use these devices for other online learning activities beyond private conversations and entertainment. It is against that backdrop that it was easy for management of the university to convince the students to migrate to remote teaching and learning. The university also has a relatively strong infrastructural base and availability of modern technologies to support that decision. It is little wonder that AUL was able to conclude the academic year successfully even during the lockdown, a decision that was commended by the parents of the students and other stakeholders.

Additionally, in teaching language-based courses, colleagues adopted a mixed method approach that accommodated asynchronous and synchronous CMC. Apart from using text-based modes on Google Classroom, some lecturers used video conferencing by relying on platforms such as Zoom, Google Meet, and WhatsApp. The audio-visual interactions helped to authenticate the online presence of the students and monitor their active participation in class activities. In order to compensate for the absence of language laboratories in online environments for practical courses like phonology and phonetics, lecturers adopted a simulation method. This involved recording the spoken language practice on WhatsApp voice notes, and transmitting such to students. The students were then required to recognise the sound production, practice the sounds, and send back their own sound productions through the same medium after about 30 minutes. The bidirectional asynchronous audio-visual method reinforced the lecture delivery using text-based online interactions through the Google Classroom platform.

Based on this study, one can deduce that remote teaching may adopt both synchronous and asynchronous methods and a mixed method depending on the platforms being used to facilitate such online learning. For instance, Google Classroom as a learning platform, to a large extent, favours synchronous CMC methods of teaching and learning where both teachers and learners interact in real-time. In an attempt to complement and improve effective remote teaching, a video conferencing platform can be used alongside the Google Classroom. Thankfully, the archival capacity of the platform allows learners to return to the platform and extract some or all of the notes posted during real-time lecture periods.

From my unscheduled interview session with two of the colleagues that taught courses in phonetics and phonology during this period, they overcame the challenges of teaching those courses online with the aid of enhanced simulations. This method assisted learners to use online teaching aids in learning sounds as well as reproducing them. The teachers made use of a software package (Audacity) to record sounds for their students. The students were required to listen to the sounds and reproduce them with Praat – sound analytical software. Also, the exam.net assessment platform provided another interesting working environment with the use of drawing tools. This tool helped learners to draw charts and tables, and engage in similar phonology-related practical exercises. It was observed that these online tools improved the learning of those language-based courses.

## 6.  Conclusion

The study has shown the growing interest in remote teaching and learning at AUL as a result of the pandemic that forced many institutions to rethink their strategies and reimagine teaching in a post-covid era. The consequential public health crisis has now provided an entirely new and exciting teaching and learning experience for both faculty and students. The initial apprehension about the difficulty in exploring the new technologies soon gave way to excitement and determination to explore the new approaches given the commitment of the university management to press forward with the migration from in-person learning to remote teaching platforms during the period. Many of the teachers have now acquired additional ICT skills as a result of the use of the new platforms for remote pedagogy. Despite the social disruptions caused by the lockdown, a compensatory social bonding between lecturers and students was promoted through online affordances based on the CMC strategy, enhancing the learning environment.

Although one cannot be blindsided to some of the challenges confronting the use of technology for online teaching in this part of the world, remote work was largely successful at AUL during the period. Some of the challenges such as high cost of data, lack of stable power supply, access to laptop and functional smartphones, and poor internet connection in some parts of the country still constitute some drawbacks to effective and productive remote teaching during the period. This study observes that the success of remote teaching at AUL was based on the commitment and clear-sighted decision by management to deploy digital platforms for a full semester of virtual teaching. The experience, though a learning curve for faculty and students, has redefined higher education pedagogy in the country and may become a viable alternative in the future (e.g. Lederman, 2020; Mishra, Gupta, & Shree, 2020; Renfrow, 2020).

## 7.  Acknowledgements

I appreciate the support received from the management of AUL and Mr Felix Oke, lecturer in the Linguistics and Languages department.

## 8. Supplementary materials

https://research-publishing.box.com/s/7xnp7wl62qift14jbkegloohmkck2wkb

## References

Gillet-Swan, J. (2017). The challenges of online learning supporting and engaging the isolated learner. *Journal of Learning Design, 10*(1), 20-30. https://doi.org/10.5204/jld.v9i3.293

Herring, S. (2001). Computer-mediated discourse. In. D. Tannen, D. Schiffrin & H. Hamilton (Eds), *Handbook of discourse analysis* (pp. 612-634). Blackwell.

Herring, S. (2004). Computer-mediated discourse analysis: an approach to researching online behaviour. In S.A. Barab, R. Kling & J. Gray (Eds), *Designing for Virtual Communities in the Service of Learning* (pp. 338-376). Cambridge University Press. https://doi.org/10.1017/cbo9780511805080.016

Kirkwood, A., & Price, L. (2014). Technology-enhanced learning and teaching in higher education: what is 'enhanced' and how do we know? A critical literature review. *Learning, Media and Technology, 39*(1), 6-36. https://doi.org/10.1080/17439884.2013.770404

Lederman, D. (2020 March 18). Will shift to remote teaching be boon or bane for inline learning? *Inside Higher Ed.* https://www.insidehighered.com/digital-learning/article/2020/03/18/most-teaching-going-remote-will-help-or-hurt-online-learning

Mishra,L., Gupta, T., & Shree, A.(2020). Online teaching-learning in higher education during lockdown period of COVID-19 pandemic. *International Journal of Educational Research Open, 1.* https://doi.org/10.1016/j.ijedro.2020.100012

NESG. (2020). *Learning in a pandemic: Nigeria's response to teaching and learning during the COVID-19 pandemic.* Nigerian Economic Summit Group. https://education.gov.ng/wp-content/uploads/2020/08/Learning-in-a-Pandemic-Report_TEP-NESG_2020.pdf

Opeibi, T., & Oluwasola, A. (2013). Innovations and reproduction in second language (L2) new media: a discursive- semiotic study of selected sms text messages in Nigeria. *International Journal of Applied Linguistics & English Literature, 2(*2), 122-132. https://doi.org/10.7575/aiac.ijalel.v.2n.2p.122

Orlando, J., & Attard, C. (2015). Digital natives come of age: the reality of today's early career teachers using mobile devices to teach mathematics. *Mathematics Education Research Journal, 28,* 107-121. https://doi.org/10.1007/s13394-015-0159-6

Chapter 3

Oyediran, W. O., Omoare, A. M., Owoyemi, M. A., Adejobi, A. O., & Fasasi, R. B. (2020). Prospects and limitations of e-learning application in private tertiary institutions amidst COVID-19 lockdown in Nigeria. *Heliyon, 6*(11). https://doi.org/10.1016/j.heliyon.2020.e05457

Renfrow, J. (2020 December 20). Ed Tech gets boost from blended learning environment. *Fierce Education.* https://www.fierceeducation.com/distance-learning/ed-tech-gets-boost-from-blended-learning-environment

Zhu, M., Herring, S. C., & Bonk, C. J. (2019). Exploring presence in online learning through three forms of computer-mediated discourse analysis. *Distance Education, 40*(2), 205-225. https://doi.org/10.1080/01587919.2019.1600365

# 4. An immersive Arabic language course in Cairo moves online

## Heba Salem[1]

### Abstract

This chapter describes the my experience as the instructor for a course rooted in community based learning theory that was forced to move online in spring, 2020, due to the novel coronavirus pandemic. The course, titled 'CASA Without Borders', allows Arabic language students in the Center for Arabic Study Abroad (CASA) program at The American University in Cairo (AUC) to leave the university environment and serve the community, while also benefiting from the experience both linguistically and culturally. This course was disrupted by the students' mandatory return to the US from Cairo as a result of the COVID-19 outbreak, and continued remotely in an online format. This chapter describes the CASA program and explains both the purpose of the CASA Without Borders course and its significance to CASA students and to the program. It also describes and reflects upon my experience of continuing the course remotely during the ongoing pandemic.

Keywords: COVID-19, online language teaching, community-based learning, Egypt.

## 1. Introduction

The ongoing COVID-19 pandemic has disrupted education across the globe, forcing many institutions to scramble to shift to remote online learning. The

---

1. The American University in Cairo, Cairo, Egypt; hebasalem@aucegypt.edu; https://orcid.org/0000-0003-4170-9537

How to cite: Salem, H. (2021). An immersive Arabic language course in Cairo moves online. In N. Radić, A. Atabekova, M. Freddi & J. Schmied (Eds), *The world universities' response to COVID-19: remote online language teaching* (pp. 79-94). Research-publishing.net. https://doi.org/10.14705/rpnet.2021.52.1265

## Chapter 4

CASA program in Cairo, for which I am both the executive director and an instructor, was no different in this regard. In addition to facing substantial challenges by the move of our Arabic language learning online in March, 2020, we also had to deal with the fact that out of concern for their safety our students were ordered to leave Cairo and return to the US prior to the closing of international airports. This was a considerable challenge, as I was at the time conducting a community based learning course called CASA Without Borders that allows students to learn Arabic by interacting with different people and institutions in Cairo. For the first time, and rather suddenly, I had to consider how to teach a community based learning course without the same level of access to community. What follows are some reflections on the situation faced in spring, 2020, and on how it might be possible to continue holding such courses in an altered educational landscape.

## 2. Description of the CASA full-year program

CASA is a scholarship awarded to competent learners of Arabic in the US that allows them to embark on a program of study abroad in Egypt at AUC. The overall objective of the CASA Full-Year program is to develop students' overall Arabic proficiency to a level that allows them to use the language as a tool for both communication and research in their graduate and post-graduate studies, and in their careers. The program aims to provide specialized language training for use in a wide variety of cultural, social, and intellectual contexts. Upon completion of the full year, program fellows reach a level of proficiency ranging between Advanced High, Superior, and Distinguished according to the American Council on the Teaching of Foreign Languages (ACTFL) rating scale, or C2 on the Common European Framework of Reference (CEFR) scale. At this level, students are sufficiently competent in Arabic to interact with Egyptians and other Arabic speakers in many different contexts, and many continue to do so after finishing the program, whether in their careers or in their personal lives. In fact, most professors and instructors of Arabic in the US who are non-native speakers of Arabic have been CASA fellows at one point in their lives.

## 3. The CASA student profile

CASA students are:

- American or non-American graduate students (depending on the grant);

- have had at least three or four years of prior Arabic language instruction;

- independent learners, brave, outgoing individuals;

- enthusiastic enquirers; and

- possess different individual areas of interest, in addition to the Arabic Language, Middle East studies, civil rights, human rights, Islamic studies, and Arabic language instruction.

## 4. The place of community based learning in the CASA program

The full-year CASA program starts in June and ends in May of the following year. Students are encouraged to engage with their surroundings and with Egyptian society throughout their fellowship year, but it is not until their final semester that their interaction with communities in Cairo is formalized through the CASA Without Borders course. This takes place, however, after extensive preparation and formal language study.

The Summer program marks the beginning of the CASA fellowship. It is a seven week long program offering 20 contact hours per week. The content course taught in the summer, titled 'An Introduction to Cairo', focuses on the four language skills using materials related to the city of Cairo, including opinion articles, works of history and geography, art, movies, soap operas, caricatures, novels, short stories, and memoirs. This course is based on community based learning theory, and helps students gain experiences related to places and people,

Chapter 4

and to then reflect on those experiences in both modern standard and colloquial Arabic[2].

During the fall semester, students are exposed to another 20 contact hours of teaching, with a focus on aural and oral language skills. Focused attention on speaking and listening abilities is one of the unique aspects of the CASA program, and it provides students with a firm grounding in an aspect of language learning that is often neglected in US-based classes, and is largely unobtainable from other sources. In addition to in-class activities, the teaching faculty in the Department of Arabic Language Instruction at AUC[3] have gathered, and constantly update, a large library of audio and video clips in order to supplement coursework and to allow students to work at their own pace outside of a classroom setting.

The program uses three courses to help accomplish those goals:

- Arabic Media, which focuses on strengthening listening and speaking skills, and which meets for a total of five hours per week;

- issues in the Middle East, which focuses on both reading and writing skills, and which meets for a total of ten hours per week; and

- enhancing ECA (Egyptian Colloquial Arabic), which meets a total of five hours per week.

During the fall semester there is also a 'meet the author' lecture series, where students get the chance to interact with the authors of many of the works that form the source material for their lessons. These lectures give them the opportunity to work on developing note-taking skills and to sharpen and strengthen their listening comprehension skills. They also introduce them to a number of prominent figures in Egypt who provide the students with an historical overview

---

2. For an example of language instruction rooted in community based learning see Ibrahim (2010).

3. https://www.aucegypt.edu/academics/studying-arabic

of Cairo, share personal experiences on a variety of topics, and offer valuable insight into the current political, intellectual, and artistic scene in Egypt.

By the end of the fall, fellows are ready for the spring semester, in which they tackle more specialized content courses directly related to their own areas of interest and specialization. The spring semester is designed to provide the fellows the opportunity to refine and apply the advanced language skills they have developed during the summer and fall by allowing them to enroll in content-based courses of their own choosing. Students are also encouraged to interact and communicate with Egyptians both in and out of the classroom, and to engage in activities that will benefit their future studies or careers.

## 5. CASA Without Borders

CASA Without Borders is a course that is offered to students in the spring. Based on community based learning theory, the course allows students to develop both cultural and linguistic knowledge via firsthand experiences with the Cairene community (Ibrahim, 2010). Arrangements for the class are made as early as November of the previous year, and the class itself runs from the end of January until mid-May when the spring semester ends. The CASA program staff and executive director work with the students to identify institutions and initiatives with which they can work (though usually on a volunteer basis) in the spring semester, allowing them to gain real-world experience using Arabic in a professional environment. The main objectives of the program are to enable students to (1) communicate effectively using speaking skills; (2) communicate effectively using writing skills; and (3) demonstrate listening and critical thinking skills.

The objectives are assessed through:

- discussions that take place both within and outside of the class;

- student presentations;

- participation in AUC's annual research conference;

- written and voice-recorded reflections; and

- a final reflection paper in which students work to identify and deal with cultural and linguistic problems they have faced throughout the semester.

Student safety is of utmost concern, so students are only allowed to choose from a list of AUC-approved institutions for their semester-long course, institutions that are not politically sensitive, and that will therefore help students avoid any unwanted negative experiences. For example, not all institutions that deal with human rights issues are able to get clearance from AUC security. What happens, then, is that students indicate their areas of interest, after which the administration connects them to the appropriate people and institutions. The students are then assigned a work position or an internship placement.

CASA Without Borders also includes a classroom component. All of the students in the course meet once at the beginning of the semester, after which individual meetings are held with the instructor on a weekly basis. Students are expected to submit weekly reflections about their work, and toward the end of the semester they all prepare presentations about their work as part of the university's yearly research conference, which allows them to share their experience with their peers and with the wider AUC community. At the end of the semester they also produce and present a final reflection paper of 1,500 words in Arabic.

From the end of January to mid-March, 2020, CASA students worked in diverse organizations, including:

- the Cairo Institute for the Hearing and Speech Impaired;

- Arab Lit Quarterly, where the student covered various cultural events;

- assisting a professor with a research survey investigating Egyptians' relationships to Pharaonic artifacts;

- the Women and Memory forum;

- Saffarni, a local initiative that works with underprivileged Egyptian children and helps expose them to foreign cultures;

- working with and teaching Syrian, Sudanese, and Nigerian refugees in Cairo; and

- working with children at risk with Banaati foundation.

Students were fully enjoying and engaged in their work and were regularly contributing to the shared digital folders that the program created for them, as well as uploading their reflections on their experience. However, in mid-March the effects of the COVID-19 pandemic disrupted the CASA program, much as it did with educational programs across the world.

## 6. Decision to move online

In mid-March of 2020, AUC made the decision to suspend all physical presence on campus and all on-campus activities, which included the CASA Without Borders course. Soon after, the program's US-based administration made the decision to evacuate the CASA students before the country's airports closed. As the instructor for the CASA Without Borders course, I immediately panicked, unsure of how to continue online with a course so heavily centered around face-to-face interaction.

At first I was busy organizing the logistics for the students' return home, especially following an announcement that Egypt's airports were going to be shut down in only a matter of days. But soon it was necessary to confront the reality that the students had all left for the US and that we needed to start meeting over Zoom, as we were doing with all of our other classes. I realized that it was necessary to meet with them to help maintain their enthusiasm. The university pushed spring break up a bit so as to give instructors time to become familiar with Zoom and to adjust to the new situation. AUC's Center for Learning and Teaching[4] has been very active from the very beginning of the pandemic, and started giving group information sessions on how to make the transition to online instruction, as well as individualized ones if needed. They stressed the importance of effective communication in online teaching, as well as the use of slideshows, tools for digital uploads, and online discussion forums.

## 7. Pedagogical considerations

The most challenging part of moving online was figuring out how to continue achieving the course's learning outcomes without the students being able to experience the immersion, interaction, and communication with Egyptians that the course is built upon. Virtual communication had to take the place of in-person communication, and some of the students' internships had to change. I met with all of the students over Zoom both individually and in groups, which involved taking into account time differences between California, the US East Coast, and Cairo. The students and I had long talks. We decided to make use of the encounters they had already had in their first five or six weeks of work in Cairo, and decided to spend the rest of the semester reflecting on those encounters and addressing their linguistic aspects.

A group of the students decided to collaborate on a translation of the book *Building and Struggling* co-authored by university professor and activist Hoda ElSadda, which was originally published in Arabic[5] by the Women and Memory Forum (ElSadda & Hassan, 2018). They would meet together, communicate and debate over Zoom, and worked hard to finish translating the whole book in order to produce the first draft before the end of the spring semester. They created a Google document in which they identified some translation issues and I held meetings with them to discuss different translation choices, with all of us speaking in Arabic, of course (see Figure 1).

---

4. https://www.aucegypt.edu/faculty/center-learning-and-teaching

5. Hudā al-Ṣadda (2018). Bināʾ wa niḍāl: min arshīf al-ḥaraka al-niswiya al-miṣriya. Muʾassasat al-Marʾa wa-l-Dhākira.

Figure 1. Sample of students' reflections

Each student then made an excellent video presentation at the end of the semester which they uploaded to the class platform in order to receive comments and feedback from their peers. Other students continued some of their work online, talking to refugees, for example, and working with Arab Lit Quarterly.

Figure 2. Presenter profiles

Another issue with moving online was that we still needed to hold the AUC conference in which the students would deliver their presentations. Although the conference had been cancelled along with all other activities on campus, I still considered it an important activity to achieve our learning outcomes and to allow me to submit the student's grades. The students' presentations at the conference (see Figure 2 above), during which they reflect orally on their linguistic and cultural experiences, are the means that I use to assess the students' overall performance in the class. As a result, we agreed to hold the conference online and I organized it over Zoom in April 2020.

## 8. Technical support

I used Google Sites as the class platform, and students uploaded their presentations to Google Slides and then linked them to the conference website (see Figure 3).

Figure 3. Stills from student presentations

Not only were the students able to watch each other's presentations and comment virtually, but an audience from the university at large was also invited to join, and encouraged to record their feedback via Google Sites. The audience consisted of more or less the same people from AUC who were expected to attend the regular conference; although, of course, attendees were fewer in number. Participants also included AUC faculty members, as well as others who were interested in the students' work and learning experiences. Professor Hoda Elsadda, the author of the book *Building and Struggling* was invited to watch the students' presentation about the book.

After one week of reviewing each other's videos, writing comments to each other, and replying to all the comments, a large Zoom meeting was held where students had the chance to talk about their feelings regarding the experience. Some colleagues of mine attended this meeting after watching the students' videos. Many of them asked the students questions, and were impressed by their deep reflection on the experience. Prof. Hoda Elsadda's reaction was as follows:

> "I would like to thank you again for the work you have done with women and memory. I am also delighted that I met some of you and only wish that I had met the whole team. I enjoyed your presentation very much, your comments on translation and the thought process that went into finding the correct word. I am also really pleased that you are interested in continuing working with [the Women and Memory Forum] after the completion of the translation of the binaa wa nidal. I think I speak for [named person] and myself when I say that we value your work and enthusiasm" (private communication, April 27th, 2020, reproduced with kind permission from Prof. Elsadda).

I have had training previously (2017-2018) on computer supported collaborative learning, and Web 2.0 technologies, such as: infographs, flipped classroom techniques, Screen Cast-o-Matic, as well as video tools, Google Sites, Google Forms for instant feedback activities, and Google Slides for the presentations. This gave me a base for all the ideas and introduced me in details to these tools, which made the transition to online easier. Meanwhile, when moved online, I had training with AUC's Center for Learning and Teaching[6]. They offered one-on-one service over Zoom when needed.

Although the sudden move online completely upended the normal format of the CASA Without Borders course, as well as all the students' other courses, there were some surprising benefits to continuing the course in an online format. Meeting with students individually over Zoom and listening to them express their feelings about the situation inspired me to make the best of a bad situation by

---

6. https://www.aucegypt.edu/faculty/center-learning-and-teaching

helping them channel their emotions into writing projects. I asked them to write about their feelings alongside their end of semester reflection paper. I gathered these writings and published them in an electronic magazine, which remains something the students are very proud of[7]. I also reached out to the university's magazine, *Caravan*, which published two of the students' compositions. The act of writing and working with me, and their other instructors on writing, as an additional component of the course was both fun and a good outlet for them, especially considering that they were forced to leave Cairo in quite a hurry, which was emotionally difficult for them.

## 9. Student feedback

Students were proud of the work they did in these difficult circumstances, and they still have the recordings of their 15 to 20 minute conference presentations, which they will be able to list on their CVs. Student feedback was overall quite positive, and highlighted the positive aspects of the course, despite its format having completely changed[8].

> "Dr Heba has been very insightful and more than helpful in every regards. I appreciate the weekly meeting and her enthusiasm. I think that the weekly writing assignments could have turned out very stiff, if it weren't for her motivation and kind demeanor".

> "Thank you Ustadha Heba for being very supportive and responsive throughout. I can't imagine what this whole experience would have been like with anyone other than you being in charge of this class and the CASA program".

As an instructor, I was initially quite worried about this community based learning course, since it depends so greatly on the students' work outside of

---

7. http://redtech.club/wp-content/CASAMagazineOnline/story_html5.html

8. See more student feedback in supplementary materials.

class, and wondered how we would be able to still fulfill the course requirements. However, with careful thought it turned out that everything could be done online, other than meeting people in person to perform public or community service. For example, the student who was working at The Cairo Institute for the Hearing and Speech Impaired, with children who need to learn Arabic sign language, found it extremely difficult to continue his work. He had to modify his approach and use a computer program to develop learning activities for the children. And although the online aspects of the course were beneficial for the students, the linguistic and cultural benefit of immersion in the Egyptian community could not be easily achieved without direct, face-to-face interaction.

The student who was working with Arab Lit Quarterly, who had previously been attending cultural events taking place in Cairo, writing about them and talking to authors, had to focus on translation instead after all public events in Cairo were cancelled, meaning she could not physically meet with authors or report on events. Even though the student had been doing her reporting in English, the act of translating her interviews from Arabic and the experience of attending cultural and literary events, as well as meeting and conversing in Arabic with diverse authors was incredibly enriching. Unfortunately, this only lasted for the first five weeks of the spring of 2020. Although she was still able to benefit from our online activities, they were no substitute for the immersive experience she would have been able to obtain had we continued as usual. In addition, the student who was working with underprivileged Egyptian children in the Saffarni initiative was only able to undertake reflection on the first five weeks of his meeting the children and explaining American culture to them in Arabic. He described giving them peanut butter and jelly sandwiches, talking to them, and showing them photos of his home in the US. However, he had to change his plans for the rest of the semester and work on the aforementioned translation project with his colleagues.

## 10. Conclusion and lessons for the future

Although the students enrolled in the spring, 2020, CASA Without Borders course eventually enjoyed the way we adapted to the situation of being entirely online, they shared my initial hesitation about the change. Without the enthusiasm that the students brought to our class the work would never have gotten done. At one point, the US-based CASA administration even discussed cancelling the course, which was impossible due to the fact that it was a registered course at AUC and could not be dropped. But despite the drawbacks of teaching a community based learning course without any student interaction with the community, the course still provided great benefits to the students, and also raised several important questions about running community based learning courses in a remote, online format.

If such a course starts totally online from the beginning of the semester, the aspect of immersion in society and the component of serving the community need restructuring and revisiting. As an instructor, teaching online forced me to think differently in preparing my courses. I felt I had to be more organized and clearer. I realized that a lot of what I do depends on my physical presence in the class and on the way I use my personality to interact with the students. Without being able to rely on my in-person interaction with the students, my instruction methods, and hence my way of thinking, had to be clearer. I was forced to pay attention to details that I do not usually think of – not out of carelessness, but because I have always been able to communicate many details to the students verbally in class, and they can ask about them anytime if they feel they need to. However, moving online made the interaction different, forcing me to present information in other modes.

I found Google Sites to be an incredibly useful pedagogical tool, and plan to use it in the future as both the platform for the class and to keep all my class material and the students work in one place, whether the course is held in person or online. Even if students' future conference presentations are able to take place in person in front of a live audience, I will still ask the students to record their presentations and upload them to Google Slides on the class platform. The fact that the students recorded their presentations and uploaded them online made it easier for me to correct the students' linguistic mistakes and give them more detailed feedback on their presentations. It also made it easier for them to obtain feedback from their peers and their virtual audience.

Although I was able to continue the course online and thus complete what the students started, it would have been difficult to start such a course entirely online from the beginning of the semester given the work that most of the students chose. Especially in Cairo, many institutes and initiatives lack both the technology and a strong enough internet connection to offer students an online internship. Working with deaf students at the Cairo Institute for the Hearing and Speech Impaired, for example, would have been very difficult to start online. And indeed, a strong internet connection is incredibly important to any attempt to do community based learning, since without one nothing can be achieved. Institutions and private homes need to be equipped with reliable internet in order to make this possible, though in some countries this is a serious problem. I myself had some issues in this regard, especially as the whole country went online in the first months of the pandemic. But the students in my course were all very understanding, and the fact that we all wanted the experience to work helped us achieve positive outcomes.

It is also important to think of alternative ways to perform community service, such as by translating a work into one's native language and making it available to another culture and readership. And although some service work cannot be performed online, there are certainly ways to build language skills through interaction with an online community of speakers. Were one to plan out a community based language learning course that takes place entirely online, there are certainly ways to use social media and videoconferencing applications such as Zoom in order to connect students with native speakers of the target language. Even though COVID-19 has disrupted education across the globe, it has also offered the possibility of rethinking what it means to interact with and serve a community, and how we can continue holding community based learning courses even in the face of a devastating pandemic.

## 11. Supplementary materials

https://research-publishing.box.com/s/jokl7y6pzbl4sj2ilqjr92lh3k9p21x1

Chapter 4

# References

ElSadda, H., & Hassan, M. (2018). *Bina'a we Nidal (Building and Struggling): from the archives of the Egyptian feminist movement.* Women and Memory Forum. http://www.wmf.org.eg/en/wmf-publishes-binaa-we-nidal-from-the-archives-of-the-egyptian-feminist-movement/

Ibrahim, M. (2010). The use of community based learning in educating college students in Midwestern USA. *Procedia - Social and Behavioral Sciences, 2*(2), 392-396. https://doi.org/10.1016/j.sbspro.2010.03.032

# 5. The University of Rwanda response to COVID-19

## Valentin Uwizeyimana[1]

### Abstract

The universities in Rwanda, like in other countries, experienced uncertainty created by restrictions and lockdowns imposed to contain the spread of Coronavirus. None of the universities were prepared to face disruptions of this scale, however, learning had to continue irrespective of the COVID-19 pandemic. Based on the case of the University of Rwanda (UR), this chapter discusses the Rwandan university's response to COVID-19, presents the lessons learnt, and provides recommendations that might help universities and researchers in the future. This chapter reports on a qualitative study that analysed the university's news articles and official communications with regards to COVID-19 that were collected during a seven-month period. The findings revealed that the university was not indeed prepared to continue its teaching and learning activities remotely online, and that the decision to go online was top-down. Furthermore, it pointed out the lack of access to the required infrastructure and tools, the lack of technical support and training, and the digital divide that exists among students, as the major challenges to a successful remote online teaching and learning process.

Keywords: COVID-19, online, language teaching, digital divide, technology, Rwanda.

---

1. University of Rwanda, Kigali, Rwanda / University of South Africa, Pretoria, South Africa; vuwizeyimana@outlook.com; https://orcid.org/0000-0003-2464-5324

How to cite: Uwizeyimana, V. (2021). The University of Rwanda response to COVID-19. In N. Radić, A. Atabekova, M. Freddi & J. Schmied (Eds), *The world universities' response to COVID-19: remote online language teaching* (pp. 95-108). Research-publishing.net. https://doi.org/10.14705/rpnet.2021.52.1266

Chapter 5

## 1. Introduction

UR is a public university located in Rwanda, the first African country that imposed the total lockdown as a measure to contain COVID-19. This lockdown was announced on 14th March 2020 to be effected on the next day (Ministry of Health, 2020). Rwanda is a landlocked country (26,338 km2 of total area) located in the centre of Africa, and inhabited by approximately 12.6 million people according to the National Institute of Statistics of Rwanda (NISR, 2014). Rwanda has Kinyarwanda as its sole national language, and Kinyarwanda, English, French, and Swahili as its four official languages (Republic of Rwanda, 2015, 2017). English is a compulsory taught subject and a medium of instructions at all levels of education, whereas the other three languages are optional taught subjects. Kinyarwanda is spoken and used in everyday activities by more than 99% of the total population of Rwanda, compared to English, French, and Swahili which are spoken by less than 5% of the total population each (Gafaranga, Niyomugabo, & Uwizeyimana, 2013; Niyomugabo & Uwizeyimana, 2018; Rosendal, 2009; Samuelson & Freedman, 2010; Uwizeyimana, 2018a, 2018b).

Rwanda is lagging behind at a significant level in terms of technology infrastructure, one of the requirements for remote online learning. According to NISR (2018, pp. 66-68), only 27.1% of the Rwandan total households have access to electricity, and 17.2% have access to the internet. Regarding the ownership of the electronic and technological devices, only 3.3% of the Rwandan total households own a computer, 10.4% own a television set, 66.9% own a mobile phone, and 73.8% own a radio set or listen to the radio on a mobile phone (NISR, 2018, p. 77). At an individual level, NISR (2018) specifies that only 36.7% of the Rwanda total population own a mobile phone, and only 10.5% of the total population aged between 15 and 24 years, as well as 8.9% of the total population aged 25 years and above, are computer literate.

The UR (2018) reported that 63% of students own laptop computers. Furthermore, the majority of UR students fall within the digital native generation (Prensky, 2001; Thinyane, 2010; Uwizeyimana, 2018b), and thus are assumed to be digital literate. However, studies found that students in Rwanda and other parts of the world are more literate and comfortable with using mobile devices than computers (Grigoryan 2018; Stockwell & Liu 2015; Thinyane, 2010; Uwizeyimana 2018a, 2018b). Furthermore, Stockwell and Hubbard (2013) pointed out that this "knowledge of how to use mobile devices for specific personal or social functions is not always a good indicator of knowledge of educational functions" (p. 4). It is in these regards that training and technical support are always recommended even for digital natives, with the purpose of not only making a positive impact on the remote online teaching and learning outcomes, but also of addressing the digital divide which was found among the current generation of university students (Brown & Czerniewicz, 2010; Thinyane, 2010; Uwizeyimana, 2018a, 2018b). This chapter verifies the basis of the above argument as it reports on a qualitative study that analysed the UR response to COVID-19.

## 2. Methodology

This study was conducted at UR. UR was selected because it is the largest, top-ranked, and sole public university in Rwanda (HEC, 2016; UR, 2020a). According to its 2019-2020 annual report, UR had 25,085 students (UR, 2020a, p. 10), and 2,072 employees composed of 1,329 academics and 743 administrative and support staff (UR, 2018, p. 29). Before the COVID-19 total lockdown, the UR programmes' mode of the delivery was face-to-face (UR, 2018, p. 22), and the majority of academic staff were not trained on remote online teaching.

In data collection, the UR website was monitored during a seven-month period starting from March and ending by October 2020. During this period, news articles and official communications with regards to COVID-19 were collected and qualitatively analysed. The findings of this analysis with regards to how UR responded to COVID-19 lockdown by shifting to remote online teaching and learning are discussed in the following sections.

Chapter 5

## 3. Findings and discussion

### 3.1. Decision-making process to go online

The UR decision to go online was top-down. This decision was communicated through the vice-chancellor's circular to students and staff as follows:

> "[i]n line with the Government of Rwanda's new measures to prevent Coronavirus transmission, the UR will stop all teaching activities from Monday 16th March 2020. Students shall be informed about the resumption of teaching in due time. In the meantime, all students are encouraged to continue their self-learning, taking advantage of online teaching materials" (UR, 2020b, p. 1).

It is clear that the UR community did not participate in this decision-making, i.e. was not given the time to prepare for its abrupt closure, probably by putting in place a remote online teaching and learning strategy rather than recommending the self-learning method. This situation created uncertainty as expressed by the vice-chancellor on 8th May 2020 as follows:

> "[i]n recent times many people have faced uncertainty about their jobs, health and schooling globally. [... w]ith the recent cabinet's guidance on progressive lifting of the lockdown and [the Ministry of Education]'s clarifications on its implication of the education sector, it is clear that we will not meet again on university campuses for some time" (UR, 2020d, p. 1).

### 3.2. Training and technical support

In its circular of 1st September 2020, the UR (2020e) recognised that remote online teaching and learning were new to the majority of its community members, and thus introduced three concepts used in remote online learning to students as follows:

"[w]hen it is live interaction, we call it 'synchronous' – as in 'of the time'; and when it is a recorded lecture, it is called 'asynchronous'. You should not be worried about these different forms. The good thing about recorded lectures is that you can go back and revisit them. [...] For those of you who are used to attending laboratories, we will be introducing you to *virtual labs* as well as giving you access to labs on campuses in due course" (p. 2, my emphasis).

After this introduction, UR organised an online induction session for undergraduate students on the 'UR e-learning platform' (Ntirandekura, 2020). Academic staff were also trained "on developing e-learning and blended modules" (Bucyansenga, 2020, n.p.).

### 3.3. Assumptions underpinning design of remote programme

Assumptions supporting the use of remote teaching and learning were based on different studies such as Elias (2011), Browne and Culligan (2008), Herrington, Herrington, and Mantei (2009), Stockwell and Hubbard (2013), and Jacobson and Turner (2010). These studies found that remote learning – with its derivatives such as 'mobile learning', 'distance learning', 'open learning' and 'e-learning' – is flexible, equitable, portable, spontaneous, personalised, contextualised, adaptable to instructional climates, and favourable for the integration of multimedia. These assumptions support the adoption of remote teaching and learning, but of course through a careful and adequate design-and-implementation process. At UR, in addition to the lack of the required infrastructure and training there was no careful and adequate planning to deal with issues pertaining to remote online teaching and learning.

### 3.4. Pedagogical and logistics considerations

UR (2020c) urged the "UR faculty and technical staff to ensure that all modules offered in all academic programmes [were] updated and uploaded on [the UR's] e-learning platform, [and that all the students were] registered for each module in [their] academic programmes" (p. 1). Meanwhile, since the lockdown was imposed in the middle of the academic year, the students were urged to spend their time "review[ing] the learning materials of the modules [they had] completed in [the previous] trimester, and even in previous years" (UR, 2020c, p. 1). Since these activities were not enough to make the teaching and learning effective, UR promised its students that the real teaching and learning and assessment activities would take place once the university re-opens for face-to-face classes as follows:

> "[p]utting learning materials online does not mean that you have been taught and can therefore be assessed. All lecturers shall resume their teaching where they left it when the university closed. Recognising that some of you don't have access to learning materials is not enough – it is making sure that this does not create disadvantage to some and advantage to others. Therefore, only when all relevant material has been taught and learnt will it be assessed. However, we recognise that those of you who have managed to engage with online materials shall probably learn more quickly when formal face-to-face teaching resumes and we encourage you to become part of a squad of peer educators when such a time comes" (UR, 2020c, p. 2).

### 3.5. Access to technology hardware

By the end of the 2017-2018 academic year, UR had the total of 7,922 desktop computers for its students and staff (UR, 2018, p. 54). Compared to the number of UR students and staff, this number of computers was insignificant, and thus the shortage was addressed by the use of laptop computers which were offered as a loan to many of the government-supported students. In this regard, 13,521 laptop computers were distributed among students during the 2017-2018 academic year (UR, 2018, p. 1). However, no laptop computers or other technological devices were provided to UR teaching staff.

It is important to recall that UR students fall within the digital native generation. According to the recent comparative studies on the use of mobile devices versus computers in teaching and learning, mobile devices were found to be the preferred technological tools for digital natives since they contribute positively to the teaching and learning of languages and other subjects, and their contribution was found to be more significant than the contribution of computers (Brown & Czerniewicz, 2010; Grigoryan, 2018; Stockwell & Liu, 2015; Thinyane, 2010; Uwizeyimana, 2018a, 2018b; Yang, 2013). Therefore at UR, mobile devices should have been taken explicitly as an alternative option to address the lack of access to a computer.

### 3.6. Availability of remote online teaching and learning software

Before the COVID-19 lockdown, UR had not developed any e-learning software or environments to be used in remote online teaching and learning apart from its Moodle-based platform. During its closure, UR requested the teaching staff to upload their course content to this platform, although it was aware that just "putting learning materials online does not mean that [students are] taught and can therefore be assessed" (UR, 2020c, p. 2). Meanwhile, students were supposed to access the uploaded materials on their laptop computers. In addition to this platform, the students were urged to "be open with one another to reduce distance", to maintain their social media groups, and to try to enhance their self-learning by using generic applications such as Facebook and WhatsApp mainly because "from time to time lecturers [would] engage with [them] in [that] way" (UR, 2020e, p. 2).

### 3.7. Remote online course delivery

In the context of universities such as UR, the notion of 'course delivery' in remote online learning can be interpreted as uploading the course content online on one side, and downloading this content by using the internet-connected devices on another side. It is from this perspective that the UR (2020a) specified the following achievement in matters of remote online teaching and learning:

> "UR lecturers have injected more efforts to upload and avail their modules online. The statistics, as of June 2020, indicate that 91% of

modules taught at UR are hosted on the eLearning platform. Particularly, during the COVID-19 pandemic lockdown, all lecturers have worked hard to finish uploading the modules online so that students can remain engaged in their learning process. The number of users [has] grown from 300 users daily before COVID-19 pandemic, to 9,000 users daily during lockdown" (p. 9).

### 3.8.   Outcomes of remote online learning

The UR (2020d) stated that it has "been able to register some successes in terms of virtual teaching in postgraduate fields, [and that] some modules have been successfully taught and assessed online and even in viva voce exams […] by videoconference" (p. 1). However, it did not publish anything with regards to the achieved learning outcomes in its undergraduate programmes. It is assumed that no measurable learning outcomes were achieved in undergraduate programmes due to the lack of access to technological devices and internet connectivity, the digital divide issues, and the lack of enough training and technical support to students and teaching staff.

### 3.9.   Student and teacher feedback on remote online teaching and learning

From March to October 2020, no news article, circular, or any other type of communication on its undergraduate student feedback was published by the UR. This might have been caused by the fact that the majority of the UR undergraduate students are from poor households in rural areas, with no training and access to the necessary infrastructure for participating in remote online learning, and thus were not able to provide their feedback.

Regarding the postgraduate students however, Niyitegeka (2020) mentioned in a news article that "[m]asters' students admit to cope with the lockdown by leveraging online technology" (n.p.). Niyitegeka (2020) specified that masters' students' supervisors were supportive, and that they were using telephone calls and e-mails as tools for teaching and learning. In another article, Nshimiye (2020) mentioned that remote online learning "has become useful to [postgraduate] students who [were abroad since they could] continue their studies despite the lockdown" (n.p.).

No negative feedback was published possibly because of the digital divide issues that exist among students. In this regard, the students who were privileged to take part in remote online learning benefited from it, and thus provided their positive feedback; whereas those who did not manage to participate, could not manage to give their negative feedback either.

UR did not publish any staff feedback on remote online teaching and learning activities in undergraduate programmes. Regarding the postgraduate programmes however, Nshimiye (2020) mentioned that COVID-19 "lockdown has brought UR to double [its] efforts in teaching online" (n.p.), and thus some postgraduate programmes which UR offers in partnership with other universities were being successfully taught online.

## 3.10. Lessons learnt and future plans

From its COVID-19 experience, UR initiated more inter-university partnerships and collaboration agreements, and increased its investment in remote online teaching and learning (Nshimiye, 2020). UR identified the lack of technical support and training as one of the challenges to effective remote online teaching and learning, and thus embarked on organising training sessions for its students and teaching staff.

In addition to these, the UR (2020a) plans that through "the Partnership for Enhances and Blended Learning (PEBL), a crosscutting module of the *'Introduction to Information Technology'* [will start] to be offered [to all the first-year undergraduate students] by [all the] PEBL participant universities through blended learning" (p. 14). Five universities, namely Makerere University (Uganda), State University of Zanzibar (Tanzania), UR (Rwanda), Kenyatta University, and Strathmore University (Kenya), are part of this programme (UR, 2020a, p. 14).

Chapter 5

The future of teaching and learning was summarised by the UR (2020d) on 8th May 2020 as follows:

> "[t]here is no going back. When we meet again [...], we will never return to full face-to-face teaching [and learning], and we will always have a form of blended learning, i.e. a combination of face-to-face and online teaching and learning. To achieve this, we are working towards a tremendous increase in internet access and bandwidth on all our campuses and eventually transform all of them into internet hotspots" (p. 3).

Lastly, the UR (2020a, p. 14) plans that some of its programmes will be hosted on third-party universities' online learning platforms through the initiated partnership agreements.

## 4. Conclusion

The world universities made an effort to shift to remote online teaching and learning following the lockdown and restrictions that were imposed to contain the spread of COVID-19. This chapter described how the UR joined this effort.

UR shifted to remote online teaching and learning due to COVID-19 total lockdown which was imposed in Rwanda in March 2020. The teaching staff had to upload the course content online, whereas students had to download the online course. These were not effective especially in undergraduate programmes as discussed in this chapter. UR was lagging behind due to various challenges such as the lack of training and technical support for students and staff, and the lack of access to the required infrastructure, technological devices, and software. Furthermore, UR was not involved in the decision-making process to go online, and thus had not planned accordingly. These are the main reasons why except in the postgraduate programmes, no learning outcomes were achieved in remote online learning at UR.

This study revealed that if both students and teaching staff are not trained on remote online teaching and learning, nor have access to the required tools and infrastructure, no positive teaching and learning outcomes will be achieved. The traditional assumption that the current university students who fall within the digital native generation are able to learn remotely online once they are provided with computers and/or mobile technological devices, is intensifying the digital divide among students rather than contributing towards the expected learning outcomes. Future studies should revisit the extent at which this assumption is relevant in the world universities' context.

## 5. Acknowledgements

The publication of this chapter was made possible through my research associateship with the Department of English Language and Linguistics at Technische Universität Chemnitz (Germany). I would like to express my gratitude to Prof. Dr Josef Schmied, the chair of this department, as well as his partners from the University of Cambridge (the United Kingdom), Università di Pavia (Italy), and the Peoples' Friendship University of Russia, for initiating and securing the funds for the 'World universities' response to COVID-19: remote online language-teaching' project.

## References

Brown, C., & Czerniewicz, L. (2010). Debunking the 'digital native': beyond digital apartheid, towards digital democracy. *Journal of Computer Assisted Learning, 26*(5), 357-369. https://doi.org/10.1111/j.1365-2729.2010.00369.x

Browne, C., & Culligan, B. (2008). Combining technology and IRT testing to build student knowledge of high frequency vocabulary. *The JALT CALL Journal, 4*(2), 3-16. https://doi.org/10.29140/jaltcall.v4n2.59

Bucyansenga, E. (2020). *As the time of UR reopening is at hand, lecturers are trained on developing e- learning & blended modules*. University of Rwanda. https://ur.ac.rw/?As-the-time-of-UR-reopening-is-at-hand-lecturers-are-trained-on-developing-e

Elias, T. (2011). Universal instructional design principles for mobile learning. *International Review of Research in Open and Distance Learning, 12*(2), 143-156. https://doi.org/10.19173/irrodl.v12i2.965

Gafaranga, J., Niyomugabo, C., & Uwizeyimana, V. (2013). Micro declared language policy or not? Language-policy-like statements in the rules of procedure of the Rwandan Parliament. *Language Policy, 12*, 313-332. https://doi.org/10.1007/s10993-013-9274-y

Grigoryan, T. (2018). Investigating digital native female learners' attitudes towards paperless language learning. *Research in Learning Technology, 26*, 1-27. https://doi.org/10.25304/rlt.v26.1937

HEC. (2016). *A report on the ranking on higher education institutions (HEIs) in Rwanda.* Higher Education Council.

Herrington, A., Herrington, J., & Mantei, J. (2009). Design principles for mobile learning. In J. Herrington, A. Herrington, J. Mantei, I. Olney & B. Ferry (Eds), *New technologies, new pedagogies: mobile learning in higher education* (pp. 129-138). University of Wollongong.

Jacobson, S., & Turner, K. M. (2010). Not your father's educational technology: a case study in mobile media and journalism education. In C. M. Stewart, C. C. Schifter & M. E. M. Selverian (Eds), *Teaching and learning with technology: beyond constructivism* (pp. 131-147). Routledge.

Ministry of Health. (2020). *Statement on new measures to prevent COVID-19 coronavirus transmission.* Ministry of Health.

NISR. (2014). *Fourth population and housing census, Rwanda, 2012. Thematic report: population projections.* National Institute of Statistics of Rwanda.

NISR. (2018). *Integrated household living conditions survey. Enquête intégrale sur les conditions de vie des ménages (EICV) 2016/17.* National Institute of Statistics of Rwanda.

Niyitegeka, J. D. (2020). *Masters students admit to cope with the lockdown by leveraging online technology.* University of Rwanda. https://ur.ac.rw/?Masters-students-admit-to-cope-with-the-lockdown-by-leveraging-online

Niyomugabo, C., & Uwizeyimana, V. (2018). A top–down orthography change and language attitudes in the context of a language-loyal country. *Language Policy, 17*, 307-318. https://doi.org/10.1007/s10993-016-9427-x

Nshimiye, R. (2020). *UR carries on online teaching services despite lockdown over COVID-19.* University of Rwanda. https://ur.ac.rw/?UR-carries-on-online-teaching-services-despite-lockdown-over-COVID-19

Ntirandekura, S. (2020). *Finalist students undergo UR e-Learning platform induction*. University of Rwanda. https://ur.ac.rw/?Finalist-students-undergo-UR-e-Learning-Platform-induction

Prensky, M. (2001). Digital natives, digital immigrants. *On the Horizon, 9*(5), 1-6.

Republic of Rwanda. (2015). Itegeko nshinga rya Repubulika y'u Rwanda ryo mu 2003 ryavuguruwe mu 2015 [The constitution of the Republic of Rwanda of 2003 revised in 2015]. *Official Gazette of the Republic of Rwanda, Special issue*. Primature.

Republic of Rwanda. (2017). Itegeko Ngenga N° 02/2017/OL ryo ku wa 20/04/2017 rishyiraho Igiswahili nk'ururimi rwemewe mu butegetsi [Organic Law N° 02/2017/OL of 20/04/2017 establishing Kiswahili as an official language]. *Official Gazette of the Republic of Rwanda, 18*. Primature.

Rosendal, T. (2009). Linguistic markets in Rwanda: Language use in advertisements and on signs. *Journal of Multilingual and Multicultural Development, 30*(1), 19-39. https://doi.org/10.1080/01434630802307882

Samuelson, B. L., & Freedman, S. W. (2010). Language policy, multilingual education, and power in Rwanda. *Language Policy, 9*(3), 191-215. https://doi.org/10.1007/s10993-010-9170-7

Stockwell, G., & Hubbard, P. (2013). *Some emerging principles for mobile-assisted language learning*. The International Research Foundation for English Language Education. http://www.tirfonline.org/english-in-the-workforce/mobile-assisted-language-learning

Stockwell, G., & Liu, Y. C. (2015). Engaging in mobile phone-based activities for learning vocabulary: an investigation in Japan and Taiwan. *Calico Journal, 32*(2), 299-322. https://doi.org/10.1558/cj.v32i2.25000

Thinyane, H. (2010). Are digital natives a world-wide phenomenon? An investigation into South African first year students' use and experience with technology. *Computers & Education, 55*(1), 406-414. https://doi.org/10.1016/j.compedu.2010.02.005

UR. (2018). *Facts and figures 2013-2018: retrospective statistical report 1*. University of Rwanda.

UR. (2020a). *Annual report 2019-2020*. University of Rwanda.

UR. (2020b). *Announcement on measures to prevent coronavirus transmission*. University of Rwanda. https://ur.ac.rw/?Announcement-on-measures-to-prevent-coronavirus-transmission

UR. (2020c). *Communication to UR students during coronavirus outbreak*. University of Rwanda. https://ur.ac.rw/?Communication-to-UR-students-during-Coronavirus-outbreak

UR. (2020d). *Letter to UR students – ongoing arrangements for learning at UR*. University of Rwanda. https://ur.ac.rw/?Letter-to-UR-Students-Ongoing-arrangements-for-learning-at-UR

UR. (2020e). *Message from the vice chancellor of University of Rwanda to students*. University of Rwanda. https://ur.ac.rw/?Message-from-the-Vice-Chancellor-of-University-of-Rwanda-to-students

Uwizeyimana, V. (2018a). *An investigation into the effect of mobile-assisted language learning on Rwandan University students' proficiency in English as a foreign language*. Stellenbosch University.

Uwizeyimana, V. (2018b). Digital native (ness), mobile technologies and language proficiency in Rwanda. *Register Journal, 11*(2), 121-138. https://doi.org/10.18326/rgt.v11i2.121-138

Yang, J. (2013). Mobile assisted language learning: review of the recent applications of emerging mobile technologies. *English Language Teaching, 6*(7), 19-25. https://doi.org/10.5539/elt.v6n7p19

# Section 2.
# AMERICAS

# COVID-19-driven sudden shift to remote
6 teaching: the case of the Languages
for the Community Program
at the Universidad Nacional del Litoral

### María del Valle Gastaldi[1] and Elsa Grimaldi[2]

#### Abstract

The Languages for the Community Program (LCP), one of the units that make up the Language Center at Universidad Nacional del Litoral (UNL), Santa Fe, República Argentina, is an extension service provided to people 17 years of age and older that live in Santa Fe or in neighboring towns, and to UNL students wishing to take language courses other than those offered in their own study programs. Since 1999 when they started, these language courses have been taught in a traditional face-to-face modality. The purpose of this chapter is to describe the way in which the first term in 2020 had to suddenly shift to remote teaching and how this shift was devised, coordinated, delivered, and evaluated in response to the unexpected context provoked by the outbreak of COVID-19. The chapter also reports the changes implemented during the second term according to the results of a satisfaction survey administered to students. Collaborative work, previous expertise, and methodological principles allowed the staff at LCP to offer a quality educational response to this paradigm shift in foreign language teaching and learning.

Keywords: COVID-19, online language teaching, IT, management, Argentina.

1. Universidad Nacional del Litoral, Santa Fe, República Argentina; mdvgastaldi@unl.edu.ar; https://orcid.org/0000-0003-3114-1984

2. Universidad Nacional del Litoral, Santa Fe, República Argentina; grimaldi@fiq.unl.edu.ar; https://orcid.org/0000-0002-3681-7835

How to cite: Gastaldi, M. d. V., & Grimaldi, E. (2021). COVID-19-driven sudden shift to remote teaching: the case of the Languages for the Community Program at the Universidad Nacional del Litoral. In N. Radić, A. Atabekova, M. Freddi & J. Schmied (Eds), *The world universities' response to COVID-19: remote online language teaching* (pp. 111-124). Research-publishing.net. https://doi.org/10.14705/rpnet.2021.52.1267

Chapter 6

# 1. Introduction

## 1.1. Objectives

The objectives of this chapter are the following: (1) report about the sudden changes that had to be implemented in response to the novel context characterized by the advent of the pandemic; (2) analyze the decision-making process of the educational response to lockdown measures; (3) examine the assumptions underpinning the design of the remote program as well as pedagogical and logistics considerations; (4) describe the training and support provided to teaching staff; (5) collect and evaluate feedback; and (6) promote future research actions.

The argumentation is developed from the angle of, respectively, the coordinator of the Extension and Professional Development area at the Language Center and chairperson of the LCP (María del Valle Gastaldi) and a member and advisor of the Extension and Professional Development team (Elsa Grimaldi).

## 1.2. Institutional context

UNL was founded in 1919 and even though from the very beginning foreign languages were incorporated into the different programs of study, this process was particularly slow. This slowness reflected the spirit of the times, when the national language had great symbolic value associated with national identity and political unity (Cogo & Dewey, 2012). The process speeded up from the early 60s onwards with the almost exclusive incorporation of English. It was only in the late 90s that the university decided to heighten the role of foreign language teaching and learning and, as a result of this decision, a special academic division was created in 1997 – the area of foreign languages – an embryo of the UNL Language Center as it is known today. Very soon, several institutional and academic steps were taken in order to improve the teaching of foreign languages in the different programs taught at UNL. Then, an important extension initiative was launched in 1999 – the LCP – aimed at people 17 years of age and older living in or around Santa Fe and UNL students wishing to take language courses other than those offered in their own study programs. For over 20 years now, this program has upheld a plurilingual educational perspective offering different language courses to the community. The first languages taught in this program were English, Italian, Portuguese, and Spanish as a foreign language, soon followed by French, German, Chinese, Hebrew, Polish, Croatian, Japanese, and Argentine Sign Language.

The courses are organized in graded levels corresponding to the six-level scale described in the Common European Framework of Reference for languages (CEFR, Council of Europe, 2001). Each course has a total of 60 or 40 hours of tuition depending on level and number of students. Moreover, 120-hour full year preparation courses for international exams are also offered as well as conversation courses, and 20-hour courses of English for Specific Purposes. From the very beginning, both general and specific-purpose courses in all languages have been taught within the communicative language teaching framework (Littlewood, 2011) in the traditional face-to-face modality. Since 2017, blended learning methodologies have been progressively incorporated, such as the development of virtual environments for English and German courses and the online placement test destined to prospective students wishing to join the LCP.

The academic year is divided into two terms, from April to July and from August to November, and a third period for summer intensive courses during February and March. On average, enrollment numbers reach around 1,000 students every term and around 200 students in the summer intensive courses.

## 2. Decision-making process to go fully online

The first 2020 term was supposed to start on March 30. By that time a new disease, designated as COVID-19 by the World Health Organization, had expanded to every part of the world and in Argentina a strict compulsory lockdown was imposed as from March 20, for two weeks. However, the risk of its spread and the news of its death toll in other countries foretold the prolongation of the lockdown and the strengthening of restrictive sanitary measures.

Consequently, the first decision taken by the authorities of the LCP was to postpone the commencement of classes while analyzing other possibilities. Nevertheless, after considering that the lockdown was to be extended beyond the proposed two weeks, it was decided to turn to remote teaching during the first term, at least. From this moment onwards, a dynamic, expedient consensus was reached thanks to the commitment, interest, and willingness of almost all the stakeholders involved in this process – executive and coordinating staff, clerical personnel and teaching staff – who had to make a paradigm shift and implement eight online foreign language courses in almost no time.

However, there were no data concerning the students' view on this shift and, consequently, it was not certain whether the enrolled students would be willing to accept taking courses under the novel modality. With this purpose, they were offered a free two-week period of online courses, after which they would be able to choose whether to attend the first term or not. Taking into account that during that period students would not pay any fees, free educational web services were adopted. Various video conferencing platforms were employed for the synchronous activities so as to comply with the generally agreed principles of communicative language teaching, namely engaging learners in meaningful interaction and communication in the target language (Richards, 2006). For the asynchronous activities, Google Classroom was selected, a free educational service which can be used as a free learning management system (Pappas, 2015), since it allows sharing files in a collaborative way.

Once this free two-week period was over, about 70% of the enrolled students opted for the new modality. The remaining 30% decided to wait for the return of classroom-based lessons and only 10% of these did so after having taken a few remote lessons, which they found frustrating as a result of connectivity problems and/or lack of technological knowledge. The opportunity was also important for teachers since it allowed them to re-think their practices, acquire new skills, understand what technology integration entails and get appropriate training to face this novel pedagogical context. Last but not least, it is important to mention the invaluable support of the administrative personnel, information technology (IT) technicians, and financial and budget assistants.

Taking all this into account, on April 20 the program officially began the first term with online courses of German, Chinese, Spanish as a foreign language, French, English, Italian, Japanese, and Portuguese, totaling 61 courses, taught by 43 language teachers and remotely attended by over 600 students, about 60% of the usual average attendance.

## 2.1. Assumptions underpinning the design of the remote program

Within the context of the coronavirus pandemic and the lockdown imposed, a number of assumptions were made as regards the feasibility of turning to remote teaching in a very short time. They were:

- stakeholders would take on an active role during the process;

- teachers would be eager to face the challenge;

- the pandemic would be an exceptional context to try out teachers' beliefs about collaborative decision making, planning and action; and

- students would be grateful for the opportunity of learning languages remotely from the safety of their homes.

Based on these assumptions, the following considerations were made by the LCP staff regarding pedagogical principles, logistics, and teacher development.

## 2.2. Pedagogical and logistics considerations

Teaching is a complex practice which implies an interweaving of different kinds of specialized knowledge. The Technological Pedagogical Content Knowledge (TPACK) framework model in language teaching (Mishra & Koehler, 2006) proposes a conceptual framework that integrates the main components of learning environments: content knowledge, pedagogical knowledge, and technological knowledge. The interaction of these three kinds of knowledge produces the type of flexible knowledge needed to successfully integrate technology into teaching and learning to make them effective and meaningful. These principles were adopted by the LCP staff when devising the online courses to be delivered. However, the fact that not all teachers had adequate experience with certain technologies was taken into account and, at the same time it was felt that acquiring these skills at such short notice presented a challenge worth taking.

During the first term different platforms were used such as Zoom, Google Meet, WebEx, and Skype in their free versions. However, all of them presented time limitations and not enough resources available to deliver synchronous teaching. For this reason, and after this weakness was particularly pointed out in a students' survey which is referred to below, during the second term the Language Center subscribed to the Zoom platform. This platform was selected for several reasons, e.g. quality of sound, possibility of using 'breakout rooms' that allow splitting a session into different separate sessions, and because it permits delivering synchronous 90-minute lessons. At the same time Google Classroom continued to be used for the asynchronous activities. As regards resources, teachers were encouraged to work with scanned, digitized material and, where possible, e-books. In all cases, and in order to participate fully, each student needed a computer, reliable high-speed internet access, microphones, speakers, and a webcam.

### 2.3. Training and support

The LCP and the Language Center have always favored continuous professional development through the frequent organization of training workshops and academic meetings. The COVID-19 emergency was no exception; teachers were encouraged to expand their knowledge and skills by taking tutorials and webinars available in social media, organized by UNL and other institutions. Based on queries from teachers, video tutorials were designed by the LCP teachers with broad expertise in technology-based language teaching using the LOOM free software available in Google Chrome. The LCP IT personnel cooperated with them in designing, uploading, and sharing this material, which was later systematized and saved in Google Drive.

## 3. Assessment

According to the legal framework that supports the LCP courses (RCS UNL 580/13 – RCS UNL109/20), after each successful passing of exams students obtain a certificate issued by UNL accrediting that they have reached the corresponding level. Levels 1 to 9 correlate to CEFR levels A1, A2, B1, B2, and their sublevels.

Turning remote also meant that exams had to be administered online, which meant having to face the challenge of designing tests which guaranteed evaluation objectives, quality, transparency, reliability, and validity. This was particularly difficult concerning the written exams but, in order not to deprive students of the possibility of obtaining their certificates, the following considerations were taken into account:

- the different levels are made up of small groups, with an average of 15 students per class;

- by the end of the term, teachers have a fair knowledge of their students and their academic performance;

- students have a right to be considered trustworthy;

- all written exams are done during a Zoom session which makes them even more transparent;

- the time allotted to complete the written exams is a relevant variable when designing them; and

- oral exams, held a week later, will undoubtedly validate the results of the written exams.

Under the traditional classroom-based modality, written tests have four sections: *listening comprehension, reading comprehension, use of English,* and *writing*.

Taking into account this particular context, the Moodle platform was adopted for the English written tests and different quiz activities were selected such as matching, multiple choice, embedded answer, or cloze tests that allow summative assessment, for the first three sections. For the writing section the essay type of question was employed which allows students to write on a particular subject according to the task. This is the only section that must be graded manually.

As regards the exams for the other languages taught at LCP, teachers preferred working in Google Classroom and the exams included the four sections but as a downloadable Assignment with an answer sheet that the students had to upload in the specified time. In June and July, oral tests were taken using Zoom, Google Meet, WebEx, or Skype according to the previous selection agreed upon by the teachers and students of the different groups. From December onwards, they will be taken by Zoom only.

Even though detailed statistical data as regards exam results are not included here, it is relevant to mention that almost 90% of the students passed their exams and almost 80% of them got the same or similar marks in both the written and oral tests.

## 4. Program evaluation

### 4.1. Teachers' feedback

Teachers' feedback was required and given by frequent interaction but not through a formal questionnaire or survey since it was not advisable to increase the teachers' workload implied by this unexpected opportunity. Most of them felt exhausted but satisfied and grateful for the challenge.

However, it is worth mentioning that it has already been decided to design and conduct a survey by the end of the second term. The aim is to gather teachers' feedback as regards their experience, their needs for further training, and their interest and availability for the next year in case both modalities still co-exist, which seems most probable.

## 4.2. Students' feedback

Given the novelty of the remote online proposal and the celerity with which it had to be implemented, very soon the need to evaluate its results emerged. Accordingly, a satisfaction survey was administered to students to know their views and impressions (supplementary materials, Appendix 1). The survey was available during the first week in June and it had a good level of response of almost 70%. The results are summarized below:

- students' general assessment of the proposal was highly positive;

- most students highlighted the professionalism and commitment of teachers; and

- students' assessment of the efficacy of the remote mode for learning the four communicative skills was positive but not highly positive. They rated the effectiveness of online learning in terms of learning how to speak and how to write a text in the target language as weak points to be improved. Nonetheless, the results of the final written and oral exams were much better than expected.

Students were also asked to make suggestions if they had any. The main ones are listed below:

- use a better, more secure platform to avoid inadequate functioning. Some suggested Google Meet or Microsoft Teams but others suggested that the university should provide a platform of its own with security enhancement to avoid privacy risks; and

- increase teacher/students and student/student interactions.

They were also asked to make a comparison between the two modalities (remote and classroom-based). Most of them agreed on the following facts:

- the remote modality is highly recommended under extreme circumstances such as a pandemic;

- it also solves transport difficulties and expenses; and

- it is highly convenient for elderly people though they are a minority, people who suffer health problems or live far from the Language Center.

However, 50% of the students expressed that, under normal circumstances, they preferred the face-to-face modality for the following reasons:

- classroom-based teaching favors face-to-face interactions between teachers and students and among students;

- this modality is better for learning oral skills and communication; and

- students do not have to worry about connectivity issues.

And there were other students (about 24%) who found advantages and disadvantages in the two modalities and suggested a combination of both.

## 5. After the emergency: the second term

Encouraged by students' responses and teachers' enthusiasm, and compelled by a further prolongation of the lockdown in Argentina, it was decided to continue with the remote modality during the second term, which started on August 18 and finished by the end of November. The enrollment numbers of the first period increased by 50%: 963 students enrolled, grouped in 83 courses of German, Chinese, French, English, Italian, Japanese, Argentine Sign Language, and Portuguese (Table 1).

Table 1.  Enrollment for the 1st and 2nd terms

| Language | 1st Term | 2nd Term |
|---|---|---|
| German | 43 | 84 |
| Chinese | 7 | 13 |
| French | 20 | 40 |
| English | 462 | 675 |
| Italian | 37 | 77 |
| Portuguese | 10 | 31 |
| Japanese | 3 | 14 |
| Argentine Sign Language | 30 | 29 |
| Total | 612 | 963 |

In response to the most important weakness pointed out by students in reference to the first term, the Zoom for Education platform was adopted for all courses, which allows delivering 90-minute synchronous Zoom-based lessons with several advantages, especially concerning speaking. According to Nation and Newton (2009) different kinds of activities are very important in teaching speaking. It is necessary to focus on aspects of speaking such as pronunciation, intonation, fluency, adequate polite language for a specific situation and last but not least tactics for holding the floor of the conversation. Synchronous meetings are a must to guarantee the context for this practice.

Enrollment for this second period was successful not only in terms of number of students but also regarding these students' location (supplementary materials, Appendix 2). Through the new online proposal, the LCP has gone national and international: 89% of the students live in the province of Santa Fe, in the city itself, in nearby towns and in other towns of the province located far from the capital city, 11% of the students are from 12 out of a total of 23 provinces in Argentina and three students are from other countries (Table 2).

Table 2.  Distribution of students according to language and country of origin

| Language | Chile | Brazil | Argentina |
|---|---|---|---|
| German | 1 | 0 | 92 |
| Chinese | 0 | 0 | 13 |
| French | 0 | 0 | 56 |

| English | 0 | 1 | 674 |
| Italian | 0 | 0 | 78 |
| Japanese | 1 | 0 | 13 |
| Portuguese | 0 | 0 | 34 |
| Total | 2 | 1 | 960 |

## 6. Conclusions

UNL, its Language Center and the LCP are educational institutions and service providers and as such they had to give a quick educational response to the community in the context of the pandemic and the lockdown that ensued. Even though taken in haste, the agreed-upon decision of going remote was adopted according to a clear set of goals, expertise, collaborative work, professional development, and effective communication. It should also be remarked that all stakeholders involved believed that it was worthwhile to face the challenge and take the risk.

The favorable results yielded by the satisfaction survey as well as by the increase in enrollment of the second term demonstrate students widely approved of the novel educational experience they went through. Hard data such as attendance, retention and completion rates as well as examination outcomes are good indicators that this non-traditional pedagogic proposal is going in the right direction.

For all these reasons, it can be concluded that remote language teaching is here to stay, even after classroom-based teaching can start again. A future is foreseen in which the two modalities will co-exist. Quoting Rapanta et al. (2020), "the current pandemic can be understood as a catalyst" (p. 941) that will speed up educational change, models, and practices in response to the society of the future.

Consequently, the research agenda on online language learning should move forward and include, among other topics, novel learning contexts and environments, use of mobile devices, and apps. Hockly (2015) claims that this new research agenda should also include "learner engagement and interaction, student self-organization, instructor presence (or lack of it), course design, and particularly, the issue of assessment and evaluation" (p. 6). Accordingly, the UNL Language Center is planning to set up a research group which will bring together researchers committed to understanding the novel challenges faced by language teaching in the context of a post-pandemic world.

## 7. Acknowledgments

The authors would like to express their gratitude to the students, teachers, IT specialists, executive and coordinating staff, clerical personnel, technicians, and assistants who made this adventure possible.

## 8. Supplementary materials

https://research-publishing.box.com/s/3r7k5j0eocyuykgvoqh8p62v9x6ieori

## References

Cogo, A., & Dewey, M. (2012). *Analysing English as a lingua franca.* Continuum International Publishing Group.

Council of Europe. (2001). *Common European framework of reference for languages: learning, teaching, assessment, companion volume.* Council of Europe Publishing. https://www.coe.int/en/web/common-european-framework-reference-languages

Hockly, N. (2015). Developments in online language learning. *ELT Journal, 69*(3), 308-313. https://doi.org/10.1093/elt/ccv020

Littlewood, W. (2011). Communicative language teaching: an expanding concept for a changing world. In E. Hinkel (Ed.), *Handbook of research in second language teaching and learning* (vol. 2). Routledge. https://doi.org/10.4324/9780203836507.ch33

Mishra, P., & Koehler, M. J. (2006). Technological pedagogical content knowledge: a new framework for teacher knowledge. *Teachers College Record, 108*(6), 1017-1054.

Nation, I. S. P., & Newton, J. (2009). *Teaching ESL/EFL listening and speaking.* Routledge.

Pappas, C. (2015). Google Classroom review: pros and cons of using Google Classroom in e-learning. *Free Educational Technology.* https://elearningindustry.com/google-classroom-review-pros-and-cons-of-using-google-classroom-in-elearning

Rapanta, C., Botturi, L., Goodyear, P., Guàrdia, L., & Koole, M. (2020). Online university teaching during and after the Covid-19 crisis: refocusing teacher presence and learning activity. *Postdigital Science and Education, 2,* 923-945. https://doi.org/10.1007/s42438-020-00155-y

Richards, J. C. (2006). *Communicative language teaching today.* Cambridge University Press.

# 7 Remote language teaching in the pandemic context at the University of São Paulo, Brazil

## Mônica Ferreira Mayrink[1], Heloísa Albuquerque-Costa[2], and Daniel Ferraz[3]

### Abstract

This chapter aims at presenting an overview of how our experiences as professors of Spanish, French, and English studies at the Department of Modern Languages (DML) of the University of São Paulo (USP) responded to the challenges put forward by the pedagogical and technological practices required since the outbreak of the COVID-19 health crisis, and the adoption of measures of social isolation in the city of São Paulo, Brazil. Our pedagogical practices are shared through a description of the institutional context and our students' narratives. The chapter is divided into three main sections. The first one presents a brief overview of the institutional context. The second briefly problematizes the decision-making process to go fully online, and the challenges of the remote program. Section three explores the experiences of the three professors and their students by discussing pedagogical practices and students' feedback. In conclusion, the text discusses the lessons learned for future actions.

Keywords: COVID-19, online language teaching, collaborative knowledge building, feedback, Brazil.

---

1. University of São Paulo, São Paulo, Brazil; momayrink@usp.br; https://orcid.org/0000-0003-3635-7768

2. University of São Paulo, São Paulo, Brazil; heloisaalbuqcosta@usp.br; https://orcid.org/0000-0002-4621-6822

3. University of São Paulo, São Paulo, Brazil; danielfe@usp.br; https://orcid.org/0000-0002-8483-2423

How to cite: Mayrink, M. F., Albuquerque-Costa, H., & Ferraz, D. (2021). Remote language teaching in the pandemic context at the University of São Paulo, Brazil. In N. Radić, A. Atabekova, M. Freddi & J. Schmied (Eds), *The world universities' response to COVID-19: remote online language teaching* (pp. 125-137). Research-publishing.net. https://doi.org/10.14705/rpnet.2021.52.1268

Chapter 7

## 1. Introduction

The impact of the global health crisis caused by COVID-19 has had overwhelming effects on many dimensions of human life, such as the economic, social, and psychological dimensions – for example, many have lost their jobs, and many have suffered from social isolation and witnessed thousands of deaths. The educational field has not been an exception, given that the sudden change from traditional face-to-face teaching to remote and online 'emergency' teaching has profoundly altered the personal daily routine of students, teachers, and the administrative staff, faculties, and other educational institutions. In these contexts, we have had to adapt ourselves – individually and collectively – to the 'new' reality. At the same time, we have sought to better understand the threat that haunted all of us and endangered the physical and mental integrity of citizens of every corner of the planet.

Within this context, three weeks after the beginning of the 2020 school year, professors[4] from the USP and their students were taken aback by the institutional decision that claimed 'USP cannot stop'. As a result, in the middle of March, they began to face the enormous challenge of reframing and adapting their educational practices within the traditional undergraduate course of modern languages. In its 86 years of history, the university has never witnessed such a situation.

Thus, this work discusses how our experience as professors of Spanish (Mônica Mayrink), French (Heloísa Albuquerque-Costa), and English (Daniel Ferraz) at the Department of Modern Languages of the Faculty of Philosophy, Languages and Human Sciences, USP have faced the challenges put forward by the pedagogical and technological practices required since the outbreak of the health crisis and the measures of social isolation in the city of São Paulo, Brazil, where we are located. Our pedagogical practices are shared through a description of the institutional context and our students' narratives. We believe they portray some of the difficulties and solutions also encountered

---

4. In this chapter we use the term 'professor' to refer to those who teach at university level.

by colleagues from other departments and areas, who were also surprised by this unknown and unexpected reality. The chapter is divided into three main sections. The first presents a brief overview of our institutional context. The second section problematizes the difficult decision-making process to go fully online and the challenges of the remote program. Section three explores the experiences of the three professors and their students, by discussing pedagogical practices and students' feedback. In conclusion, the lessons learned and planning of future actions are discussed.

## 2. Institutional context

USP is a public university, supported by the State of São Paulo, Brazil. It offers undergraduate courses in all areas of knowledge, free of charge. There are also postgraduate programs in all fields of knowledge, offering Master's and PhD degrees. Their objective is to educate highly qualified human resources for teaching, research, and scientific and technological development. In addition to undergraduate and postgraduate courses, USP offers one year certificates and up-to-date courses for the community.

Since its foundation in 1934, USP has played a fundamental role in advancing research in the country, whether in scientific, technological, or social fields. Currently, USP is responsible for more than 20% of all scientific production in Brazil. It is ranked #115 in Quacquarelli Symonds Global World Rankings 2021. The DML was the highest ranked department at USP (#38) in the area of arts and humanities. The languages and literature courses at USP are attended by approximately 5,000 students. They offer undergraduate and postgraduate courses in English, French, German, Italian, and Spanish, covering the areas of language, linguistics, teacher education, literature, cultural studies, and translation.

More specifically, the DML (English, French, German, Italian, and Spanish) offers undergraduate courses for Brazilian students coming from all over the country. It currently has 49 tenured professors and seven assistant professors, all of whom have a doctoral degree and many, in addition, have already undertaken post-doctoral research. Most tenured professors work in undergraduate and postgraduate levels, and develop research and activities for the external community, which are more directly articulated with the community outside the university. Only a few professors from the languages and literature courses have dedicated themselves to research on teaching and technology. This peculiar characteristic may explain, to a certain extent, some of the difficulties faced over the past few months. In the midst of the serious global health crisis that surprised Brazil and the world, university teachers were impelled to rapidly adapt to modalities that were completely different from the ones that had traditionally been developed for years.

In terms of technical support – even before the pandemic – USP had already entered the digital era. There are several online platforms where the public can access the knowledge produced at the university. There are courses, events, and classes recorded in various channels: Canal USP (USP channel of communication) and e-Aulas (e-Classes/Moodle), among others. The university also offers a wide digital structure to professors and students. Most student enrolment and administration procedures are carried out online. On the teaching side, almost all processes are digitized and online, such as students' registration, managing of downloadable attendance lists files, grades, and reports. At USP[5], professors and students can actually access more than 25 university digital domains (from human resources departments to class management).

The academic community at USP has access to the Moodle platform, which is available as pedagogical support for face-to-face courses at the undergraduate, graduate, and community levels[6]. In DML, it has been used mainly as a repository and communication channel between professors and students. However, previous studies (Mayrink & Albuquerque-Costa, 2015, 2017) had already pointed out other possibilities of use, some of them not traditionally explored by USP users,

---

5. https://uspdigital.usp.br

6. Before the pandemic Moodle was used mainly as support for the development of extra-class activities. With the pandemic outbreak most of the teachers started using it as the main platform for remote teaching.

such as interaction tools. These possibilities showcased a favorable potential for online language teaching at the university.

The urgency in the migration from face-to-face to remote teaching ended up highlighting the Moodle platform as one of the main options to meet the new pedagogical needs that arose from the social isolation of professors and students. The technical support from staff, in addition to local initiatives such as the provision of direct communication channels of support for teachers and students, were important allies in the basic training of those who had never used Moodle tools.

Most significantly, guidance on the use of this platform was offered by the Information Technology Department, where different workshops to present other tools such as Google Meet and Zoom were designed and offered to members of teaching staff. This technical support provided professors with technological options that could adequately respond to the pedagogical objectives and didactic choices they wished to develop. Given the specificity of the work with the teaching and learning of languages, it was important to seek technological alternatives that offered interaction between professors and students, and among students, providing them with real opportunities for linguistic exchange. However, as will be seen below, the experiences that professors began to build over the months pointed to the use of complementary platforms and tools that could be better suited to their teaching practices, according to the specificities of the subjects they teach.

## 3. Decision-making process and challenges of the remote program

Under the motto 'USP cannot stop', professors and students were taken aback as most undergraduate and graduate courses were practically 'forced' to become virtual online courses. Practically overnight, professors and students had to find ways to negotiate all aspects of higher-level education, and this situation raised some questions related to the following topics: contents (would contents be the same as those initially planned?), interaction (if professors and students were used to interacting in classes, what kinds of interaction would remote teaching promote?), assessment (would evaluation be the same?), technology knowledge and expertise (were professors and students tech savvy enough to adapt to this new technological reality?), not to mention the number of students who ended up with depression and anxiety during the process of adaptation to remote learning (how would we deal with professors' and students' anxieties and depression?). As the decision-making process came to us in a top-down approach, many of these questions have not been answered yet.

The languages and literature students' profile is quite heterogeneous. In the initial years of the course, we welcome many students with little or no proficiency in the foreign language, while there are also those who are highly proficient. This heterogeneity requires teachers to plan classes that address content that is sufficiently accessible for those who are taking their first steps in a foreign language but also challenging for those who are linguistically proficient. The development of oral and written comprehension and production is one of the objectives to be pursued throughout the course. At the same time, language studies are carried out to deepen knowledge in the areas of phonetics and phonology, syntax, semantics, pragmatics, discourse studies, sociolinguistics, among others.

We understand that in order to achieve these objectives it is essential to provide teaching strategies that allow negotiation in the building of knowledge, and this is a challenge when it comes to teaching in the remote mode. The work we have developed in the areas of Spanish, French, and English seeks to preserve the spaces for permanent interaction among the different participants in the process in the remote modality. In this sense, with the support of the Moodle platform and other tools (Google Meet, Zoom, etc), we have offered different possibilities of students' engagement with the content to be studied. To this end, we have sought a balance in the use of tools and strategies that guarantee more intense interpersonal and interactive classes by developing proposals that adjust to what Valente (2011) calls "being virtually together" (p. 29). At the same time, we have allowed students a more individual, autonomous, and subjective interaction with the contents.

## 4. Pedagogical practices and students' feedback

The guiding principles of our practice in a remote context are based upon Vygotskian assumptions of valuing the collaborative building of knowledge, in which the most competent peers (teachers and students with a greater degree of mastery of content) play a pivotal role in the mediation of learning (Vygotsky, 1930/1998). Also essential in this process are the mediation instruments, which make up the different technological tools used to facilitate interactions, access, and the practice of language.

By the same token, our practices are based on Freire (2005), for whom the education of critical and active citizens, capable of critiquing the status quo and naturalized perspectives, is paramount. Even though Freire sought to rethink elementary education carried out in Portuguese language, much of his critique reverberates in university education carried out in foreign languages departments around the country. Obviously, 'banking education' (Freire, 2005) does not refer to every university professor's pedagogy, and perhaps the generalization and universalism conflated here should also be put under scrutiny. In many contexts, we still hear from students that this is the case: too many lecture classes, very few possibilities for discussion, negotiation, interaction, and questioning from students. This is perhaps the Achilles' heel we try to avoid (ourselves included). The more we see university as a place of critique, questioning, and projection of social alternatives, the more we act to keep it as our place of critique (Ferraz & Duboc, 2021). In this sense, in this case study we do not offer 'solutions' for online remote teaching and learning of languages. However, we can offer the reader some of our pedagogical practices and their outcomes by bringing our students' voices to the fore[7]. In order to do that, each of us will showcase below the ways we have dealt with remote language.

---

[7]. As we are worried about improving our teaching practices, we always consider the importance of giving students plenty of space to evaluate the learning process they have gone through along the semester. In this particular case study, all the data presented were collected in July 2020 (end of the first academic semester), when students were asked to write reports in the language they were studying (Spanish and French comments were translated into English). We have been granted permission to publish their comments.

With regards to Spanish studies, Mayrink – right after the first week of social isolation – intensified the use of the Moodle platform in order to continue her *Spanish Language I* and *Spanish Language III* classes[8]. At first, during this transitional period to the new remote education, the environment was prepared for the provision of materials and resources, as well as for the development of individual and group asynchronous activities. After a week, the students and professor decided to hold synchronous meetings, using the Google Meet tool, twice a week, in accordance with the face-to-face course. However, the first experiences presented difficulties of various kinds (problems with network connection, lack of resources, such as ample access to wi-fi, availability of camera and microphone, adequate physical spaces to attend synchronous classes, among others). Such restrictions prevented the development of prolonged interactions and led the groups to negotiate synchronous and asynchronous class times.

These challenges, added to the personal difficulties faced by the students (family members infected with coronavirus, reconfiguration of their work routine, depressive states), also influenced decision-making from the point of view of didactics. In order to promote greater balance and flexibility of the proposed activities, meeting times, and evaluation methods, it was important to guarantee the recording of synchronous meetings so as to make them available to students who could not participate in these interactions. This promoted a greater participation of students individually and in groups. The activities that involved the design of videos and murals, audio for animations, recording of personal texts, among others, were appreciated by students. At the end of the semester, their feedback was very positive:

> "I liked the way it was done [...], in the conditions that we had [...]. Of all classes I had, this was the most dynamic, the one that most kept the student-teacher interaction, [...] without being that passive thing. I liked that you always brought different formats for classes, such as power point, online exercises, Moodle, some videos. I think these activities

---

8. The courses were offered twice a week and the groups had an average of 30 students each.

complemented each other in a very good way, and the many interactions allowed us to practice and talk" (M.R.).

"Professor, this was the subject that best worked for me [...]. I don't know if it was the dynamics or because this is a language class [...] the use of the Moodle platform was the best" (E.).

"The course was very organized, you could find everything on Moodle [...] there was a lot of support material. Not to mention the recorded classes for those who couldn't attend synchronous classes. So it worked really well. [...] I think that the fact that the class was small also helped (...) I really learned a lot. I feel more confident with my Spanish [...] I can only thank you because you handled Moodle very well" (M.).

In relation to French, Albuquerque-Costa has discussed with the students[9] – who were beginning their first experience as French teachers – how to develop their own classes using different platforms. The syllabus content was adapted to accommodate the discussion of topics like:

- creating virtual classes to welcome their own students. Also, they discussed how they could modify the spaces of the platforms using images, animated effects, and messages to connect and motivate the students;

- sharing the plan of the course with the students and explaining in detail what they were supposed to do; and

- choosing oral and writing support related to the objective of the class. A very interesting discussion was developed on this topic, for example, their methodological steps to create activities and pedagogical choice to organize their courses.

---

9. Albuquerque-Costa taught a group of 18 students.

One point that is important to mention is that students realized that sometimes they had to use more than one virtual platform to develop their oral and writing activities. This probably shows they have had training in digital literacy. Below, some of her students' feedbacks are shared.

> "Taking college courses remotely was both a challenging and enriching experience. It was challenging to reconcile online classes with the family routine, but on the other hand, it was enriching in the sense that I was able to learn more autonomously. In the discipline of French, there was understanding with the atypical situation of remote education and, therefore, consistent with the activities and assessments required during the course. My learning took place in a more autonomous way, but always guided by the professor [...]. Another change in relation to the face-to-face modality was the more frequent use of the computer and digital tools. What I was able to learn from the remote teaching experience was mainly the organization for studies and autonomy in the learning process" (J.O.).

> "I had already used Moodle in subjects where I should read texts, but this semester was different, as there were classes and activities to do. I didn't do them all due to lack of time... I'm working from home too. From the discipline, I liked the Exposé activity... I did it little by little and exchanged messages in the Moodle forum, which I didn't know" (L.M.).

With regards to English, Ferraz has discussed and negotiated the syllabus contents of the two courses, *Discourse studies* and *Semantics*[10], with his students since the first weeks of classes. As the pandemic hit us, this negotiation was transferred to online settings. In addition, the assessment system was discussed and adapted to pandemic times as they went through a very interesting evaluation experience: as soon as the pandemic broke out, the professor scheduled online meetings through Google Meet, outside of class hours. In the meetings, students discussed

---

10. Both courses had approximately 40 students each.

new forms of assessment and how each group and student would like to be assessed, for example through response papers, video recording, assessment, or interviews with the professor.

Assessment negotiation is just one of the many examples of the adaptation to remote language teaching. Like in Mayrink's experience, the professor and students also talked about the difficulties brought by lack of access or slow internet connection, the lack of interaction in classes, the lecture-like classes and their consequences in terms of the impact on the learning process, the choice of the pedagogical practices and methodologies for remote education, and the fact that many students felt depressed and anxious in relation to the COVID-19 pandemic, isolation, and mandatory remote education. Despite these difficulties, most students' feedbacks were positive.

> "First of all, I would like to thank you again for the lessons and your posture during this pandemic moment. I was able to enjoy immensely all the classes and the content taught, so thank you so much for continuing the course and always listening to the students' side!!" (H.M.).

> "I wanted to say that your classes are opening my mind to issues that I didn't know existed. I am admiring the classes" (M.S.).

> "Good evening, professor! I would like to thank you again. I'm truly happy that you enjoyed the content. It was really singular to me to try this experience. I loved your course and the fact that you created some different options for the evaluation" (P.S.).

The pandemic has affected both students and professors and all of them have been forced to discover new paths that can guide them on this unpredictable situation. Pedagogical and technological challenges associated with personal difficulties in dealing with the disease, a new routine, and a mental strain make it clear that we cannot expect our teaching and learning activities to be a mirror of a regular course. We need to be sufficiently open-minded to reconsider and redefine our practices so as to find, together with our students, the best ways to move on. Nevertheless, individual attitudes do not guarantee the success of the enterprise. It is absolutely necessary that the university provides both professors and students with excellent conditions to circumvent any difficulties that might hinder the progress of the teaching and learning process in such an unusual context as a worldwide pandemic.

## 5. Conclusion

There is still a lot to learn when it comes to dealing with mandatory remote teaching, a process that – at least in our university – was ordained top-down and overnight. The first lesson that we learned from this experience shows that it is necessary to unsettle the idea that digital and face-to-face environments are on opposite sides. In fact, this conundrum is not new. Our practices contend that many characteristics of face-to-face teaching can and should come to terms with digital settings: contents adaptation, assessment negotiation, and creative ways of interacting. As we have pointed out throughout the paper, these should actually be lessons for every language teacher, teacher educator, or professor with or without pandemic times, with complementary or full online education.

Another lesson points to the fact that we have focused on language teaching and learning and its linguistics dimensions, when in fact language as a social practice, as put forward by Freire (2005), has been an important dimension in our work. In the future, we believe that the university should acknowledge a constant formative and technological support policy that backs up the construction of new remote, online teaching possibilities in regular courses, in post pandemic times.

In this context, we believe that blended learning could be a very productive alternative for university language courses, since it may enhance the possibilities of learning by combining different spaces and times. As pointed out by Moran (2015), this teaching modality provides an expanded classroom which allows the teacher to communicate with the student in a face-to-face environment as well as in a digital context. This also promotes a more balanced interaction with the students altogether and with each one of them individually. However, as emphasized by Moran (2015), in order to achieve this goal, it is imperative that the university is open to review its curricula, as well as its conception of time and space. Besides, those who are responsible for developing teaching education programs have to think about the new demands of the 21st century so that future language teachers feel prepared to contribute to the development of didactic activities, methodologies, and learning environments. Finally, we believe that all these forthcoming practices put forward other possibilities of research that can be shared in a broad academic community in order to expand the studies in the area of language learning and teaching.

# References

Ferraz, D. M., & Duboc, A. P. (2021). *Language education and the university: fostering socially-just practices in undergraduate contexts*. Pimenta Cultural. https://doi.org/10.31560/pimentacultural/2020.540

Freire, P. (2005). *Pedagogy of the oppressed*. Continuum.

Mayrink, M. F., & Albuquerque-Costa, H. (2015). A extensão da sala presencial para o Moodle: espaço de aprendizagem, reflexão e pesquisa nos cursos de Letras Francês e Espanhol da USP. In K. A. Silva, M. Mastrella-de-Andrade & C. A. Pereira Filho (Eds), *A formação de professores de línguas: políticas, projetos e parcerias* (pp. 215-232). Pontes.

Mayrink, M. F., & Albuquerque-Costa, H. (2017). Tecnologias digitais no ensino de línguas. Ensino presencial e virtual em sintonia na formação em línguas estrangeiras. *The Especialist (PUCSP), 38*(1), 1-14. https://doi.org/10.23925/2318-7115.2017v38i1a10

Moran, J. M. (2015). Educação Híbrida: um conceito-chave para a educação, hoje. In L. Bacich, A. Tanzi Neto, A., & F. M. Trevisani (Eds), *Ensino Híbrido: personalização e tecnologia na educação* (pp. 47-66). Penso.

Valente, J. A. (2011). Educação a distância: criando abordagens educacionais que possibilitam a construção do conhecimento. In V. A. Arantes (Ed.), *Educação a distância* (pp. 13-44). Summus.

Vygotsky, L. S. (1930/1998). *A formação social da mente*. Martins Fontes.

# 8. Creating communities of practice: The Harvard Language Center's role in supporting language instruction during the pandemic

## Andrew F. Ross[1] and Sarah Luehrman Axelrod[2]

### Abstract

When Harvard University moved all instruction into an online modality in response to the COVID-19 pandemic, The Language Center positioned itself as a critical source of guidance on best practices in this new environment. For Harvard, an institution that has always prioritized face-to-face instruction above all other formats, 2020 has been a watershed moment that has forced faculty to reconsider nearly everything about the way they organize and deliver their courses. Owing to the pandemic crisis, we find ourselves in a moment in which the efficacy of these modalities in language learning is, despite initial concerns, being proven day after day. In the context of this crisis, The Language Center has developed training and support mechanisms for this transition, focusing on desired learning outcomes, centering instructor and student experience, and positioning the language faculty to be able to successfully employ hybrid and online approaches to instruction that will continue to serve them well after the crisis abates. This contribution describes the strategies and actions that The Language Center took to ensure the success of the remote teaching and learning of languages at Harvard University in the first term of the 2020-2021 academic year, after the emergency evacuation of campus in March

---

1. Harvard University, Cambridge, Massachusetts, United States; andrew_ross@fas.harvard.edu; https://orcid.org/0000-0002-4509-0551

2. Harvard University, Cambridge, Massachusetts, United States; slaxelrod@post.harvard.edu; https://orcid.org/0000-0001-7187-7297

How to cite: Ross, A. F., & Axelrod, S. L. (2021). Creating communities of practice: The Harvard Language Center's role in supporting language instruction during the pandemic. In N. Radić, A. Atabekova, M. Freddi & J. Schmied (Eds), *The world universities' response to COVID-19: remote online language teaching* (pp. 139-152). Research-publishing.net. https://doi.org/10.14705/rpnet.2021.52.1269

Chapter 8

of 2020, and offers a model for other centers engaged in academic support. While extensive insights on the success of these efforts are still pending, given the timing of this crisis and the interventions undertaken, early feedback suggests that faculty have found provided resources to be useful, and their intention is to adopt aspects of technologically-mediated instruction in their face-to-face teaching going forward.

**Keywords: COVID-19, remote online instruction, training and support, Harvard Language Center, USA.**

## 1. Introduction

In March of 2020, central leadership at Harvard University made the determination that all courses would be conducted online for the remainder of the semester due to concerns about the nature, spread, and consequences of COVID-19. Furthermore, it was announced that all courses offered in June, July and August would be taught online as well, and that a decision would be made at that time as to whether the remainder of 2020 would allow teaching face-to-face, in a hybrid framework, or in an online modality. In early July, the institution decided to move all instruction for the academic year 2020-2021 online, although a limited number of first-year students would be invited to live on campus in socially-distanced housing during first semester (i.e. the term spanning from September to December) and fourth-year students would be invited back to campus for second semester (the term spanning from January to May), so as to be able to finish out their Harvard experience on campus. Faculty and staff are presently encouraged to work from home, where practicable, and a COVID testing regimen has been set up for those who must be on campus to perform work, including students.

The magnitude of this decision and its impact cannot be overstated. Teaching and learning at Harvard has historically been conducted face-to-face, and where possible, in small classes that afford a highly personalized educational experience. Language courses were capped at 18 students prior to the pandemic; in the current online modality, they are capped at 12. For both faculty and students, teaching and learning online through the medium of technologies both synchronous and asynchronous is entirely new. The Language Center has stepped forward to take a proactive role in managing and facilitating a minimally disruptive transition to remote instruction, and a thoughtful approach to online teaching and learning in the COVID crisis.

## 1.1. Institutional context

Harvard University, founded in 1636, is the oldest institution of higher education in the United States. It is comprised of Harvard College, which houses and educates undergraduates, as well as a number of graduate schools including the Kennedy School of Government, Harvard Law School, the Harvard Business School, the Harvard Medical School, the Graduate School of Education, the School of Divinity, the School of Engineering and Applied Sciences, and the Chan School of Public Health. Its student body is highly diverse: in 2019, Harvard welcomed 10,285 students and scholars from 155 countries. In academic year 2019-2020, Harvard enrolled a total of 23,731 students at all levels, across all programs. Within the college, which will be the focus of this study, 819 students from 103 countries are included in the 6,716 undergraduate students enrolled in the 2019-2020 academic year.

Of the students attending Harvard College, 37% self-identify as White, 21% are Asian, 11% are Hispanic/Latinx, 9% are Black/African-American, and 8% are multiracial. The ratio of female to male students is approximately 1:1. Harvard's students are also economically diverse; the institution provided USD193M in grants to enrolled students in the fall of 2019, supplemented by USD11M in federal grants and external grants of USD12M. These awards are typically made on the basis of demonstrated financial need. Harvard is highly selective; its admit rate has declined over the last 20 years to approximately 4% of applicants.

Harvard University employs 4,500 people in the Faculty of Arts and Sciences. Of these, slightly less than 2,000 are faculty and researchers. The remainder

## Chapter 8

are administrative and professional staff, and support personnel. The Language Center at Harvard has a staff of three administrative professionals and supports the approximately 80 languages taught at Harvard.

### 1.2. Assumptions

A few assumptions underpin the move to online teaching and learning, which should not itself be conflated with the emergency measures taken for remote instruction in the immediate wake of the move from campus (Ross & DiSalvo, 2020). The first of these is that most students have access to a basic toolkit of affordances and applications that will allow them to be successful online learners. These include internet access which Harvard has supplemented where necessary through the distribution of WiFi hotspots connecting to mobile networks for students who were unable to return to campus. Most students have access to their own computers or a shared computer; where this is not possible, Harvard has distributed laptops, iPads, and other essential devices such as webcams to students and faculty alike. All students have access to Canvas, the university's learning management system, and to tools such as Zoom, AnnotationsX (a collaborative reading and annotation tool produced at Harvard), and specific groups of students – those in language courses – are provided with VoiceThread[3], a platform for asynchronous interaction and discussion around media, Extempore[4], an application to allow for oral production and evaluation outside of class, and support for teletandem activities. In those cases where teaching staff find themselves abroad and unable to return to the US, Harvard reimburses the local purchase of technology that they need to perform their work successfully.

A second set of assumptions revolves around faculty and student experience with, and facility in, using these affordances and applications. For many faculty used to teaching face-to-face, the experience of moving instruction online has been challenging. A survey done by The Language Center early

---

3. https://voicethread.com

4. https://extemporeapp.com

in the first semester of 2020-2021 (see supplementary materials), however, indicates that the majority of respondents did not feel a need to completely redesign their curricula for the move to remote instruction in Spring 2020. Some adaptations in terms of task design and communication, as well as in restructuring their courses for online delivery, sufficed in the short term, but often these changes required learning one or two completely new tools at most, as well as incorporating a training module for students in the use of those tools. Many, however, took significant time between May and August of 2020 to rethink and redesign their courses in preparation for the forthcoming semester, based on their experiences and student feedback on the remote instruction experience. Data from the survey suggests that a plurality of faculty members will incorporate technologies and strategies that they have used during the current crisis in post-COVID iterations of their classes.

## 2. Training and support

Harvard's community was fortunate to learn of the decision to go fully remote for the 2020-2021 school year in July of 2020, well in advance of the start to the semester, and faculty and staff were thus given adequate time to think and plan for how existing course offerings could be moved online. During this pre-semester planning phase, The Language Center reached out to every language program in the Faculty of Arts and Sciences to offer help in preparing instructors to teach online. In effect, this situation gave The Language Center a chance to foreground our capabilities and support model and establish ourselves as a knowledge base for faculty within the context of the crisis. Our plan for assisting faculty with remote language teaching involved two stages: pre-semester training and ongoing support. We assumed that many instructors would be interested in working with us *a priori*, but certainly not all, and we therefore expected that much of the ongoing support would reach back to the fundamentals taught in the pre-semester training. So, while there is significant overlap between these two components, we are aware of the need for faculty to feel that the training they receive at any given moment is neither beyond them nor beneath them, which therefore required us to be versatile and nimble in what we offered and how we

## Chapter 8

offered it. Our pre-semester training mostly took the form of pre-announced Zoom webinars on specific Harvard-licensed tools, while our ongoing support continues to be more situational and one-on-one. In the first instance we aim to be anticipatory, and in the second we aim to be responsive.

We note that the timing of this contribution, which we are writing as Harvard and the rest of the United States continue to grapple with the pandemic, renders us unable to present a quantitative summary of the impact of our efforts. We believe that it is still worthwhile, however, to reflect in this moment upon how we approached the sudden onset of remote learning and the need to pivot the entire university to a remote-only academic year in 2020-2021. In this moment, while it would be irresponsible to refer to early feedback and impressions we have obtained as hard data, or even identify causality in the relationship between our work and what learning outcomes may be apparent, there is value in assessing our own decisions and their immediate ramifications from where we stand now, particularly given the fact that recent experience so often impacts decisions for the future, whether data-driven or not.

The Language Center coordinated with a number of other campus units, including the Derek Bok Center for Teaching and Learning[5], the Academic Technology Group[6] within Harvard University Information Technology (HUIT), the dean of the college, and the Division of Continuing Education, to deliver a series of topical workshops to faculty and teaching staff who were abruptly asked to move to an online modality. These ranged from a five-day intensive workshop for summer school instructors on designing and delivering an online language course, to a mandated three-day workshop for faculty in languages and literatures, to more focused workshops on creating learning communities in this environment, the use of specific tools, and assessment in online courses.

Of primary importance to us was to maintain consistency in our approach to training faculty, and to establish a set of principles that underlay everything we

---

5. https://bokcenter.harvard.edu/

6. https://atg.fas.harvard.edu/

did. Firstly, cognitive load (Sweller, 2011) is a concern, both for instructors and for students. Anyone designing or using online learning materials and strategies must be mindful of how many tools they are asking their students and in many cases their teaching staff to deploy for the first time. We encouraged those in the role of creating syllabi and crafting lesson plans to think critically about whether the tools they were using were enhancing the quality of teaching and learning in a given setting, or simply being used for their own sake. We strongly encouraged instructors to make training and support a key part of their own course plans, as well, by first teaching students about the tools they would need and then gradually building in new information atop that foundation as it grew stronger. Harvard language instructors, having been trained in a communicative approach to language teaching (see Brandl, 2008), were no strangers to the concept of scaffolding (see Lightbown & Spada, 2006, p. 131), and this particular subset of our training materials on careful scaffolding and avoiding cognitive overload lined up well with principles to which our population already subscribed.

Secondly, we worked in close concert with academic technology staff at the university and took great care that our training directed faculty to learn and use the tools that Harvard had licensed and was prepared to support. At times, faculty in transition to remote learning had understandably reached for free, open-source tools that they had found either by consulting colleagues at other universities or by searching the internet themselves. When this led them to consult us for help, our job was to meet them where they were and help them find a way to realize their teaching objectives using the platforms that the university had approved and could support. For example, if a professor wanted to use an open-source blogging platform for students to research and discuss relevant topics in language, we helped them transition that same project, together with all its important pedagogical functions and objectives, to a Canvas-based discussion forum. This not only guaranteed that Harvard technology staff would be able to assist them in the event of difficulties but also protected them and their students from possible data privacy and accessibility issues.

Our third principle of faculty support stemmed from that very concern: that our training and support materials complied with Harvard's university-wide standards for data protection and user accessibility. Early in the process, we explicitly committed to helping faculty work within Harvard-supported educational resources, which had been thoroughly vetted and found to comply with the university's stringent policies on privacy and accessibility. In addition to making sure we and our constituents were using these approved tools for teaching and learning, we also made sure that we frequently reminded faculty that the university's concerns should be theirs as well. Our website has a detailed online teaching and learning section[7] that contains curated and annotated deep links to university policy on accessibility, data privacy, and copyright and fair use. Through Harvard libraries, for example, students or faculty can access data-driven consultations on the accessibility and user-friendliness of Harvard-owned websites. Harvard's Accessibility Education Office[8] hosts a website full of detailed, easy-to-understand information about how to increase the accessibility of web-based learning content, and Harvard's Office of the General Counsel[9] has a website where community members can read in detail about how copyright and data privacy laws affect the practice of online teaching. We consistently and clearly encourage faculty members with whom we consult to learn not only how to work within the university's regulations, but also how to benefit from the guidance thereon.

## 3. Delivery

Harvard has historically privileged face-to-face instruction of languages, and small class sizes, even to the extent of allowing students to petition to learn languages that are almost never taught in US classrooms. These courses tend to be very small, with perhaps one or two students electing to learn Gullah, Mongolian, Nepali, or Icelandic for their very specific purposes. The use of technology, including that which has been readily available through the institution, has in many cases been seen as unnecessary for, if not an impediment

---

7. https://language.fas.harvard.edu/resources-remote-instruction-language-courses

8. https://aeo.fas.harvard.edu/

9. https://ogc.harvard.edu/

to, instruction, because its affordances have not been seen as significantly contributing to highly personalized instruction for a small cohort of students. The COVID-19 crisis has perhaps for the better changed that perspective.

In preparation for Fall semester, all faculty who were to be teaching were required by the dean of the college to sign up for training in how to move a face-to-face course into an online environment. The Language Center helped coordinate and deliver a three-day workshop for language instructors that focused on the adaptation of curriculum and teaching strategies to an online format. In working with language program directors in a number of departments, we incorporated research-supported, outcome-driven methodologies of language teaching into the core of our guidance. All languages at Harvard are taught with a student-centered focus, though individual departments are given considerable license to decide which methodologies to embrace; our role is not to prescribe but to support and optimize, and language faculty at Harvard – particularly the language program directors – are well-acquainted with the research of instructed second language acquisition. Therefore, the common denominator in our remote teaching workshops was to foreground the use of student-centered, interactive, and task-based activities, and to help teachers find ways to minimize one-way transferral of information for students to absorb, as in a lecture format delivered via Zoom or other technology. For the languages with very small enrollments, this was perhaps a simpler matter than for those with multiple sections as well as teaching fellows – graduate students who teach and provide instructional support as part of their professional development and financial aid package. The instructors of less-commonly-taught languages, for instance Yoruba, Vietnamese, Gullah, or Norwegian, needed to understand how to use Harvard's videoconferencing platform, Zoom, how to distribute (typically self-created) materials to their students, how to receive completed work from students, and how to assess student outcomes reliably. These classes have tended to look similar to their pre-COVID counterparts; plenary sessions via Zoom in which materials are presented, drill activities are conducted, and students' spoken language abilities are assessed. Canvas, the university's learning management system, has typically been used in the past as a document repository and as a site for students to upload completed assignments. In a few cases, instructors in these courses are adopting other tools to support their students' learning. African languages faculty, for example, are using VoiceThread as a digital storytelling platform, allowing students to explore the nature of oral transmission of culture and to respond to prompts that are culturally authentic, if mediated by technology.

The rupture inherent in a move to online has in some cases provided language programs – particularly those which are well-staffed and supported, an opportunity to rethink their curricula entirely, and in some cases to move from commercial textbooks toward educational resources that are either open, or available for license from peer institutions. The German department has moved from a commercially-produced textbook to an online resource created at Princeton University, called Der|Die|Das[10]. Rather than retrenching to a reliance on an 'easy' solution provided by publishers, they have made a clean break from an environment and set of resources that no longer was meeting their needs. The Spanish department developed its own curriculum, modeled to some degree on the educational resource adopted by the German department.

It should be no surprise that course organization and scaffolding student use of online platforms and materials have proven to be essential in designing online language classes. In March 2020 The Language Center developed an orientation module that was made available to all faculty building courses in this modality. The module contains a course 'map', a set of surveys on learner preferences and self-perceived ability in the language, an inventory survey that asks students to relate their level of comfort and ability using particular technologies, and an inventory of the affordances they have available to them. This module has been widely deployed and adapted across online courses and serves to prepare faculty to address student needs *ab initio*.

We are seeing a few different models of course organization across language divisions at Harvard. Some large programs, such as Spanish and French, have

---

10. https://www.dddgerman.org/

opted to create a single Canvas instance into which all sections of a multi-section course are enrolled; students must select the assignments and communications channels that pertain to their section. Other languages, such as German and Portuguese, have opted to create a Canvas site for each section. Most courses are organized by module, a division which correlates to week or unit, depending on the program's choice.

## 4. Lessons learned and planning for the future

This past year has provided The Language Center with an unprecedented opportunity for teaching new material to a wide and diverse audience, and we have learned that the principles that we are urging them to espouse are just as important for our own instruction. In teaching our community the skills and affordances needed for effective online instruction, we have striven to model evidence-based pedagogical strategies, not just for the sake of example but for ensuring maximal uptake of best practices.

Firstly, language instructors are just as susceptible to cognitive overload as their students, and we need to be mindful of that when teaching and modeling new tools. When teaching a workshop on our learning management system, Canvas, we have had to recognize a wide variety of comfort levels with the platform and pace content appropriately. We cannot expect faculty to learn to create an effective and clear assignment without first teaching them how the content editor works, and if someone needs to learn how to embed a media file, they cannot be expected to retain that skill if they are learning it on top of five other brand new functions they have never used before. Learning outcomes must always be front of mind, for us as well as for those we hope to teach, and our teaching modules must be tailored and focused to respect the amount of new information an instructor can credibly retain. We created a Canvas shell for instructors only in which every member could use instructor privileges to experiment with the platform's many affordances, its main objective being to encourage instructors to *do* things rather than merely *ask* things in the course of deciding how they would teach. The principle of creating low-stakes tasks as a gateway to effective learning and strengthening of skills has been proven effective in language pedagogy (Rubio, 2015), and it is equally so for those learning the lexicon of online instruction.

We think it important to frame our current situation as an opportunity for thinking about the future. We intend to focus ongoing language center efforts in three areas: creation of a series of self-paced training modules for instructors who need to learn how to implement online teaching tools in their courses, exploration of different models for flexible instruction even when face-to-face instruction again becomes possible, and continued advocacy for technology in language instruction.

In an attempt to begin assessing the impact of our interventions in the language teaching community at Harvard, we have begun collecting informal feedback regarding instructional sessions on remote language teaching that we conducted in March and again in June of 2020, in which we modeled synchronous and asynchronous approaches tailored to the specific needs of the instructors who were in that moment preparing to teach. The responses we have received to date indicate that they were, indeed, helpful in the process of course planning, and as such we plan to make a flexible, self-paced version of these sessions widely available to language teaching staff across the Faculty of Arts and Sciences, or the college).

We envision a series of modules addressing the various synchronous and asynchronous tools Harvard has licensed for educational use, with a particular focus on how these affordances can help faculty work toward the specific learning outcomes they hope to produce. If instructors could access this repository at any time, they might feel freer to repeat certain modules when they inevitably need a refresher on some of the things they had previously learned. Furthermore, we hope that teaching staff will continue to use the various online tools they worked with in 2020 to enhance their teaching when we return to in-person instruction. The Language Center will host a post-term debriefing session to allow faculty to share their experiences with their course's structure, delivery, and outcomes, but we are already gathering information on these elements via informal conversations.

On an institutional level, we hope that pedagogical objectives will cement themselves in the foreground of discussions around the implementation of other models of hybrid instruction. There are currently many individual models of 'flexible' instruction, though few institutions have the technological resources to adopt a fully HyFlex model, which implies that any student can choose on any given day whether to attend any given class in person or from a remote location, or indeed not to attend (Beatty, 2019). HyFlex – currently of great interest to administrators – assumes, of course, that faculty are sufficiently equipped and supported to deliver this type of exceedingly flexible teaching without hindering the learning objectives they are pursuing, and that the structure of the course lends itself to a model in which synchronous face-to-face, synchronous remote, and asynchronous modalities can be equitably leveraged by students. In the past, higher education has seen online programs implemented as a response to the financial or logistical needs of their institutions, irrespective of whether online teaching makes sense for the subject matter at hand. Now that there is more data on which online affordances work best in which contexts and how some tools can be leveraged effectively as an accompaniment to face-to-face learning, it should follow that resources for development of online teaching and learning programs be allocated, at least in part, based on which disciplines can benefit the most from a more flexible model of instruction.

Harvard's language faculty and students have met this moment with exceptional creativity and an inspiring collaborative spirit, and we hope to preserve a record of the work that has emerged as a result. Faculty who participated in an end-of-term debrief and symposium (December 2020) shared a number of innovative practices incorporating dynamic assessment techniques, project-based learning, and in at least one case, the move away from publisher-produced materials to a 'custom' curriculum. In addition to making people feel good about their successes by showcasing and celebrating them, we plan to create a repository of best practices that have distinguished themselves this year. From here, we can move forward with a more organized overarching structure that will guide future decisions about where, when, and in what way to implement online and blended learning not as crisis management but as an integral part of the most effective pedagogical approach to language teaching and learning.

## 5. Supplementary materials

https://research-publishing.box.com/s/o3ztmhwle94oymiyiqcet5z1ut0uop88

## References

Beatty, B. J. (2019). Evaluating the impact of hybrid-flexible courses and programs. Highlights from selected studies. In B. J. Beatty (Ed.), *Hybrid-flexible course design. Implementing student-directed hybrid classes* (pp. 1-15). EdTech Books. https://edtechbooks.org/hyflex

Brandl, K. (2008). *Communicative language teaching in action. Putting principles to work.* Pearson.

Lightbown, P. M., & Spada, N. (2006). *How languages are learned* (3rd ed.). Oxford University Press.

Ross, A. F., & DiSalvo, M. (2020). Negotiating displacement, regaining community: the Harvard Language Center's response to the COVID-19 crisis. *Foreign Language Annals, 53*(2), 371-379. https://doi.org/10.1111/flan.12463

Rubio, F. (2015). Assessment of oral proficiency in online language courses: beyond reinventing the wheel. *The Modern Language Journal, 99*(2), 405-408. https://doi.org/10.1111/modl.12234_4

Sweller, J. (2011). Chapter two – cognitive load theory. *Psychology of learning and motivation, 55,* 37-76. https://doi.org/10.1016/b978-0-12-387691-1.00002-8

# Section 3.
# ASIA

# 9 Sudden shift to online learning during the COVID-19 pandemic: the case of Arabic at Qatar University

## Abeer Heider[1]

### Abstract

The present chapter focuses on the immediate impact of the COVID-19 pandemic on the higher education sector, presenting the case of the Arabic for Non-Native Speakers Center (ANNS) at Qatar University. It evaluates what actions the center has undertaken to pledge its integrity to the cause of higher education throughout the pandemic and considers a sample of students' responses to a survey about the approaches and strategies adopted when learning shifted online. In order to speak to the book project rationale, the questions herein addressed concentrate on what has changed in language teaching practices as a result of COVID-19; on which changes might become permanent changes and which are expected to return to their pre-pandemic conditions; on reconsidered language pedagogy and new educational purposes and on informational progress for remote teaching. The chapter also aims to identify a number of techniques to be researched further.

**Keywords: COVID-19, online language teaching, student perceptions, technology-enhanced learning, Qatar.**

---

1. Qatar University, Doha, Qatar; abeer_s@aucegypt.edu; https://orcid.org/0000-0003-0416-9658

**How to cite:** Heider, A. (2021). Sudden shift to online learning during the COVID-19 pandemic: the case of Arabic at Qatar University. In N. Radić, A. Atabekova, M. Freddi & J. Schmied (Eds), *The world universities' response to COVID-19: remote online language teaching* (pp. 155-166). Research-publishing.net. https://doi.org/10.14705/rpnet.2021.52.1270

Chapter 9

## 1. Introduction

Since the arrival of COVID-19 and the consecutive lockdown in all countries, higher education institutions have had to proceed speedily toward online delivery to guarantee the continuity of teaching and learning. It seems that this transition was less challenging for those countries that had invested in the online sector and approached digitalization as a tactical strategy. The pandemic forced an adjustment to educational techniques, on account of the infeasibility of conducting physical classes, in effect requiring the educational sector to experiment with educational means and approaches to achieve distance learning (UNESCO, 2020).

At Qatar University, the ANNS modified their existing educational program and transitioned to virtual learning, replacing face-to-face lessons with online procedures, completely or partially. Solutions for teaching and learning online have progressed since then, and consequently, in spite of the complications in the transformation to an utterly different methodology for teaching, the ANNS rose to the challenge of finding solutions to enable the continuity of teaching and learning during the pandemic.

There are many indications that this global crisis will change many aspects of life (e.g. Johnson, 2020; Minello, 2020), and if distance learning proves to be effective, education may be one of those sectors that finds itself profoundly and permanently changed. Arguably, several effects of the pandemic, although not immediately observable, are regrettably very significant and will rise in the medium- and long-term. Universities have therefore been called upon to answer the central question: How do we understand whether distance learning is indeed successful or not? As discussed by a summer 2020 post published in Qatar University Newsroom[2], in order to answer this question, it is essential to collect and analyse data extensively and place focus on quality higher education.

---

2. https://www.qu.edu.qa/newsroom/Qatar-University/Education-and-Learning-Post–Pandemic---Covid–19?

Many educational leaders acknowledge that the shift in modality was the result of an unpredictable contingency situation. At the same time, they acknowledge that they ought to start to plan for online teaching in the future with better pedagogical support and resources, prognosticating that the continuance of the crisis will amplify over time (for example, see the post and related comments on *El Corona Teaching*, which appeared in the educational blog[3]).

In this study, the case of the ANNS is considered and in particular how the center has responded to the unexpected shift to online learning following the closure of the university as a result of the COVID-19 pandemic. After describing the institutional context and scope of the ANNS, students' responses to an informal survey were analyzed in order to distill their views and perceptions of technology-mediated modes of learning. In particular, the questions posed to the students concerned the kinds of support systems and collaborative efforts which enabled the learning process during the initial phase of COVID-19 for learners taking one of the ANNS' courses, and the use of technology in the ANNS during the first wave of the pandemic. Students' confidence and satisfaction with distance modes of learning was also elicited through survey items. The first question is addressed in Section 2, while the second and third in Section 3 and 4. Section 5 draws some conclusions on some of the lessons learned and a number of techniques to be researched further.

## 2. Institutional context

On 15th March 2020, the Government of Qatar announced a state of emergency in the country and established a set of measures to fight the spread of coronavirus. The following actions were taken on behalf of educational institutions: all educational facilities were closed, extracurricular activities were nullified, sports and other types of in-person activities were discontinued, both indoors and outdoors. Institutional measures have included rigorous health checks, adaptation of schedules, contributions of research on alleviating the pandemic,

---

3. https://edumorfosis.blogspot.com/2020/04/el-corona-teaching.html

ensuring the continuity of the pedagogical scenario through remote education, bibliographical and technological resources' endorsement, and also socio-emotional encouragement to the university community.

In this context, Qatar University embraced the use of the latest technologies from the very beginning of the emergency and employed virtual platforms for its faculty and students, in line with Qatar's efforts to keep the education system going and as effective as before the pandemic. Moreover, the university also allowed for faculty to continue their meetings remotely, so that university life would continue regularly but through virtual platforms. As far as digital resources are concerned, the Center for Excellence in Teaching and Learning played a crucial role in setting up a repository of tools[4] as well as pre-recorded guides to online teaching and learning available both in Arabic and English[5] to help faculty and students alike to cope with the new learning environment. Along the same lines, best-practice guides to evaluating students in a distance setting were made available to the university community[6]. Qatar University also provided faculty, staff, and students with a unique hotline number for remote technical support and requests[7]. The ANNS shared the same concern to continue providing education for the whole term for all students and to accomplish crucial learning outcomes.

### 2.1. ANNS' students

Students in the ANNS come from extremely diverse backgrounds, namely Turkey, Azerbaijan, Cameroon, Serbia, Bangladesh, Ukraine, Indonesia, Malaysia, India, Russia, Ghana, Greece, and Pakistan. As stated in the ANNS website,

---

4. http://www.qu.edu.qa/offices/cetl/distance-learning

5. http://www.qu.edu.qa/offices/cetl/distance-learning/teaching_online

6. http://www.qu.edu.qa/offices/cetl/distance-learning/evaluating-students

7. http://www.qu.edu.qa/coronavirus

> "[t]he center serves future scholars, teachers of Arabic and Islamic sciences, journalists, diplomats, employees of Non-Governmental Organizations or cultural centers, and many others. Each year, a number of the ANNS students are accepted into other departments at Qatar University upon completion of the center curriculum, including Arabic Language, Computer Science, and Business"[8].

With the movement to remote learning, students have been involved in classroom activities twice a week along with their participation in media-based classes and listening and speaking practicums. Students of the ANNS have had to reorganize their lifestyles to adapt to a situation of incarceration. Inescapably, the loss of interaction and acculturation that are part of the daily lives of higher education students has taken its toll. The separation that is unavoidably linked with confinement is likely to have a harmful impact on students' socio-emotional stability, particularly with pre-existing issues of this nature. However, the established practice of remote education, that is, that in which educators proceed to instruct a regular class through live streaming and which can be regained on a delayed basis, appear to be welcomed by students because they are the ones that best replicate the dynamics to which they are already accustomed through exposure to digital media.

## 2.2. ANNS' faculty and program

As mentioned on the ANNS website,

> "[t]he center employs a number of full-time Qatar University faculty [members] with academic credentials and varied experience in teaching Arabic to non-native speakers. Classes are small, with an average of 10-15 students in the Beginning and Intermediate levels, and approximately ten in the Advanced level"[9].

---

8. http://gpc.qu.edu.qa/artssciences/departments/anns

9. http://gpc.qu.edu.qa/artssciences/departments/anns

In teaching modern standard Arabic, the ANNS uses the communicative language approach (see Facchin, 2019 and Littlewood, 2011 that discusses different traditions in the teaching of Arabic as a foreign language, particularly Chapter 6 on 21st century developments and communicative approaches). This includes a focus on learners' exposure to language varieties used throughout the Arabic speaking world, both in print and electronic media, in educational and academic settings, as well as other aspects of daily life. The courses offered by the center are designed to develop all communicative skills, i.e. listening, speaking, reading, writing, as well as to cover media in Arabic and modern and classical literature. Before the lockdown, the center would also organize monthly excursions and cultural activities around Doha where Arabic is used. Trips to museums, the Al Jazeera television studios, and recreation sites were an integral part of the center extracurricular program to help students link the language acquired in class to the larger Qatari and Arab contexts[10].

## 3. Technical support offered by ANNS

The ANNS has encouraged its staff to take part in a variety of training sessions organized by the university's Center for Excellence in Teaching and Learning aimed at illustrating principles and forms of digital learning and education at large, e.g. by introducing the key differences between face-to-face and online education, by distinguishing between synchronous and asynchronous forms, and illustrating the different tools. Different videoconferencing applications and platforms were explored, namely WebEx, Zoom, and Microsoft Teams. The learning management system chosen by the university and used by the ANNS was Blackboard and Blackboard Collaborate and Echo360 for video management and recording. In all, the experience of the ANNS with the use of the Zoom platform was positive enough to guarantee the completion of all teaching programs for the whole semester. In this respect, we share Oyedotun's (2020) view that "there is no doubt that the online mode has proven to be the saving grace for the completion of the semester in difficult times" (p. 2).

---

10. http://www.qu.edu.qa/artssciences/departments/anns

Moreover, Qatar University has provided both its employees with high-tech computers to be able to work remotely and its students with help with online resources, offering extra support through its Student Learning Support Center[11].

The ANNS has introduced special assistance for both students and staff due to the pandemic. For example, it has used digital technologies to provide:

- tools for lectures such as WebEx in order to host interactive webinars or large-scale virtual events;

- the Zoom platform for video meetings and interactive lectures;

- Microsoft Teams for communication between lecturers and students and for file storage and integration of applications;

- solutions for home office, including Blackboard Learn, an interactive learning management system suitable for higher education institutions; and

- pedagogical advice for professors on how to make teaching digital, and for students on how to maintain study habits when going digital, and the creation of a help desk for digital services assistance for students and staff.

## 4. Collected responses from the students

In a moment when face-to-face classes are necessarily substituted with the online format, it is crucial to examine students' perceptions of the latest reality during the COVID-19 crisis (see Cohen, 2017). The author of this chapter, in her capacity as lecturer of the ANNS, has informally collected and analyzed responses from as many students as possible, aged between 19 and 30 regarding

---

11. http://www.qu.edu.qa/students/success-and-development/student-learning-support

## Chapter 9

this transition. Students who took part in the survey were asked to comment on questions about the new learning environment and the activities in which they had been involved when learning shifted online, their experience with collaborative language learning methods as a result of the emergency situation, the level of support and collaboration they received, and the challenges and opportunities experienced. A total of 40 students completed the questionnaire. The analyses of the responses demonstrate the following.

First, the faculty's professional positive attitude advantages students in addition to the ANNS. All of the students' responses showed that some learners, who tended to be diffident and unwilling to partake in regular setting interactions, turned out to be more motivated during online sessions. Some of the students who previously felt uncomfortable in an in-person class found themselves feeling more empowered to perform their best when their webcams were turned off. In view of the fact that remote teaching and learning may be a new experience for the center as much as for the students, faculty should be clear, but realistic, regarding how they expect students to interact and function. The students pointed out that they missed being in the face-to-face classes; however, they felt safe in their online classes, which positively affected their performance. Additionally, three daily meals were offered, so as to allow the students to be secure and therefore able to focus on their studies. The online classrooms were appropriately organized, faculty was structured to keep its educational setting while students were involved in remote learning activities, and thus the experience was professional, secure, and not disturbing.

Second, students value faculty who maintain a confident and consistent approach. Teachers continued to show up on time in online classrooms. A number of activities and interactions had become unavailable to be taught online, as a consequence, alternative means needed to be established. Students, however, did not expect the online classes to be captivating to the same extent as with the face-to-face classes. Exams and activities were challenging, but nevertheless the students were delighted to explore absolutely modern methods, in particular play-acting educational video games such as Quizlet, Kahoot, and Socrative. In the present case, ANNS was felt as a privileged place, as both the center and the students shared their ideas and emotions with one another and talked about their experiences as appropriate.

Third, students made a number of self-critical comments concerning acknowledging the limits of their own technical proficiency. Developing universally accessible models of learning is a vital feature of remote learning, and one way to start this process is by recognizing that whereas certain trainees may be capable of quickly figuring out how to partake in online instruction, others may need more support and endorsement. Fortunately, the teachers did not experience any complications with the access to online classrooms, as the connection to the internet in the dormitories of Qatar University has been sufficiently reliable.

Finally, students desire faculty to be untroubled with technology. There are many existing ways of teaching remotely. Both the teachers and students watched videos in online classrooms and discussed subject matters, which was similar to the pre-pandemic teaching period. The teachers encouraged students to deal with Microsoft Teams and Blackboard, so the educational conditions were settled and there have not been feelings of frustration. Additionally, if the center demands students to make notes, there is an option to provide them with the PowerPoint file as a starting point.

## 5. Conclusions

### 5.1. Planning for the future

The colossal attempts to adjust to new online-based forms of cooperation by both teachers and students also require that the ANNS monitor how teaching activities are executed and what are the requirements, of any types, that can appear in the academic community.

At the university level, emphasis must inescapably concentrate initially on how to handle the procedures, specifically teaching continuity, in the middle and promptly after the crisis, and in addition, to gain benefit of the lessons learned to take into consideration the teaching and learning processes in higher education.

The ANNS has observed diverse implementations for remote education that can be efficient, despite the fact that a matter which is still not fully resolved is the determination of the student's identity when live streaming classes. Moreover, streaming can be problematic to access if the quality of connectivity required is not sufficient. However, technology can be exploited as a support tool rather than the sole medium of interaction. We therefore agree with the UNESCO-IESALC's (2020) statement that

> "if virtualization is to be the primary informative instrument to uphold the performance of education, the tremendous technological gap must be taken into account. Its existence must be acknowledged, not to repudiate virtualization, but to structure approaches along with support devices that will facilitate it all the more actively" (p. 42).

Thinking today about what comes next, it is essential to begin with the principle of reality and produce plans of action that do not depend simply on a particular technology, but on several, to guarantee that all students are kept in mind or, which is similarly or increasingly important, that technological solutions do not further disadvantage those who are already underprivileged. The ANNS must discover the most suitable amalgamation of technologies and resources to enhance the academic effect. It is sufficient to carry out a realistic practice, implementing the principle that additional efforts should be inducted into those technologies, instructional materials should be circulated and supports offered to improve the quality of in-person teaching and strengthen hybrid methodologies; alternatively stated, hybrid methodologies coalesce the greatest of face-to-face instruction with the prospect of technology to support pedagogical renovation and enhancement (UNESCO-IESALC, 2020 and see also their website[12]).

---

12. https://www.iesalc.unesco.org/en/

## 5.2. Lessons learned

In this chapter we have reported on the influences of the crisis on the Qatar University language program to document the experience of ANNS' students. For the students, the most instant impact has clearly been the temporary interruption of face-to-face teaching at the ANNS and, in the absence of any indication of how long it will continue, the immediate impacts on lifestyle, expenses incurred and financial burdens, and, of course, learning progression and international mobility.

Despite all this, and in line with UNESCO-IESALC (2020), the ANNS will have missed a valuable opportunity if they cease to reflect inwardly, with the engagement of students and teachers, regarding the experience acquired in times of crisis about the teaching and learning procedures. The crucial issue is whether the experience gained might be capitalized upon for a remodeling of these techniques, optimizing the benefit of person-to-person courses while making the most of the technologies, which then begs the question of how much further the ANNS can go.

This reflection may be specified if the ANNS takes initiative in increasing the pedagogical proficiency of teachers, in promoting pedagogical innovation and in spreading the findings arising from their evaluation. We have a saying that in each calamity, there arises a window of opportunity. Perchance, in this instance, there lies a possibility for a pedagogical reconsideration. It is consequently anticipated that the ASSN will undertake the direction of an essential pedagogical revival that encourages both high quality and equality.

## References

Cohen, A. (2017). Analysis of student activity in web-supported courses as a tool for predicting dropout. *Educational Technology Research and Development, 65*(5), 1285-1304. https://doi.org/10.1007/s11423-017-9524-3

Facchin, A. (2019) *Teaching Arabic as a foreign language. Origins, developments and current directions*. Amsterdam University Press.

Johnson, P. (2020). A bad time to graduate. *Observation. Institute for Fiscal Studies.* https://www.ifs.org.uk/publications/14816

Littlewood, W. (2011). Communicative language teaching: an expanding concept for a changing world. In E. Hinkel (Ed.), *Handbook of research in second language teaching and learning* (vol. 2, pp. 541-557). Routledge. https://doi.org/10.4324/9780203836507.ch33

Minello, A. (2020 April 17). The pandemic and the female academic. *Nature.* https://doi.org/10.1038/d41586-020-01135-9

Oyedotun, T. D. (2020). Sudden change of pedagogy in education driven by COVID-19: perspectives and evaluation from a developing country. *Research in Globalization, 2*, 1-5. https://doi.org/10.1016/j.resglo.2020.100029

UNESCO (2020). UNESCO COVID-19 Education Response. Crisis-sensitive educational planning. Education Sector Issue Notes, Issue Note 2.4, *Developed by UNESCO International Institute for Education Planning, Section of Education for Migration, Displacement and Emergencies & Section of Education Policy* (pp. 1-4). UNESCO.

UNESCO-IESALC (2020). *COVID-19 and higher education: today and tomorrow. Impact analysis, policy responses and recommendations* (pp. 1-44). http://www.guninetwork.org/publication/report-covid-19-and-higher-education-today-and-tomorrow-impact-analysis-policy-responses

# 10 The response of the University of Isfahan to COVID-19: remote online language teaching

## Adel Rafiei[1] and Zahra Amirian[2]

### Abstract

This study describes the changes in the instructional system experienced by the language departments in the University of Isfahan, Iran, during the 2020 COVID-19 outbreak and the consequent national lockdown. After providing a very brief scenario of a regular academic year in higher education in Iran, this chapter focuses on the changes made to the instructional system in response to this worldwide pandemic and the non-academic measures taken across the university in general and language departments in particular. After pointing to some challenges of online instruction, the advantages and disadvantages of remote instruction with regard to the four language skills from both teachers' and students' perspectives will be discussed. A review of the assessment procedures in the platform used by the University of Isfahan will then be provided. This case study will come to an end by providing some outlook for the future.

Keywords: COVID-19, online language teaching, teacher-feedback, student-feedback, Iran.

---

1. University of Isfahan, Isfahan, Iran; a.rafiei@fgn.ui.ac.ir

2. University of Isfahan, Isfahan, Iran; z.amirian@fgn.ui.ac.ir

How to cite: Rafiei, A., & Amirian, Z. (2021). The response of the University of Isfahan to COVID-19: remote online language teaching. In N. Radić, A. Atabekova, M. Freddi & J. Schmied (Eds), *The world universities' response to COVID-19: remote online language teaching* (pp. 167-178). Research-publishing.net. https://doi.org/10.14705/rpnet.2021.52.1271

## 1. Introduction

The University of Isfahan was established in 1946. Over the last 70 years, it has evolved into one of the top academic institutions in Iran. The university has 14 faculties with over 15,000 students and 650 academic staff. The faculty of foreign languages has over 1,500 students (with around 1,000 undergraduate and 500 post-graduate students) and 54 teaching staff. The faculty has five departments, including the department of English language and literature, the department of German, Armenian, and Chinese language and literature, the department of Arabic language and literature, the department of French and Russian language and literature, and the department of linguistics.

Each academic year at the University of Isfahan, like at most universities in Iran, consists of two terms named Autumn and Spring semesters. The Autumn semester starts around mid-September and ends late January while the Spring semester begins early February and ends late June. Iranian New Year holidays are in the Spring semester. New Year holidays start from 20th March and last around 20 days.

The first cases of COVID-19 were reported in the third week of the Spring semester on 19th February 2020. In a few days, with an increasing number of daily cases, universities in Iran closed their campuses and opted for remote online instruction.

## 2. Objectives

The primary objectives of this study are as follows:

- to describe the instructional measures taken by the University of Isfahan to tackle the problems raised by the pandemic; and

- to describe the non-instructional measures taken by the University of Isfahan to tackle the issues raised by the pandemic.

## 2.1. The instructional measures taken by the University of Isfahan during COVID-19

In line with other higher education institutions in Iran as well as the schools, the University of Isfahan had some emergency responses in order to effectively and urgently tackle the instructional and non-instructional problems raised by the national lockdown. Although the University of Isfahan was equipped with some previous virtual teaching experience, the immediate change of the whole educational system was a far-reaching task. The university had the following concerns.

- To what extent could the technical infrastructure of the university afford this volume of virtual classes?

- How could the infrastructure be improved and strengthened?

- To what extent could teachers, students, and staff adapt to the new educational system?

- Did all students have access to computers and high-speed Internet?

When the lockdown was nationally announced, there were three weeks to the beginning of the New Year holidays in Iran. Given this situation, the university took the following measures in response to the concerns mentioned above. First, it was announced that virtual classes are optional. Besides, teachers were free to use any platform they found appropriate, although they were encouraged to use BigBlueButton, the platform that has been used in the university in some virtual courses for years. With this decision, the initial shock largely subsided, and the university had time to strengthen its infrastructure and train the teachers, students, and staff by the end of the New Year holidays. To introduce the teachers and students to the platform used for teaching, the university designed and conducted various workshops and posted some instructional videos on the university website. The university also telephoned each student to ensure their access to computers and the Internet. In case a student did not have access to a computer/smartphone, the university attempted to solve the problem through charities. If the issue remained unresolved, the student was recommended to cancel the semester.

Meanwhile, the administrative staff of the university had a lot of virtual meetings in order to find ways to go through the educational and technological challenges that occurred due to the sudden outbreak. After empowering the technological infrastructure of the university, the university offered online classes from the very first day after the New Year holidays. The classes were to be held on the university platform, and the catch-up classes, i.e. additional classes, were automatically scheduled by the system for each course.

Some training workshops were also arranged for both the teachers and the non-academic staff in order to make them familiar with the BigBlueButton, the platform of choice for the delivery of remote courses. These workshops also helped the academic staff learn how to handle usual technical problems. Some guidelines about the assessment of the students were also suggested.

### 2.2. The non-instructional measures

Some non-instructional measures were also taken by the university. First, all students were telephoned and consoled. They were asked about their own and their family members' infection or possible loss due to the COVID-19. Students were also asked whether their parents (or themselves) lost their jobs in this critical situation and if they were in financial trouble. Some food packs were donated to students in need in line with the National Donation Movement across the country. In addition, those who could not afford smartphones or the cost of the Internet connection were identified and helped through charities.

The second measure was that all non-academic staff who suffered from underlying conditions, including diabetes, heart disease, cancer, or kidney disease were allowed to stay home and do their job online. This attempt reduced the rate of infections and relieved the vulnerable staff. Moreover, in different points of time when the country suffered from a sudden increase in number of infected people and consequently in the number of the dead, only a small number of non-academic staff (one third, half, or two-third, based on the severity of the conditions) were present at the university, and others did their jobs at home.

## 3. Teacher feedback

To get feedback from the teachers, an online questionnaire was developed to learn about their problems, opinions, experiences, best practices, and requirements of online language classes. In order to collect data, nine teachers were randomly selected from different departments: five from English, two from French, one from German, and one from the Chinese language department.

Based on the feedback received, the most significant challenges in teaching language skills in online classes are inadequate interaction (65%) and technical problems (35%). The most significant advantages are the availability of teaching resources and tools (50%), the ability to record the classes (25%), and low student stress (25%), respectively.

Most teachers believe that students participated less in online than in face-to-face classes. According to them, students sometimes avoid interaction on the pretext of technical problems and lack of access to high-speed Internet. However, they claim that the problem will be removed if the technical infrastructure is good enough and the instructors are proficient in working with the platform.

The next four questions looked at teaching language skills. Regarding reading and writing skills, most teachers prefer online classes to regular face-to-face classes. According to the teachers, in online reading and writing classes, providing feedback is more comfortable, students are more focused, and online text correction tools are available. Low intensity of students' interaction is considered as the only drawback of these classes.

Despite the positive opinion of teachers about online teaching of reading and writing skills, they have very different opinions about listening and – especially –

speaking skills. All respondents – except one – believed that teaching speaking skills is more effective in face-to-face classes. Regarding teaching the listening skill, the teachers' opinions were more moderate. Only two of nine teachers were in favor of online classes. According to the teachers, the most significant drawbacks of teaching speaking/listening online are low student participation and lack of face-to-face interaction. Easy recording of classes is the only advantage mentioned for these classes.

Regarding the most critical technical problems, the teachers mentioned the following: low Internet speed, the platform limitations, and insufficient mastery of the teachers and students of the platform. The most crucial non-technical challenge from the teachers' point of view is how to engage those students who refuse to participate in class activities under the pretext of technical problems, and more importantly, how to take a valid exam.

All participants in the study stated that in addition to the university-approved platform, they also use other messaging applications, especially WhatsApp, for further coordination and sending content, etc. All the participants have taken the final exam with the help of WhatsApp video calling.

For the post-corona period, one teacher wants to continue online classes, three want to go back to the face-to-face classes, and five teachers prefer a blended method provided that the technical infrastructure is strengthened.

## 4.   Student feedback

The students' feedback was examined through an online questionnaire too. The link was sent through WhatsApp to student populations of different departments in the faculty of foreign languages including English, French, and Chinese. Around 128 students voluntarily filled in and submitted the questionnaire. However, since this study mostly focused on the quality of learning language skills, the target student populations were those who were passing language skills courses in their second to fifth semesters. Last year's students were, therefore, excluded. First semester students were excluded as well because due to the pandemic their semester started later. The researchers supposed that since these students have not yet experienced usual face-to-face learning in the context of higher education, they may not be able to pinpoint the distinctive features of virtual learning or come up with a rational comparison between traditional and virtual learning contexts. As a result, the responses to 90 questionnaires were carefully examined.

The first item asked about the quality of virtual teaching in general at the University of Isfahan; 33.3% of the respondents rated it as good; 44.4% described it as having medium quality; 11.11% supposed it to be weak; and 11.11% rated it as very weak.

Concerning the efficacy of the number of teaching hours, that was 60 minutes a week for every two credit course, 44.4% believed it was good; 33.3% rated it as very good; 11.1% rated it as moderate; and 11.1% rated it as weak. Those who rated this item as moderate or weak believed that more time is needed for the students to participate in classroom activities or find the opportunity to talk or ask their questions. They thought this amount of time does not provide them with enough opportunity to speak or write and practice their communicative skills.

Four items of the questionnaire dealt with the quality of learning the four language skills in the online setting. Regarding reading skills, 33.3% of the respondents rated it as good; 33.3% rated it as moderate; 11.1% believed it is weak; and 22.2% believed it is very weak. The low possibility of focusing on the text was mentioned as their problem. They stated that they were unable to zoom the text because either the platform did not have such capability or they did not know how to zoom the text.

With regard to the writing skill, 44.4% rated it as good; 11.1% rated it as moderate; 33.3% of the respondents believed it is weak; and 11.1% rated it as very weak. The possibility of writing in the chat-box to answer the questions raised by the teacher was mentioned as a good opportunity for improving writing skill. Moreover, since there was no traditional pen and paper final exam, the teachers assigned different tasks or essay-type quizzes for the students. This was considered as an opportunity by some of the students while others viewed it as a misfortune that takes a lot of their time.

Regarding listening, 33.3% of the respondents rated it as very good; 33.3% rated it good; 11.1% considered it moderate; 11.1% supposed it is weak; and the remaining 11.1% of the respondents ranked it as very weak. Generally speaking, the students were satisfied with online teaching because it provided them with the opportunity to practice their listening. As a matter of fact, listening was supposed to be the most privileged language skill in the online teaching environment because the teachers recorded their lectures, and it was possible for the students to listen to them as many times as was required. However, those who were dissatisfied and rated it as weak or even very weak were mostly from less privileged, rural areas of Iran who did not enjoy high-speed Internet, and therefore had problems with the quality of the voice and even got disconnected many times.

Finally, regarding the speaking skill, 33.3% of the participants rated it as good; 33.3% rated it as moderate; 11.1% considered it as weak; while 22.2% believed that it is very weak. Those who rated it as good and moderate stated that they have very low anxiety and stress in online environments, and they are not embarrassed of talking in front of their classmates. They said that some teachers assign them speaking tasks or require them to present lectures in the classroom. Such kinds of activities provide the best opportunity for the students to improve their speaking ability in a low-stress environment. On the other hand, other students blamed online teaching sessions as being short, depriving them of finding the chance to talk or participate in classroom discussions and activities.

Another item of the questionnaire investigated students' attitudes toward learning different language skills in the online setting on a five-item Likert scale of very positive to very negative. Statistically speaking, the attitude of students toward all four language skills was nearly the same: 14.3% of the participants have a very positive attitude toward all four language skills; 42.9% had a positive attitude toward listening, while 14.3% had a positive attitude toward speaking; 28.6% of the respondents had no opinions with regard to reading, writing, and speaking skills. However, as mentioned above, the students believed that they could best improve their listening skills. Due to the speed of the Internet and in order to prevent the noise and even the probable disconnection, the teachers close their webcams; therefore, the students are only exposed to the teacher's voice without his/her picture. This makes the students more attentive to what they hear. Consequently, it would improve their listening abilities. In addition, the classroom sessions are recorded by the teachers so that the students, especially those who missed the class due to the infection with COVID-19 or various technical problems, could use the recorded file at their convenience as many times as required.

Speaking was the second skill favored by the student respondents. They believed those tasks and practices which require them to talk are highly effective especially because they enjoy a less embarrassing learning experience in the online setting. Writing ranked third. The respondents believed that since most of the time they write in response to the teacher's questions instead of talk, they have more opportunities to practice their writing skills. They also believed that they have more time to organize their writing or revise what they have written in the chat-box while listening to the teacher. However, reading was the least favored skill; the respondents believed that they do not have enough concentration on the passage especially because the font of the texts is very small on this platform, and they cannot (or do not know how to) zoom the text and make it more readable. To sum up, listening and speaking were the most challenging skills for the students, while the least challenging skills were reading and writing.

The final item of the questionnaire asked the respondents about their preference for the mode of instruction after the pandemic: 55.6% of the participants preferred a classical face-to-face classroom while 44.6% preferred a good blend of classical and online instruction. Interestingly, no one selected online instruction as his/her preference. This may be due to the fact that online instruction is associated with the COVID-19 outbreak in the minds of students, and this may lead to a sense of disgust among them. The other reason may lie in the fact that some students come from less privileged families who cannot afford smartphones, laptops, and even the cost of the Internet connection, or they may come from rural areas and do not enjoy high-quality Internet.

## 5. Assessment

In the first Spring Semester that coincided with the outbreak of COVID-19, the university required teachers to have formative assessment through the term and report the results regularly to the head of departments. Accordingly, based on the nature of different courses, the teachers assigned various tasks and activities during the term to observe students' learning and development. Giving lectures, taking quizzes, taking open-ended exams, assigning short essays, or taking oral tests through BigBlueButton or other platforms were among the popular options. Most students were happy with this assessment procedure. They believed that the gradual nature of such an assessment decreased their test-related anxiety, specifically in this situation that they were worried about technical problems and the disconnection on the day of the final exam. Of course, some teachers took the final exam as well because they believed that the summative assessment would give integrity and formality to the course; however, it only formed a small part of the total score of the students.

However, for the next semester, the teachers were required to take the exams using the testing platform provided by the university. A detailed video clip made by one of the teachers designing his own test on this platform was provided for all the teachers in order to help them learn how to follow different steps in order to take their own online tests. Some workshops were also held in order to help the teachers design their tests on this platform. However, it was suggested to the teachers that if they are offering the courses to post-graduate students whose tests are essay-type and project-based by nature, or if they are teaching to international students who have problems working with this testing platform, they can substitute any other convenient platform and report the results and share the documents with the heads of departments.

## 6. Conclusion

As a matter of fact, although not pleasant, the experience of COVID-19 was a giant leap for the online instruction in Iran in general and in the University of Isfahan, in particular. Before the COVID-19 outbreak, the University of Isfahan had the experience of holding online courses, workshops, and even the entire educational programs for some fields of study on a small scale. However, at that time, both the teachers and students hesitated to hold or attend online courses because they only thought about the drawbacks of online teaching. This seemingly unpleasant experience taught us that it *is* possible, and more importantly, it can be a good complement to our traditional classroom-based teaching. Future programs can be developed in a way that they blend both types of instruction in an appropriate way in order to reduce the efforts and costs for both the university and the students.

Moreover, based on this experience, it can be inferred that some workshops or different optional courses, especially those offered to post-graduate students or international candidates, can be more effective and more convenient if held online even after the pandemic. Online courses and workshops not only are more convenient for the participants, but also they are more cost-effective for the university because a greater number of students will participate without much cost for accommodation purposes. However, for achieving the best outcomes and the most satisfaction of both students and teachers, the university should enhance its infrastructure with regard to technological facilities. In addition, both teachers and students require more training in order to work more efficiently and more smoothly with the teaching and specifically the testing platform defined by the university. Therefore, planning ongoing, up-dated workshops, and providing instructional voice clips or video clips on how to work with the teaching or testing platforms are in urgent need, especially for first-year students.

## 7. Acknowledgments

The authors are sincerely thankful to the vice-chancellors of the University of Isfahan and their staff, who welcomed all the questions and warmly provided the information required for describing the immediate measures taken by the university at the time of the pandemic. The authors are also grateful to all teacher and student participants, without whose help and cooperation the process of data collection of this study would have been impossible.

# 11. A blended learning model supported by MOOC/SPOC, Zoom, and Canvas in a project-based academic writing course

## Li Zhang[1] and Yunjie Chen[2]

### Abstract

Blended learning has played an important role in teaching English as a second or foreign language around the world. However, little research has been conducted on blended learning that is entirely online owing to the coronavirus pandemic. We aim at exploring the model of blending Massive Open Online Courses (MOOC) and Small Private Online Courses (SPOC), Zoom conferencing, and the Canvas course management platform. The new approach of blended online learning incorporates the pre-class autonomous learning of knowledge in MOOC/SPOC, in-class internalization of knowledge through case studies and discussions on Zoom, and after-class application of knowledge to the completion of a research project. A questionnaire and interviews were conducted to explore learners' perceptions of the effectiveness of the model. Learners have a positive attitude about the new approach of blended online learning, but still hope that the in-class activities can be implemented face-to-face offline. The model will contribute to teaching and learning with the blended approach against the current coronavirus pandemic.

Keywords: COVID-19, online language teaching, academic writing, MOOC/SPOC and Zoom, Shanghai Jiao Tong University, China.

---

1. Shanghai Jiao Tong University, Shanghai, China; zhangli@sjtu.edu.cn; https://orcid.org/0000-0003-1793-9850

2. Shanghai Jiao Tong University, Shanghai, China; katherine_06@sjtu.edu.cn; https://orcid.org/0000-0002-0411-5097

How to cite: Zhang, L., & Chen, Y. (2021). A blended learning model supported by MOOC/SPOC, Zoom, and Canvas in a project-based academic writing course. In N. Radić, A. Atabekova, M. Freddi & J. Schmied (Eds), *The world universities' response to COVID-19: remote online language teaching* (pp. 179-197). Research-publishing.net. https://doi.org/10.14705/rpnet.2021.52.1272

## 1. Introduction

Leakey and Ranchoux (2006) define blended learning as "the adaptation in a local context of previous CALL and non-CALL pedagogies into an integrated program of language teaching and learning drawing on different mixes of media and delivery to produce an optimum mix that addresses the unique needs and demands of that context" (p. 358). In brief, blended learning is to combine face-to-face instruction with computer mediated instruction (Graham, 2006), which can also be conducted via a mobile phone nowadays. Research has shown that blended learning is beneficial for reducing learners' anxiety in communication (Liu, 2013), improving interaction between students and between students and teachers, increasing learners' motivation of autonomous learning, facilitating the flexibility and curiosity in learning, and enabling students to learn more actively (Mahalli, Nurkamto, Mujiyanto, & Yuliasri, 2019).

Many people have long got used to the traditional face-to-face teaching and learning, and do not have much intention or motivation to use technology for blended learning even though they have been encouraged to do so. However, due to the COVID-19 pandemic, face-to-face instruction seems rather impossible. Even with blended learning, which combines both online and offline instructions, the traditional form of teaching conducted offline has to be replaced by online interactions. This situation poses a challenge for both teachers and students, who are not quite prepared to transfer the real classroom to the online context in such a short period of time. Therefore, it is all the more necessary for educators and practitioners to cooperate and share ideas, resources, and experiences of online teaching and learning. In this study, we intend to share our experience in a project-based academic writing and presentation course that blends online MOOC/SPOC autonomous learning with Zoom class instructions, supported by the Canvas course management platform so as to show how the blended learning in the digital context can be realized. In order to serve the purpose of online instruction against the special circumstance of coronavirus pandemic, blended learning in this study refers to the integration of different online platforms to facilitate learning that can be achieved by blending online learning and offline face-to-face classroom instruction.

We propose a model of blended learning for a project-based academic English course (see Figure 1). The model is composed of three parts: pre-class, in-class, and after-class. It includes Objectives, Flipped classroom learning (instructional videos, questions, reading materials, test), Activities, Assessment, Summary, and Project-based usage, and is simplified as OFAASP.

Figure 1. The OFAASP model of project-based blended learning

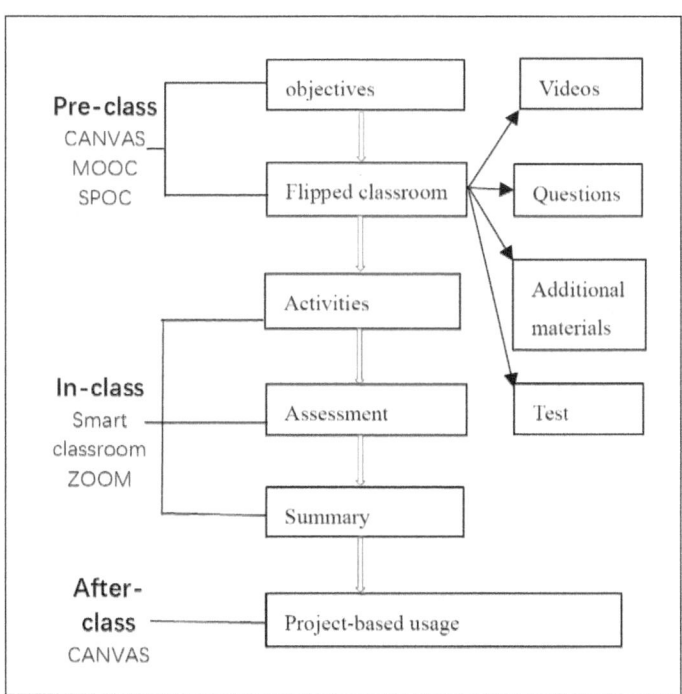

In the following example of a case study, we are going to show how this model is implemented and realized in our course. Two questions will be addressed in our research.

- How is the model implemented in the academic writing course?

- What are learners' perceptions of the effectiveness of the model?

## 2. Implementation of the model

### 2.1. Course objectives

This is an elective course intended for improving students' academic writing and presentation skills in English and preparing the students for publication and conference presentation in the future. All undergraduates of different majors could take the course, after which they were expected to be able to:

- find sources for research, locate necessary information rapidly in research papers, read critically to form ideas for research;

- learn the structure and components of a research paper to tell an academic story with good logic; and

- grasp strategies for delivering a good speech at the conference.

### 2.2. Course design

We designed a teaching model that integrated online platforms such as MOOC/SPOC, Zoom, and Canvas. Students were required to learn knowledge autonomously on MOOC/SPOC before class. They performed activities through interactions in Zoom (or a smart classroom in the post-pandemic era) which helped them to internalize the knowledge. Finally, they applied the knowledge to a research project and imitated the process of publication and conference through the method of 'learning by doing'.

#### 2.2.1. Before class: MOOC/SPOC learning

Students were required to learn autonomously before class on MOOC[3] or SPOC[4]. They watched videos to learn the basic knowledge that they were

---

3. https://www.icourse163.org/course/SJTU-1206705804?tid=1461155452

4. Only available to the students in Shanghai Jiao Tong University

supposed to grasp in the unit. Take 'Abstract' for example, this unit includes three instructional videos: the essential components of an abstract, sentence templates for writing the abstract, and choosing keywords. After watching the videos, students were required to finish exercises or take multiple choice tests to check their understanding of the videos. We got to know students' problems through the exercises and tests before class so that we could focus on the problematic points in class. There were also communications in the discussion board where students could share opinions with each other and interact with the teacher online (see Figure 2).

Figure 2. Online learning on MOOC/SPOC before class

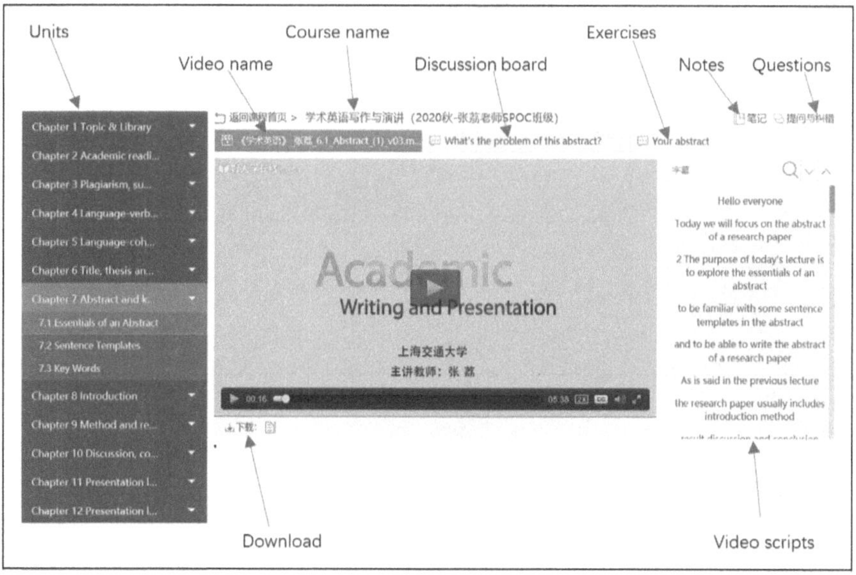

### 2.2.2. In class: Zoom conference

The teacher and the students met online in Zoom every week at a fixed time required by the course schedule and conducted activities such as case studies or discussions in the virtual classroom for the purpose of internalizing the knowledge through these activities (see Figure 3). Students were encouraged to put up their virtual hands in Zoom and use the microphone to voice their opinions, or to express their ideas via the Zoom Chatroom by typing what they wanted to share. In addition, they could make use of the 'notepad' to mark directly on the screen, another way to show their thoughts.

Figure 3. In-class teaching and learning in a virtual Zoom classroom

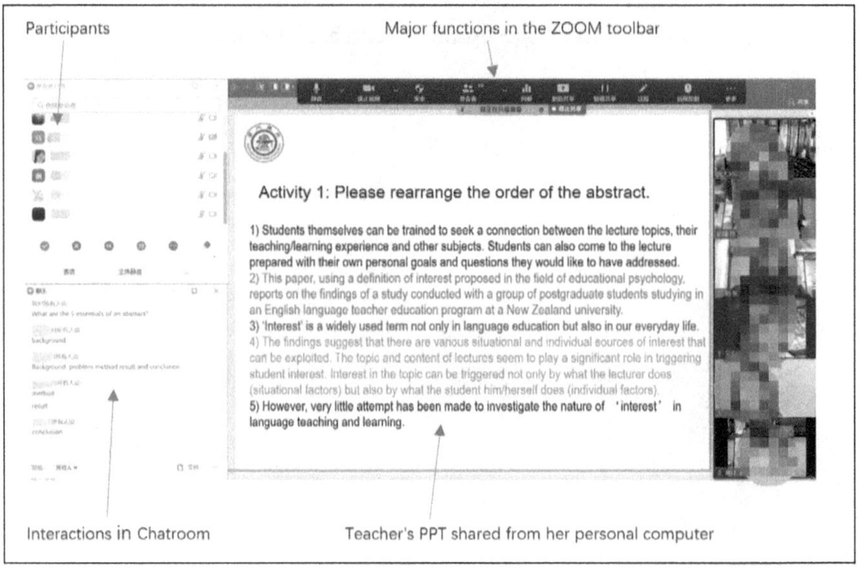

### 2.2.3. After class: Canvas management and WeChat interaction

Finally, students applied the knowledge in project-based writing by imitating the process of research paper publication and academic conference, which manifested our approach of 'learning by doing'. They submitted to Canvas their homework 'assignments' all through the course, such as outline, first draft, peer review, second draft, final research paper, and PowerPoint slides for presentation. The teacher also made use of Canvas to arrange the process of learning before, in, and after class and to inform the students about Zoom conference times and entrance codes in 'Announcement' (see Figure 4). To cooperate well in the tasks, students worked in groups of three and had frequent discussions about their homework by WeChat, a very popular app for online synchronous and asynchronous communications in China.

Figure 4. Canvas course management software frontpage

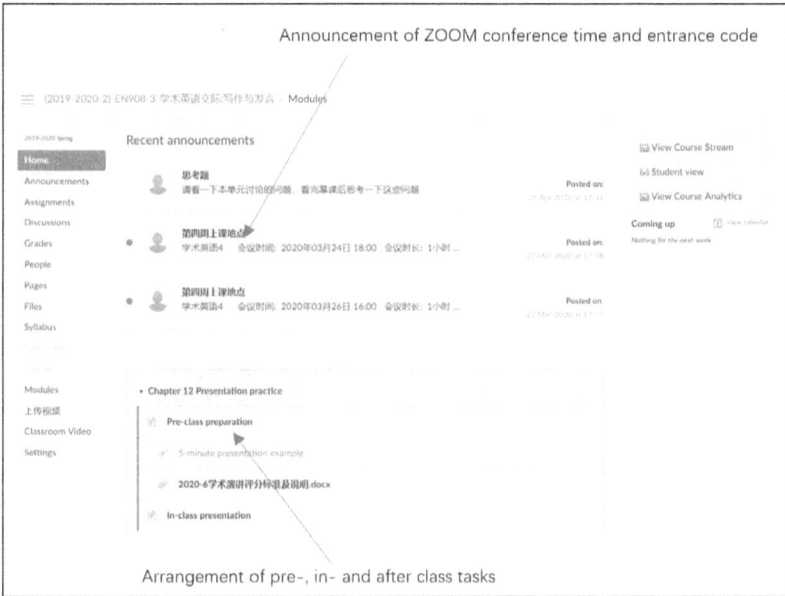

## 2.3. Evaluation of learning

We adopted a formative evaluation method to assess students' performance. The final score was composed of 40% for research paper writing, 20% for presentation, and 40% for other performance, which includes:

- **pre-class**: autonomous learning on SPOC 10%;

- **in-class**: presence and participation 10%; and

- **after-class**: reading 5%, outline 5%, first draft 5%, peer review and second draft 5%.

Chapter 11

Students' autonomous learning experiences were recorded on the MOOC or SPOC platform in terms of total time of learning, percentage of video and exercise completion, and postings in the discussion board, with a corresponding total progress of learning for each student (see Figure 5).

Presence and participation were checked by means of a QR code released every ten seconds from the campus website[5] and the messages saved or recorded in Zoom.

Figure 5. Online learning record on MOOC/SPOC

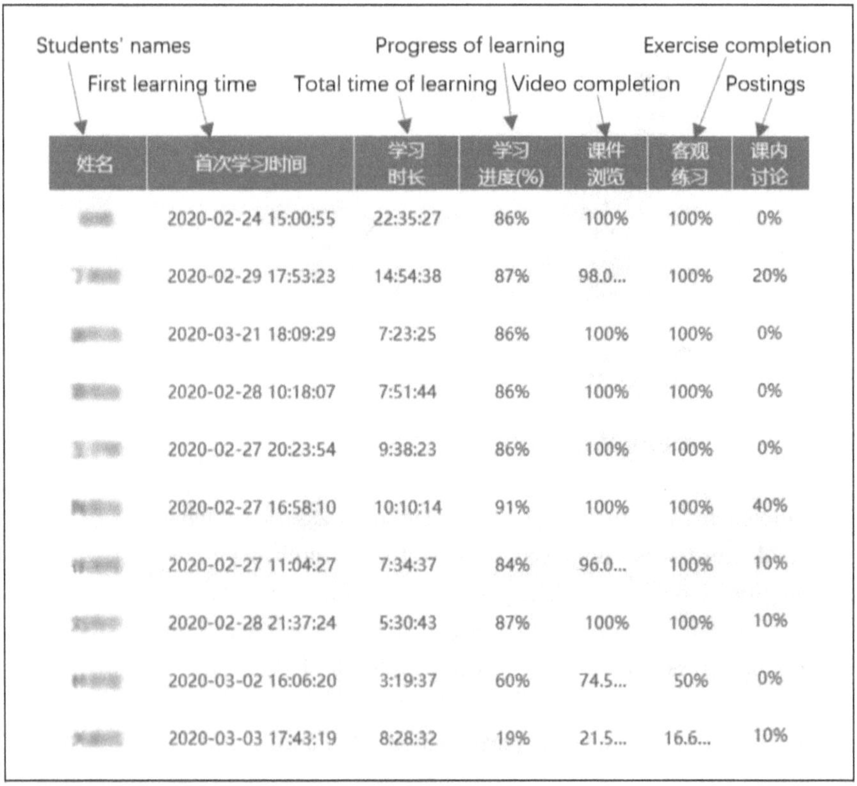

| 姓名 | 首次学习时间 | 学习时长 | 学习进度(%) | 课件浏览 | 客观练习 | 课内讨论 |
|---|---|---|---|---|---|---|
| | 2020-02-24 15:00:55 | 22:35:27 | 86% | 100% | 100% | 0% |
| | 2020-02-29 17:53:23 | 14:54:38 | 87% | 98.0... | 100% | 20% |
| | 2020-03-21 18:09:29 | 7:23:25 | 86% | 100% | 100% | 0% |
| | 2020-02-28 10:18:07 | 7:51:44 | 86% | 100% | 100% | 0% |
| | 2020-02-27 20:23:54 | 9:38:23 | 86% | 100% | 100% | 0% |
| | 2020-02-27 16:58:10 | 10:10:14 | 91% | 100% | 100% | 40% |
| | 2020-02-27 11:04:27 | 7:34:37 | 84% | 96.0... | 100% | 10% |
| | 2020-02-28 21:37:24 | 5:30:43 | 87% | 100% | 100% | 10% |
| | 2020-03-02 16:06:20 | 3:19:37 | 60% | 74.5... | 50% | 0% |
| | 2020-03-03 17:43:19 | 8:28:32 | 19% | 21.5... | 16.6... | 10% |

Column labels (annotated): Students' names | First learning time | Total time of learning | Progress of learning | Video completion | Exercise completion | Postings

---

5. http://qd.sjtu.edu.cn

## 3. Effectiveness of the model: a mixed-method approach

### 3.1. Research design

A mixed-method approach was adopted to investigate students' opinions of the effectiveness of the model. A questionnaire investigation was conducted six weeks after the students had experienced online learning guided by the OFAASP model in the hope that we could know students' opinions about blended learning and adjust our teaching in time if necessary.

Another questionnaire survey was carried out at the end of the course to inquire about students' learning outcomes and five students were interviewed to give further explanations of the questionnaire results. Students also posted on Canvas their opinions on the learning outcomes.

### 3.2. Participants

Enrolled in the course were 90 undergraduate students who were divided into three classes of 30 students each. Sixty-six students finished the first questionnaire investigation about the perception of blended learning and 69 completed the second survey about the learning outcome. Table 1 demonstrates the basic information of the students.

Table 1. Information of participants in the two investigations

| Category | Specification | First | Second |
|---|---|---|---|
| Gender | Male | 32 | 33 |
| | Female | 34 | 36 |
| Year | Freshmen | 44 | 40 |
| | Sophomore | 13 | 16 |
| | Junior | 5 | 7 |
| | Senior | 4 | 6 |
| Major | Science, engineering, agriculture, medicine | 56 | 57 |
| | Social science, humanities, economics | 10 | 12 |

## 3.3. Instruments

The first questionnaire included three items of choices about personal information, 15 items about blended learning on a five-point Likert scale, and one open-ended question about their feelings about current learning and suggestions for the next step. The second questionnaire consisted of six items about personal information, nine items about learning outcomes on a five-point Likert scale, and 18 items for students' own ratings of their abilities and qualities on a 100-point scale before and after the course.

To avoid confusions in the questionnaire results, we interviewed five students on a voluntary basis. The interview includes such questions as below.

- Do you think blended learning has promoted or impeded your grasp of knowledge? Why? Compared with face-to-face learning, which is better?

- What strategies have you adopted in learning before, during, and after class?

- Do you have difficulties in blended learning, how do you overcome them?

Students also posted on the Canvas discussion board their opinions about what they have gained in the course with regard to academic reading, writing, presentation, and research ability.

## 3.4. Data collection and analysis

The two questionnaire investigations were conducted online by means of Wenjuanxing[6], a popular online questionnaire platform in China. Students were given a link to the platform in WeChat and filled the questionnaire either on

---

6. https://www.wjx.cn/

their mobile phones or computers. Then, data were collected from the platform and analyzed using SPSS statistic software. Means, percentage, and standard deviation were calculated in the first questionnaire to find out the students' opinions about blended learning. Paired-sample t-test was conducted to show the difference in students' abilities before and after the course.

## 4. Results and discussion

Table 2 shows students' perception of the effectiveness of learning after six weeks.

Table 2. Students' perceptions of the effectiveness of blended learning

| Evaluation contents | Strongly agree | Agree | Do not know | Disagree | Strongly disagree | Mean | Standard deviation |
|---|---|---|---|---|---|---|---|
| **General evaluation** | | | | | | | |
| Having clear objectives | 39.39% | 53.03% | 7.58% | 0% | 0% | 4.3182 | .61166 |
| Considering Canvas helpful for study management | 45.45% | 50.00% | 4.55% | 0% | 0% | 4.4091 | .58117 |
| Preferring blended teaching method | 31.82% | 48.48% | 18.18% | 1.52% | 0% | 4.1061 | .74687 |
| Preferring learning-by-doing | 48.48% | 50.00% | 1.52% | 0% | 0% | 4.4697 | .53262 |
| **Autonomous learning before class** | | | | | | | |
| Watching videos | 39.39% | 46.97% | 13.64% | 0% | 0% | 4.2576 | .68636 |
| Gaining basic knowledge from videos | 46.97% | 48.48% | 4.55% | 0% | 0% | 4.4242 | .58337 |
| Raising questions after self-study | 12.12% | 43.94% | 40.91% | 3.03% | 0% | 3.6515 | .73364 |

| | | | | | | | |
|---|---|---|---|---|---|---|---|
| Learning additional materials effectively | 39.39% | 54.55% | 6.06% | 0% | 0% | 4.3333 | .59052 |
| **Internalization of knowledge in Zoom classroom** | | | | | | | |
| Understanding knowledge through online activities | 43.94% | 51.52% | 3.03% | 1.52% | 0% | 4.3788 | .62672 |
| Participating actively in Zoom discussions | 19.70% | 57.58% | 22.73% | 0% | 0% | 3.9697 | .65562 |
| Completing in-class tests effectively | 16.67% | 62.12% | 21.21% | 0% | 0% | 3.9545 | .61848 |
| Clarifying knowledge points through summaries | 39.39% | 54.55% | 6.06% | 0% | 0% | 4.3333 | .59052 |
| **Application after class** | | | | | | | |
| Being able to apply knowledge to writing | 34.85% | 54.55% | 9.09% | 1.52% | 0% | 4.2273 | .67472 |
| Getting timely feedback from teachers | 50.00% | 48.48% | 1.52% | 0% | 0% | 4.4848 | .53328 |
| Communicating with group members frequently | 25.76% | 53.03% | 18.18% | 3.03% | 0% | 4.0152 | .75432 |
| Completing tasks though cooperative work | 43.94% | 43.94% | 9.09% | 3.03% | 0% | 4.2879 | .75986 |

Generally speaking, students had positive attitudes toward blended teaching that was totally conducted online. They benefited a lot from the project-based learning and regarded learning-by-doing as a very effective approach (Mean=4.47, Agreement=98.48%). However, problems arise with regard to completing videos and raising questions in pre-learning, communicating, and focusing attention in Zoom, and applying knowledge in research paper writing.

Therefore, it is necessary to carry out the formative evaluation in the middle of the term so that we can adjust our teaching immediately (Black & Wiliam, 2009). Besides, students still preferred face-to-face interactions even though they could accept online instructions via Zoom (Mean=4.11, Acceptance=86.36%). This finding is in line with the previous research by Platt, Raile, and Yu (2014) who find that students preferred face-to-face learning over online learning. Therefore, even though technology has developed over time, face-to-face education is still necessary and cannot be totally replaced by online teaching (Fish & Snodgrass, 2020), and blended learning with face-to-face instructions in the classroom is still encouraged after the pandemic.

### 4.1. Autonomous learning before class

Results from the first questionnaire investigation show that although students were required to watch videos in MOOC/SPOC before class, 13.64% of them skipped this process and attended classes in Zoom without any preparation. The interview after the survey revealed that some students regarded pre-class learning as unnecessary because they thought that the key points would be repeated in class. Therefore, we adjusted our teaching plans by directly studying examples and cases. When the students met difficulties in the in-class activities, they would realize the importance of pre-class autonomous learning in a flipped classroom (Du, 2020).

Besides, students were expected to raise questions whenever they encountered problems in understanding while doing their autonomous learning. They were also encouraged to bring their questions to class because only by raising questions could students achieve a better understanding of knowledge and make progress in their ability to think (Mazer, Hunt, & Kuznekoff, 2008). However, we found in the questionnaire that students were not very good at raising questions (Mean=3.65). Thus, we redesigned the exercises on the MOOC/SPOC by making them more challenging so as to provoke deeper thinking. Also, we added some open-ended questions in the discussion board, aiming to challenge their thoughts and expand their scope of thinking.

## 4.2. Participation in class

Students were less likely to participate in online discussions (Mean=3.97) owing to the inconvenience brought about by the undesirable fact that they were only connected by screens in the Zoom classroom. Group discussion was not easy to be implemented in Zoom because the teacher could hardly monitor the whole class for effective discussions and there is often a feeling of disconnection with students. To solve this problem, we designed special tasks and raised purposeful questions to engage every student, leaving group discussions to students themselves after class through WeChat when they were working together to write a paper. We also found that although oral discussion was reduced in online teaching, the Zoom Chatroom enabled those who were too shy to voice their opinions in face-to-face interactions to become more actively involved and more willing to express their ideas by typing in what they had to say.

Some students found it hard to 'pay full attention to online courses'. According to Wu (2015), the focus of attention can be achieved through the regulation of one's brain or behavior. We tried to design interesting and thought-provoking activities to provoke thinking so that students could stay focused. Besides, we employed various ways of communication in Zoom when dealing with different types of questions. For example, students turned on their microphones when there was much to be expressed, which was close to face-to-face teaching; or they typed in words in the Chatroom when the answer was short and relatively fixed; they also used the 'notepad' to mark on the screen to boost the sense of participation.

## 4.3. Application after class

According to the results of the questionnaire, most students could apply the knowledge to their writing project (Agreement=89.39%) while some students do not know how to use the knowledge in practice even though they understand what was taught in class. Actually, application of knowledge is not only the essence of project-based learning (Seman, Hausmann, & Bezerra, 2018) but also the focal point for our OFAASP model. In order to help students better achieve their learning objectives, we redesigned more practical tasks to effectively help students form a deeper understanding of knowledge. For example, we provided some cases for study or some model research papers for reference. We also motivated them to cooperate and interact more frequently with each other, sharing their unique learning strategies and helping each other to make progress together. In addition, teachers can act as the scaffolding by participating in the online discussions, answering questions or giving feedback (Alharbi, 2017). In this way, students would be closely connected with the teacher and their confusion could be cleared up in time.

### 4.4. Quantitative analysis of learning outcomes

Table 3 shows students' perceptions of learning outcomes. The means for most items are above four, which shows that the course is helpful for learning. As is shown in Figure 6, their academic reading, writing, presentation, and even their research abilities were significantly improved from an average of above 70+ to 80+ ($p<0.001$). Therefore, the learning outcome meets the knowledge and ability goals of the course.

Table 3.   Students' perceptions of learning outcomes

| Items | Numbers | Min | Max | Mean | SD |
|---|---|---|---|---|---|
| The course meets my expectations | 69 | 2.00 | 5.00 | 4.3043 | .75351 |
| I can grasp knowledge through practice | 69 | 3.00 | 5.00 | 4.4783 | .55859 |
| I have learned how to use Endnote | 69 | 2.00 | 5.00 | 4.1304 | .83864 |
| I am able to use COCA[7] and Phrasebank to help writing | 69 | 2.00 | 5.00 | 3.8116 | .75294 |
| I know how to find resources | 69 | 3.00 | 5.00 | 4.5507 | .52960 |
| I know how to review the literature | 69 | 2.00 | 5.00 | 4.0870 | .65841 |
| I know how to write different parts of a research paper | 69 | 4.00 | 5.00 | 4.3913 | .49162 |
| I know the structure of research papers | 69 | 3.00 | 5.00 | 4.4348 | .52799 |
| I know how to cite and list references | 69 | 3.00 | 5.00 | 4.3913 | .59945 |

---

7. Corpus of Contemporary American English

Figure 6. Students' perception of improvement

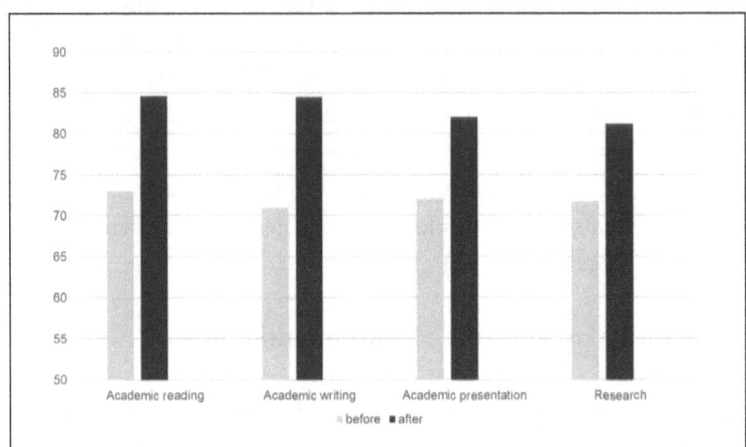

## 4.5. Qualitative analysis of students' reflective comments

At the end of the course, students posted on Canvas their comments on the course and the following comments are to show what they have gained in their ability and quality.

> "I must admit that I was not interested in academic research at all before I took this course. However, during this semester, the course has gradually aroused my interest in academic writing and motivated me to conduct my own research".

> "The literature review part helps me to improve my experience and skills of reading academic essays. When I have an essay to read, I now know where to read first and how to get the main ideas that the author is trying to convey, thus saving a lot of time and energy".

> "I am able to write an academic paper, which is unbelievable before the course. This experience also helps me a lot when I have to write a paper

in other courses or projects. I think this is very helpful for my future development".

"I know how to stand on the stage to give a presentation, although I am a shy person who doesn't love to speak out, and through this course I know how to speak loudly and bravely. Though my oral English is not so good, speaking out in front of people is really a breakthrough for me".

The above comments from students show that the course is helpful for the improvement of their academic research, reading, writing, and presentation abilities.

## 5. Conclusion

This study suggests an online blended learning model that incorporates the pre-class autonomous learning of knowledge on MOOC/SPOC, in-class internalization of knowledge through interactive activities in Zoom, and after-class application of knowledge in a project-based practice. Results show that students generally have positive opinions about online blended learning and the course benefits students in the improvement of academic writing and presentation abilities. But problems still arise with regard to pre-class MOOC/SPOC learning and online interaction in Zoom. Therefore, we can do further research by comparing scores of their performance rated not only by themselves by also by peers and the teacher. Future research can also be conducted as to how to have a smooth transition from Zoom to a real classroom in the post-pandemic period.

## 6. Acknowledgments

The authors would like to thank the Center for Teaching and Learning Development in Shanghai Jiao Tong University for their support of the projects No. JYJX20 0132 and No. CTLD20T 0047.

# References

Alharbi, W. (2017). E-feedback as a scaffolding teaching strategy in the online language classroom. *Journal of Educational Technology Systems, 46*(2), 239-251. https://doi.org/10.1177/0047239517697966

Black, P., & Wiliam, D. (2009). Developing the theory of formative assessment. *Educational Assessment Evaluation & Accountability, 21*(1), 5-31. https://doi.org/10.1007/s11092-008-9068-5

Du, Y. (2020). Study on cultivating college students' English autonomous learning ability under the flipped classroom model. *English Language Teaching, 13*(6), 13-19. https://doi.org/10.5539/elt.v13n6p13

Fish, L. A., & Snodgrass, C. R. (2020). Changing business student perceptions of program factors in online versus face-to-face education. *Business Education Innovation Journal, 12*(1), 123-131.

Graham, C. R. (2006). Blended learning systems: definition, current trends and future directions. In C. J. Bonk & C. R. Graham (Eds), *The handbook of blended learning: global perspectives, local designs* (pp. 3-21). Pfeiffer, Wiley & Sons. https://doi.org/10.5465/amle.2008.31413871

Leakey, J., & Ranchoux, A. (2006). BLINGUA. A blended language learning approach for CALL. *Computer Assisted Language Learning, 19*(4-5), 357-372. https://doi.org/10.1080/09588220601043016

Liu, S. Y. (2013). Web2.0-based blended learning in college English teaching. *Proceedings of the 2013 International Conference on Information, Business and Education Technology (Icibet 2013), 26*, 156-159. https://doi.org/10.2991/icibet.2013.138

Mahalli, Nurkamto, J., Mujiyanto, J., & Yuliasri, I. (2019). The implementation of station rotation and flipped classroom models of blended learning in EFL learning. *English Language Teaching, 12*(12), 23-29. https://doi.org/10.5539/elt.v12n12p23

Mazer, J. P., Hunt, S. K., & Kuznekoff, J. H. (2008). Revising general education: assessing a critical thinking instructional model in the basic communication course. *The Journal of General Education, 56*(3-4), 173-199. https://doi.org/10.1353/jge.0.0000

Platt, C. A., Raile, A. N. W., & Yu, N. (2014). Virtually the same? Student perceptions of the equivalence of online classes to face-to-face classes. *MERLOT Journal of Online Learning and Teaching, 10*(3), 489-503.

Seman, L. O., Hausmann, R., & Bezerra, E. A. (2018). On the students' perceptions of the knowledge formation when submitted to a project-based learning environment using web applications. *Computers & Education, 117*, 16-30. https://doi.org/10.1016/j.compedu.2017.10.001

Wu, J.-Y. (2015). University students' motivated attention and use of regulation strategies on social media. Computers & *Education, 89*, 75-90. https://doi.org/10.1016/j.compedu.2015.08.016

# 12. Online training of prospective language teachers: exploring a new model

## Hang Zheng[1] and Lianyue Zhang[2]

## Abstract

This chapter reports on a language teaching practicum course of a Master of Teaching Chinese to Speakers of Other Languages (MTCSOL) program in China in Fall 2020. Driven by the challenges of the COVID-19 pandemic, this report presents a model to guide practice in online language teacher training via virtual learning communities. In the course, native and nonnative students in the MTCSOL program formed study groups in which they conducted discussions regarding the lectures and completed teaching demonstrations through videoconferences. All students provided online feedback on their peers' teaching demonstrations. The content analysis of post-task interviews revealed that both native and nonnative students benefited from online interactions. Nonnative students had opportunities to practice language and professional skills, while native students developed intercultural communication competence. Peer feedback was also highly rated, as feedback receivers had different perspectives on how to improve their teaching, and feedback providers learned from their peers' strengths and weaknesses. We argue that the model can (1) promote learning autonomy and cultural exchange and (2) boost teachers' self-confidence, which could thus become a desirable new model for language teacher training.

Keywords: COVID-19, online language teaching, virtual community, feedback, Sun Yat-sen University, Zhuhai, China.

---

1. Sun Yat-Sen University, Zhuhai, China; zhengh73@mail.sysu.edu.cn; https://orcid.org/0000-0001-7888-7359

2. Qingdao University, Qingdao, China; zhanglianyue06@163.com; https://orcid.org/0000-0001-7200-4906

How to cite: Zheng, H., & Zhang, L. (2021). Online training of prospective language teachers: exploring a new model. In N. Radić, A. Atabekova, M. Freddi & J. Schmied (Eds), *The world universities' response to COVID-19: remote online language teaching* (pp. 199-214). Research-publishing.net. https://doi.org/10.14705/rpnet.2021.52.1273

## 1. Introduction

With the global spread of the COVID-19 epidemic, many countries have implemented border controls. This change has massively impacted international education and student exchanges. The consequences of this shift are particularly evident in second language (L2) teaching and learning. In China, for example, because most international students (Chinese degree pursuers or short-term Chinese learners) were unable to return to China after the winter recess, all Chinese classes for international students were moved online for the 2020 Fall semester. This change posed severe challenges for MTCSOL programs designed for international students. As professional degree programs, MTSCOL programs must, on one hand, introduce theories and, on the other hand, cultivate the ability to solve practical problems in the classroom by providing students with knowledge and training on teaching skills and techniques. For international students, attention also needs to be paid to the improvement of their target language. The contemporary curriculum also includes the goal of cultivating student teachers' intercultural competence and their ability to integrate foreign cultures in classrooms (Gay, 2013).

Nonnative MTCSOL students opt for programs in the target language environment because immersion learning contexts can rapidly increase their language proficiency (Xiao, Taguchi, & Li, 2019) and enrich their target cultural understanding (Taguchi, Xiao, & Li, 2016). Immersion programs also often provide hands-on training by allowing students to participate in experienced teachers' classrooms.

Turning to online learning poses major obstacles to nonnative MTCSOL students' linguistic and professional development. First, most MTCSOL programs have not been prepared for the rapid conversion to online teaching, either technologically or pedagogically. Second, hands-on teaching practicums are difficult to conduct in online environments. Third, isolated learning environments significantly affect students' target language use. Consequently, international students have limited access to natural language learners to practice their teaching skills and native speakers to improve their language proficiency.

## 2. Objectives

The example we present below is from an online teacher practicum course for MTCSOL students at a Chinese public university. The purpose is twofold: to adapt to the new teaching and learning settings and to explore the possibility of establishing a new model for language teacher training.

As a compulsory course for the MTCSOL program, the teaching practicum course introduces junior graduate students to various aspects of Chinese L2 classroom teaching through critical discussions of prominent theories, interaction with experienced teachers, and engagement with fellow students' teaching demonstrations. The goal is to expand students' expertise as Chinese teachers in the classroom and other learning settings and to develop their ability to make informed decisions in future instructional contexts.

In the program that we are investigating, Chinese Native Students (NSs) and Non-Native Students (NNSs) complete the course in separate sections. Both sections are taught by the same instructor using the same syllabus.

In the 2020 Fall semester, NSs resumed regular on-campus classes. However, all NNSs' classes were converted online. Due to this situation, both NS and NNS classes changed, as demonstrated in Table 1.

Table 1. Class design for NSs and NNSs before and after COVID-19

|  | **Native student class** | **Nonnative student class** |
|---|---|---|
| Before COVID-19 | **Whole-class tasks (Classroom)**<br><br>• Lectures and discussions<br><br>• Watch expert teacher videos<br><br>• Teaching demo in front of the whole class | **Whole-class tasks (Classroom)**<br><br>• Lectures and discussions<br><br>• Watch expert teacher videos<br><br>• Teaching demo in front of the whole class |
|  | **Practicum (Classroom)**<br><br>• Observe and teach an actual Chinese class | **Practicum (Classroom)**<br><br>• Observe and teach an actual Chinese class |

| After COVID-19 | **Whole-class tasks (Classroom)**<br>• Lectures and discussions<br>• Watch expert teacher videos<br>• Teaching demo in front of the whole class | **Individual tasks (Online)**<br>• Asynchronous lectures<br>• Asynchronous expert teacher videos<br>• Asynchronous Q&A with the instructor |
|---|---|---|
| | **Small group tasks (Online)**<br>• Discussions with 1 NS and 1 NNS peers<br>• Prepare teaching demo with 1 NS and 1 NNS peers | **Small group tasks (Online)**<br>• Discussions with 2 NS peers<br>• Prepare teaching demo with 2 NS peers<br>• Make teaching demo video with 2 NSs |
| | **Peer feedback (Online)**<br>• Anonymized feedback on NS and NNS demos | **Peer feedback (Online)**<br>• Anonymized feedback on NNS demos |

Table 1 shows that major changes occurred to NNSs' classes, including individual tasks, small group tasks, and peer feedback. The following section will explicate the rationales of these tasks and how they are operationalized.

## 3.  Method

### 3.1.  Instruments

For both international and Chinese students, the course materials are published on the course website built on Chaoxing, an online learning platform (similar to Moodle) designed for and widely used by higher institutions across the Chinese mainland.

Students who enroll in the course may access the system with their college account. International students in our study reported no difficulty logging onto the system. Students must also use videoconferencing platforms, such as Tencent, Voov, or Zoom, to perform group tasks.

## 3.2. Participants

Seventeen NNSs are advanced Chinese learners from ten countries: Egypt, Russia, the Czech Republic, Thailand, Poland, Malaysia, Indonesia, Vietnam, France, and South Korea. The 17 NNSs and 34 NSs are assigned to 3 member mixed groups. Each group includes one NNS and two NSs. The three students complete all group work together.

## 3.3. Course tasks

The NNS course primarily involves five sequenced tasks, as shown in Figure 1. Tasks 2 through 4 are all group work.

Figure 1. NNS course tasks and procedure

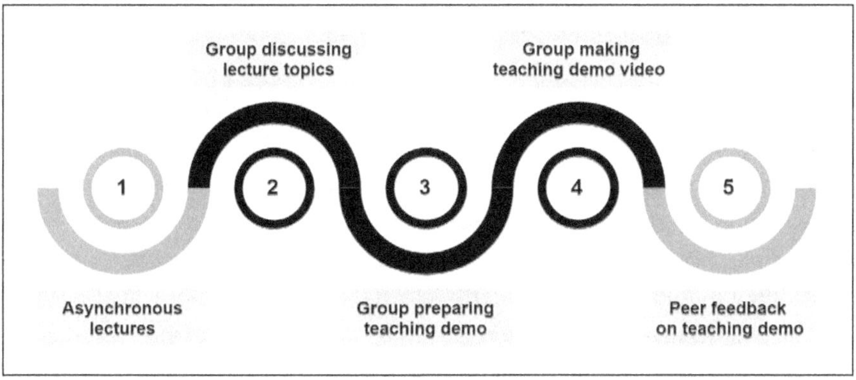

*3.3.1. Asynchronous lectures*

Task 1 involves students watching asynchronous lectures and participating in the asynchronous discussion forum. The main function of the asynchronous task is that teachers can remain present and attend to students' needs, so students can feel a sense of belonging to a learning community (Meskill & Anthony, 2005). In this course, asynchronous lectures are brief and focused audio-visual PowerPoint presentations created and uploaded by the instructor. Students can only watch the lectures on the platform, which enables teachers to monitor students' learning processes, as the system can track the total time each student spends on a lecture. After watching the lectures, students can post their questions on the discussion forum. The instructor responds to all questions in a timely fashion.

*3.3.2. Group work*

As shown in Figure 1, most course tasks (Tasks 2 to 4) are group work. Small group interactions between learners are often used in L2 classrooms. The interaction hypothesis states that learner interactions may draw learners' attention to their ungrammatical utterances, stimulate learners to practice language forms in meaningful contexts, and promote autonomous learning (Gass, 1997). The output hypothesis suggests that interactions between NNSs and NSs can stimulate learners to notice the distance between interlanguage and target-like forms and reflect on their own language use (Swain, 2000).

In Tasks 2 and 3, students are required to conduct group meetings by videoconferencing, discussing lecture-related topics, and preparing teaching demonstrations. Videoconferences create a virtual face-to-face situation which allows remote interlocutors to synchronously exchange both verbal and nonverbal information. Nonverbal information, such as gestures or facial expressions, can be captured by the interlocutors fairly clearly, even with minor signal latency. All videoconference sessions are recorded by the team leader and submitted to the instructor.

In Task 4, NNSs are required to make a teaching demonstration video with their NS partners using videoconferencing. The purpose of teaching an artificial lesson is to demonstrate approaches and techniques that students have learned in class. In the video, the NNS 'teacher' teaches two NS 'students' a 10-minute lesson assigned by the instructor. Some groups choose to use the full-screen model to present the PowerPoint slides without showing the speakers' faces; other groups choose to present the slides as well as show all interlocutors' faces (see Figure 2).

Figure 2. Screenshot of a teaching demonstration (reproduced with kind permission from the students)

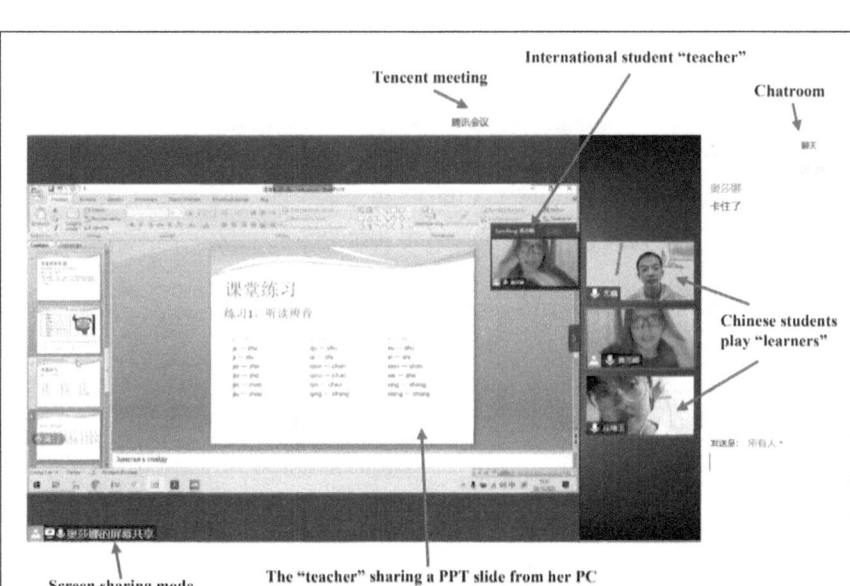

NNSs' teaching demo videos are uploaded to the course website for both NNSs and NSs enrolled in the course to watch.

### 3.3.3. Peer feedback

After watching each teaching demonstration, both native and nonnative students are required to provide feedback on each other's teaching demos. In L2 acquisition, peer feedback was proven to improve feedback givers' awareness of their own performance and provide feedback receivers with different perspectives (other than the teacher's perspective) on how to make improvements (Rollinson, 2005).

The review-reflect-revise process can also encourage students to be more independent learners. In this course, students are asked to provide feedback on the following three questions.

- What do you think are the best parts of this teaching demonstration?

- Do you have any suggestions on how this teacher can improve his or her teaching?

- What have you learned from this teaching demonstration?

The instructor collects and anonymizes the feedback, compiles it in a Word document, and then gives it to the student 'teacher'.

### 3.4. Data collection and analysis

Because the course began in August 2020 and is still in progress, we report our observations and reflections on the online section as of the date of manuscript submission.

Thus far, four groups have completed all group tasks. The instructor initiated a one-on-one online text interview with these students using the following questions.

- What do you think about the remote teamwork learning model?

- Which changes would you suggest to improve the model?

- Which major difficulties have you experienced in using this model?

Students' peer feedback and interview responses were analyzed using exploratory content analysis.

## 4. Findings

Overall, both native and nonnative students hold a positive opinion of the online group interactions and peer feedback.

## 4.1. Online group interactions

Regarding the group discussions, as demonstrated in Excerpts 1-3, nonnative students had opportunities to practice the Chinese language and understand Chinese culture, and NSs developed intercultural communication competence.

- **Excerpt 1 (Thai student)**
  "我喜欢，因为我一边练习汉语一边更好了解中国人，中国文化什么的。我觉得我的组的中国学生很热情。我有不懂的地方，她们给我解释，很清楚。" (I like it, because I can practice Chinese while better understanding Chinese people, Chinese culture, and so on. I think the Chinese students in my team are very enthusiastic. They explain to me, very clearly, the places that I don't understand).

- **Excerpt 2 (Czech student)**
  "其实不管怎样我都喜欢，因为我比较想跟中国学生交流。现在疫情的问题没办法当面，能在网上讨论已经是很不错了，我对线上讨论没有什么不满的。" (In fact, I like it anyway because I do want to communicate with Chinese students. Currently, there is no way to discuss face-to-face because of the epidemic. It is good enough to be able to discuss online. I have no dissatisfaction with the online discussion model).

- **Excerpt 3 (Chinese student)**
  "能锻炼我和留学生交流的能力，为以后课堂教学做铺垫吧。" (I can practice my communication skills with international students, thus paving the way for future classroom teaching).

## 4.2. Peer feedback

Regarding peer feedback, as demonstrated in Excerpts 4-6, feedback givers provided both comments (see Excerpt 4) and suggestions (see Excerpt 5) and often made self-reflections when giving feedback (see Excerpt 6). After reading feedback, receivers also made self-reflections on their teaching performance (see Excerpt 7).

- **Excerpt 4 (a native student to a nonnative peer)**
  "一开始直接了当复习上节课内容，这种导入承前启后，也挺自然的。" (In the beginning, (the teacher) reviewed the content of the previous lesson directly. This kind of introduction serves as a link between old and new knowledge and is also quite natural).

- **Excerpt 5 (a nonnative student to a nonnative peer)**
  "老师可以用母语或者英语来解释新词，也多做一点互动。" (The teacher may use learners' native language or English to explain the new words and have more interactions).

- **Excerpt 6 (a native student to a native peer)**
  "我学到了在讲生词的时候应该讲它的适用范围，让大家会认的同时会用。" (I learned that when teaching a new word, we should teach its scope of application so that everyone can recognize it as well as know how to use it).

- **Excerpt 7 (Russian student)**
  "关于例子，很多同学说少。我自己先也写比较多例子，但是我故意地把它们删除，因为这是学生的第二课，他们除了'你好'以外什么都不知道，所以我把简单的一两个例子放在PPT上。" (Many students said the examples were too few. I wrote many examples initially, but I deliberately deleted them because this is just their second lesson. They don't know anything except 'hello'. So I put one or two simple examples on the PPT).

### 4.3. Challenges and suggestions

Both native and nonnative students reported challenges in technology use and time differences among group members. Nonnative students also conveyed challenges in language proficiency, stating that "I feel I could not fully express my opinions" or that "I don't always know how to express my ideas. That's why I particularly value the opportunities to talk to Chinese students".

When asked about their suggestions, nonnative students expressed the fact that they liked the model as it was, saying that "nothing needs to be changed" and that "I do not think there is any problem with it". The other two stated that they had no opinion on the model. Some NSs expressed that they hoped to have larger-scale meetings or additional meetings in the future. For example, students stated: "I hope to add more team members, especially foreign students", "it would be better if the instructor could join us occasionally, so it could help us to answer difficult questions", and "I hope to have more chances to talk to international students".

## 5. Discussion

Based on our observations of students' progress and our evaluations thus far, we believe that the course design we have developed can offer a desirable permanent model for remote language teacher training rather than just a temporary change. There are three major potential achievements of this model.

### 5.1. Promoting learning autonomy

When classes are suddenly moved online, students are forced into a situation where they must rely more on themselves to learn. One desirable outcome is that online learning fosters learning autonomy (Little, 1991). The question is what instructors can do to promote and monitor autonomous learning processes. In regular classrooms, autonomous L2 learning comprises learners' engagement, self-reflection, use of the target language, and collaboration (Little & Brammerts, 1996). Our study shows that these aspects can be achieved via virtual learning communities created by instructors. The native-nonnative teamwork ensures peer collaboration and the use of the target language. Peer feedback encourages students to reflect on their teaching behaviors. Each task is monitored by the instructor through online platforms, which ensures learner engagement.

## 5.2. Developing teachers' beliefs

Meijer, Verloop, and Beijaard (1999) highlighted that teachers' beliefs about their teaching stem from classroom practice and that these beliefs continue to guide their behavior in future classrooms. Combined with theoretical knowledge and teacher expertise, these beliefs are the premise for teachers' further refinement of their teaching practices (Verloop, Van Driel, & Meijer, 2001). In our study, the three integrative and reflective training practices allow prospective teachers to "critically examine their own beliefs and teaching styles and to explore other avenues of professional development" (Lord & Lomicka, 2007, p. 514).

## 5.3. Stimulating cultural exchange

Modern language teaching aims to engage in various forms of communication across cultures and communities (Huhn, 2012). In this unprecedented period, when countries tend to shut their doors to one another, the successful implementation of global understanding and cultural tolerance depends upon classroom teachers. Thus, it is important to cultivate students' global perspectives and intercultural communication competence before they become teachers. In this study, native-nonnative interactions not only improve students' professional skills but also enhance their intercultural awareness, which will mobilize their future students' cultural resources and cultivate the values of diversity, equity, and inclusion in their future classrooms.

# 6. Conclusion and future classes

In response to the worldwide COVID-19 crisis, we initiated an attempt to develop online teacher training classes. The model is still being tested, and the observations reported here are by no means conclusive. However, we believe that the model can be more than a temporary adaptation and has potential for application to language teacher training programs in the future. The virtual communities built for nonnative and native student teachers can promote learning autonomy, help shape teachers' beliefs, and ultimately train foreign language teachers with global perspectives. The computer-assisted teaching model also archives longitudinal data, which enables us to trace and analyze learners' progress over time and to uncover the complexity of student teacher development.

Despite the positive feedback regarding this new model, some obstacles and drawbacks of the model must be noted for future classes to consider.

First, different countries may use different desktop videoconferencing tools. Thus, international students may have to spend time adapting to new or less familiar platforms to complete group work. Students reported that unstable connections could sometimes be "a waste of time" and "interrupt our discussion". One principle proposed for online synchronous L2 learning tasks is *practicality*, referring to "the fit between the task and the capability of the videoconferencing tool(s) to support task completion" (Wang, 2013, p. 593). Future classes may consider choosing one fixed videoconference platform with a relatively larger user base and providing a training session on how to use that platform before the group work begins.

Second, at the beginning of the course, we found that some international students were not as open as others to peer feedback, particularly critical feedback from Chinese students. To address this situation, the instructor wrote a letter to all students that addressed some points of giving and receiving feedback guided by the three key attitudes proposed for teacher reflection, namely, *open-mindedness*, *responsibility*, and *whole-heartedness* (Dewey, 1933). To feedback providers, the instructor wrote,

> "[p]lease be honest as well as respectful so you can help your classmates improve their teaching without hurting your peers' feelings. Remember, you will also receive feedback from your classmates, so put yourself in others' shoes".

To feedback receivers, the instructor wrote,

> "[p]lease be open-minded because your classmates only mean to help you make progress, and your classmates' perspectives are unique as they are both teachers and learners and can be more thorough than I can. Remember, you will receive feedback – probably more reserved – from your students in the future. An important quality of a good teacher is the ability to embrace different opinions".

One cause of the situation could be that native and nonnative students may have different standards and perspectives regarding what is 'good' versus what is 'poor' performance. Future classes involving collaborations between native and nonnative student teachers should consider *learner fit*, which emphasizes the individual proficiency level and the way in which the interlocutor aligns with that level (Wang, 2013).

Finally, one component missing from the model is interactions between NNSs. Because nonnative students come from countries in different time zones, finding a mutually convenient time to meet online is not always feasible. However, interactions between nonnative learners are important in L2 acquisition. Research has found that different partnerships may influence students' perceptions of the learning experience and even affect learning gains (Tocaimaza-Hatch & Santo, 2020). Partnerships among NNSs can reduce learners' anxiety and provide them with more time to speak the target language (Brown, 2001). Our interviews also revealed that some international students felt nervous when interacting with two Chinese students simultaneously. Future classes may consider developing another form of group work involving students in matched partnerships.

## 7. Acknowledgments

We would like to thank Professor Chenguang Chang for his feedback on an earlier version of this article as well as the reviewers for their insightful comments. The project is supported by the Fundamental Research Funds for the Central Universities (SYSU, 20WKPY111) granted to the first author. The project is also supported by the Ministry of Education in China Youth Funds of Humanities and Social Sciences (18YJC740144) granted to the second author.

# References

Brown, R. E. (2001). The process of community-building in distance learning classes. *Journal of asynchronous learning networks*, *5*(2), 18-35.

Dewey, J. (1933). *How we think: a restatement of the relation of reflective thinking to the educative process*. Heath.

Gass, S. (1997). *Input, interaction, and the second language learner*. Lawrence Erlbaum.

Gay, G. (2013). Teaching to and through cultural diversity. *Curriculum Inquiry*, *43*(1), 48-70.

Huhn, C. (2012). In search of innovation: research on effective models of foreign language teacher preparation. *Foreign Language Annals*, *45*(1), 163-183. https://doi.org/10.1111/j.1944-9720.2012.01184.x

Little, D. (1991). *Learner autonomy I: definitions, issues, and problems*. Authentik.

Little, D., & Brammerts, H. (1996). *A guide to language learning in tandem via the Internet*. Trinity College, Centre for Language and Communication Studies.

Lord, G., & Lomicka, L. (2007). Foreign language teacher preparation and asynchronous CMC: promoting reflective teaching. *Journal of Technology & Teacher Education*, *15*(4), 513-532.

Meijer, P. C., Verloop, N., & Beijaard, D. (1999). Exploring language teachers' practical knowledge about teaching reading comprehension. *Teaching and Teacher Education*, *15*(1), 59-84. https://doi.org/10.1016/s0742-051x(98)00045-6

Meskill, C., & Anthony, N. (2005). Foreign language learning with CMC: forms of online instructional discourse in a hybrid Russian class. *System*, *33*(1), 89-105. https://doi.org/10.1016/j.system.2005.01.001

Rollinson, P. (2005). Using peer feedback in the ESL writing class. *ELT journal*, *59*(1), 23-30. https://doi.org/10.1093/elt/cci003

Swain, M. (2000). The output hypothesis and beyond: mediating acquisition through collaborative dialogue. In J. P. Lantolf (Ed.), *Sociocultural theory and second language learning* (pp. 97-114). Oxford University Press.

Taguchi, N., Xiao, F., & Li, S. (2016). Effects of intercultural competence and social contact on speech act production in a Chinese study abroad context. *The Modern Language Journal*, *100*(4), 775-796. https://doi.org/10.1111/modl.12349

Tocaimaza-Hatch, C. C., & Santo, J. (2020). Social interaction in the Spanish classroom: how proficiency and linguistic background impact vocabulary learning. *Language Teaching Research*. Advance online publication. https://doi.org/10.1177/1362168820971468

Verloop, N., Van Driel, J., & Meijer, P. (2001). Teacher knowledge and the knowledge base of teaching. *International Journal of Educational Research*, *35*(5), 441-461. https://doi.org/10.1016/s0883-0355(02)00003-4

Wang, Y. (2013). Task design in videoconferencing-supported distance language learning. *CALICO Journal*, *24*(3), 591-630. https://doi.org/10.1558/cj.v24i3.591-630

Xiao, F., Taguchi, N., & Li, S. (2019). Effects of proficiency subskills on pragmatic development in L2 Chinese study abroad. *Studies in Second Language Acquisition*, *41*(2), 469-483. https://doi.org/10.1017/s0272263118000128

# Section 4.
# EUROPE

# 13. Tracks for Russian university students' multilingual development within remote education during the pandemic

### Anastasia Atabekova[1], Alexander Belousov[2], and Oleg Yastrebov[3]

## Abstract

The chapter explores language and non-language university students' practices of foreign language learning within the unscheduled shift to remote studies in Russia due to the COVID-19 emergency. The RUDN University Law Institute experience is considered as an example. The paper explores common and specific features of foreign language, translation, and interpreting skills training within the Law Institute language and non-language programmes. The research rests on the case study methodology, considered from the policy-making and managerial point of view. The findings reveal both common features and specificities of multilingual university education of non-language and language students. The study also confirms the need for the educational institutions to draft specific guidelines on language courses implementation for different target audiences during the COVID-19 pandemic.

Keywords: COVID-19, remote online teaching, foreign language, translation and interpreting skills, multilingual development, degree programmes, LSP, RUDN University, Russia.

---

1. RUDN University Law Institute, Moscow, Russia; atabekova-aa@rudn.ru; https://orcid.org/0000-0003-2252-9354

2. RUDN University Law Institute, Moscow, Russia; belousov-aa@rudn.ru; https://orcid.org/0000-0002-3435-0485

3. RUDN University Law Institute, Moscow, Russia; yastrebov-oa@rudn.ru; https://orcid.org/0000-0003-4943-6910

How to cite: Atabekova, A., Belousov, A., & Yastrebov, O. (2021). Tracks for Russian university students' multilingual development within remote education during the pandemic. In N. Radić, A. Atabekova, M. Freddi & J. Schmied (Eds), *The world universities' response to COVID-19: remote online language teaching* (pp. 217-233). Research-publishing.net. https://doi.org/10.14705/rpnet.2021.52.1274

Chapter 13

## 1. Introduction

The goal of the present case study is to consider various tracks for university students' multilingual development within mandatory remote learning during the current pandemic.

The case study population includes 1,129 students of at Bachelor of Arts (BA), Master of Arts (MA), and PhD jurisprudence programmes, professional conversion programmes and masters' courses on legal Translation and Interpreting (T&I) – the educational field is linguistics. The materials considered cover legal regulations, evidence from the university practice, students and teachers' comments (over 3,102 items that include legal orders, students' and teachers' items of oral and written communication), while the methodology is based on the analysis of regulations, observation of students and teachers' activities during online classes, analysis of students' live oral and chat-based reactions, students' academic records and messages to the administration, as well as consideration of teachers' reports and oral information during the Foreign Languages Department regular meetings.

Among further case study variables are federal and institutional regulations (Sections 2 and 3), particular programme contents, opinions of teachers and students, and their languages of study (Section 4). Some conclusions are drawn on features of remote education that are common to the various educational programmes analysed and others that are specific to each individual track (Section 5).

## 2. Federal level

Russia has been affected by the COVID-19 since February 2020 when the information systematically came from other countries. Since mid-March the Russian Federal Ministry of Science and Education has transitioned universities to fully distant education. The quarantine regime was gradually introduced across the country, Moscow was in lockdown from March 30th to June 9th, 2020. Due to the vast territory, the regional socio-economic differences that influence the educational capacities of respective universities, and the diversity in terms of higher education institutions programmes, as well as the student population socio-cultural specifics across the regions, the ministry had to shape solid federal policies and tailor them to regional and local levels. The ministry thus initiated comprehensive measures and adopted a number of regulations, starting from the 14th March (see Order No. 397[4] and Order No. 566[5]) and held regular nationwide video conferences[6] with all the Russian universities' rectors to monitor the situation and tailor measures to local conditions.

During the period from March 16th to March 19th each university launched a situation task force to provide university campus emergency transition from on-site to remote format, to monitor student and staff health, to foster sanitary measures and social distancing, to ensure medical service, administrative and financial support for students and staff, and to maintain the smooth operation of the university infrastructure. In order to raise public awareness thereof, during the above mentioned period each university launched a special website to inform students, their parents, and teachers on the various aspects of university operation during the COVID-19 emergency. These sites have posted federal legislation and respective university internal regulations that standardised the procedure and requirements for the universities' activities during the health emergency since March 19th, 2020, including information in several languages to meet international students' needs[7].

Russian higher education institutions, as other universities across the world (Marinoni, van't Land, & Jensen, 2020), had to enhance their digital environment for training. Almost every Russian university now has its own Learning

---

4. https://www.garant.ru/products/ipo/prime/doc/73645128/

5. http://www.consultant.ru/document/cons_doc_LAW_350030/

6. Video Conferences on Education during COVID-19 (2020). Russian Federation Ministry of Science and Education YouTube Channel, https://www.youtube.com/channel/UCtKQPCIdo9bDaSAw9y8A69Q

7. https://covid-19.rudn.ru/index.html#measures

Management System (LMS), while it's scope, capacity, and quality depend on the institution size, the financial situation of the region, etc. However, before COVID-19 most universities' LMS which traditionally included multimodal educational toolkits for disciplines, testing systems, survey tools, etc., operated as a supportive blended learning component to the traditional full-time/part-time learning in class (Pevneva & Edmunds, 2020).

## 3. Institutional level

### 3.1. RUDN University framework for remote learning

The university has designed a special site on the COVID-19 issues on its corporate digital platform[8]. This site specifies the education process, its requirements, and resources and procedures, among other topics. The site covers the following common issues which have been agreed upon at the point of transition to remote education:

- curricula changes;
- classes timetable on the university-tailored Microsoft (MS) Teams platform;
- procedure for student's individual studies in case of illness, stay in another country/region within another time zone, etc.;
- resources and tools for online learning;
- support service for teachers and students on the use of digital tools (University LMS, MS Teams, cloud servers, virtual whiteboards, and other resources);
- recommendations for video recording of online classes (for those who failed to join);
- tools and regulations for mid-term and final assessment, for graduation and admission;
- exam proctoring system;

---

8. http://eng.rudn.ru/

- rescheduled laboratory classes;
- individual online consultations for students;
- surveys of students and teachers regarding remote education in emergency;
- organisation of traineeships and internships;
- issues of tuition fees decrease due to remote format;
- situations where students are absent from classes;
- certificates issue procedure (transcripts/extracts from the grade book, etc.); and
- student volunteering activities to help peers and teachers.

## 3.2. RUDN University profile within multilingual education

RUDN University was established in Moscow in 1960. Traditionally this university enrols students from over 150 countries across the world and currently integrates about 30,000 students. RUDN operates as a comprehensive university with faculties and institutions that offer over 470 programmes on various specialties at various levels of higher education. One of the RUDN educational process specifics includes a multilingual education through various formats, including standard foreign language classes for all university students at bachelors, masters, and PhD levels, a qualification programme for specialised translation skills training for non-language students of various specialties, and degree courses for language students. Each university faculty has a department of foreign languages that runs the above courses.

The above landscape explains why RUDN University has had to provide comprehensive and audience-specific solutions to foreign language teaching (including Russian for foreigners) and T&I skills training of language and non-language BA, MA, and PhD students amidst the emergency transition to remote education. The mentioned training rested on a university-wide framework for distance learning and depended on the language/non-language nature of programmes, the kind of degree programme and the theoretical/applied nature of a particular programme subject.

## 4. Tracks for students' multilingual development at RUDN Law Institute

The Foreign Languages Department of RUDN Law Institute runs different programmes, including the following:

- foreign language training in four languages (English, French, German, Spanish) for students who study only Jurisprudence at BA, MA, and PhD levels;

- a four year long professional conversion programme with a qualification diploma in legal translation in eight languages (Arabic, Chinese, Japanese, and Korean, in addition to English, French, German, Spanish); and

- a two-year long MA course in legal T&I (English-taught theoretical disciplines, working language pairs combine two of the above mentioned eight languages with Russian).

The above courses have obvious difference in their content scope and workload, see supplementary materials.

### 4.1. Common features of different programmes

The mentioned programmes differ in many aspects. However, they required a number of common administrative features during the COVID-19 lockdown. First, training on the MS Teams platform was recommended due to the need for the students, teachers, and institute and department administration to have an easy access to the educational process and its monitoring. The change of platform was not recommended as the break between classes within the overall institute timetable was ten minutes.

A strict schedule was set for students to submit their home assignments to the teacher each week; submissions were not accepted after a particular deadline.

Each teacher of the department checked weekly about 200 students' assignments (from all the Law Institute language programmes). A similarly strict schedule was set for teachers to check students' papers and deliver them back before the respective online class for discussion, as students needed to distribute their preparation time over all the curriculum disciplines.

Compared to the above, before the COVID-19 lockdown there were two stages of evaluation, namely mid-term (the middle of the Autumn or Spring semesters) and the corresponding end-of-term assessment. By the respective dates of the mid- and end-term evaluation procedure, students could submit the assignments that they had failed to produce in due time or ask for consideration of their improved and revised assignments.

Furthermore, the content of each discipline taught either in four or in eight languages required a strict and transparent balance in terms of the same list of task types for each week, the same number of assignments (number of test items, the number of characters in the assignment texts), and the same assessment criteria (proportion of scores and errors, error types). All this became especially critical from the angle of equal educational rights of students who study different languages within the same programme and discipline. Students strived to maintain their high academic record to uphold their academic reputation and obtain a bursary.

During traditional teaching, workload balance and assessment were not so critical as programmes in various languages differ in terms of coursebook unit materials, number and type of exercises, and specific individual preferences within the group. Moreover, sometimes students fail to prepare written assignments for their class activities and nonetheless manage to compensate the lacking material through active engagement in classwork. Workload and assessment criteria became sensitive in the online format as the scope and quality of students' preparation for online classes were more obvious and transparent. The same applies to the work of the teacher who had to prepare more explanatory materials (additional visual/printed data to be uploaded in the online classroom) and provide more detailed information to each student regarding his/her submitted assignments and online class performance evaluation (oral, printed/typed info about the type and number of errors).

The online format set forth a strong argument for the flipped classroom methodology (e.g. Abeysekera & Dawson, 2015) with respect to both applied and theoretical disciplines across the programmes. Most students strongly supported the format as it allowed them to follow individual pathways of material processing while leaving room for preliminary individual consideration of the data, conceptual as well as applied exercises.

Furthermore, written communication with students and among teachers took more time. The department meetings were conducted once a month before the COVID-19 lockdown; during this period, they were held weekly. They covered the following themes:

- up-to-date information on the students' attendance, performance, problems, and the psychological climate in the groups;

- special training and support for those who were isolated for quarantine in the university campus dorms with COVID-19 infection in light forms and wanted to continue their studies; and

- coordination and possible change in resources and technical issues in the same groups of T&I programmes several teachers worked in.

At the same time, students wanted to get detailed recommendations on their performance and explanations about marking of their assignments. Before the pandemic students could get all the replies during face-to-face classes and consultations. During the lockdown they only had the opportunity to address their questions via their university e-mails. Teachers had to reply in writing as well. Both teachers and students, regardless of the programme they were affiliated to, unanimously complained about their increased workload in general, beyond the online contact hours, due to preparation issues, as well as to the burden of working in front of the computer screen for longer, in comparison to traditional education. Students and teachers also reported challenges related to the quality of internet connection.

## 4.2. Programme specificities and challenges

*4.2.1. Non-language students of BA in Jurisprudence programme (only European languages)*

- **1st year students (beginners, European languages), general language.** The course covers phonetics and pronunciation training, basic grammar, and speech pattern training in standard communicative contexts, related to students' everyday academic life and socio-cultural activities. Students had limited speaking capacity, and teachers tried to develop communication of question-reply format and engage students in role plays. This was often slowed down by technical and sound issues that caused disappointment and gave a negative impression of the technology-facilitated classes. It also fostered the feeling of disrupted personal contacts, though the teachers worked with cameras 'on' and asked the students to do the same during their replies and communicative activities. Other challenges referred to the use of Russian both in oral and chat-based communication by students who wanted clear explanations, and teachers who had to meet students' requests for online contact-hour time.

- **1st year students (non-beginners, European languages), general language.** The course covers grammar knowledge revision and communication skills development within the context of official and everyday life. Public topics of social importance are the subject of discussions. The challenges mentioned with reference to beginners' groups were less obvious. Teachers had to be more attentive to students' personal compatibility in the online group and consider their personal learning styles. Video, audio recordings, and assignments related to mini group projects produced positive student feedback. Students gradually adjusted to the use of a foreign language for oral and chat-based

## Chapter 13

communication. The teachers' comments on grammar or vocabulary mistakes were not always accepted as students were rather confident in their communication abilities. Within the online settings they were eager to focus on this activity and not on the discussion of errors, which could take place after the lesson. At the same time, some students (about 15-25%) wanted to discuss their mistakes and scores as a top priority within the online class itself. They often preferred to do this in Russian, which led to some disruption within the learning environment.

- **2nd and 3rd year students, legal language disciplines**. The course covers the texts in English about branches of law and aims to help students learn background legal terminology and speech patterns that are specific to oral and written communication in legal settings. The activities included online training of terminology pronunciation and use in context, discussion, presentations, written translation as a home task. The challenges referred to some extensive use of Russian in cases when troubles emerged in the group while searching for and selecting legal term equivalents within bilingual contexts. Third year students worked more rapidly and efficiently. Their better results are likely to be associated with the fact that they were more experienced in law branches and knew the subject context.

- **2nd year students, background course on legal documents translation**. The course content covers the translation of personal documents, standard format of contracts, powers of attorneys, and appeals to the government bodies. The course objectives are in line with those of the legal language disciplines above. However, this course uses a variety of learning materials and document samples. A problem occurred with the document layout which is known to have specifics in each national legal culture. At the beginning of the course teachers could hardly persuade students that this point did matter for legal translation quality. Ensuing discussions took time and effort and often meant waste of time for explanations in Russian and not in a foreign language. The positive signs consisted in the students' extensive outsourcing of supporting bilingual information to defend their choices. This practice developed bilingual analytical skills, helped students to get used to providing comprehensive oral explanations and written commentaries and glossaries to the documents.

- **1st and 2nd year MA in Jurisprudence students (beginners and non-beginners, European languages).** The language module covers academic foreign language and foreign language for legal purposes. The materials for groups of beginners and non-beginners differ in terms of complexity. However, students understand better the need to improve their language skills in relation to their further career. Therefore, students were ready for online project work, for oral reports preparation, and for debates on legal topics. Unfortunately, learners were less ready to discuss errors during the online classes. Thus, the online tests for grammar and vocabulary training served as an efficient solution. Relevant data were obtained from the observation of students' performance of tasks and teachers' reports analysis. The programme assumes that the masters thesis oral defence shall be in a foreign language. This is mandatory for all RUDN master's students regardless of their specialisation. Thus, to train students for the corresponding procedure in terms of language, communication strategies and tactics, report text structure, etc., the course includes simulations based on the material related to the masters students' specialisation in law. What can be done orally and individually within traditional classroom or consultations, required additional time for teacher's online work with a student, both in oral and written forms.

- **1st and 2nd year PhD students (non-beginners).** This level focuses on training students for legal research conducted in a foreign language. It incorporates training with regard to students' specialisation and a particular topic of legal research, the development of skills for legal text analysis, and information processing and its translation. The course content looks more specialised when compared to the masters level. This warrants a higher level of individualised materials to be incorporated into the course. On the other hand, group members are already specialists in law and they can use their professional background to ask questions and engage in discussions during online classes. However, these higher levels of specialisation of masters and PhD students require language teachers to acquire, maintain, and enhance his/her legal knowledge in a foreign language as well. Moreover, extra hours of online individual consultations are required to work with students who have to pass the exam in a foreign language. In Russia this is a condition for PhD students' admission to the thesis defence procedure. Under the Russian federal regulations, the exam requires that the student fulfilled the individual translation assignment (the text size is about 15,000 characters) and drafted a report on a monograph written in a foreign language. Such a procedure required teachers to deliver practically individual online supervisions to each student.

### 4.2.2. Non-language students of BA in Jurisprudence programme with professional conversion course with a qualification diploma in legal T&I (eight languages)

This programme provides a deeper and more intensive learning of foreign language T&I skills training when compared with the language module for non-language students.

The online learning features of this programme students can be detailed into several aspects: as far as 1st year students (beginners and non-beginners, European languages groups) are concerned, students' higher motivation and stronger commitment to learn a foreign language should be mentioned. It resulted in an overall better academic achievement in the groups. The course contents and learning environment did not differ much from the features described earlier with respect to non-language students (see 4.2.1.).

However, some specific comments should be provided with reference to 1st year students who decided to learn Oriental languages as beginners. They had their first semester in March 2020, when they started practicing hieroglyphs, tones, etc. In a traditional class format, in the case of our Law Institute, these classes are conducted by native speakers of Arabic, Chinese, Korean, and Japanese. The teachers consciously use a very limited amount of Russian for explanations as they have visual support tools at hand (pictures, symbolic figures, white board, etc.). However, the use of these tools within online communication required techniques of uploading the respective data in the chat or through ppt or video files. This meant additional work for the teacher. The technology issues related to the quality of sound turned out to be sensitive when it concerned oral communication in tonal languages.

- **2nd and 3rd year students (European and Oriental languages).** The course contents included the translation of legal documents (the experience was similar to that described in section 3.2.1), Computer-Assisted Tools (CAT) for legal translation, and consecutive interpreting practice. CAT tools for legal translation revealed students' interest in applied projects related to the topic under study. Unfortunately, the online format of ppt presentation or word format did not always allow students to incorporate the data of translation memory due to the electronic tables' complexity. The group often had to limit themselves to listening to oral speaker's narratives. This decreased the audience's interest in the topic. There were also some initial difficulties with the description of the tools in the relevant foreign language. The consecutive interpreting training was a real challenge. If the video/audio recording was used students often faced trouble with the sound quality. Other challenges stemmed from the situation when students concentrated on the picture right in front of their faces and put less effort into activating their audio channel.

- **4th year students.** They had to do their translation internships and pass the final qualification exams that included written and oral part. The internship stage did not cause any trouble as it traditionally takes place in the offline individualised format. The exam proctoring system allotted more time for the students' passports demonstration. The exam included the written translation of an academic legal text. The oral part covered sight interpreting of a legal text in a foreign language into Russian, consecutive bilingual interpreting on legal topics, the report in a foreign language on individual legal research. The consecutive interpreting was the most challenging part, as in earlier years. The challenges with this exam item did not depend on the online format of the exams, even though poor sound and sound breaks were taken into account.

*4.2.3. Master's students in legal T&I*

The course covered theoretical disciplines, applied subjects with no translation or interpreting components, and T&I. The distant format of the MA course revealed the most efficient training formats in each of the disciplines.

Flipped classroom techniques were used to organise the study of theoretical subjects that are mandatory under the Russian federal higher education system requirements. Students got all the material from the university LMS. To foster student skills in the English-based discussion of theoretical topics, teachers selected for each discipline open access video lectures delivered by English speaking prominent scholars in the related research field and the online classes focused on the oral discussions.

Applied disciplines with no translation/interpreting component were successful in the case study format. They were first designed by teachers and more materials were then prepared by students. Applied disciplines with a translation component caused no trouble because students were interested in the assignments as the materials provided a direct link to their future profession. English (or second foreign language)-based discussions of translation procedures and their relevant outcomes created some additional impetus.

Sight interpreting of written texts caused additional workload for teachers who had to prepare the text as the presentation slides to be uploaded to the screen, with written teacher comments on the errors (that had to be anticipated and envisaged ahead of the lesson) in the chart. Consecutive and conference interpreting sometimes turned into trouble due to technical issues, for instance, low sound quality due to dispersion.

## 5. Concluding remarks

The emergency transition to online learning revealed some common and some specific features with regard to the learning practices of the language and non-language university students within the unscheduled shift to remote studies. The common features refer to administrative, organisational, technology, and disciplinary issues. The above situation in the particular Russian university under study goes in line with other universities' experience both in Russia (Almazova, Krylova, Rubtsova, & Odinokaya, 2020) and other countries (Neupane et al., 2020; Zalite & Zvirbule, 2020) that mention similar critical points.

The Spring 2020 lockdown in Russia confirms a number of points. In terms of teaching quality, strict and comprehensive planning of all aspects of the educational process as mutually dependant components are strongly required from the national and local university management. The teachers' role as psychological facilitators increases, in addition to their didactic duties and responsibilities, while the importance of students' academic and social maturity becomes more crucial. Specific awareness-raising activities seem relevant for 1st year students to help them understand academic policies and practices in the digital environment.

As far as specificities are concerned, the academic context analysed here mostly focuses on a particular field of university education (cf. Brammer & Clark, 2020; Usak, Masalimova, Cherdymova, & Shaidullina, 2020). The present study reveals which specifics relate to the particular language programmes' contexts and to the corresponding teachers and students' activities.

The emergency transition to remote learning made it possible to identify the strong and weak parts of educational programme contents, check the relevance of various training techniques, and tailor them to particular language programmes and disciplines. The observation of the learning process in groups that operate within different language programmes confirms that the teacher needs to prepare more specific materials, written explanations, and comments for each particular subject.

Furthermore, the RUDN Law Institute emergency move to remote multilingual education of various student audiences reveals that guidelines for the academic faculty should be drafted to coordinate, balance, and specify training tasks during the situation under study. Moreover, the learning/teaching of languages and translation skills within the particular programme contents requires a more individualised approach from each teacher to each student in terms of lesson planning and management within remote training during the pandemic emergency.

The present study has some limitations as the multilingual education features were considered within a single university institute. Further studies will integrate faculty and students of other specialties and expand to other universities.

## 6. Supplementary materials

https://research-publishing.box.com/s/04343651h3d3m49dkybrzwnx5chkvrzx

## References

Abeysekera, L., & Dawson, P. (2015). Motivation and cognitive load in the flipped classroom: definition, rationale and a call for research. *Higher Education Research & Development, 34*(1), 1-14. https://doi.org/10.1080/07294360.2014.934336

Almazova, N., Krylova, E., Rubtsova, A., & Odinokaya, M. (2020). Challenges and opportunities for Russian higher education amid COVID-19: teachers' perspective. *Education Sciences, 10*(12), 368. https://doi.org/10.3390/educsci10120368

Brammer, S., & Clark, T. (2020). COVID-19 and management education: reflections on challenges, opportunities, and potential futures. *British Journal of Management, 31*(3), 453-456. https://doi.org/10.1111/1467-8551.12425

Marinoni, G., van't Land, H., & Jensen, T. (2020). T*he impact of COVID-19 on higher education around the world. IAU Global Survey Report*. International Association of Universities. UNESCO House.

Neupane, D., Kattel, K.,Tha, R., Shrestha, A., Acharya, B., Thapa, R., KC, F., Bc, B., Joshi, Y., Basnet, N., Maharjan, M., & Bhuju, D. (2020). Academic institutions at the time of COVID-19 pandemic. *International Journal of Science and Research (IJSR), 9*(5), 91-95.

Pevneva, I., & Edmunds, P. (2020). Online learning vs. extreme learning in mining higher education under COVID. *E3S Web of Conferences, 174*, 04001. https://doi.org/10.1051/e3sconf/202017404001

Usak, M., Masalimova, A. R., Cherdymova, E. I., & Shaidullina, A. R. (2020). New playmaker in science education: COVID-19. *Journal of Baltic Science Education, 19*(2), 180-185. https://doi.org/10.33225/jbse/20.19.180

Zalite, G. G., & Zvirbule, A. (2020). Digital readiness and competitiveness of the EU higher education institutions: the COVID-19 pandemic impact. *Emerging Science Journal, 4*(4), 297-304. https://doi.org/10.28991/esj-2020-01232

# 14 Teaching online in translation studies: a teacher-researcher's feedback from France

## Geneviève Bordet[1]

## Abstract

This chapter focuses on the impact of the COVID-19 pandemic on language classes in a Paris university in 2020. The first case studied is a Master of Arts (MA) class in translation studies. The forced and sudden switch to online learning was well accepted by students who cooperated with the academic staff to choose an online platform, in the absence of any available institutional resource. Although online teaching proved efficient in terms of learning output, it implied a lot of extra work to ensure interaction between teacher and students. Besides, important discrepancies appeared between students as regards equipment and connection. The second case is taken from language classes with Bachelor of Arts (BA) students. Communication was compromised by students' reluctance to activate their webcams, seen as a threat for their privacy. Material problems such as poor connection were thus compounded by the digital divide among them. This situation reveals disparities between students while opening opportunities for change. The priority should be given to an assessment of students' needs in a context of pandemics, at an international level.

Keywords: COVID-19, remote language teaching, digital divide; needs' assessment; interaction, France.

1. Université de Paris, Paris, France; gbordet@eila.univ-paris-diderot.fr; https://orcid.org/0000-0003-0037-9236

How to cite: Bordet, G. (2021). Teaching online in translation studies: a teacher-researcher's feedback from France. In N. Radić, A. Atabekova, M. Freddi & J. Schmied (Eds), *The world universities' response to COVID-19: remote online language teaching* (pp. 235-248). Research-publishing.net. https://doi.org/10.14705/rpnet.2021.52.1275

Chapter 14

## 1. Introduction

This chapter addresses the consequences of language studies' sudden switch to remote learning due to the COVID-19 pandemic and the resulting lockdown in the context of a French university. The process was made even more difficult considering that the new 'Université de Paris' was born in January 2020 from the merging of Université Paris Diderot-Paris 7 and Université Paris Descartes-Paris 5. This is part of the current restructuration of French universities, with a view to creating larger entities, so as to make them more visible in the competitive academic world while at the same time cutting costs (Nature, 2020). In March 2020, the restructuring process was just starting, which made adaptation to an emergency situation even more difficult. The programme discussed in this chapter deals with translation studies as part of the Paris Diderot Applied Languages Department. In this multidisciplinary university, mastering of languages is a shared issue. Beside the applied languages and the English studies departments, students from other disciplines take part in courses addressing the specific linguistic needs of various disciplines. They all have access to a language resource centre. Besides, a recently created Linguistic Resources Development Service (PERL)[2] aims at providing teachers and students resources based on new technologies, including blended and online programmes. The Applied Languages Department offers four MA, three of which are based on apprenticeships in the industry. They focus respectively on Languages for Specific Purposes and Translation (LSPT), technical writing, intercultural communication, and digital culture management. Another MA aims at training future researchers in translation and corpus studies of English for specific purposes. One shared objective of these MA's is training future language service providers in various professional contexts. Another shared feature is the importance given to a functional approach to languages, based on translation studies, corpus studies, and terminology (Baker, 1996; Bordet, 2017). Thus, the LSPT MA includes part-time training in vocational settings as well as an individual applied research project. This project implies the choice of a highly specialised field in which the translation and terminology project is set. The field

---

2. Pôle d'Élaboration de Ressources Linguistiques: https://perl2018.wixsite.com/perl-uspc

chosen may be as diverse as agroecology or digital marketing, etc. The students explore a hitherto unknown field, interrogating a bilingual corpus which they compile themselves in the source and target language and carry out a contrastive study of its terminology and phraseology (Aston, 1999; Kübler, 2011; Zanettin, 1998), with the support of one or several experts from the field (Bordet, 2013; Froeliger, 2013). The resources collected provide the student with the required contextual knowledge for a satisfactory translation from a functional (Nida, 2001; Nord, 1997) and a pragmatic point of view (Newmark, 1988). The project is supervised by academic staff and translation professionals. While this project was traditionally completed during the second year of an MA, a modification of the curriculum made it possible recently to introduce a preparatory step during the second term of the MA first year. The objective of this first step was an initiation to both the use of information technology for information retrieval and processing as well as to the fundamentals of terminology. One expected positive impact is to reinforce coherence between the first and the second year of the programme, while making the workload lighter for the second year students. This paper focuses on the impact the lockdown had on this specific class.

## 2. Context

For the LSPT second year translation studies students, the two first weeks of March are traditionally dedicated to individual presentations in which the students give a 20-minute talk justifying their work in grasping the fundamental issues in the area chosen and in tackling questions of terminology and translation. In 2020, the COVID-19 pandemic disrupted this procedure as on the 14th March the French government announced the beginning of a lockdown (in French 'confinement') initially for two weeks. To ensure that there was no gap in the learning process, the decision to take the class online was immediately taken, with the agreement of the academic staff and professionals involved. Moodle platform is the only technological support that was made available by the university. This platform, however, turned out to be excessively restricting since it only catered for transferring written and visual teaching contents so that it could not be used to organise online classes.

Chapter 14

The second limitation was that the platform was only available for permanent university staff, thus excluding the many non-university professionals involved in the programme. In the absence of official alternatives, the MA's students and the teaching staff explored what free-access platforms were available. Our exploration was widely based on email exchanges between teachers and also with students, who proved most cooperative and strongly motivated in these exceptional circumstances, despite the economic and housing difficulties some of them had to face. This point will be taken up again later as well as its impact on learning conditions, in the second part.

The aim of this brief introduction has been to describe the context in which we had to proceed to a sudden change so as to adapt to a new situation. This involved a complete reappraisal of our teaching approach. As mentioned above, this paper deals with the impact of this change on the introductory course to the second year MA research project during the second term of the 2019-2020 academic year. However, it will also include new prospects based on our teaching experience during the first term of the 2020-2021 year, with undergraduate classes dedicated to language learning.

### 2.1. A new programme in a context of 'forced' innovation

As mentioned above, the case discussed here is a specialised translation studies MA class. Introducing the students to information retrieval and terminology since the MA's first year was an innovation following a 2016 modification of the Bachelor, Master, and Doctorate (BMD) system[3]. While up to 2016, students coming from other MA's could apply to register for the second year of translation studies MA, admission from the first year became compulsory. This implied a reinforced continuity between the two years of the MA. The LSPT MA is in fact a highly selective programme considering that there are many more applications for admission than places available. It is also very intensive. In the second year, students have to adapt to a new professional environment in the industry one week out of two and attend workshops and classes at the university during

---
3. BMD: a European educational system defined by the Bologna process with a view to standardising education at a European level: https://www.eua.eu/issues/10:bologna-process.html

the other week. At the same time, they have to deal with short term deadlines for assignments and long term time management for the research project. The modification to the BMD cycle offered the opportunity to launch the research project with an information retrieval and a terminology class during the second term of the first year, so as to lighten the workload in the second year.

The MA's capacity is 40 students. The students are divided into two groups according to their second foreign language, a high-level command of English and French being a condition required to integrate the programme. The students are selected based on language tests exclusively. Consequently, while a majority of the students come from language studies departments, others may come from Science, Technology, Engineering, and Mathematics (STEM) and law fields for instance, as long as they give evidence of an outstanding proficiency in those languages. The age range is usually very wide, since this MA is frequently selected by older students as an opportunity for professional reorientation.

In 2019, the course received, through the French government organisation 'Campus France'[4], an unusually high number of applications from various countries, in Africa and South America, but also from Italy, Russia, China, and Taiwan. For this reason, a third of the 2019-2020 class came from these countries and this year that was affected by the COVID-19 pandemic was the first year in France for these non-French students.

## 2.2. The MA first year information retrieval class before COVID-19

During the second semester of the academic year 2019-2020, each of the two groups of MA first year students was scheduled to attend six sessions, one week out of two, for two hours, with the same teacher. The objective was to provide the students with the techniques and tools required for the choice of a specialised domain and the collection of a comparable corpus, representative of its discursive production, as a basis for their research project. This implied developing the students' awareness of the diversity and the complexity of

---

4. https://www.campusfrance.org/fr

Languages for Specific Purposes (LSPs) (Swales, 2000), while providing support to each student's research process. Therefore the class was designed to combine theoretical and pragmatic input from the teacher and exchanges between the students as to their ideas and findings. The final result was to be a written report presenting a research proposal and including a description of the domain, a commented sample of the future corpus, and a selection of texts submitted for translation. These written reports were to be presented during an individual oral exam. The final objective was not only to provide the students with the required techniques but also to make sure that each of them was able to persuade the supervisors of their final reports of the relevance of their research proposal at the end of the first year. Therefore the first year report was intended as both a feasibility study and a communication document.

### 2.3. Working out online teaching strategy

When the lockdown was announced by the French government on 14th March 2020, each of the two LSPT groups had attended only two face-to-face sessions, one every two weeks. The class had started with students' pair work about their ideas for their research project. This led to a whole group brainstorming on possible ideas of specialised domains and topics. The second session focused on a presentation of the resources offered by the online platform of the university library and their application to research on various topics. It was also an opportunity to develop students' awareness of the variety of available discursive genres (Dressen-Hammouda, 2003) for each topic. The instant switch to online classes was made easier by the fact that the students and some teachers had already had to use online learning platforms in December 2019 and January 2020, due to massive public transport strikes in Paris, which made physical access to university very difficult.

Three platforms were successively tested. After the first online session, two of these, namely Blackboard[5] and Renater[6], decided to impose restrictions on

---

5. https://www.blackboard.com/teaching-learning

6. National network for research and education: https://rendez-vous.renater.fr/home/

the group size, which caused a third switch to Zoom[7]. With Zoom, there was no problem with group size and the access procedure was very easy. However, we could only use it through private connection, which implied that we had to disconnect and reconnect every 45 minutes, which of course resulted in a loss of teaching time. It should be mentioned that this problem was solved for the year 2020-2021, since the university decided on an institutional subscription.

A new teaching strategy was adopted. Online classes were dedicated to input on research methodology, presentation of Information Technology (IT) resources, and techniques for corpus collection: use of the university library catalogue online, Open Archives, Google Scholar, Boolean search in databases, etc. In the homework following the online sessions, each student applied the resources and research techniques presented in class to his/her own project and domain of choice. The teacher then sent individual feedback to each student, sometimes requiring follow up from the student.

Each online session started with feedback to the group, based on examples taken from the students' work. To do so, the screen-sharing function was used alternatively by the teacher and one of the students for group discussion. Students could either take part orally or using the 'conversation' space. The same space could be used to share useful links and resources.

The switch to online teaching did not imply major modifications to the way in which students' work was evaluated. The students' reports were sent by email as well as downloaded on the Moodle platform. They were then presented orally by the student to the teacher in charge of the class and a colleague specialised in corpus studies, thanks to individual Zoom sessions. They were commented on by the teachers, who sent the students a written feedback. Track-change was used for syntax errors, and comments to highlight specifically interesting points to be developed in the project or to require more information. Once the required revisions had been made, the reports were marked and finally sent on by email to potential supervisors, according to the chosen combination of languages, which

---

7. https://zoom.us/

included mostly English to French, but also Italian to French, Chinese to French, and Chinese to English.

### 2.4. Impact of the switch to exclusive online teaching

Since the course under discussion was new, it is not possible to compare the quality of work delivered by the students with previous realisations. However, considering the aims of the team who initiated this class, it may be said that it totally fulfilled the expectations. It was clear, from the students' reports and the oral exchanges that followed, that students had fully integrated the functional approach of LSP and translation studies (Kübler & Volanschi, 2012), based on corpus observation and contextualisation of translation choices.

Although, as expected, there was still much exploration necessary to master the field they had chosen, the students knew enough about it to be able to select the variety of genres and disciplinary discourses which were representative of this field. For instance, one student chose to deal with ecotechnologies as applied to sustainable building. Using a Venn diagram, she showed that this very specific topic involved a wide range of fields such as urbanism, sustainable development and circular economies, and documents such as patents, regulations, research papers, and product sheets. So students knew where to find adequate resources and were able to justify their relevance for their project. In other words, they were now in a position to start a fruitful cooperation with their supervisors at the beginning of the second year. They were also able to ask field experts the relevant questions.

The online class sessions and the teacher's regular individual feedback combined with informal online meetings strengthened the mutual relationship, especially since informal online meetings gave time for discussions about students' motivations and professional plans. They also made it possible for the students, aged between 22 and 40, to express their stress and worries about the public health emergency and its multiple implications.

Indeed, while the learning outcome was very obviously positive, the students' and teachers' quality of life were strongly impacted by this change of situation.

This was partly due to individual socio-economic factors, such as housing conditions and social environment. Some students found themselves totally isolated and motivation was hard to sustain. It is most likely that the Facebook group traditionally created by the students for informal exchanges was very useful in this case. The students who had just arrived from abroad, mostly Northern Africa, found themselves in a very difficult position since their housing conditions were most precarious, sometimes staying with more or less close family relatives, often sharing a room with the children, with infrequent access to a computer.

One main difficulty was the closing of public and university libraries, which had up to then provided the required conditions for concentration. While a large part of documentary resources was available online, and commented on in class, this did not offset the impossibility to have access to reference books.

More generally, the social and cultural phenomenon commonly referred to as the digital divide was made more visible than ever, mostly in terms of equipment and connection. Some individual oral interviews were moved from Zoom to WhatsApp due to lack of appropriate connection. In the absence of an institutional response, solidarity between students and teachers turned out to be the most effective answer, in the form of individual loans of computers. In one extreme case, a final oral exam was conducted with a student seated in a car, which appeared to have been lent to him for the duration of the exam since he had been sleeping in the streets for several days. Obviously, these difficulties were strongly aggravated by the housing shortage in Paris.

Another negative side-effect was the obvious increase in the teacher's workload due to individual interviews and informal meetings, added to individual weekly feedback.

To sum up, while the quality of teaching and learning does not seem to have been impaired, this comes with the price of students' stress and teachers' workload increased.

## 3. Additional feedback from current language teaching situations with undergraduate students

The experience described above was totally improvised and lasted only two months considering the fact that the lockdown was imposed mid-March while university face-to-face classes had to end by the beginning of May. By contrast, the 2020-2021 academic year started in the context of a six month old public health emergency due to COVID-19. Although we were only six weeks into the first semester at the time of writing this chapter, this second experience has brought further insight into the changes due to the COVID-19 crisis; this time with undergraduate language first and second year BA students. Language classes at this level imply a different stance for the teacher. While I was both transmitting information and coaching my MA's students in a new approach of language, language classes with new students set the focus on interactions, with the teacher among students. Another important difference is that first year students not only had no experience of university but also, in this specific case, had not attended high school classes for the last four months of the previous school year. The Baccalauréat examination (equivalent of A-Level in the UK) was based on the first six months of the year. The resulting social isolation of these new students made bonding with these students as a teacher a challenge. The first obstacle was convincing them to switch on their cameras so that I could identify them. Despite my repeated requests and explanations about the importance of visual interactions, the students remained extremely reluctant. In a recent assignment where they were required to take a stance for or against distance learning, several students explained that this reluctance was not due to the refusal to have an interaction with the teacher, but to privacy concerns and other students being able to watch their environment (see Figure 1 below). This reaction seemed to lessen with years and was much easier to overcome with third year students. However, creating interactions in distance learning remained a core issue. In the same assignment, students expressed their frustration of not being able to talk to the teacher and to ask questions after class. The technological substitutes, such as a frequently asked questions space on the Moodle platform or simply email questions to the teacher did not seem to fully meet their needs. However, other informal techniques seemed to provide a lead in that direction. One striking example is that of a second year student who waited for others to switch off their connection and to end the programme, to lunge forward to say "if you still have time, I do have a question". As a result, I now wait a few seconds before clicking on the button to end the class. Beyond the anecdote, this little story sheds light on the importance of managing time instead of space, switching to new signals.

It should also be mentioned that the digital divide which was made visible among MA students was even more visible among BA students, not only in terms of equipment and connection, but also due to lack of skills in handling digital communication.

Screen capture below provides an illustration of students' reactions when required to switch on their camera.

Figure 1. Digital divide: students' apologies for not switching on their camera

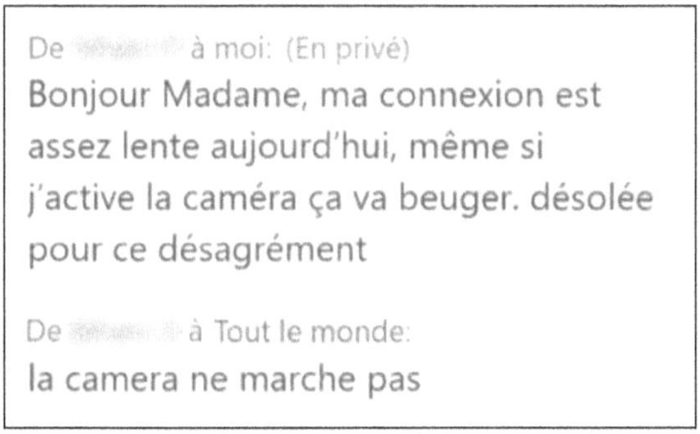

> De ▓▓ à moi: (En privé)
> Bonjour Madame, ma connexion est assez lente aujourd'hui, même si j'active la caméra ça va beuger. désolée pour ce désagrément
>
> De ▓▓ à Tout le monde:
> la camera ne marche pas

## 4. Conclusion

The conditions of an emergency and resulting improvisation encountered have led to rapid changes but also to an increased obligation to assess students' needs in this new context. Distance teaching and learning does not only impact the way content is presented but the whole relational context. It highlights the role of group socialisation in the learning process and gives evidence of the importance of informal exchanges before and after class.

## 4.1. Opportunities

Learning platforms also open up new teaching possibilities, thanks to the array of technological functions they offer. One example is the possibility of sharing the screen with the students. From a practical point of view, this function solves the irritating problem of teaching in large classrooms where the students sitting in the back rows can hardly see the screen. It also makes it much easier for the teacher to improvise and to decide to share resources according to students' emerging difficulties or demands. More importantly, it allows the students themselves to show their own screen, comment their work, and share criticisms and suggestions with the group. The chat function makes it possible to share references and online links or to contact the teacher without having to speak up. The Zoom 'poll launching' function is used by some teachers to get anonymous feedback from students as to the points they have not understood or even their decreasing or increasing level of motivation! New tools create new opportunities and new modes of communication, even though many problems remain to be explored, one of the main issues being the organisation of exams and more generally techniques of knowledge validation of learning outcome.

Beyond these practical issues, this situation of 'forced' innovation paves the way for a collective reflection on the objectives of university education and its various forms. Teaching and learning needs must be assessed, making clear the distinction, and complementarity between knowledge transfer, academic socialisation, and acquisition of individual skills. For instance, this recent experience shows that MA students are more likely to benefit from online knowledge transfer, while BA students obviously need to integrate the academic community through interactions with peers and teachers so as to develop new communication skills. Therefore, this unprecedented situation imposed on the academic community offers an exceptional opportunity for a critical use of technologies, where needs' assessment comes first.

## 4.2. Risks and limitations

Of course, these positive outcomes also imply risks. In a context of cost saving and ever-increasing economic liberalisation, there is a strong temptation to turn course content into prepacked products which can be marketed for various audiences (cf. Schmied, 2021). We might even see the emergence of a distinction between 'designers' and 'disseminators', the teachers finding themselves in charge of sharing knowledge that has been imposed on them. This type of information broking is already familiar to the academic world, where researchers have lost control of their own publications, to the benefit of powerful electronic publishers (Larivière, Haustein, & Mongeon, 2015). In countries like France, imposed distance learning might also provide a tempting opportunity to make up for the current lack of investment in student housing, university libraries, and other such facilities. Finally, these risks and these opportunities both contribute to providing evidence for the urgent need for the international academic community to share these new experiences and confront them with the diversity of the students' educational needs.

## References

Aston, G. (1999). Corpus use and learning to translate. *Textus, 12*, 1000-1025.

Baker, M. (1996). (Ed.). Corpus-based translation studies: the challenges that lie ahead. In H. Somers (Ed.), *Terminology, LSP and translation: studies in language engineering in honour of Juan C. Sager*. John Benjamins Publishing Company. https://benjamins.com/catalog/btl.18.17bak

Bordet, G. (2013). Brouillage des frontières, rencontres des domaines : quelles conséquences pour l'enseignement de la terminologie et de la traduction spécialisée? *Asp, la revue du Geras, spécial Domaines, territoires, et frontières en anglais de spécialité, 64*, 95-115. https://doi.org/10.4000/asp.3851

Bordet, G. (2017). Translation, ESP and corpus studies: bridging the gap in a French context. *International Journal of Language Studies, special issue: English for specific purposes: the state of the art, 11*, 31-52.

Dressen-Hammouda, D. (2003). Contributions of an integrated genre theory of text and context to teaching LSP. *ASp. la revue du GERAS, 39-40*, 73-90. https://doi.org/10.4000/asp.1306

Froeliger, N. (2013). *Les noces de l'analogique et du numérique.* Editions des Belles Lettres.

Kübler, N. (2011). Working with different corpora in translation teaching. In A. Frankenberg-Garcia, L. Flowerdew & G. Aston (Eds), *New trends in corpora and language learning* (pp. 62-80). Continuum.

Kübler, N., & Volanschi, A. (2012). Semantic prosody and specialised translation, or how a lexico-grammatical theory of language can help with specialised translation. In A. Boulton, S. Carter-Thomas & E. Rowley-Jolivet (Eds), *Corpus-informed research and learning in ESP: issues and applications* (pp. 103-134). John Benjamins Publishing Company. https://doi.org/10.1075/scl.52.05kub

Larivière V., Haustein S., & Mongeon P. (2015). The oligopoly of academic publishers in the digital era. *PLOS ONE.* https://doi.org/10.1371/journal.pone.0127502

Nature. (2020). Egalité: France's research reforms must balance competitiveness with well-being. *Nature, 587,* 7-8. https://doi.org/10.1038/d41586-020-02853-w

Newmark, P. (1988). Pragmatic translation and literalism. *TTR: traduction, terminologie, rédaction, 1*(2), 133-145. https://doi.org/10.7202/037027ar

Nida, E. (2001). *Contexts in translation.* John Benjamins.

Nord, C. (1997). *Translating as a purposeful activity. Functionalist approaches explained.* Routledge. https://doi.org/10.4324/9781315760506

Schmied, J. (2021). Remote online teaching in modern languages in Germany: responses according to audiences and teaching objectives. In N. Radić, A. Atabekova, M. Freddi & J. Schmied (Eds), *The world universities' response to COVID-19: remote online language teaching* (pp. 353-368). Research-publishing.net. https://doi.org/10.14705/rpnet.2021.52.1283

Swales, J. M. (2000). Languages for specific purposes. *Annual review of applied linguistics, 20,* 59-76. https://doi.org/10.1017/s0267190500200044

Zanettin, F. (1998). Bilingual comparable corpora and the training of translators. *Meta: journal des traducteurs/Meta: Translators' Journal, 43*(4), 616-630. https://doi.org/10.7202/004638ar

# 15. Braving remote instruction at Vilnius University: response to the COVID-19 pandemic

### Loreta Chodzkienė[1], Julija Korostenskienė[2], and Olga Medvedeva[3]

## Abstract

This chapter examines the experience of teaching English-related courses at Vilnius University (VU), 'the oldest and largest Lithuanian institution of higher education, in the spring 2020. We discuss arrangements made in the organizational process and implementation of the subjects within the areas taught in English by the staff members of the Institute of Foreign Languages, Faculty of Philology, VU. Limiting our account to the period when the instruction was changed abruptly from face-to-face to remote, we focus on three areas of instruction: the intra-course logistics of transferring students to the remote synchronous method of instruction, the delivery of a course syllabus in the lockdown conditions, and student reflections on the experience.

**Keywords:** COVID-19, remote, online, language teaching, language learning, leadership programme, qualitative data analysis, LSP, Lithuania.

---

1. Vilnius University, Vilnius, Lithuania; loreta.chodzkiene@flf.vu.lt; https://orcid.org/0000-0002-7735-0645

2. Vilnius University, Vilnius, Lithuania; julija.korostenskiene@flf.vu.lt; https://orcid.org/0000-0001-9703-8678

3. Vilnius University, Vilnius, Lithuania; medolga0707@gmail.com; https://orcid.org/0000-0002-1380-9381

**How to cite:** Chodzkienė, L., Korostenskienė, J., & Medvedeva, O. (2021). Braving remote instruction at Vilnius University: response to the COVID-19 pandemic. In N. Radić, A. Atabekova, M. Freddi & J. Schmied (Eds), *The world universities' response to COVID-19: remote online language teaching* (pp. 249-263). Research-publishing.net. https://doi.org/10.14705/rpnet.2021.52.1276

## 1. Introduction

The first case of coronavirus infection was identified in Lithuania on February 28th 2020[4]. After putting all efforts toward preventative measures[5] long before COVID-19 received pandemic status, the Government of the Republic of Lithuania made the difficult decision to introduce the national quarantine on Monday, March 16th 2020[6]. The week running 9-13 March celebrated Lithuania's Independence Day on Wednesday, March 11th 2020 and was the official state holiday. On March 12th at 12:25 pm, VU officially announced the impending quarantine regime through a pan-university email released in Lithuanian and English and addressed to both the staff and the students. The staff were advised to cancel face-to-face classes and switch to a remote mode of instruction starting Friday, March 13th. The initial quarantine period was to extend until March 27th, with the possibility of further extension.

It is natural that, even in challenging times, the academic school seeks both to ensure maximum possible safety to its members on the one hand, and on the other, to provide for an interrupted study process. Below, we share the experience of tackling the organizational issues and delivering courses within the three distinct areas taught in English by the Institute of Foreign Languages, Faculty of Philology, VU: the elective course on 'Language and Leadership'; the compulsory course English for Law Students; and the study program 'English and Another Foreign Language (Spanish, French, Norwegian and Russian)' run by the Faculty of Philology. In particular, we focus on three different aspects of the lockdown: (1) the logistics of the shift to the remote synchronous mode of instruction of the course Language in Leadership (LL), (2) the good practice of delivering the course English for Law Students, and (3) the analysis of the language students' attitudes toward the pros and cons of the remote teaching following the spring quarantine. Methodologically, our study relies on the aspects of qualitative content analysis and case study.

---

4. https://lrv.lt/en/news/first-coronavirus-case-confirmed-in-lithuania

5. https://koronastop.lrv.lt/en/news/lithuanias-efforts-to-combat-covid-19-come-into-worlds-spotlight

6. https://lrv.lt/en/news/quarantine-announced-throughout-the-territory-of-the-republic-of-lithuania-attached-resolution

## 2. Institutional context

Established in 1579, the VU is the oldest and largest Lithuanian higher education institution. The 12 faculties, seven institutes, and four study and research centers of the university offer the widest range of study programs in the country. Besides study programs, VU offers a rich variety of elective courses, coming under the umbrella notion of General University Education (GUE). The mission of GUE courses is to "go beyond the boundaries of fields of study and study programs", promoting "interdisciplinarity, dialogue, and sociality typical for university studies and science"[7]. LL is one of these pan-university GUE courses, first launched in 2019. It is an innovative interactive interdisciplinary course delivered in English, and, at the time of writing this article, the only English-language GUE course offered by the Faculty of Philology. LL, conceived and developed primarily for international students at VU, is also open for local students. The course comprises 16 lecture hours and 32 seminar hours. When COVID-19 hit in the spring semester of 2020, LL was running for only the second time.

Interdisciplinarity and availability to all VU students are two reasons why all GUE courses are scheduled for Thursdays and Fridays, at 15:00 and 17:00, seeking to minimize schedule clashes across the various specialties.

## 3. LL – braving the turn to the remote synchronous instruction

Unsurprisingly, when the pan-university email was released on March 12th at 12:25 pm announcing the switch of instruction to the remote mode starting on March 13th, to be enhanced by the national lockdown starting on 16 March, this came just two and a half hours before the LL seminar classes and put LL participants into a logistical predicament. Many international students, especially those living in geographical proximity, hastened to book tickets and return home to avoid being locked down in a foreign country with no clear plans

---

[7]. https://www.vu.lt/en/studies/academic-info-for-students/regulations

for reopening. Others chose to stay in Lithuania, viewing the situation from a more long-term perspective and considerations of safety, subsequent return to resume face-to-face studies (hoping the quarantine period would be brief), and mandatory self-isolation following the quarantine. As a result, only three students turned up for the seminar at 15:00 on March 12th (and none at 17:00). The class time was thoroughly emotionally charged, imbued both with the academic dedication and solidarity on the one hand, and with the understanding of the looming unknown and, most likely, the abrupt last occasion to meet on the other. Amidst this uncertainty, however, there was a clear understanding and determination to develop the logistics for an uninterrupted synchronous mode of instruction. To that point, LL employed Moodle for storing course materials, collecting home assignments, as well as providing all information announcements. Another option already available to VU staff yet regarded with little interest at the time – which is the exact opposite of its present-day use – was Microsoft Teams (MS Teams), part of the Microsoft 365 package. Whatever the initial lecturer's exposure to the technology, availability of MS Teams offered the valuable opportunity to run the LL sessions on March 19th in the remote synchronous mode, sustaining both the continuity of academic instruction as well as the leadership vision of the course as of fundamental value, as advocated in the course title and manifested, in particular, through perseverance and ability to withstand difficulties. Therefore, careful planning was needed.

Two potential problems were identified. Firstly, despite the students' almost guaranteed presence on social networks, the likelihood of their previous exposure to MS Teams was rather weak. The second problem was of technical nature: availability of a reliable connection in the face of the sharply increased load on university servers, quality of participants' internet connections, the equipment available to them, and so on. In the absence of previous exposure to consistent remote teaching, and as a reserve plan alongside the LL course page on MS Teams, an LL course page was created on Facebook, the former intended as the main platform, and the latter as a back-up resource. A general announcement was sent through Virtual Language Environment (VLE) with wishes of well-being and successful resolution of travel arrangements (since a number of students were in the process of moving to their homes), as well as the request and instructions: (1) to befriend the LL course page on Facebook and (2) to join the course on MS Teams using the code provided.

At the time, MS Teams had already been available through the university system, and introductory seminars on MS Teams were delivered by Dr Saulius Preidys, Head of the university Information Technology Service Center (ITSC). During the first quarantine week, Dr Preidys relentlessly ran multiple sessions per day so as to facilitate the transition to remote teaching. One just cannot underestimate the most dedicated contribution of Dr Preidys and the three members of his team.

On the first days of the lockdown, MS Teams had not yet been widely used. With basic skills in their operations, step-by-step guidelines on setting up MS Teams were developed specifically for the LL participants by the course teacher. Consequently, while the staff were allowed to deliver classes asynchronously during the first weeks of the quarantine, LL switched to remote synchronous teaching within the regular interval between two successive seminars.

The day before the first meeting on MS Teams, the students were contacted again through Moodle (alongside communication via Facebook and university email, responding to individual students' queries) with the guidelines on connecting for the first remote meeting, considering the likelihood of lack of previous exposure to MS Teams among the students. On the day of the seminar, a welcome message was posted on MS Teams 30 minutes before the seminar, greeting the students and informing them that the seminar would begin shortly. This early greeting, conceived to reflect the 30-minute break between lectures at VU, has become a tradition and has been employed since then in all lectures and seminars conducted on MS Teams.

At the beginning of the first remote seminar, it did take some time for students to join the meeting. There were to begin with minor technical issues, such as noise, unstable network, opening multiple meeting sessions, but with the combined efforts of all course participants, these were soon resolved. Overcoming the state of being a novice user of MS Teams herself, the teacher introduced the students to the basic functions of the platform, such as starting and ending a meeting, screen sharing, downloading a document, etc. Overall, making the students feel comfortable during class time was perceived as an important objective for the seminar setting.

Facts that soon became common caveat areas, at this initial time were new. Besides technical issues of internet connection and server overload, these included ensuring students' involvement in classwork while their cameras were off, and upholding and fostering the leadership idea, one manifestation of which was efficient use of class time. The teacher was the only uninterrupted connection point during class sessions, and solutions for empowering students in the face of occasionally imperfect technical resources available were to be developed. One of them was the creation of a number of channels, or *Discussion lounges*, within the LL team, the name of the channels carefully designed to create an atmosphere of a large international forum. The physical on-camera presence of the teacher throughout the class, somewhat surprisingly, provided a certain stability benchmark and was perceived enthusiastically by the students. On one occasion, when the teacher's camera went off, a few students immediately expressed their concern: "We don't see you anymore!". The students' involvement and lively reaction were also suggestive of the successful construction and implementation of the, albeit simulated, face-to-face communication even though the students readily put up with the less than regular opportunity to see each other while team-working synchronously in breakout rooms referred to, within the context of the course, as the Discussion Lounges.

Despite its challenges, the quarantine period provided an invaluable experience in technological immersion, the use of MS Teams for classwork ultimately to become a criterion of the efficiency of the course itself.

## 4. Legal English studies in a remote mode

The legal English course offered to the second year law students comprises 270 hours; the content of the course is agreed with the law faculty administration;

it complies with the major subjects, taught in the respective terms (third and fourth terms): civil law, criminal law, EU law, international law.

As in most language for specific purposes studies, students aim at acquiring language skills needed for professional communication, which for law students includes reading and interpreting professional texts, and exchange of opinions in writing and orally; besides, about one quarter of the workload is dedicated to academic skills, namely reading and summarizing academic articles, and giving presentations. With the ratio between face-to-face sessions and independent work being 1:2 (96 hours of class work and 174 hours of self-study), the transition to distance learning was quite smooth and painless. The university VLE, even before the lockdown, was used as a tool for communicating weekly tasks, for sharing and storing learning resources and authentic materials, and for time management and control.

Although the switch to distance learning was quite sudden, it did not cause any serious disruption or inconvenience. Within about two weeks, the studies were fully transferred to MS Teams as that platform proved to be very well adjusted to teachers' and students' needs: calendar and message facilities, storing and sharing the learning materials, quizzes and other testing possibilities, collaborating in mini groups (channeling) either with or without teacher's interference.

All the reporting on students' individual tasks (submission of summaries of academic articles, course paper presentations, and mock professional correspondence) was done in MS Teams, without any difficulties or failures. During the course, the students had several opportunities to 'try out' the tasks that not only provided practice in certain language skills (debates, presentations, etc.), but also to get used to being 'restricted' in human interaction and to making the most of the existing tools and ways.

The biggest challenge for teachers was to carry out the course exam under the new conditions. The exam traditionally consists of two parts, the assessment of writing and of speaking skills.

There were two main points to consider: (1) how to exclude or, at least minimize cheating in writing; and (2) how to organize the oral exam, so that students could demonstrate not only the prepared speaking, but also their skills in a spontaneous exchange of opinions or ideas.

To prevent cheating, the following measures were taken:

- students had to base their written responses on the specially selected authentic materials/documents. There was very little chance of finding something similar on the net; the tasks (opinion essay, professional advice on a legal issue) required one's independent reaction to the prompt;

- students had to observe the time limit; the exam started and was to be submitted at the same time for all the second year students; and

- students had to have their cameras in the 'on' mode throughout the whole exam (50 minutes).

The oral part of the exam included two stages: (1) individual preparation for discussion (with the relevant authentic materials at hand), and (2) participation in a mini-group discussion to complete the task.

During the term sessions, students had sufficient practice in group discussions. They had mastered the relevant functional language and other language requirements ('turn taking' conventions, interaction, discussion dynamics, etc.). The discussions were carried out simultaneously in several groups (four students per group), so that all the students had equal time for preparing and presenting their opinions. The group discussions were recorded and the recordings were submitted at the end of the exam. These recordings were viewed by one or two teachers and assessed according to the agreed assessment criteria.

Overall, the transition to the remote mode of teaching the legal English course was void of serious problems or setback, most probably due to the nature of the target skills and the initial ratio between face-to-face and self-studies. The IT facilities and services offered by VU were sufficient. Nevertheless, the quarantine period showed that the adequate use of MS Teams and other communication platforms requires additional technical skills, teachers' confidence, and openness to new/alternative ways of teaching.

## 5. Student feedback

This part explores the 63 third-year students' feedback on the organization and implementation of the study program 'English and Another Foreign Language (French, Spanish, Norwegian, and Russian)' during the first wave of the COVID-19 pandemic. The survey is based on the evidence provided by 63 respondents who either participated in two focus groups (24 students in total) to discuss the issues of the study process in the spring 2020 or completed an online questionnaire which targeted at discovering:

- the overall dynamics of the students' attitudes toward remote teaching-learning during the spring 2020 semester;

- the advantages and disadvantages of the remote teaching-learning mode; and

- the students' attitudinal tendencies toward remote teaching in general.

Both forms of data collection allowed us to obtain an abundance of emotionally vivid reflections on the target mode implemented in the spring 2020. The analysis of the recorded texts was based on qualitative content analysis (Bitinas, Rupšienė, & Žydžiūnaitė, 2008); analytical and descriptive approaches were applied.

From the respondents' point of view, the spring 2020 lockdown brought much uncertainty to all the citizens across the country. The atmosphere in the academic environment reflected people's general mood which, consequently, led students to focus more on their existential issues rather than concentrate on education. The respondents elaborately report on their time spent following every piece of news either in the media or on social networks "with a hope that this will end soon, and they will be at their university again" (S1). Both members of the academic staff as well as students regarded the pandemic upheaval temporary, which would take just a number of weeks, and then bring all of them back to the university premises. To manage the teaching-learning process to continue, the MS Teams and VLE platforms were recommended for use by the university ITSC. VMA[8] was not a novelty for the teachers since they have been employing it for several years. The instructions of the application of the MS Teams platform were shared online[9]. The students were extremely eager "to feel the taste of online teaching" (S27) since they had been told about it so many times, though almost never had an opportunity to experience it in practice.

> "Thanks to global digitalization, Linguistics is on the list of subjects which can successfully survive being taught only online with absolutely no damage to our knowledge and skills!" (S38).

Their excitement grew due to the fact that non-residents of Vilnius could return home and spend time together with their family members. Enjoyment of parental care without 'worries about food' or 'constant rental issues' added some extra appeal to the novelty of the whole study process. The initial stage of the remote teaching-learning mode listed a number of advantages that were ranked in the following way (Table 1).

Table 1. Advantages of the remote mode

| | |
|---|---|
| 1. | Longer sleeping hours |
| 2. | No morning worries about make-up, what to wear, and what to eat |
| 3. | No need to waste time on commuting or sitting in the traffic jams |
| 4. | Common monthly budget saved |

8. The functions of VMA (Vilnius University's virtual learning environment) are equivalent to the ones of Moodle: https://www.vu.lt/en/covid-19/teaching-online/tools-for-online-teaching#virtual-learning-environment-vma

9. https://www.vu.lt/covid-19

| 5. | Much freedom when your camera is turned off |
|---|---|
| 6. | Less stress than in contact classes |
| 7. | Access available from everywhere |
| 8. | It is easy to combine part-time job and study activities at a time |
| 9. | The use of technology makes classes more appealing |

However, the elation stage, listing the benefits of flexibility of the remote teaching did not last long. The shift to remote teaching clashed with the respondents' expectations in a way, and that is why it could not escape some criticism.

"At the beginning of remote teaching, there was a bit of confusion from both sides, professors and students" (S20).

"Some lecturers were quite quick, others took a bit more time to get adapted to the online system" (S5).

"It was easy for the students because we are more tech-savvy and it took us just a few days to get used to it" (S5).

"Not all the lectures were held on time, changes in the timetable occurred every week, professors were using different platforms for communication" (S20), thus, "working online became a bit chaotic" (S12), leading to misunderstanding, such as where to look for homework and information.

"Some lecturers were exceedingly kind, understanding, and flexible, and everybody could feel their support" (S48), however, not all of them "were able to distribute workload" (S52), which led students to sleepless nights and too much time spent at the computer. Since the majority of the students did not use their webcams "there was a lack of real communication" (S22) "leaving professors talking to themselves" (S19), "preventing students from asking questions" (S3) and putting them into difficulties to concentrate on the theme.

As soon as the initial technical issues were tackled, the period of confusion transformed itself into a routine. Very soon, the majority of the respondents admitted that they "could easily dedicate themselves to such a type of their studies" (S3). They started learning on their own, found that "writing tests or presenting projects was not as stressful as in the class environment" (S26). In occasional cases, some teachers were thought of as being pretty harsh by setting ridiculously short time slots for tests "trying to prevent students from cheating" (S20). Doubts about the quality of studies disappeared.

> "At first, I thought that the quality of the studies would decrease sharply, that we would not be able to learn something, that we would not be able to communicate properly as we did in contact classes. But after some time, [...] all the teachers[10] taught in alternative ways and made that period even more interesting than it would have been in classes" (S19).

Many respondents became aware of their own responsibilities.

> "Over time, I started to overcome my time-management problem and learned to use that extra time that I had properly. In the end, I managed to devote more time to studies than usual and learn more than in the previous semesters" (S20).

> "I had to become amazingly fast at using IT because there was an opportunity to gain information from sources. It became a key to my success" (S8).

Apparently, the pandemic changed students' personalities, their worldviews: the first stage of stress was over and they got used to the routine "a kind of a comfortable one" (S52). However, this wasn't the case for all of them. Yet, there appeared different types of distractors, or disadvantages, preventing them from full engagement in the study process (Table 2).

---

10. In the Lithuanian context, university teachers (assistants, associate professors, and professors) are called teachers in general. The same term of a 'teacher' is used in secondary and tertiary levels. However, when foreign teachers start working at the university, they usually teach students to call them professors.

Table 2. Disadvantages of the remote mode

| 1. | Inability to separate home environment from study environment |
|---|---|
| 2. | Difficult/tiresome to sit in front of the computer all day long |
| 3. | Unstable internet connection/improperly functioning devices |
| 4. | Shortage of living space/devices (among family members) |
| 5. | Social interactions disrupted ('stuck at home') |
| 6. | A plethora of distractors: telephone calls, constant constructions outside, family members' interruptions |
| 7 | Motivational downturn |
| 8. | Lack of coping mechanisms: concentration, self-discipline, and time management |
| 9. | Depressive mood swings |
| 10. | Worsening eyesight |
| 11. | Debatable efficiency |
| 12. | Some teachers' poor proficiency in IT application |

It can be added that students' personality types have possibly contributed much to the level of their ability to adapt to the new mode. The shy or reserved ones did not feel comfortable and blamed IT for damaging their self-esteem:

> "I was afraid of speaking, expressing my opinion, showing my face though the camera; the lectures were so unreal all the time! I started avoiding them, and that led to a large number of missing lectures. I have always been afraid of technologies; they do not cooperate with me. I found myself judging this whole situation as it took away the joy of sitting in the classroom and being able to communicate in a normal way as humans do!" (S41).

The more outgoing ones suffered from "missing social contacts" and a "limited environment". The events happening outside, including the media reports on the soaring number of COVID-19 cases, made the young people feel desperate:

> "the question whether I should be engaged in endless homework until nightfall or whether I should perform my civic duty? Volunteering had always been on my mind [...] and I was about to help my society" (S8).

Chapter 15

According to Pacansky-Brock (2017, p. 53), in order to achieve specified learning results, a diverse student group requires engagement, an understanding who they are and what the level of their willingness to adapt is. However, the reflections quoted above reveal the students' greater concern about surviving the unusual circumstances of the spring 2020 semester as much as possible rather than searching for the ways of adaptation to satisfy their own needs.

Having considered all the positives and negatives of the remote teaching mode presented by the language students, there might be a question raised on how many supporters of this mode were left? Actually, just two of them, stating the fact that "online learning is not a bad thing at all!" (S11). All the rest found teacher-student live interaction crucial for their advance toward foreign language proficiency with "a few online theoretical lectures" (S35).

## 6. Conclusions

In this article we sought to provide an account for the arrangements and study process through the prism of several courses delivered in English at the Faculty of Philology, VU. In particular, we presented an overview of setting the organizational logistics for the elective course LL on the threshold of moving from face-to-face to remote synchronous mode of instruction. We then discussed the delivery of the course English for Law students in light of the adjustment of the curriculum and examination tasks to the remote instruction mode. Finally, we referred to the study program 'English and Another Foreign Language' and examined its students' perceptions of the study process during the quarantine. The selected approach has revealed two perspectives. In our discussion, we hoped to portray the work conducted by the teachers during the pandemic, in which accompanying factors, such as reconsidering and remodeling both the environment of the classroom and the assignments, especially for seminar settings, ultimately leading to extra work time during remote instruction, were essentially taken for granted. The feedback solicited from the students and presented in the final section of our study reveals the true size of the iceberg of COVID-time teaching: it is feeling at a loss, overcoming fear, learning time management, mastering the new technologies as well as the communication skills of the new reality, and – at all times – persevering in the face of the unknown, striving for quality performance, and sustainable professional approach.

## References

Bitinas, B., Rupšienė, L., & Žydžiūnaitė, V. (2008). *Kiekybinių tyrimų metodologija*. Socialinių mokslų kolegija.

Pacansky-Brock, M. (2017). *Best practices for teaching with emerging technologies* (2nd ed.). Routledge.

# 16. Stumble or fall? Responses to moving language learning online at Durham University during the 2020 pandemic

**Mark Critchley[1]**

## Abstract

This chapter offers a chronological narrative of the steps taken by the Centre for Foreign Language Study (CFLS) at Durham University to move language teaching, learning, and assessment online following the announcement of the global COVID-19 pandemic in March 2020. This includes immediate steps to suspend classroom teaching, a move to online assessments, preparations for teaching of summer language courses, and steps to convert existing curricula and teaching materials for online delivery in 2020-2021. The chapter concludes with some lessons learned, and plans for the future.

**Keywords:** COVID-19, online, language teaching, assessment, training, university-wide programme, UK.

## 1. Introduction

The CFLS provides access to language learning to anyone in the university, and the local community who is not otherwise registered for a specialist degree in Modern Languages and Cultures. We offer language courses in a variety of formats in 18 languages, not including English. In March 2020, we were supporting 2,100 language learners, 1,150 studying elective language modules

---

1. Durham University, Durham, United Kingdom; mark.critchley@durham.ac.uk; https://orcid.org/0000-0001-7010-1796

How to cite: Critchley, M. (2021). Stumble or fall? Responses to moving language learning online at Durham University during the 2020 pandemic. In N. Radić, A. Atabekova, M. Freddi & J. Schmied (Eds), *The world universities' response to COVID-19: remote online language teaching* (pp. 265-277). Research-publishing.net. https://doi.org/10.14705/rpnet.2021.52.1277

that count towards their respective degree, and a further 950 on evening courses. We were supporting a core team of 22 language teachers, a further 37 teachers delivering evening courses on a freelance or part-time basis, and an administration team of five individuals. CFLS is a sub-department in the School of Modern Languages and Cultures (MLAC). In turn, MLAC offers four specialist undergraduate degree programmes, and a range of postgraduate and undergraduate joint honours programmes. CFLS operates autonomously from MLAC, although shares governance via a School Education Committee and Board of Examiners. We have had an unfulfilled plan to develop online delivery of language courses for a number of years.

At Durham University, the pandemic has evolved in four phases:

- the initial suspension of face-to-face teaching and immediate response to deliver the final week of teaching and assessment;

- the conclusion of formal examinations in April and May, including Boards of Examiners;

- the planning and preparation of summer language courses to start in June 2020; and

- the planning and preparation for the resumption of teaching in the new academic year.

This chapter offers a chronological narrative behind the decisions and actions undertaken from a management and coordination perspective.

## 2. Staying safe

The decision to suspend face-to-face teaching was announced to the departments by the senior management team at Durham University on the afternoon of the 10th of March 2020. This was a timely, unilateral decision made early by the university's senior management team to mitigate risk of exposure to the coronavirus within the university community. At that point, we were in the penultimate week of teaching. Students were encouraged to complete classes in that week, and then seek ways to return home, with the final week of timetabled teaching to be delivered by alternative means. For CFLS, the announcement presented three immediate problems: first, we had scheduled summative assessments due to take place the following afternoon. In one case, this involved one exam venue for 150 students. We decided to progress with this exam, not to re-schedule, but to divide the students into four smaller groups distributed across separate rooms. We also had other assessments scheduled the following week, by which time many students would have left Durham. In each case, it was decided to proceed with the assessment, but to provide the students with an assessment task remotely via the university Virtual Learning Environment (VLE), then submitted to the relevant module teacher by email. This fortunately only involved around six separate courses and 100 students, with the assessments themselves comprising typically 25% of the course mark. The risk was mitigated by keeping the assessment as a real-time task, undertaken live and supervised by the course teacher.

Secondly, CFLS had 60 evening courses ongoing, with ten days left until course completion. An immediate decision was made to suspend face-to-face teaching for the final week, with teaching materials for those and previous sessions made available to learners via the VLE. Teachers, who in this case are all part-time, were advised not to come onto campus, and were encouraged to offer a virtual Skype session where this was considered feasible and viable. Approximately half continued with a final session online, usually using Skype. Fortunately, our evening courses are not assessed, the courses were almost at an end, and the circumstances were such that learners in any event were not necessarily immediately focussed on their learning.

Finally, we still had one week of teaching remaining for our elective modules. These are assessed modules, with marks counting towards students' degree outcomes. The final week of teaching usually helps wrap up the course, and helps to prepare the students for the final speaking assessments that take place

Chapter 16

after the Easter break. It was decided to proceed with delivery of teaching sessions in the final week online. To this end, the central university Information Technology (IT) service had stepped in promptly as soon as the suspension of classroom teaching was announced. Durham University uses Blackboard as the platform behind our VLE, and already had a licence for limited use of Collaborate, Blackboard's online teaching platform. This licence was extended almost immediately, and made available to all courses and all teachers across the university. The university also rapidly acquired institution-wide licences for Microsoft Teams and the Zoom video-conferencing software, and established centrally-coordinated training in the use of Collaborate and Microsoft Teams through our Durham Centre for Academic Development (DCAD), accessible at scale to staff across the university.

With this support, we therefore took the decision to proceed with some real-time remote teaching in the final week, supported with asynchronous teaching materials, and using office hours as a means for individual students to raise concerns and get more focussed support. This interim solution worked well, allowing teachers themselves to decide what they considered to be the best and easiest solution for their individual circumstances, and allowed teaching to conclude without significant impact on the learning of the students. Furthermore, teachers were encouraged to start working from home immediately. With progress of the pandemic at a national level, on Monday March 16th we took the decision in CFLS that all staff would move to remote working from home. Ultimately, at this point, the priority was to reassure students about their progression, to provide a stopgap emergency solution to continue to provide teaching to the end of term, and to remove as many individuals as possible from the university campus to minimise risk of the virus spreading into the university community.

## 3. Catching breath

Having managed to reach the end of the academic term, we then had time to take stock, and the university focus moved towards end of year exams. For elective language modules we only had to concern ourselves with speaking assessments, usually undertaken individually or in pairs with an examiner in a small teaching room. For students studying a specialist languages degree, they would have to take a speaking assessment and a written examination.

For speaking assessments, the main decision to make was one of submission format. How might we replicate a conventional speaking assessment when we cannot meet the students? Would we attempt to keep the usual exam format, with students meeting examiners via video in real time, or would we ask students to submit a recording of themselves in response to instructions and submit this for marking by the examiner? For degree students, MLAC took the decision to change the format of the speaking assessments, requiring all students to submit a recording of themselves. The assessment format itself was modified to a more reflective submission that allowed students to demonstrate their full range of speaking ability in the target language. The assessment task would be released to students at a set time, with a recording to be submitted within a 48 hour time window.

For CFLS, we retain more flexibility. When consulting with teachers, some preferred the idea of allowing students to pre-record a submission, thereby avoiding issues with internet connectivity, and to hopefully allow the students to be more relaxed. Others preferred to keep the format of a real-time assessment, undertaken by video link. CFLS allowed module convenors to make their own decisions on their preferred format, albeit having a consistent approach in each format and across all courses. For all courses, approximately half of students had a live video assessment and half submitted a pre-recording.

Teachers briefed students as to the modifications to assessment methodology, and spent time over the Easter break modifying assessment tasks and preparing to undertake assessments virtually. To this end, we were able to take advantage of a consultation forum set up with other language teachers in other university language programmes across the UK. Durham University is a member of the Association of University Language Communities in the UK and Ireland (AULC), and the Director of CFLS also happens to be the current Chair of

AULC. It was recognised early in the process that all university language teaching, learning, and assessment would need to adapt, and common approaches shared across the wider language teaching community would work well. As a result, an online community of language teachers across the UK was established in mid-March on Microsoft Teams, with 127 individual participants, and a variety of discussion fora, related to asynchronous teaching, online summative language assessments, online support for languages using non-Roman scripts, and mitigation strategies for students. This network did not in and of itself provide any significant breakthrough. However, it did allow language teachers across the country to gain some reassurance that the issues they were facing were being similarly addressed in other institutions. This did a great deal to ease anxiety amongst the language teaching community, and to allow teachers to then focus their efforts in areas of greatest concern, locally, in their own contexts.

When it came to the assessments themselves, we encountered a number of issues:

- for pre-recorded oral assessments, it proved not possible to submit video due to large file sizes. As a result all pre-recordings were audio only;

- several students, but not as many as first feared, had connectivity problems. For those who were unable to upload, we managed to organise an alternative live assessment, usually via mobile video;

- a number of students clearly over-prepared, and on occasions read from scripts, contrary to the usual spontaneity desired from a speaking exam. In isolated cases, we also suspected instances of self-plagiarism or impersonation, which proved difficult to confirm in every case; and

- we had a number of students who had fallen ill themselves with coronavirus, or had complex domestic circumstances, including caring for other family members who were unwell, and we had to re-schedule a higher than usual number of assessments.

## 4. Interim solutions

CFLS runs three sets of extra-curricular language courses, usually evening courses, with start dates in October, January, and June each year. These lie outside the main academic programme of the university, and those registering pay a course fee. By the end of March, the UK was in full lockdown, a situation that would not really be lifted for a further three months. These circumstances presented two main challenges:

- the pandemic created uncertainty in the prospects for recruitment of international students, and the potential deferral by UK students. There was a resulting anticipation of significant financial income shortfalls for Universities across the UK, and an immediate call for restraint on all expenditure, and a reduction in non-essential activities; and

- uncertainty across higher education meant that casualised teaching staff, including many language teachers on fixed term or temporary contracts, faced the prospect of a loss of work if language courses were withdrawn, or if solutions to be able to deliver language courses online were not found.

Durham University made clear that we wanted to continue to offer language learning opportunities during the lockdown, both to our students and the local community, and we wanted to make sure we could continue to offer employment to our language teachers. As a result, a business case was submitted and approved through the emergency budgeting procedures in place at the time, to proceed with delivery of language courses online in June, these also presenting an excellent opportunity to test new online delivery methods.

Our evening courses are taught by freelance language teachers. At this point in time (April 2020), CFLS had only three teachers who had anything more than a couple of weeks experience with online teaching, with a handful of others familiar with digital language teaching tools. The majority of our part-time teachers had no experience at all and, as a result, we had to quickly adapt, and put together a training programme to prepare teachers for remote course delivery. The Durham Centre for Academic Development had by this time put together a thorough training programme to help all teaching staff transition towards online teaching. This included bespoke training on individual learning platforms (Teams, Collaborate), and generic online teaching skills. However, this was not discipline-specific and, as a result, lingering questions remained about teaching language specifically. From our past experience in delivering pilot academic reading skills courses online, we knew that progress was 25% slower when teaching online. As such, we recognised early on that the main effort would need to focus on effecting a culture shift, especially through re-balancing the use of contact time and student self-study accordingly.

The process of training our part-time teachers was undertaken through a four-part training programme, focussing on:

- programme and course objectives, adapting teacher and learner behaviours, and maintaining a consistent approach;

- different approaches to online teaching and use of contact time;

- different approaches to student self-study and the link to contact time; and

- use of online tools and software to aid remote teaching and learning.

The training was delivered by a team of six, comprising the Director, four of the core teaching team who had more experience of remote teaching and learning, and an external consultant, who has been offering technical and online support to language teachers in the UK for more than ten years. The programme offered four hours of direct training time, supplemented by the generic online teaching training offered by the university centrally, and peer-to-peer sharing, where small groups of teachers would get together online to test out exercises and activities, and become individually and collectively more comfortable with the technology.

Twenty-six part-time teachers were trained over the course of four weeks in May 2020. Upon completion of the programme, all of the teachers were issued with a Teacher Pack, effectively a guide to the Centre's expectations of online teaching. We also prepared a Student Pack, so that learners subscribing to our courses knew what to expect, were briefed to expect problems from time to time, and what they needed to do to support their own learning.

We have subsequently run the training programme twice more; once internally for core teaching staff in CFLS and some in MLAC, and again for remaining part-time teachers who are involved in delivery of a larger online programme in October 2020. All-in-all 67 language teachers have been through a short, bespoke training programme focussed towards language teaching between May and September 2020.

## 5. Reality dawns

The one constant throughout the summer of 2020 was the uncertainty: would the pandemic die down or come back even stronger, how many students would arrive and what would be their expectations, was face-to-face teaching possible, were there enough teaching rooms? From the outset of lockdown in late March, Durham University was giving clear signals that all staff should prepare for the possibility of teaching being online for the academic year 2020-2021. An early decision was made to deliver all large group teaching online in all academic disciplines. All small group teaching would be undertaken face-to-face in a classroom where possible, applying risk assessments and social distancing in line with UK Government guidelines. The university went to enormous efforts to re-configure teaching spaces and a timetable to match. However, it was obvious that it would be impossible to undertake all small group teaching within the conventional university weekly timetable. Considering the pitfalls of trying to teach language classes whilst either the teacher or the students were wearing face masks, it was decided in late June that all language teaching would be delivered online only, at least for the first term before Christmas, and most likely for the full academic year. This meant that staff could continue to prepare teaching materials for online delivery safe in the knowledge that this would not be time wasted. This helped ease anxiety and, even if teaching staff realised they had a lot more work to do, at least they were reassured a clear decision had been made, and one that they generally supported.

The university also acknowledged the additional work that would be required to prepare to teach online. The objective is to ensure all departments across the university offer a high quality, online product. This recognises the innate quality that already exists in all teaching, but that the move online must not attempt to simply replicate the classroom in the virtual sphere. At the same time, to design a high quality, purpose built online course takes many months. A nominal workload allocation was assigned for all language modules, 75 hours per module to review and re-design curricula and teaching materials to be suitable for online delivery and online learning – both synchronous and asynchronous. As a result, language teaching staff were given the clear message that 'good enough' should be the aspiration. We needed to work to optimise our course curricular and materials for online delivery, but not try to re-create a perfect online language module in the course of a few weeks.

The fact that we made an early decision to move everything online did much to reduce anxiety. We then set up a weekly drop-in session for CFLS staff, so that we could check in with each other, check on mutual well-being, and respond to the many questions that colleagues would inevitably have. As an extension of the AULC Team, we also set up a weekly drop-in session nationally from the end of June, whereby colleagues from across AULC could meet informally on Teams. We never had more than 16 people attend any one session (out of the 127 signed up on Teams), but over the course of the summer we met up with around 100 colleagues from 21 different UK universities. Participants were generally at the management end of the spectrum, rather than teacher-practitioners. In this way, we were able to informally share ideas, thoughts, and challenges with each other, and compare notes. This very quickly demonstrated a very similar approach at all universities in the UK. Without exception, at the universities who engaged, all language teaching is taking place online only in 2020-2021. The only differences relate to use of class contact time, group sizes, and overall teaching hours. Nevertheless, the fundamentals of approach are very similar.

Armed with the reassurance that our approach was sector-standard, the problems that were regularly raised in Durham were ones of a practical nature. The actual tasks of modifying curricula and producing teaching materials for online delivery almost passed by without comment. The recurring themes were, and to an extent still are as follows.

- What do we do with student attendance and engagement?

- Should all teaching sessions be recorded?

- Do all recordings need to be captioned to comply with UK legislation?

- How do we stop plagiarism for remote assessment of language tasks?

None of these issues has yet been entirely resolved, and they remain under review both in CFLS and at university level.

## 6.  Lessons learned and planning for a post-pandemic future

October 5th 2020 saw the first day of teaching in the new academic year at Durham University. Staff have been trained. Teaching materials have been prepared. Students have registered. International student numbers are down, but not as much as originally feared, whereas domestic student numbers are up, in part due to issues with the marking of post-16 school qualifications during the pandemic, which became subject of a government review and u-turn. Registrations to elective language courses are similar to 2019-2020, but demand has soared, 30% higher than 2019-2020. Meanwhile, registrations to evening courses are down, largely, we believe, to problems in marketing, and possibly due to student anxiety about excessive online learning.

# Chapter 16

We have the usual problems about students wishing to change courses, some students not attending, and some students with positive tests for COVID-19, or self-isolating. However, so far, the hard work over the summer is largely paying off. The issues will come when assessments begin in early December, and we can then properly evaluate how effective the online delivery model has been in comparison with past years.

The most useful lesson we have learned is to cooperate and collaborate with peers. Taking advantage of available networks with colleagues in other Universities has proved a lifeline, providing us all with reassurance and confidence knowing that our plans were in line with our peers. We have also learned that the transition to online teaching, long anticipated as a major step with significant barriers, has been less problematic than any of us could have envisaged. Certainly, the additional work imposed has been significant, and the pressures of this workload and the impact it has on family life and personal well-being cannot and should not be underestimated. Nevertheless, we are well set up for a more flexible future.

CFLS will continue with online delivery of language courses, fulfilling a long-term plan to deliver language courses outside the university. This will become a key element of our portfolio, with face-to-face teaching at its heart, and always teacher-led, that will offer flexibility and choice to learners. The principle advantages for online delivery are perceived to be:

- the ability to maximise the viability of less widely taught languages through wider reach online;

- the ability to deliver courses to defined groups across institutional boundaries, unconstrained by location (e.g. multi-institution PhD partnerships); and

- access to a wider pool of professional language teachers in a peripheral geographic region.

To support this, we will review and develop the online training programme and replicate this on an annual basis. We also need to continue to critically reflect on different approaches to blended learning, maximising the benefits of online or digital teaching and learning resources in a genuinely blended learning environment for students.

## 7. Acknowledgements

This chapter is dedicated to colleagues in the CFLS at Durham University, who have actually put in the hard work to be ready to deliver language courses online.

# 17. Reflection on digital language teaching, learning, and assessment in times of crisis: a view from Italy

## Maria Freddi[1]

### Abstract

This chapter is a reflective account of the author's experience as a teacher of English at the University of Pavia during the first wave of the SARS-CoV-2 pandemic. It considers the design and delivery of an English for architecture and construction engineering course as well as the assessment stage of a text analysis course. It proceeds by presenting and discussing the decisions implemented as a consequence of the crisis situation and reflects on principles of English language teaching, learning, and assessment in general and English for Specific Purposes (ESP) in particular. In doing so, it addresses the book project rationale as an opportunity to reflect on the adjustments made to various planning and design factors informing language education during the health crisis and thought to be generalisable to language teaching, learning, and assessment in the global digital world. It concludes with thoughts on what the future of digital language teaching, learning, and assessment could look like.

Keywords: COVID-19, online language teaching, assessment, ESP, target situation analysis, learner-centred approach.

---

1. University of Pavia, Pavia, Italy; maria.freddi@unipv.it; https://orcid.org/0000-0003-2893-1790

How to cite: Freddi, M. (2021). Reflection on digital language teaching, learning, and assessment in times of crisis: a view from Italy. In N. Radić, A. Atabekova, M. Freddi & J. Schmied (Eds), *The world universities' response to COVID-19: remote online language teaching* (pp. 279-293). Research-publishing.net. https://doi.org/10.14705/rpnet.2021.52.1278

Chapter 17

## 1. Introduction

The present chapter reports on the author's experience as a teacher of English of a course designed and delivered right in the middle of the first outbreak of SARS-CoV-2 (Spring term 2020), and as responsible for the assessment stage of a text analysis course taught prior to the pandemic crisis. The account is accompanied by reflections on general English language teaching principles (e.g. Ur, 2012) and ESP (e.g. Basturkmen, 2010, Gollin-Kies, Hall, & Moore, 2015, Hafner & Miller, 2019) and applied to the specific situation. In doing so, it addresses the book project rationale as an opportunity to reflect on the adjustments made to various planning and design factors informing language education during the pandemic and thought to be generalisable to language teaching, learning, and assessment in the global digital world.

The first experience is an English for architecture and construction engineering course, which was redesigned and delivered entirely through the internet during the lockdown of March-May 2020 in Italy. This means that the teacher first met her students through the online mode, and developed and maintained the virtual relationship up to and including the final examination stage. The second concerns the assessment at the end of a text analysis (English Language 2) course for undergraduate students of modern languages. While the English Language 2 classes took place before the pandemic crisis, the assessment procedures were carried out exclusively online. In what follows, all stages in course design are presented and discussed in the broader framework of ESP pedagogy and revisited in light of the changed situation. Assessment done on the English Language 2 – Text Analysis Course is then discussed.

## 2. ESP course design

### 2.1. Context

As usually done when planning and designing a Language for Specific Purposes (LSP) course, the first factor that is taken into account is the context, both in terms of target situation analysis and needs analysis, i.e. analysis of learners' needs and of stakeholders (typically faculty from the disciplines and professionals from the industry, e.g. Gollin-Kies et al., 2015). English for Architecture and Construction Engineering is normally delivered for small groups of an average 10-15 students in their last year of a five-year degree programme inclusive of a master's in architecture and construction engineering. The course is elective and usually chosen by students who are close to graduating and therefore keen on improving their employability prospects. The course takes the form of a 32-hour lab divided into 18 hours of more frontal teaching and the remaining 14 hours of more practical activities, which, prior to the health crisis, were focused on developing writing skills and in particular on writing up the design project report in English.

Although attendance is not mandatory in the majority of the degree programmes in Italian state universities, participants who choose this course tend to have a higher attendance rate than average for a number of reasons: engineering students in general attend classes more regularly than in other degree programmes, they are used to lab sessions and value attendance more than in humanities courses, where attendance is perceived as superfluous and thus devalued unless it offers practical benefits, such as, for example, when it is associated with continuous assessment. As said, the English for Architecture and Construction Engineering Course is optional and placed in the last year of study, when students are about to finish their studies and therefore very close to entering the relevant professions. Instrumental motivation therefore is usually very high (cf. Ur, 2012) as well as satisfaction with the course learning objectives, as demonstrated by the steadily positive feedback given in students' questionnaires at the end of each course.

### 2.2. Course objective and intended learning outcomes

The overall course objective consists in developing the writing skills relative to the project description and report. These are learner genres students are exposed to during their five years of study and therefore are familiar with, at least in their own native language. Moreover, they are part of the design master's thesis and correspond to some of the written genres typical of the building professions, i.e. the project descriptions for the portfolio and for the architecture project competition (Spector & Damron, 2017).

The development of writing skills builds on the auxiliary skills of vocabulary and grammar. Because the technical vocabulary of architecture and construction encompasses a large range of specialisations and related terms, the goal of the course was to develop awareness of the digital and printed resources that can be used to find the specialised vocabulary and phraseology needed. The expected learning outcomes therefore included acquisition of the basic lexicon of architecture complemented by awareness of the tools available to broaden the technical vocabulary. As far as mastery of grammar is concerned, the course similarly aimed at developing knowledge of some of the internet-based corpus tools that can be used for grammar checking and self-editing. Explicit grammar teaching was limited to specific areas deemed necessary following needs analysis, e.g. modified nominal structures, but avoiding excessive use of metalanguage (e.g. *noun + noun clusters* was used instead of *noun phrases*). Furthermore, the items chosen were never treated as exclusively grammatical, i.e. without separating lexis from grammar (e.g. modified noun phrases and technical vocabulary, use of prepositions of place expressing orientation in space).

As a by-product of genre mastery, students were expected to develop a more systematic understanding of the design process on the assumption that enculturation into the genres brings about enculturation into the disciplines, in this case the design disciplines, and helps develop membership into the community of practice – as stressed by many contributions in Gruber and Olman's (2019) collection on language and science, and in research on academic literacies by Nesi and Gardner (2012) and Schmied (2018), among others. The fact that exposure to the genres occurred in another language than the learners' native language reinforced the students' reflective process.

### 2.3. Evaluation and assessment

Assessment consisted in writing a design project report of one of the students' own projects that they were allowed to choose from any they had to design for one of the disciplinary courses during their academic career (e.g. architectural composition, building technology). The report was evaluated for both its organisation (internal structure, genre conventions, and verbal-visual integration) and language accuracy. In particular, appropriateness of technical vocabulary and of the lexico-grammatical structures taught and practiced in class (e.g. noun modification) was assessed too. The report had to be sent to the teacher some days prior to the exam date and discussed orally on the date of the exam to address the teacher's questions and critiques.

## 3. Moving online: course redesign and implementation

As a result of the pandemic and the changed context, the course objectives and learning outcomes had to be revisited and the course redesigned accordingly. Additionally, new content could be created as well as new methods experimented with to replace traditional face-to-face teaching, learning, and assessment.

### 3.1. Target situation re-analysis

In the emergency of the lockdown, the University of Pavia left lecturers free to decide whether to record their classes on a talking presentation software such as PowerPoint and upload the entire course for asynchronous use by the students, or to deliver synchronous teaching sessions using a videoconferencing tool, according to the official schedule of the semester (instructions along these lines were issued by the rector of the university as early as 27th February 2020). After initial discussion of whether using Skype for Business could be a viable option, Google Meet was the tool resorted to, Google being the chosen provider of the university mailing system and thus including the videoconferencing tool for free. At the time, the number of institutional accounts on Zoom were not sufficient to cover all teachers and courses offered and exclusively reserved to graduation sessions across all university departments. This changed with the start of the new academic year and the courses delivered in the Fall of 2020, after the university decided to provide its teaching staff with a Zoom account for the online courses (see Conclusions).

Because of the small number of participants, the mainly practical nature of the course (a language lab in its vocation) and well-identified learning objectives, I decided that live streaming would be a more desirable choice than pre-recorded lessons. The decision was further based on the fact that even before the pandemic I had been using the Learning Management System (LMS) of the university, a customised version of Moodle called Kiro[2]. Kiro is a dynamic and interactive e-learning platform that offers features such as sharing documents and links to websites, posting news to participants, assigning and correcting homework, and more generally managing the whole course. This platform had been an integral part of my courses for a number of regular face-to-face teaching years supplemented by distance learning tools, but not exclusively replaced by them. However, before moving the course entirely online, I had not exploited Kiro to the full and actually used just a few of the many features available. For example, I had never trialled the various assessment options, which allow to put together and administer tests of various kinds with both open-ended and multiple-choice questions. In what follows I will discuss some of the features of the new course combing the enhanced use of the LMS and live classes on Google Meet in light of some of the values of good language teaching and learning, as, e.g. in participatory experience-centred approaches and collaborative language learning (Hafner & Miller, 2019; Larsen-Freeman, 2000, pp. 153-155).

## 3.2. Course objective and assessment revisited

The first consequence of going entirely digital was the breaking of physical barriers, more internationalisation, and a more naturalistic English as lingua franca context. Thanks to the course being online, colleagues who teach academic English at Aalto University, Finland could participate in the first meeting and in the final students' project presentations, thus taking part in a collaborative teaching project where English was spoken not just among L1 speakers of Italian, but also with speakers of different L1s, including English. This learning situation is closer to real life situations at the workplace,

---

2. https://idcd.unipv.it/kiro3/

a tendency that has been observed by reviews of ESP pedagogy (Hafner & Miller, 2019). Under normal conditions, such collaboration would have been much more costly and time-consuming for the visiting teachers, instead with staff virtual mobility it had less impact on the teachers' home duties, while, at the same time, it brought great benefit to students at the receiving institution for the reasons outlined above. Although the telecollaboration stemmed from an ongoing EU-funded research project on language and communication education for engineers[3], it was accelerated by the digital environment.

This collaborative teaching and international context allowed me to revisit the course learning objectives and led to the inclusion of oral presentation skills as an additional goal of the course. Evaluation was thus included in the final classes, when students' 10 minutes oral presentations were assessed. Students presented online by sharing their screens and using 3D animation software for architecture project renderings, thus engaging in the learning process more actively as in project-based learning (cf. Hafner & Miller, 2019). After each presentation, the teachers could comment and ask students questions. Marking criteria focused on the mastery of architectural discourse conventions and effectiveness of communication rather than strict oral proficiency. Also, continuous assessment was deemed the most appropriate form of evaluation at a time of crisis that challenges strictly normative views of testing and prefers formative assessment centred on scaffolding and "on a continuous feedback loop" (Gottlieb & Katz, 2020, p. 48). This had a double effect, on one hand it allowed to incorporate psychological factors more explicitly into the course, something that would not normally happen or, at most, would have been a concession without the intervening exceptional circumstances. On the other hand, it brought constructive feedback to the centre of the course.

### 3.3. Being social

As one way of tapping into psychological and affective factors affecting communication and language learning, teaching sessions were sometimes

---

[3]. https://www.thebadgeproject.eu/

opened with the feel wheel[4], a way to establish interpersonal connection as well as expose students to new general English vocabulary relevant to the emotional states caused by the pandemic crisis (as suggested in one of the trainings in which I participated, see 3.7 below).

The schedule was the same as the one originally agreed for the conventional classroom, with two classes taking up a four-hour morning slot, with a break around 11 am for students to make their own coffee. Sometimes the feel wheel was used when reconvening after the break just to make a smooth transition into the more technical content.

### 3.4. Enhanced feedback

Feedback is valued in LSP pedagogy as part of a broader student-centred philosophy of teaching and learning that tries to address very specific needs and motives for learning a language, where learning equals being capable of putting into practice. The digital environment augments the need to provide specific and constructive feedback, as a way to maintain social contact and preserve continuity in the learning process.

Detailed and timely feedback meant regular assignments and more careful calibration of workload on the part of the teacher, both in terms of what was feasible for students from one meeting to the next and reasonable correction time for the teacher. Because most of the feedback was written and uploaded on Kiro, it also required the teacher to think about the phrasing so as to make it simple, unambiguous, and useful all at once. The enhanced role of feedback (Gottlieb & Katz, 2020; White, 2017) has been an opportunity for intensive error analysis.

### 3.5. Collaborative project-based learning

All of the contents and methods created anew for this course were collected on the LMS and successfully employed to enhance teaching and learning.

---

4. https://imgur.com/gallery/tCWChf6

The most notable of these was the glossary collaboratively constructed by the students and the teacher. The model was initiated by the teacher, but students contributed to refining it and to overcoming some of the limitations of the e-learning platform affordances. The aim of the glossary was not to replicate the many monolingual or bilingual technical dictionaries already available for free consultation, but rather to give students a chance to contribute entries of their own choice that they would encounter during the course, and instead of providing a definition of the terms, complement them with examples taken from the different authentic sources included in the teaching material.

The glossary took the shape of a digital list of terms accompanied by a rich illustrative apparatus of examples showing the use of the terms in their natural context of occurrence, on the recognition that it is not the term as such, but the collocation and patterning that are difficult to learn for the L2 speaker. A drop-down menu of so called 'aliases' allowed for the inclusion of synonyms (e.g. *floor, storey, story*) and equivalent Italian terms. This kind of jointly constructed glossary had the advantage of reinforcing the learning process based on principles of redundancy in second language learning and acquisition (Larsen-Freeman, 2000) and learner autonomy and collaborative project-based learning in ESP (Hafner & Miller, 2019). By adding a lemma they encountered while reading or listening to authentic sources, students were deliberately choosing what was salient for them and reinforcing the acquisition of the item also by selecting the relevant examples. By adding the Italian equivalent term, they were then learning bilingual correspondences in the terminology. If the term chosen was already present in the list because another course participant had contributed it, then there was still room for adding new examples. The development of the glossary prompted metalinguistic reflection on polysemy, synonymy, and equivalence, when, for example, the same term in English corresponds to two different terms in Italian (e.g. *floor* meaning both 'piano' (*storey*) and 'pavimento' (*the surface of a room you walk on*), and on optimal ways of representing semantic and field relations between terms, e.g. when trying to group items belonging to the same field, e.g. *crenellation*, *portcullis*, *mullioned windows*, etc. as features of gothic (and neo-gothic) architecture; *profiles, joist*, and *installations* used when describing structures and systems, etc. or ranging across sub-fields, e.g. *design development*, *bid*, *brief*, *component*.

### 3.6. Students' evaluations

Students' feedback at the end of the course was unanimously positive and pointed to the digital environment as a strength rather than a weakness of the course, as can be seen in the following two quotes from the questionnaires:

> "è stato molto interessante e mi ha permesso di implementare la mia conoscenza dell'inglese, in particolare legata alla professione che dovrò affrontare nel futuro (*It was very interesting and it allowed me to implement my knowledge of English, in particular as it is linked to my future profession*)".

> "nonostante sia un corso di inglese, si focalizza sugli aspetti architettonici ed ingegneristici, dando un valore aggiunto al corso ed aprendo la possibilità ad un mondo lavorativo oltre l'Italia. La collaborazione il 'BADGE PROJECT' è un buon metodo, in grado di porci obiettivi che magari si sarebbero trascurati (*Although it is an English course, it focuses on architecture and engineering features, giving added value to it and opening up possibilities of working abroad beyond Italy. The BADGE PROJECT collaboration is a good method that gives us objectives that would otherwise have been overlooked*)".

### 3.7. Teacher development

The next two considerations regard research-informed teaching and fast teacher development as an unexpected outcome of the shift online. In order to favour maximum accessibility, a mechanism was put in place to enable the videorecording of the entire course after obtaining permission from participants. This yielded a wealth of ethnographic data that would lend itself to thick qualitative descriptions of the whole course. A first output was a 10-minute video produced by the author (see supplementary materials), i.e. an edited version of the students' final presentations with the teachers' evaluations to capture some of the learners' achievements as well as needs to inform the design of the next course.

Moreover, after opting for the synchronous delivery combined with the e-learning platform, I felt the need to get fast and reusable training on distance teaching. The crisis became an opportunity for teacher development in many areas, including innovation, which would not have otherwise occurred. Because locally no real internal training had been offered besides assistance with the technical features of the LMS, I looked out for possibilities, as offered for example, by other universities, notably the Graduate Program in Applied Linguistics and Language Studies (Linguística Aplicada e Estudos da Linguagem, LAEL) webinar series of the Pontifical Catholic University of Sao Paulo, Brazil[5], and by materials publishers, e.g. National Geographic Learning of Eli Publishing, the latter specifically dealing with online English language learning (see Shin & Borup, 2020). Although not directly concerned with online teaching, the LAEL webinars allowed me to participate in the audience and learn how to use the interactive affordances of the videoconferencing tools on the students' side (especially the chat and the Q&A). The many opportunities for professional development had now become easily accessible and worthwhile and put the teacher in contact with a global community of practitioners sharing similar needs and experiences.

## 4. Moving online: re-examining assessment

The other experience I will briefly discuss is assessment at the end of a course for undergraduate students of modern languages. The course, the compulsory second year of a three-year program for students majoring in English and one or two other languages (among French, German, Russian, Spanish), depending on the individual curriculum, had been delivered in the first semester before the COVID-19 outbreak through traditional face-to-face teaching. However, because of the changed situation in June, the final assessment had to be done remotely. The exam usually consisted of a reading comprehension and text

---

5. http://corpuslg.org/lael_english/

analysis followed by the oral examination on the course contents, titled 'Making sense of text'. Despite the initial pressure from the Department of Humanities to avoid written tests altogether, for my course this represented a unique opportunity to learn to use Kiro's testing options. I therefore tried to maintain the same test format as in the paper-based version, i.e. a text with comprehension and analytical-descriptive questions, and experimented with test items design as allowed by Kiro, particularly, short guided open-ended questions, multiple-choice, gap-fills, and longer open questions inviting for more writing.

Turning the written test into a computer-based one involved rethinking not so much the test format as the connection between test items and course syllabus, carefully choosing from the syllabus items and balancing them in the written test as a guarantee of test validity (see Gollin-Kies et al., 2015). This was facilitated by the affordances of the digital platform in which each question had to be labelled with a tag corresponding to each content item in the syllabus. This brought about a deep evaluation of the syllabus as well as systematic analysis of each test item individually (*what is item x testing?*) and in relation to the overall test (*how does item x fit the whole test?*). The digital format allowed storing the items easily into a reusable database and even though the questions are text-based, one can draw from the database to put together different tests based on the same reading text to be used in successive testing sessions or for formative assessment. The digital test was then trialled as a mock exam to help students familiarise with it and to receive feedback on the practical limitations or difficulties linked to the format (e.g. time needed to scroll up and down the screen to go back to the text after reading each question). It also helped clarify the phrasing of the instructions and prompts, which I could then streamline in my preparations of the test for the final exam.

The test was administered using an improved Kiro platform called KiroTesting[6], which allows for timed tests, combined with a Safe Exam Browser software, impeding internet navigation throughout the duration of the test, and a Zoom videocall for the teacher to be able to actually see the students while taking the

---

6. https://kirotesting.unipv.it

test. The time-consuming part, especially for the first testing session in June, was the rollcall, which was meant to check the students' set up and video framing on Zoom. For this first testing session, I could count on the IT assistant, who was connected to the videocall and had access to KiroTesting. The session went smoothly: only three out of 52 examinees experienced issues with the testing platform or the internet connection and were allowed to retake the test the following day. The overall students' performance was good and the pass rate comparable to that of the paper-based test the year before. When informally asked to give feedback on what it had been like to take the test remotely, some students said they enjoyed taking the test from home in a familiar environment and not having to commute to Pavia just for the exam. Others said they preferred the pen and paper version. The test experience would deserve a more systematic evaluation of the students' perceptions. Should the digital format be maintained, it will be done as a step forward in the research on online language assessment. From the teacher perspective, the digital administering proved convenient and timesaving to the extent that it did not involve deciphering the students' handwriting. However, marking was not too efficient and rather time-consuming because the nature of the test items, all open-ended (see supplementary materials), made it impossible to check answers automatically.

## 5. Conclusions

In all, the unforeseen movement toward digital language teaching and learning seems to have brought about new pedagogical possibilities that build on and boost already existing good educational practices (e.g. enhanced feedback, collaborative work, task-based learning, additional learning objectives, assessment). Sudden and dramatic changes such as those brought about by the pandemic reshaped the teaching context by turning what were local limitations and constraints into a global space without borders and with enhanced means that allowed for new forms of collaborative work. Break-down of physical barriers and reduced means limitations meant improved accessibility, a positive change that could be sustained. A blended paradigm that combines in-presence contact with the students and more practical and collaborative learning activities online seems to be the scenario of the future, where learner's centredness and empowerment are at the heart of successful language learning. Blended learning is versatile and can offer learners more opportunities for social interaction through the tools of digital communication (e.g. the chat), more autonomy (e.g. the web searches), and additional advantages such as promoting real life language use.

At the time of writing this, I have just completed the English Language 2 Course redesigned and delivered fully online as in Fall 2020 Pavia and the whole Milan region are entering a second lockdown. The university has now acquired Zoom licenses for all its staff, has developed how-to-teach-with-zoom guidebooks through the Information Technology (IT) department, and is requesting lecturers to teach live, record the entire course and save it on a Google Drive shared folder and make both the livestream and the recordings accessible through links on the local e-learning platform Kiro. This has raised controversy over unsolved copyright issues. At the same time, I have revisited the syllabus, more carefully planning the sequencing and grading of contents, experimenting with interactive tools such as break-out rooms with the students, and reusing KiroTesting for formative assessment during the course. What has been achieved has a lot of potential for dynamic innovation (Grgurovic, 2017), but the teachers need more training to fully embrace the digital paradigm and exploit its pedagogical possibilities to the full. What we, as language practitioners need in the future is more opportunities for teacher development, from more technological and pedagogical training to more international exchange on teaching practices to take the conversation beyond the local and toward the global. I believe this project is one such opportunity.

## 6. Supplementary materials

Ten-minute video: https://drive.google.com/file/d/1gP9Y8mPg6SydUtF1hXIX8c8CASDMDArv

Text analysis test items: https://docs.google.com/document/d/1kcZx7v18Y3JDk1JZpzAU65Hsrd3uLZg8d9n0UTZu16g

# References

Basturkmen, H. (2010). *Developing courses in English for specific purposes*. Palgrave.

Gollin-Kies, S., Hall, D. R., & Moore, S. H. (2015). *Language for specific purposes*. Palgrave.

Gottlieb, M., & Katz, A. (2020). Assessment in the classroom. In C. A. Chapelle (Ed.), *The concise encyclopaedia of applied linguistics* (pp. 44-52 ). Wiley Blackwell.

Grgurovic, M. (2017). Blended language learning: research and practice. In C. A. Chapelle & S. Sauro (Eds), *The handbook of technology and second language teaching and learning* (pp. 149-168). Wiley Blackwell. https://doi.org/10.1002/9781118914069.ch11

Gruber, D. R., & Olman, L. (2019). (Eds). *The Routledge handbook of language and science*. Routledge.

Hafner, C. A., & Miller, L. (2019). *English in the disciplines. A multidimensional model for ESP course design*. Routledge.

Larsen-Freeman, D. (2000). *Techniques and principles in language teaching* (2nd ed.). Oxford University Press.

Nesi, H., & Gardner, S. (2012). *Genres across the disciplines: student writing in higher education*. Cambridge University Press. https://doi.org/10.1017/9781009030199

Schmied, J. (2018). A global view on writing research articles for international journals: principles and practices. In J. Schmied, M. Hofmann & A. Esimaje (Eds), *Academic writing in Africa: the journal article. REAL 15* (pp. 1-18). Cuvillier.

Shin, J. K., & Borup, J. (2020). Global webinars for English teachers worldwide during a pandemic: "they came right when I needed them the most". In R. E. Ferdig, E. Baumgartner, R. Hartshorne, R. Kaplan-Rakowski & C. Mouza (Eds), *Teaching, technology, and teacher education during the COVID-19 pandemic: stories from the field* (pp. 157-162). Association for the Advancement of Computing in Education.

Spector, T., & Damron, R. (2017). *How architects write* (2nd ed.). Routledge.

Ur, P. (2012). *A course in English language teaching* (2nd ed.). Cambridge University Press.

White, C. (2017). Distance language teaching with technology. In C. A. Chapelle & S. Sauro (Eds), *The handbook of technology and second language teaching and learning* (pp. 134-148). Wiley Blackwell. https://doi.org/10.1002/9781118914069.ch10

# 18 University of Cambridge Asian, Middle Eastern and Persian studies during the pandemic

## Mahbod Ghaffari[1]

### Abstract

This case study will focus on the COVID-19 lecturers' experience in the Faculty of Asian and Middle Eastern Studies (FAMES)[2] at the University of Cambridge. After a brief background about how the academic year works in the University of Cambridge and an introduction about the situation after the outbreak of COVID-19 in the UK, the author will discuss about the measures taken by the faculty and the way the teaching was conducted in the FAMES in general and Persian language courses in particular. Then, the challenges and problems regarding online teaching in Department of Middle Eastern Studies (DMES) will be highlighted. Finally, a short explanation about the way the examination and assessment were handled in the faculty will be provided. The findings show excellent management and steady leadership turned the classic classroom-based teaching to remote and online teaching. Also, professional collaboration and performance of lecturers along with the ongoing technical and training support were the main factors to go through the critical phase of the pandemic's impact successfully. It seems that the language teachers have gained valuable experience and skills in teaching languages differently, which can be deployed in future post pandemic situations.

Keywords: COVID-19, online language teaching, Persian language, UK.

---

1. University of Cambridge, Cambridge, United Kingdom; mg695@cam.ac.uk; https://orcid.org/0000-0002-4709-2462

2. https://www.ames.cam.ac.uk/

How to cite: Ghaffari, M. (2021). University of Cambridge Asian, Middle Eastern and Persian studies during the pandemic. In N. Radić, A. Atabekova, M. Freddi & J. Schmied (Eds), *The world universities' response to COVID-19: remote online language teaching* (pp. 295-305). Research-publishing.net. https://doi.org/10.14705/rpnet.2021.52.1279

# Chapter 18

## 1. Introduction

In this section, a brief introduction of the academic year in the University of Cambridge, the institutional context, and the outbreak of the COVID-19 in the UK will be provided.

Usually, each academic year in the University of Cambridge consists of three terms named Michaelmas, Lent, and Easter term[3] respectively, of which Easter term includes the assessment and examination period. Therefore, usually, examination is conducted only once in an academic year.

> "All Cambridge undergraduate courses are assessed through examinations in broad subject areas called Triposes. Each Tripos is divided into one or more Parts and you need to complete a number of Parts in one or more Triposes to qualify for the B.A. degree"[4].

In the FAMES, there are two separate departments and hence two different triposes: Department of Middle Eastern Studies, where the students study Arabic, Persian, Hebrew, and/or Hindi languages, and Department of Asian studies, where the students study Chinese, Japanese, or Korean languages. Either of these Triposes will last four years before the students graduate and are awarded a Bachelor of Arts (BA) degree.

Year three of their study is called the Year Abroad[5] and the students need to spend this third year of their four-year course in a country or countries relevant to their course. This is an excellent opportunity to increase their fluency and understanding of the language. It also provides the opportunity to start work on their dissertation, which must show evidence of a substantial use of the sources, whether oral or textual, in their language of study.

---

3. https://www.cam.ac.uk/about-the-university/term-dates-and-calendars
4. https://www.camdata.admin.cam.ac.uk/structure-undergraduate-courses-cambridge?
5. https://www.ames.cam.ac.uk/undergraduates/what-can-you-study/year-abroad

The first cases of COVID-19 were reported in the UK on 15 Feb 2020[6], which was in the middle of the university's Lent term, which was planned to end on 13 March 2020. So, in the last couple of weeks of that term, the anxiety and stress amongst students and staff could be seen as the news was indicating that the number of daily cases was increasing, particularly in other countries. Very soon, more precisely, 10 days after the end of the Lent term, the national lockdown was announced in the UK[7].

The university's vice chancellor published messages[8] accordingly, and different working groups were set up. The Cambridge Centre for Teaching and Learning[9] gave some guidelines and consulted staff to help them with practical advice. That was the starting time, when departments, faculties, and the university started to think about the possible ways to address the issue and the brainstorming of how the teaching could be conducted after Easter.

It was early April that the university decided to have the lessons online, and for that reason, a lot of meetings were started for the best way of delivery. Although I am a member of the FAMES, I am working at Cambridge University Language Centre too. They were pioneers in deciding to use the Zoom platform for online delivery of their lessons. So, the meetings, training sessions, and practice sessions on how to use Zoom were really helpful. That made me prepared in advance for what I would plan to do when teaching would start in the FAMES.

In our DMES virtual meetings, I shared my findings and learnings with my colleagues and also delivered a couple of training sessions for the academic staff (particularly lecturers of different languages) on how to use Zoom in the classroom. I should emphasise that teaching online and using such platforms were not easy for many lecturers. However, my previous experience in designing remote online and offline language resources as well as my experience

---

6. https://www.theguardian.com/world/live/2020/feb/15/coronavirus-first-fatality-in-europe-confirmed-wuhan-COVID-19-death-toll-symptoms-cruise-ship-liner-quarantine-live-updates

7. https://www.gov.uk/government/speeches/pm-address-to-the-nation-on-coronavirus-23-march-2020

8. www.cam.ac.uk/notices/news/an-update-from-the-vice-chancellor-on-the-coronavirus-outbreak

9. www.cctl.cam.ac.uk

## Chapter 18

in online language teaching gave me confidence that I could easily continue my teachings online. Actually, I had been involved in developing content and the preferred way those contents could be designed, adapted, and delivered digitally when I was dealing with a Multimedia software for teaching Persian language and introductions to Iranian culture, which was named 'Alefba-ye Iran' and designed and produced by 'RayMehr Company' in 2007. I also had been in charge of content and design of the first interactive online Persian language teaching website named "www.PersianLanguageOnline.com", created by the Persian Language Foundation in 2014, which was acquired by the Iran Heritage Foundation in 2018. On the other hand, I have been teaching online, particularly using Skype since 2009 and also using other websites which were helpful for language teaching, such as Oovoo.

Hence, when I was introduced to Zoom by Cambridge University Language Centre in April 2020, I found that the platform had many features and advantages which could be helpful for online delivery of the lessons. It was very user friendly: you could have 100 students logged in to your class and you could see them on your screen; the breakout rooms provided the opportunity to divide students into pairs and groups in order to practise speaking skills and conversation; recording the session was straightforward and reasonably easy to be shared with those unable to attend so they could make use of it; the chat box was available to communicate with the student and write words and phrases for them; the whiteboard was helpful to write in Persian script, so the students could see the cursive handwritten form they would experience in normal in-person classes; and above all, you could share your screen with the students to work on particular text, watch a particular clip, etc. Finally, as we are using Moodle in the University of Cambridge and we have already lots of e-content over there, Zoom was easily compatible with Moodle. So, I decided to use Zoom over other platforms such as Microsoft Teams and Google Meet and suggested it highly to all other colleagues in the faculty.

Therefore, considering all my experience and knowledge of offline, digital, and interactive or online live remote teaching, I put myself forward to help other members of the faculty in using online technology and representing them in the

School of Humanities Online Learning, Teaching, and Assessment Group of the University of Cambridge.

## 2. Objective

The objective of this chapter is to highlight the actions which were taken in the FAMES after the lockdown during the Easter term, and this section particularly focuses on Persian case study.

As it was mentioned earlier, the faculty offers different Asian and Middle Eastern languages at the undergraduate level for four years. The number of students accepted and admitted for the undergraduate programme is about 40 students (20 students in the department of Middle Eastern studies and 20 students in the department of Asian studies) per year, and hence the classes are not exceeding 12 students and accordingly much smaller in size in comparison with other courses and other universities. In the department of Middle Eastern studies, usually 90% of students have a combination of two languages of the Middle East or one language from the Middle East and another language from the Department of Modern Medieval Languages and Linguistics. Therefore, they may have up to ten contact hours of language classes per week and these would form about 50 to 60% of their degree.

Apart from language classes, all students will have some other classes on history, literature, anthropology, cinema, etc. of the regions. These are called content papers, which are more like lectures with discussions. Also, students will have dedicated supervision sessions every week for the language or non-language subjects they take. These are usually in groups of one to four students.

It should be noted that the advantages of having language classes of small size made the online teaching of languages perfectly feasible. This is also applicable to very small supervision sessions as well as lecture type classes of bigger size which do not need the active engagement of students for language learning. Hence, it was fairly manageable to conduct online language classes in the faculty.

Chapter 18

In the case of Persian studies, there were 12 students in total, of which 5 were doing Persian Elementary, 2 were doing Persian Intermediate, and 5 were doing Persian Advanced with the same lecturer. Each group had at least 4-5 sessions per week. Each session of language class was 50-60 minutes, and the students were connecting through the provided Zoom link. The teaching task was straightforward and done as usual. It should be acknowledged that the teaching time in online mode was the least difficult part of the whole process. Students were engaged and involved actively in the learning process, the breakout rooms were used properly for pair work and group work activities, and the reading texts and listening materials were accessible via Moodle and also were screen shared with or played for the students respectively. In addition, the videos and online interactive Persian teaching websites were of great help during the Easter term.

## 3. Support

The University of Cambridge reacted promptly to the advent of COVID-19 in order to support students, lecturers, and staff to make them prepared and equipped for online remote teaching. At the faculty and department level, a considerable amount of meeting and consultation sessions were held in order to find the needs and requirements as well as best possible solutions towards the critical situation. Despite the guidelines and advice the university and the faculty provided, the lecturers were given freedom in deciding the best practices for the classes that they were teaching.

Regarding technical and technology support, the faculty provided all teaching staff with Zoom premium accounts to address the shortcomings of basic accounts. The devices needed for marking the students' assignments were requested by some language teachers and were purchased quickly. The university acquired Panopto as a recording platform for the academic staff to create and share the videos of their lectures. Different training sessions on using technologies such as Zoom, Panopto, and other platforms as well as online and remote teaching principles, techniques, and strategies were provided by different parts of the university. Ongoing support and training were in the core of the plan in a way that it was really impossible to attend all, and the teaching staff had to choose only the ones they found most beneficial from the many webinars and the training sessions provided.

## 4. Challenges

There were also some challenges, some of which needed more time than in normal classes. Among which, I can refer to preparing the materials for online classes, including scanning the texts which were not available in digital format and uploading the written and oral materials in the Moodle. Also spending a huge amount of time on the computer for lesson preparation as well as having the classes online for a few hours in row were tiring, and problems such as eye fatigue, back pain, and other physical health problems were unavoidable. What should be added to this is the after class workload, which was doubled. The students were submitting their homework and assignment online in different formats, and marking them digitally was time consuming, tiring, and problematic. Unavailability of printers and learning how to mark the digital language homework were big issues. However, the devices such as Penpads (which have been provided by the faculty if asked) were helpful to some extent to do the marking on the computer without the need of using a mouse or printing much homework (which is, on the other hand, not environmentally friendly). The colleagues who were in possession of tablets or iPads had fewer issues of such kind.

The other challenge was to find the perfect time where all students of a particular class could log in and attend the class, as some of them had returned to their home countries, which were in different time zones. We had students who were in Canada, Egypt, France, the UK, and the USA. Moreover, it was needed that all participants, including the teacher, be in an appropriate place with the proper desk, chair, and light and without any disturbing noise as well as having reliable internet connection. There were a couple of instances when somebody entered a student's room and distracted not only that particular student but also all other participants. Moreover, there were times when one student lost connection and could not connect any more to one particular session. Despite all these downsides and challenges, the Easter term went well, with above 95% attendance and covering all the required topics and materials and preparing the students for the examination and attendance.

Regarding Arabic and Hebrew language classes, the experience of the lecturers were to some extent similar to the Persian ones. All language classes and supervision sessions were conducted online through Zoom. For other content papers (lecture type classes) and their supervision, the lecturers were using a mix of platforms including Microsoft Teams, Zoom, Google Meet, and Skype.

## 5. Assessment

For the assessment and examinations, after several meetings and consultations with all teaching staff, the university decided to have formal examinations for final year students and summative assessment for other year group students. In the case of Persian studies language papers, all oral exams (including listening and speaking skills) were conducted online where each individual student was attending exam sessions separately in their dedicated time. For written exams (including reading and writing exams), the same examinations which were provided for normal situations were made available on the specific date for the students to access them. They needed to complete the assessment in the normal exam duration and finally scan and upload their work into the system to be marked by the examiners. The exam results were in line with the lecturer's expectations based on the students' one year performance, and also there was no meaningful difference in comparison to the results in the previous years.

## 6. Discussion

For getting the feedback from the students and teachers, a couple of questionnaires with open questions were sent to the lecturers. The questions were mainly asking about the problems, opinion, experience, best practice, requirements, and support. The students' feedback was gathered in online sessions and through the emails received. Also, another survey was conducted by School of Humanities Online Learning Teaching Group, in which many language teachers and students participated. Some feedback was gathered from this survey.

Based on the feedback received, the online teaching was welcomed warmly by the students because not only they have been more familiar with modern technology as well as different features and advantages of social media and virtual world but they were also less worried and stressed about the pandemic. However, different feedback was received regarding the productivity of teaching language remotely. Some believed that body language was missing, which has a great role in understanding spoken language, and there had been less opportunity to focus on speaking skills in comparison to classroom-based teaching. However, they found that online learning is as good for reading skills, enhancing vocabulary, and understanding grammar.

In the same way, the language teachers had mixed experience about online teaching. Some were really struggling and had negative feedback, and some were supporting it and wanted to use their materials and experience even post COVID-19. Some language teachers believe that face to face language teaching is irreplaceable and remote teaching doesn't allow for a sense of real contact with and among the students. There are associated costs with remote teaching: teachers might have home responsibilities with family around or have a partner as a key worker, some of them are single parents and hence school/childcare setting closure should be accounted, and finally, their working environment has been less than ideal and they would prefer uninterrupted access to their offices at the faculty. These groups of lecturers found that they didn't have sufficient time to seek training in remote teaching. They found their students were less active with inadequate concentration. Also, they found online teaching exhausting, tiring on eyes, and very demanding with a lot of strain on them physically and mentally. On the other hand, some lecturers find remote language teaching and particularly the Zoom platform interestingly useful and surprisingly easy. They believe it works really well and is quite intense.

## Chapter 18

What has been learnt and can be considered as the findings of this case study of online language teaching in the FAMES can be summarised in a few points.

Apart from all the shortcomings and problems with online remote teaching, the higher the familiarity of the teachers with technology, the easier and less stressful the online teaching experience. It may start with a steep learning curve, but it would get easier with familiarity and through time. This has been true and visible in the first term of the new academic year 2020-2021. Although the interaction with the students via online platforms is tricky, it can be carefully and professionally managed after gaining more training and experience. Teaching online can be highly effective with no major pedagogical hurdle particularly for small group teaching and supervisions. However, the pace in online teaching would be slower than in-person teaching. In general, it needs a great amount of adaptability. Mastering how to use one particular platform is much better than not having enough deep knowledge of many platforms at the same time, and, among those, the Zoom platform is one of the most appropriate for online language classes. More tailored training courses would be much more beneficial for supporting the lecturers and addressing their needs and solving their problems. Availability of digital or online content will help the lecturers in saving time and energy spent for digitalising the hard copies of their teaching materials. Access to offices and an adequate working atmosphere with all the needed materials, technology, and devices around will make online teaching more straightforward and pleasant both for lecturers and students. Online teaching can be a way forward, but if it is blended with in-person teaching, it will solve many problems and overcome the downsides and disadvantages.

## 7. Conclusion

The FAMES took action immediately concerning the outbreak of COVID-19 and the sudden changes of the educational requirements. Due to different teaching staff expertise, beliefs, and approaches in the faculty, with limited technologies in place, excellent management and steady leadership were absolutely essential for turning the classic classroom-based teaching to remote and online teaching.

The exceptionally professional and quick collaboration and performance of colleagues to adapt to this sudden change, along with the ongoing technical and training support were the main factors to make the lecturers and students able to go through the critical phase of the pandemic's impact successfully. The language teachers of the faculty gained valuable experience and skills in teaching languages differently. They are now more comfortable in using technology inside and outside classrooms, developing their materials appropriate for remote and online teaching, and addressing their new pedagogical needs. Not only are they better prepared to continue their teaching whilst there is the COVID-19 pandemic condition but also to deploy these skills and advantages in future post pandemic situations.

# 19 University of Cambridge Modern and Medieval Languages: response to COVID-19

## Silke Mentchen[1]

## Abstract

This case study will describe and analyse how the experiences of online language teaching at the University of Cambridge gained during the first UK lockdown helped to inform planning for the next academic year. Emergency measures implemented for the third term of the academic year 2019/2020 were evaluated. A curriculum of blended teaching combining synchronous and asynchronous modes was developed and is being implemented now. Particular attention will be paid to modes of examining and teaching, the role of the teacher, and the use of technologies. It will become clear that inclusive and interactive teaching will continue and that some of the newly acquired skills may stay with us. However, other aspects of language teaching such as building a sense of a learner cohort have been found to be much more difficult to replicate online.

**Keywords: COVID-19, online language teaching, blended teaching, asynchronous modes, German language, UK.**

---

1. Cambridge University, Cambridge, United Kingdom; scm30@cam.ac.uk; https://orcid.org/0000-0002-2622-2715

**How to cite:** Mentchen, S. (2021). University of Cambridge Modern and Medieval Languages: response to COVID-19. In N. Radić, A. Atabekova, M. Freddi & J. Schmied (Eds), *The world universities' response to COVID-19: remote online language teaching* (pp. 307-320). Research-publishing.net. https://doi.org/10.14705/rpnet.2021.52.1280

Chapter 19

## 1. Introduction

In this chapter, the response to the COVID-19 pandemic at the University of Cambridge will be described and analysed. The intention is to consider two teaching terms, differentiating between the required reaction during an emergency and the typical measures taken for the first term of a new academic year. The focus will be on pedagogical approaches as well as on pragmatic, technical, and medical considerations. By examining the institution's decision-making process, the intention is to show that wide consultation, albeit time consuming, has resulted in inclusive and pedagogically successful teaching programmes.

## 2. Context

Modern and Medieval Languages is one of two degrees offered by the Faculty of Modern and Medieval Languages and Linguistics (MMLL)[2]. Languages offered as part of the degree course comprise: French, German, Italian, Portuguese, Russian, and Spanish. Students must study two of these languages and are also able to study introductory courses in Catalan, Dutch, modern Greek, Polish, Portuguese, and Ukrainian as part of their degree. French is the only language currently not available for study at *ab initio* level. Modern languages offered by the faculty can be studied as part of joint degrees in combination with languages offered by other faculties. It is also possible to study a modern language from MMLL alongside history.

This case study will concentrate on undergraduate language teaching. Modern and Medieval Languages admits approximately 160 students each year and in 2019 there were roughly 70% female and 30% male students[3].

The full-time degree takes four years with the third year spent abroad. We teach in three eight-week terms.

---

2. www.mmll.cam.ac.uk

3. https://www.undergraduate.study.cam.ac.uk/apply/statistics

- Term 1: October/December.

- Term 2: middle of January/middle of March.

- Term 3: end of April/middle of June. This third term is dedicated to revision and examinations, with only the first four weeks reserved for teaching. In effect, the degree comprises 20 weeks of teaching per year.

### 2.1. Staff

It is somewhat difficult to identify precisely the number of staff employed by the faculty, as we draw on a pool of university tenured staff, college based staff, post docs, and part time staff.

### 2.2. Technical support

The university has a university-wide Information Technology (IT) service[4]. MMLL does not employ IT specialists with expertise in language teaching.

At the end of March 2020, when the UK entered into a first lockdown, language teachers organised many peer-to-peer conversations, either on the phone or by email correspondence. There was a clear demand for guidance on how to make the various technologies work for the particular faculties' needs. Members of staff organised themselves in groups, using platforms like Zoom, Microsoft Teams, and Google Docs to exchange ideas and work out common ground. The university's information services reached out to individuals involved in teaching, and the first of these consultative meetings took place at the beginning of April. Each faculty within the school nominated a representative for a working group on online teaching. Meetings started at the beginning of May and were a useful conduit for information.

---

4. https://www.uis.cam.ac.uk/

## 3. Decision-making

Cambridge University comprises over 30 colleges. Colleges are responsible for admitting and housing students, organising small group teaching called 'supervisions', and looking after students' welfare. Decisions therefore must be made at various levels. The university's vice chancellor published messages[5], starting on March 13, informing staff and students of discussions and decisions concerning COVID-19. In addition, open consultations and various working groups were set up. The Cambridge Centre for Teaching and Learning[6] issued guidelines and consulted staff, and several 'clinics' were organised to help teachers with practical advice. Decisions made at the highest level included the transition of all lecturing to online mode and the introduction of a 'safety net' for final year examinations.

The senior management team consulted with students and staff, and the Language Teaching Officers as a group consulted and agreed on basic principles and approaches for teaching. Surveys were sent to part time staff as well as full-time lecturers.

Expectation management was deemed important at the beginning of lockdown. The term 'emergency remote teaching' to describe the faculty's approach was used. The situation changed rapidly, with new information, for example advice about face coverings emerging. Some decisions had to be made quickly: students on their year abroad who had to return home (on travel advice issued by the UK government) urgently needed information on study requirements. All oral examinations for first and second year students scheduled for April and May were cancelled. Other issues concerned the lockdown of facilities and access of staff to their offices and to the libraries.

---

5. https://www.cam.ac.uk/notices/news/an-update-from-the-vice-chancellor-on-the-coronavirus-outbreak

6. https://www.cctl.cam.ac.uk/

## 4. Teaching and examining

### 4.1. Teaching for the academic year 2020/2021

The third term differs from other terms in that its main purpose is revision. Lectures have concluded and students are taught in small group supervisions where they can concentrate on topics in preparation for exams. Correspondingly, language classes, which continue, focus on revision and consolidation. Mock exams and extensive written feedback to student's work are central. It is important to note that the faculty was faced with what was very much understood to be an emergency. Both students and staff were working from home. However, all students were familiar with the curriculum and knew their teachers and peers. This helped to maintain trust, co-operation, and an overall positive attitude.

For their third term, students did not return to the university campus. The main concern here was inclusivity: access to the internet, quality of broadband, suitability of equipment, and access to a quiet study space could not be assumed for all. For this reason, a blended programme was evolved, making use of recordings combined with Q&As. The Cambridge system of detailed and individual (written) feedback was used extensively. Teaching for a number of classes took place synchronously online. Student feedback to this approach was mixed. While some expressed anxiety about having to attend online live classes preferring instead to work at their own pace, soliciting help when needed, others found live classes much preferable to asynchronous provisions.

The university introduced a 'safety net' for all final year students: any student whose marks during the end of year examinations in 2020 were lower than their results in the previous year would be classed in that higher category[7].

After consulting with students, MMLL developed a plan for examinations. Some of the language examinations, which involved testing of correct application of grammar rules and vocabulary, would not provide meaningful results if conducted

---

[7]. https://www.cam.ac.uk/coronavirus/students/archive/assessment-201920/assessment-principles-and-policies-easter-term-2020

online as open-book exams. However, in order to send a clear signal to students that they had made progress and should continue work on their language skills over the summer, progress tests were introduced at the beginning of the academic year 2020/2021. Results of these tests would not have any effect on the student's future career as a linguist; rather, they were meant to reassure students and certify that they had reached the appropriate level of proficiency.

For translation examinations, which were to go ahead, the format was changed so that candidates were permitted to use online resources (dictionaries, for example) but were advised not to use machine translation available from Google or DeepL. A task in which students had to choose a specified number of challenges per passage and explain, in English, how they solved the problem was introduced. This could include comments on style, vocabulary, and grammar. The intention here was to confirm that students had produced their own work.

Communication with students was maintained via the faculty's webpage and via email. An FAQ page was produced and a generic email address to deal with any questions concerning examinations was created. In total, MMLL administers over 200 different examinations. Student feedback on the whole was favourable.

Plans for the first term of the new academic year evolved. Given that most students would be back on campus, synchronous online teaching delivery and some face-to-face teaching were possible. The university decided that all lectures should be online. This would free up lecture halls to make face-to-face teaching in comparatively smaller groups possible. Language classes were included in the types of teaching for which face-to-face classes would be allowed. However, for MMLL language teaching, it was decided that online teaching would be preferable[8].

After discussions considering the effects of online teaching on the health of both students and staff, it was agreed that parity of the learning experience would be guaranteed by conducting most classes online. No one would be disadvantaged

---

8. For a comparison of online and on campus teaching see Salmon (2020).

should they not be able to attend. Reasons for non-attendance could be the need to shield, the requirement to self-isolate, not being able to return to Cambridge, or having tested positive for COVID. Of course, it would also be statistically likely that any number of the teaching staff would not be able to teach in person. Further uncertainties about childcare infrastructure, for example, only added to the concerns.

In this context, it may be interesting to note that the UK's government advisory body SAGE released a statement on the 3rd of September 2020 in which they recommended online teaching:

> "[a] clear principle from the hierarchy of risk control is that elimination (e.g. removing in-person activities) is the most effective approach to control transmission, followed by substitution (e.g. changing the activity to substantially reduce interaction). Alongside any adjustments to enable in-person provision, it is important that access to online learning is also considered, both in terms of accessibility of materials for different students and in their ability to engage effectively including whether they have appropriate equipment, working spaces and internet connections"[9].

At the time of writing this case study, the UK's Student Union and the UK's University and College Union have launched joint campaigns to move all teaching online[10].

The need to build a sense of community for continuing students and especially for freshers was recognised. Using platforms such as Padlet and OneNote (these are just two examples from a much longer list) to enable meaningful collaborations amongst students was discussed. This was crucial for students

---

9. https://assets.publishing.service.gov.uk/government/uploads/system/uploads/attachment_data/file/914978/S0728_Principles_for_Managing_SARS-CoV-2_Transmission_Associated_with_Higher_Education_.pdf.
Also see the minutes of a meeting of SAGE on the 21st of September in which the recommendation that "all university and college teaching to be online unless absolutely essential" is included in a "short-list of non-pharmaceutical interventions. https://assets.publishing.service.gov.uk/government/uploads/system/uploads/attachment_data/file/925854/S0769_Summary_of_effectiveness_and_harms_of_NPIs.pdf

10. https://www.ucu.org.uk/article/11035/UCU-and-the-National-Union-Students-issue-joint-statement-calling-for-action-over-university-Covid-crisis

entering university life after a school year with many disruptions and without A-levels, normally a requirement for university entry[11]. Many students in Cambridge suffer from what is known as 'imposter syndrome'[12]. They feel inferior when comparing themselves to their peers. Doubting their own abilities can lead to low motivation. Frequent and positive feedback combined with an increased number of small tests or quizzes to consolidate attained knowledge (and confidence) can help[13].

The university's virtual learning environment is Moodle, and many language teachers had been exploring the use of interactive tasks using H5P[14] for example, or else have prior experience in creating interactive online exercises in collaboration with the university's language centre[15], which were all now integrated more fully into lesson plans[16].

It should be mentioned here that the librarians worked extremely hard to offer as much online access as possible. Also, Cambridge University Press, along with other publishers, made a good number of their publications available online[17].

All concerns discussed above have produced a teaching programme using a mix of synchronous and asynchronous teaching with some hybrid teaching as well.

### 4.2. Examinations for the academic year 2020/2021

At the time of writing we are assuming that some in-person examination will be possible. It is intended that language examinations testing textual comprehension and production, as well as correct application of grammatical

---

11. https://www.gov.uk/government/publications/coronavirus-covid-19-cancellation-of-gcses-as-and-a-levels-in-2020/coronavirus-covid-19-cancellation-of-gcses-as-and-a-levels-in-2020

12. See https://www.counselling.cam.ac.uk/GroupsAndWorkshops/copy_of_studentgroups/Impsyn

13. See a study at Harvard from Reuell (2013)

14. https://h5p.org/

15. For examples see: https://www.langcen.cam.ac.uk/opencourseware/opencourseware-index.html

16. Other tools used include, for example: Mentimeter, Kahoot, Flipgrid, and Quizlet

17. https://www.cambridge.org/core/

knowledge and vocabulary recall will be conducted in this way. Translation is tested in both directions at all levels of the Cambridge Modern and Medieval Languages degree. Translation examinations will be online and open-book and will be conducted using a modified format: students will need to supply a specified number of comments explaining their translation choices. This is therefore a substantial change to our practice. The final year language exam for which students have to analyse and react to a passage of 800 words will also remain a take-home examination. Allowing a high number of examinations to be open-book and online helped to make the examination process more inclusive. Students are allowed to type, they can take rest breaks, and can demonstrate their knowledge without having to rely on recall.

Since some of the cohort had not been able to spend enough time in their intended destination during their year abroad, it was decided to make the final year oral examinations optional. The exams were carried out online and worked well.

Statistics seem to indicate that the use of open-book examinations resulted in a change of gender statistics. It seems that female students performed better under these new conditions[18].

The school paid for Zoom licences for teachers and also used Microsoft Teams, incorporating H5P and Panopto.

The role of the teacher has to adapt even more to that of becoming a curator of resources, a facilitator, and the one who puts in place a clear structure with clearly signposted learning goals[19]. Students need to learn how to become even more independent and self-reliant. New learning outcomes will almost automatically include the use of different technologies, online tools, and software.

Language classes vary greatly in delivery format, while some entail five hours a week of contact time, others only take place fortnightly. Much thought is

---

18. Statistics for this are not available at present.
19. For a discussion of using scaffolding in online teaching see McLoughlin and Marshall (2000).

Chapter 19

going into using the flipped classroom approach[20] and exporting activities like watching videos, reading texts, or translating out of the classroom. All courses have clear plans for the whole term so that students can work ahead or catch up. Most resources are digital (some exceptions include languages with non-Latin alphabets where the use of handwriting and hard copies of texts are deemed essential) and students hand in work and receive feedback online.

### 4.3. Student and teacher feedback

Consulting students was key. Communication (in both directions) seemed absolutely crucial to making this new teaching model work. Cambridge is particularly well prepared for such, as each student is assigned a director of studies (for academic issues) and a tutor (for pastoral questions). The intent is that early warning signs of students falling behind or disengaging be spotted quickly.

Many teachers have expressed enthusiasm for the development of new learning materials. As a team, we have learnt to rely on each other's expertise. For example, a quick call on Microsoft Teams using screen share has helped to solve many technology problems. Meetings have had to become more frequent out of necessity, and although this increase has created more time pressure, many have found this conducive to team spirit. However, we are also concerned about long working hours and occupational health issues. Additionally, difficult family situations, and the fact that many of us have family abroad, has meant an increase in anxiety and stress.

## 5.  Discussion

There was (and still *is*) very little, if any, face-to-face teaching. It is not possible to use team work or working in pairs because of safety distancing rules. Furthermore, the sharing of documents is not allowed. The wearing of facial

---

20. See Von Lindeiner-Stráský, Stickler, and Winchester's (2020) flipping German project

coverings (even if a distance of two metres or more can be maintained) was recommended by the university in October 2020. This measure makes language teaching very difficult.

## 5.1. Asynchronous online teaching

The use of pre-recordings is employed for lectures. Dividing one 50-minute lecture into 'chunks' works best. It is both easier to record these lectures and to watch them. For language teaching, asynchronous tools are used for four main purposes.

- Delivery of administrative information about the course can be presented in a video: for example how to navigate the VLE, where to find resources, and how to plan and organise work and homework. Depending on the language level, these are either recorded in English or in the target language.

- A 50-minute session can be divided into two sections: a 15-20-minute recorded session introducing a topic (grammar, topic for discussion, vocabulary, etc.) followed by a 30-35-minute live session online in which the topics are discussed.

- There are many interactive tools available to stimulate work outside the classroom: Quizlet and Phase 8, for example, can be used to make vocabulary acquisition more collective and manageable.

- What is normally referred to as 'homework', i.e. extending the lesson and delegating further work on a particular subject to the individual learner, should also be seen as asynchronous learning.

## 5.2. Synchronous online teaching

Synchronous online teaching is used for most classes. A wide variety of tools is used to aid interaction during a class session. For example,

- using the chat function to try out new vocabulary, answer questions, and identify grammatical structures, etc;

- Google Docs/OneNote/OU blogs or Open Forum within Moodle: these can be used to allow students to work collaboratively on a single document. This method works well in translation classes, for example. Several groups can work in breakout rooms on parts of a passage at the same time; and

- polling/quizzes: a variety of tools are available to enliven teaching and to engage students. The main ones used are the polling function on Zoom, Kahoot, and Mentimeter.

The principal objectives of a class have not changed substantially, but its main functions of helping learners to use resources, allowing various speeds for learning processes, providing feedback and consolidating knowledge have been amplified by the new learning environment. What is missing is the interaction between people in a physical room: reading body language, sitting next to someone, meeting friends. However, a few measures can be used to replicate parts of this experience. For example, a Zoom link can be made available to students before the teacher enters the meeting. Students may use this time to chat about their lives outside the classroom. Also, tools like Padlet, Miro, and Flipgrid, for example, can be employed to encourage learners to use the target language to say something about themselves – places they would like to visit, music they enjoy, films they can recommend, and articles they have found interesting. All this can help to build a sense of community. If integrated into the teaching programme, with clearly defined tasks, these tools serve as useful additions to the learning experience and its success.

Different learner levels require different online teaching approaches. It is more straightforward to engage a class of final year students in a discussion about migration in Germany, for example, than to make sure every student in a class of beginners has understood a particular text. This has always been the case, of course, but this difference in pedagogical approach has been highlighted during online teaching. For the teaching at beginners' level it is even more crucial to be able to give frequent and extensive individual feedback.

Teachers are also fully aware that all skills need to be addressed. Switching between utilising audio, video, and text as teaching resources **as well as** media for homework and contributions is absolutely vital. In fact, in some ways, this approach is more natural in the new learning environment.

## 6. Looking ahead and conclusion

The university is developing policies on recording of teaching. For language teaching, the faculty has argued successfully that classes should not be recorded as this has proven to be inhibiting to some students. We are also discussing how long any such recordings should be kept. Should they expire after a term or should it be possible to 'binge watch' an entire series of lectures in the days before the examinations?

Which of the online options should be retained in a post-Covid world? For modern languages in the UK, the new online platforms will be used to continue work on outreach and widening participation.

Online language teaching can work well provided that all involved feel confident. This is not the case during a pandemic. Concerns about mental health and health generally overshadow much of the experience of being a student. However, first anecdotal evidence seems to suggest that most teachers and students have been pleasantly surprised by how well many classroom activities can be exported into the online teaching format. Subject-specific reasons why language teaching does not lend itself well to face-to-face teaching in the current situation have led to a mix of synchronous and asynchronous teaching. This measure has offered many opportunities to develop inclusive and interactive learning. Some of these adaptations will survive beyond the pandemic mode: the migration of introductions of topics to video recordings, using online marking, and conducting meetings online. Some of the skills developed by both teachers and students will remain (adaptive use of technology, use of digital resources). This may be the silver lining we all need to find. However, it also seems clear that interpersonal exchanges, the development of a sense of a learning community, and an identity as a learner as part of a cohort are much more difficult to replicate. Equally, concerns about workload and the feeling of loneliness and isolation are much harder to tackle.

## References

McLoughlin, C., & Marshall, L. (2000). Scaffolding: a model for learner support in an online teaching environment. In A. Herrmann & M. M. Kulski (Eds), *Flexible futures in tertiary teaching. Proceedings of the 9th Annual Teaching Learning Forum, 2-4 February 2000*. Curtin University of Technology. http://www.c3l.uni-oldenburg.de/cde/support/readings/loughlin2.htm

Reuell, P. (2013 April 3). Online learning: it's different. *The Harvard Gazette*. https://news.harvard.edu/gazette/story/2013/04/online-learning-its-different/

Salmon, G. (2020 May 28). Testing the equivalence of online and on campus learning. WONKHE. https://wonkhe.com/blogs/testing-the-equivalence-of-online-and-on-campus-learning/

Von Lindeiner-Stráský, K., Stickler, U., & Winchester, S. (2020). Flipping the flipped. The concept of flipped learning in an online teaching environment. *Open Learning: The Journal of Open, Distance and e-Learning*. https://doi.org/10.1080/02680513.2020.1769584

# 20. COVID-19 and the Autonomous University of Barcelona: current trends on language teaching and learning strategies

## Sonia Oliver del Olmo[1]

### Abstract

When COVID-19 emerged, it meant many changes as to health specific measures for prevention as well as social, political, and educational considerations to cope with a completely new situation which necessitated very quick responses. In this sense, this worldwide pandemic implied challenges in terms of decision-making at the highest level, the key involvement of universities' technical support (taking into account pedagogical and logistics considerations) and very specific training for teaching staff to design materials and facilitate both remote tuition and students' assignments delivery and feedback. In this chapter, I will describe the design and development of a new interactive scenario where lecturers and students keep their teaching and learning practices working under very exceptional circumstances as it is the case of the Autonomous University of Barcelona (UAB). This institution has shown a very effective plan based on constant technical support and training, staff's full commitment to their new remote online language teaching and students' flexibility and willingness to learn within their English Studies degree despite an unfavourable context *a priori*.

Keywords: COVID-19, online language teaching, decision-making, support and training, Spain.

---

1. Autonomous University of Barcelona, Barcelona, Spain; sonia.oliver@uab.cat; https://orcid.org/0000-0002-8385-6001

How to cite: Oliver del Olmo, S. (2021). COVID-19 and the Autonomous University of Barcelona: current trends on language teaching and learning strategies. In N. Radić, A. Atabekova, M. Freddi & J. Schmied (Eds), *The world universities' response to COVID-19: remote online language teaching* (pp. 321-336). Research-publishing.net. https://doi.org/10.14705/rpnet.2021.52.1281

---

© 2021 Sonia Oliver del Olmo (CC BY)     321

## 1. Introduction

The Royal Decree 463/2020 of March 14th, declaring the state of alarm for the management of the health crisis in Spain, caused by COVID-19, urged the educational system to cope with exceptional circumstances. In response to that, the UAB[2] had to fix criteria for the application of restrictions collected in ongoing official Resolutions by which new public health measures were, and still are, adopted to contain the pandemic in Catalonia. This unexpected situation implied challenges in terms of decision-making at the highest level, the key involvement of the institutional technical support for pedagogical ongoing academic activities and very specific training for the teaching staff to design materials to facilitate remote tuition, effective delivery of students' assignments, and efficient feedback.

This chapter will describe the design and explain the development of this new interactive scenario where teachers and students had, and still have, to keep their learning and teaching practices working under very exceptional circumstances.

First, I will provide details of the institutional context of the UAB to later deal with the technical support provided and the specific training offered to teachers, researchers, and administrative staff. In addition, I include specific recommendations for teachers and students and their respective training courses to aid pedagogical and logistics challenges posed by the pandemic.

Furthermore, I will depict the new learning scenario where issues such as student's participation and their assignments' delivery, teacher's feedback, and student's self-assessment are key.

Finally, some conclusions as to the efficiency of the institutional emergency plan and a possible further line of research on the topic are included.

---

2. https://www.uab.cat/web/universitat-autonoma-de-barcelona-1345467954774.html

## 2. Institutional context and emergency response

The UAB is a state university in Spain which was founded in 1968. Most of its teaching and extracurricular services are located in Bellaterra Campus, in Cerdanyola del Vallès, Barcelona. The UAB has 37,166 students, 3,262 lecturers, 107 Bachelor of Arts (BA)'s degrees, 328 postgraduate programmes and 90 PhD programmes. Now more than 50 years old, the UAB has already consolidated itself among the main university rankings. Furthermore, and as mentioned by Fessenden (n.d.), in recent years, this university has seen recognition for its efforts in promoting quality in teaching, attracting international talent, and obtaining a growing impact in research. In fact, the UAB has steadily shown an obvious improvement in its classifications in the most prestigious and influential international rankings, occupying an outstanding position among Spanish universities in world rankings, such as the Quacquarelli Symonds World University Rankings, the Times Higher Education World University Rankings, and the Academic Ranking of World Universities.

The UAB had to reorganise teaching and assessment practically from one day to the next in March 2019, in other words, immediately after the state of alarm declaration, our institution steadily developed a specific website: *Information for COVID-19* (UAB, 2020) to keep students, teachers, research, and administrative staff constantly updated.

This institutional website (see Figure 1 below) includes key issues, such as a communication protocol for cases affecting members of the university community (students, teachers, or administrative staff developing symptoms of COVID-19), the UAB's contingency plan and organisation protocol to contain the epidemic outbreak in the territory of Catalonia, considerations related to teaching and assessment practices, such as field practices and outings, and Information and Communication Technologies (ICT) teaching resources available.

More specific information was also provided as to each academic centre or division, our libraries' service, international mobility, and possible Frequently Asked Questions (FAQ) within this exceptional context, as shown in Figure 2.

Figure 1. Information about COVID-19 website (UAB, 2020)

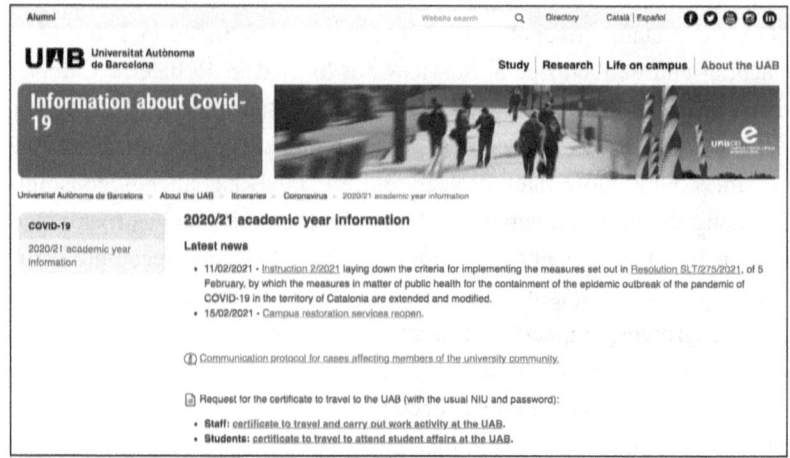

Figure 2. Coronavirus 2020/2021 academic year information (UAB, 2020)

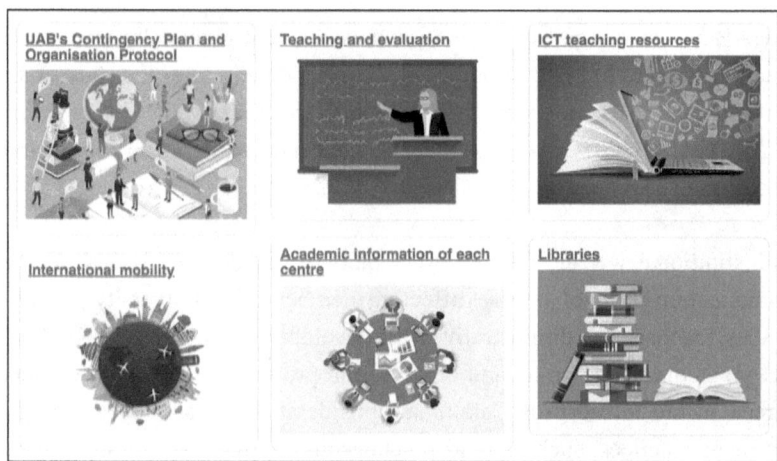

In addition, the *Information about COVID-19* website includes links to web channels, such as *Canal Salut*[3] (Health Channel in English), the latest news

---

3. https://canalsalut.gencat.cat/ca/salut-a-z/c/coronavirus-2019-ncov/

from the Spanish Ministry for health, consumption, and social welfare[4], and the Centre for Disease Control and Prevention updated measures[5].

The COVID-19 website also displays statements from university and government institutions, namely *Generalitat de Catalunya* (the Catalan government) and the coordination with the Ministry of Universities in Spain. There are also reports on the regulatory impact of online assessment procedures: data protection and guaranteeing the rights of students (see supplementary materials Appendix 1 UAB data protection regulation), remote evaluation procedures, and external internships. Lastly, the website includes the final degree and Master of Arts (MA) theses academic calendars and has a section on universities and research with UAB's university sector plan, specifying the end of lockdown and transition from phase 0 to phase 1 in the universities' sector and research centres (where labs and animal farms were open despite the total lockdown of the campus).

The specific information provided in the UAB's *Information about COVID-19* website also includes selected guides on good communication practices in the Moodle classroom, the use of face masks, home management of waste in positive homes or in quarantine by the COVID-19 and the Official College of Psychology of Catalonia's recommendations for psychological management during confinement. Last but not least, there is a FAQ section dealing with queries about restrictions of activities due to the pandemic in Catalonia and questions and answers about COVID-19 in the university setting[6].

## 3. ICT support and specific technical training

In this section, I will focus on the technical instructions that were regularly given to the teaching and research staff in the UAB and the institutional

---

4. https://www.mscbs.gob.es/profesionales/saludPublica/ccayes/alertasActual/nCov/home.htm

5. https://www.cdc.gov/

6. See a selection of these specific questions in supplementary materials Appendix 3.1 Questions addressed to the lecturing staff and Appendix 3.2 Questions for students.

recommendations as to the use and management of ICT by teachers and students during the academic year 2019-2020 immediately after the pandemic set in.

Right from the beginning of the COVID-19 health crisis, the *Centre d'Assistència i Suport* (CAS), which is the central Computer Service support in the UAB, issued key recommendations to the teaching and research staff within the institution. First of all, they warned us to be careful with the use of passwords, to keep the operating systems updated and to install and keep our Personal Computer (PC)'s antivirus updated, too. The technicians reminded us to have a personal firewall and keeping back-up copies at all times, not to download files from unknown sources or open suspicious emails. In this sense, CAS showed great concern as to UAB staff's suitable usage of spam filters and avoiding suspicious websites whenever possible. Furthermore, the CAS experts highlighted the importance of not providing personal or financial details online nor leaving applications or documents open after usage. Finally, our technicians recommended that we turn off our PCs when not in use and to call their CAS service in case of any doubt or possible technical problem.

The UAB technical support created a specific *Canal TIC* blog (ICT blog) with relevant updates on equipment maintenance, regulations, and a series of useful advice for teachers and students as soon as we went teaching online in March 2020, immediately after Spain was declared in state of emergency. The ICT blog was designed to fit teachers and research staff's needs. There is also a News section, where the UAB university community can check periodic updates, in particular safety tips and recommendations to work remotely, the instruction 8/2020 on the protection of data in the field of virtual working meetings, and a series of videos of Teams' webinars on virtual teaching as shown in Figure 3.

Thanks to the UAB rector's resolution, it established an exceptional criterion for the use of electronic identification and signature during the state of emergency period and instructions regarding the organisation of services including Sports Service (SAF), which did not charge any membership fee and provided a whole range of home training and exercises through their SAF application.

Figure 3. ICT blog (UAB, 2020)

On the one hand, teachers were recommended to check the infographic about *La universitat en línia, una oportunitat per innovar* (Online university, an opportunity to innovate) and provided a compilation of useful tools for teaching remotely. For those 'new' to the online teaching environment they urged to review *First Steps in Moodle* documents with tips to record sessions and tools to carry out online evaluation. Regarding assessment, the institution reminded us to always keep in mind the data protection regulation, to use software for comparing and detecting similar works (plagiarism), and to prevent teleworking risks. Regarding the latter, the experts advised us to follow UAB's security specific recommendations and insisted on using the link to Online Help and Support within the virtual campus environment of our university.

On the other hand, the UAB's Technical Support recommended to our students suitable tools to work remotely, software only for students, instructions on how to record a video, and to do a presentation, as well as information on online assessment tools. Besides encouraging students to follow the security tips and reminding them that there was a specific Help section in the virtual campus homepage, CAS experts strongly advised students to approach online learning positively.

## 4. ICT training courses for remote teaching

The UAB saw in online teaching an opportunity to innovate. In this vein, some general advice was given to the university community on the proper use of technologies and tools. Therefore, in this section I will include both the instructions given to the teaching staff when they started remote online teaching due to the COVID-19 pandemic early in 2020 and the specific institutional ICT training courses. The official instructions that our institution provided when we started with our online teaching and learning processes are reproduced below. The key points are accessibility and need for simplification, internet security, and privacy as regards recording of online classes.

> "Do not forget that not everyone has the latest computer equipment or a high-speed internet connection and that at moments of maximum usage the system works slower than usual: simplify the processes as much as possible and add additional time for students to download and upload documents from and to the system, if necessary. Try to avoid having students upload photos or scanned documents (this can be complicated on mobile devices).
>
> Whenever possible, always use 'corporative tools' such as Office365 (Teams, Forms, OneDrive, etc.) and Campus Virtual-Moodle. Avoid using free software such as Gmail, Zoom, Houseparty, etc., since the majority of these do not offer enough guarantees in terms of data protection and security. In addition, use of differing tools can create confusion for students.
>
> Always be explicit when alerting students that the online session will be recorded, offering the possibility of disconnecting the camera to those who wish to do so. You must alert them before commencing the recording (proof that the procedure is being followed correctly)" (UAB, 2020).

At the start of the second semester (Spring 2020) the area of personal development and technical support at UAB organised a series of training courses in office automation and quality for this extraordinary period of virtual teaching and remote working. During the first months after the Royal Decree declaring the state of emergency in Spain, our institution mainly focused on delivering specific courses on computer applications and programmes. ICT resources were provided for the optimisation and improvement of learning and teaching processes, for creating materials, learning strategies and assessment tools, communication and connectivity in a remote working environment (virtual), and the organisation of tuition and meetings using Teams to support teaching practices. In this regard, it was key to know how to use the institutional official platform (Teams) chosen for teaching during the pandemic, accessing its calendar, their live sessions/ meetings, dealing with the waiting room, and recording a lecture (if required).

Later on, UAB's courses were more oriented towards personal skills development, in other words targeting personal excellence and professional effectiveness (see Bates, 2000; O'Sullivan et al., 2020), enhancing critical thinking and ethical commitment as cross-curricular skills of university students (e.g. Fry, Ketteridge, & Marshall, 2009), and dealing with committed teaching: strengthening the link between the university and the social environment (Zins, Weissberg, Wang, & Walberg, 2004).

Eventually, we started the current academic year 2020/2021 with a wider range of specific training courses for administration, teachers, and research staff[7]. In this vein, the training courses, designed and developed by the UAB personal development and technical support (see Figure 4), were organised around the six following areas:

- computer tools and applications/programmes;
- personal skills;
- regulations;
- courses for teaching and research staff (*Personal Docent i Investigador*);
- prevention; and
- resources.

---

7. See the link: https://infogram.com/1p12v0nllknr97fmvkj5107j30u6r5w92e3?live

In *computer tools and applications/programmes*, lecturers can apply and learn about how to work in the Cloud with Microsoft Office 365 and One Note virtual, how to use Teams to support university teaching, good practice in remote Teamwork Management, and collaboration functionality using Teams as well as communication and connectivity in a remote working environment. In *personal skills*, the courses available deal with resilience (how to manage changes positively), virtual work by objectives, interpersonal communication while working remotely, stress management, uncertainty, fear and self-management, transforming insecurity and fears into tools for professional success, and helping ourselves and others with our communication. In *regulations*, staff become aware of the institutional norms on data protection of personal nature and the specificities of the remote working environment (virtual); *courses for teaching and research staff* include management by objectives, learning to learn, project management remotely, team management, participative and creative techniques, professional efficiency 4.0, and hybrid team management; *prevention* offers courses on prevention at work and safety in a remote working environment, capacitation on collecting liquid nitrogen for research, and oral communication using a mask. Finally, *resources* display a series of ICT recommendations, the ICT channel for News in Teams, and the specific Stream Channel where lecturers and research staff can find videos on how to use Teams for university teaching and learning.

Figure 4. Specific training courses for teaching staff and researchers (UAB, 2020)

## 5. Pedagogical and logistics considerations

This section will deal with pedagogical and logistics considerations as to recommendations for teachers and online teaching challenges. These concern student's participation, assignments' delivery, and feedback and student's self-assessment.

### 5.1. Recommendations for teachers

As previously stated, the UAB recommended using Teams as the institutional tool since it is very comprehensive and is integrated with the rest of Microsoft tools. However, there is also the possibility of using Zoom, Meet, Hangouts, Skype, or Jitsi. The latter, with open code and without having to register or download anything. Once lecturers received training on how to create materials, online teaching management, a wide range of tools and gadgets, and methodological resources, they were also instructed as to their daily teaching practice. In other words, the institution suggested planning communication with students to facilitate and enhance participation, and explain to them how virtual teaching would work in the following months. They also recommended publishing a working plan in PDF, using a short video and the Forum tool to allow for public tutorials where students could share doubts and learn from each other's issues. All this was combined with using Teams to have a live session, a synchronous chat with students, the instant messaging application in Moodle, or the UAB Webmail for individual tutorials to provide students with feedback.

Throughout the end of the academic year 2019-2020 it was shown that planning a calendar so that students can see key dates at first sight and announce news or upcoming events through the Moodle classroom is key. Moreover, explaining a topic using a PPT, for example, and recording it has become a very popular practice among the teaching staff. Once recorded, teaching materials can be published and uploaded to the virtual campus, and online assessment tools such as questionnaires are used both by students and teachers. On the other hand, Teams is constantly used for assignment delivery, work presentations, and public defences of university students' work, namely, a subject's oral presentation, BA papers, MA theses, or even doctoral dissertations.

### 5.2. Online teaching challenges

Even though remote tuition has opened new possibilities for university students and teaching and research staff, it has also posed many challenges, especially as regards encouraging and keeping student motivation and participation, sending/ receiving teacher feedback, and dealing with student assessment online, among other issues.

Teachers were trained to enhance student participation through the use of Socrative or Mentimeter online computer applications. These questionnaires allow for anonymous responses but the teacher can also ask to identify the student by including their names or UAB's identification code which are also very useful in keeping a register of group's participation and check the subject's attendance list.

As far as student assignment delivery and feedback are concerned, computer applications, such as *Additio o IDoceo*, allow both for student assignment delivery and sending teacher's personal reports. However, Moodle enables the university community to edit work (underline, write...), mark it, and add comments to it. Teachers can even send a message to students informing them that the assessment results are available through Google or Microsoft, i.e. combining correspondence (Morodo, 2020).

As for student self-assessment for practice, Google Forms and Microsoft Forms permit users to create forms and self-correct questionnaires quite easily. There is also the possibility to set up messages to explain why an answer is correct or incorrect. The Questionnaire tool in Moodle performs this function too, but it is rather more complex. However, teachers can design answers with negative scores and make sure that the one who is answering is the student himself/ herself. In fact, the creation of rubrics was one of the main concerns among the teaching staff at the beginning of the semester 2019-2020, but eventually teachers ended up using CoRubrics for student assessment, peer-assessment, and self-assessment. Moodle was also a suitable option when using rubrics to assess student progress and performance as the Questionnaire tool in Moodle allows making questions and answers (test type) with positive or negative scores with different values.

## 6. Students and teachers new learning scenario

Throughout the past months both students and teachers have had to deal with a new organisation of learning-teaching processes and have had to cope with key issues, such as family responsibilities, time management, teleworking, home computer equipment, connectivity, and social isolation (psychological factors). In Noguera's (2020) training course, teachers discussed how to move from face-to-face to distance tuition, they reflected on their teaching, learning, and remote assessment and thought about how to exploit the possibilities of using a virtual classroom and other tools. In fact, teachers had to keep teaching and assessing student skills and attitudes but most of them were not so familiar with remote online language teaching. As a matter of fact, there was a clear lack of time and we had to learn as we kept on teaching. Furthermore, both teachers and students needed some extra training on synchronous classrooms, the use of technology, and social interaction. To keep student motivation high and avoid their dropout, teachers were asked to design short offline activities and enhance coordination among the teaching staff. The institutional technical support offered by CAS was key to help teachers go on with their work by incorporating new resources, making students responsible for their own language learning, opening to new methodologies, and reinforcing active English learning. In this sense, teachers were recommended to use the potential that mobile phones offer to record videos and audios, to take photos, to write short texts, and to vote and answer questionnaires (Mentimeter, etc.) as well as to display images and documents.

Nevertheless, at times both teachers and students felt overwhelmed with work, some users still lacked technological skills and some students seemed confused at the beginning of online teaching in times of confinement. Not having face-to-face contact made students pester the administrative, teaching, and research staff by sending countless numbers of emails (24hx7), some of them including connectivity issues.

## 7. Conclusions

When the COVID-19 worldwide crisis emerged, it meant many changes as to health specific measures for prevention besides social, political, and education considerations to cope with a completely new situation, which required very quick responses. As to the teaching practices in this new reality, the UAB recommended that teachers focus on pedagogy and not so much on the platform chosen by the institution (Teams). Our institution's experts suggested that both teachers and researchers spend time thinking about how to use the new technologies in their own teaching practices and reflect on how to exploit the potential that interactivity offers to the teaching-learning community since most students are digital natives and English online teaching may have relevant advantages (Oliver del Olmo, 2017; Pérez-Cañado, 2011).

The UAB as an institution perceived this abrupt change as a clear opportunity to innovate since, in principle, it meant opening to new teaching methodologies, which allowed students and teachers to explore other foreign language learning methods and tools. However, during this process, teachers had to re-think what the main objective of their tuition was in terms of contents and skills or competences and how to proceed by using the most suitable methods and activities.

Collaborative work, on the other hand, urged teachers to find out how to group students and be very aware of the importance of timing tasks properly by using resources accordingly. In addition, teachers had to consider which devices were already available for students and which evidence was the most optimal for collection in order to assess their progress in a fair way. In this respect, our institution has shown a very effective plan based on constant technical support and specific training for students and teachers.

Finally, I would like to state that thanks to UAB's teaching staff's full commitment to their new remote online language teaching and the university students' flexibility and willingness to learn, in rather unfavourable circumstances, this methodological challenge has evolved into a very intense and meaningful opportunity to learn in many aspects. A further study on this issue may include both a quantitative and qualitative research methodology by incorporating interviews with teachers, researchers, and administrative staff involved in the process and passing questionnaires of student satisfaction regarding online teaching and learning strategies. Our results might shed some light on good practices and possible areas of improvement for the current and, most likely, persisting online language teaching at university level.

## 8. Supplementary materials

https://research-publishing.box.com/s/ylh38voerncroy8gl0eow02vo74r1gfz

## References

Bates, A.W. (2000). *Managing technological change. Strategies for college and university leaders*. Jossey Bass.

Fessenden, M. (n.d.). *AMTS academic use: Universitat Autonoma de Barcelona, Spain– teaching ruminant nutrition*. AMTS. https://agmodelsystems.com/amts-academic-use-universitat-autonoma-de-barcelona-spain-teaching-ruminant-nutrition/

Fry, H., Ketteridge, S., & Marshall, S. (2009). Understanding student learning. In S. Marshall (Ed.), *A handbook for teaching and learning in higher education: enhancing academic practice* (3rd ed., pp. 8-26). Routledge. https://doi.org/10.4324/9780203891414

Morodo, A. (2020). *Computer programmes and digital resources for the improvement and optimization of the learning and teaching processes. Online training course for UAB teaching and research staff*. Department of Personal Development and Technical Support, June 2020.

Noguera, I. (2020). *Organization of teaching in times of confinement. Online training course for UAB teaching and research staff*. Department of Personal Development and Technical Support, June/July 2020.

## Chapter 20

Oliver del Olmo, S. (2017). El uso de las tecnologías (lingüísticas) en la lectoescritura en el aula de inglés L2: retos metodológicos en la práctica educativa. In E. Viviana Oropeza Gracia, V. Zamudio Jasso, & J. M. Gasca García (Eds), *Enseñanza y aprendizaje de lenguas: nuevos escenarios. Universidad Nacional Autónoma de México (UNAM)* (pp. 53-72). Centro de Enseñanza de Lenguas Extranjeras. Colección Lingüística, volumen 21.

O'Sullivan, Í., Dobravac, G., Farrell, A., Kacmarova, A., & Leijen, D. (2020). (Eds). *Centralised support for writing, research, learning and teaching: case studies of existing models across Europe*. COST Action 15221: We ReLaTe. https://www.maynoothuniversity.ie/centre-teaching-and-learning/ctl-projects/current-ctl-projects/cost-action-15221-we-relate

Pérez-Cañado, M. L. (2011). The use of ICT in the European higher education area: acting upon the evidence. In F. A. Suau Jiménez & B. Pennock Speck (Eds), *Interdisciplinarity and languages. current issues in research, teaching, professional applications and ICT* (pp. 21-43). Peter Lang. https://doi.org/10.3726/978-3-0353-0145-8/7

UAB. (2020). *Information about Covid-19*. Universitat Autònoma de Barcelona. https://www.uab.cat/web/about-the-uab/itineraries/coronavirus/2020/21-academic-year-information-1345823683302.html

Zins, J. E., Weissberg, R. P., Wang, M. C., & Walberg, H. J. (2004). (Eds). *Building academic success on social and emotional learning: what does the research say?* Teachers College Press.

# 21 COVID-19 emergency teaching: from CULP to remote CULP

## Nebojša Radić[1]

### Abstract

In this chapter I describe the emergency delivery of the Cambridge University institution-wide Language Programme (CULP) during the COVID-19 lockdown in March-July 2020. I am the Director of the Programme and report from a managerial point of view. I begin by outlining the institutional context and the student and teaching staff backgrounds. I proceed by describing the decision-making process, the rationale behind the decisions, the steps taken in preparation for the online, remote delivery of the teaching, and the delivery itself. The chapter reports on measurable student performance as well as formal and informal student and teacher feedback. The chapter concludes by drawing the relevant conclusions about this unique professional experience, the changes we witness in communication, teaching, and learning patterns, and outlining a possible way forward.

Keywords: COVID-19, online language teaching, training and support, course-design, university-wide programme, UK.

## 1. The institutional context

The University of Cambridge is defined by a long-standing tradition, its collegial structure, and the international profile of its students and staff. The academic year is divided in three eight-week terms: Michaelmas, Lent, and Easter. The

---

1. University of Cambridge, Cambridge, United Kingdom; nr236@cam.ac.uk; https://orcid.org/0000-0001-6859-5775

**How to cite:** Radić, N. (2021). COVID-19 emergency teaching: from CULP to remote CULP. In N. Radić, A. Atabekova, M. Freddi & J. Schmied (Eds), *The world universities' response to COVID-19: remote online language teaching* (pp. 337-351). Research-publishing.net. https://doi.org/10.14705/rpnet.2021.52.1282

Language Centre supports the teaching and learning of languages throughout the university. It does so by offering support in Academic Development and Training to International Students (ADTIS)[2], a self-access learning centre that hosts resources in 180+ languages, a dedicated technical section for the design and production of multimedia resources for online delivery, and a taught programme of world languages (CULP). CULP offers general language courses as well as courses for specific purposes such as academic reading for postgraduates in the Schools of Arts and Humanities and Humanities and Social Sciences, or for students of Clinical Medicine as well as historians and musicians to some 2,000 students per year. CULP offers tuition in 16 languages[3] and up to six levels[4]. All courses are aligned with the relevant international frameworks of reference for languages such as the Common European Framework of Reference (CEFR), HSK and JLPT[5], and are formatted to offer 30 hours of face-to-face classroom teaching and require around 45 hours of self-study. General language courses are offered at three points during the year and in three different formats. In Michaelmas and Lent (first and second term), over a 15-week period, students attend two hours of classroom teaching and self-study for around three hours. In the Easter term, the same number of contact hours and self-study is distributed over a period of eight weeks and in Long Vacation (summer period) over four weeks. The vast majority of CULP courses do not use textbooks but digital, multimedia learning resources that are available online via a dedicated virtual learning environment (Moodle). It is also important to mention that Cambridge does not feature a credit system. Most language centre students, therefore, take language classes on top of their regular studies. Languages are studied for a degree in the faculties of the School of Arts and Humanities[6].

---

2. Former English for Academic Purposes (EAP).

3. Arabic, British Sign Language, Chinese, French, German, Greek, Hebrew, Italian, Japanese, Korean, Persian, Portuguese, Russian, Spanish, Swahili, and Turkish.

4. Basic 1, Basic 2, Intermediate 1, Intermediate 2, Advanced and Advanced+ in European languages and Basic 1, Basic 2, Elementary 1, Elementary 2, Intermediate 1 in Arabic, Mandarin Chinese, Japanese and Korean. Not all levels are available in all languages, though. This is subject to demand.

5. HSK: Chinese Proficiency Test; JLPT: Japanese Language Proficiency Test.

6. Please see in this collection the contributions from Silke Mentschen who teaches German in the Faculty of Modern and Medieval Languages and Linguistics (MMLL) and Mahbod Ghaffari who teaches Persian in the Faculty of Asian and Middle Eastern Studies (AMES).

## 1.1. The students

CULP is an institution-wide language programme that enrols graduate and postgraduate students as well as university staff and a small number of members of the general public. The programme offers a range of specialist and general language courses to some 2,000 students per academic year. In 2019, Easter courses attracted 242 students. This year however, we announced very early towards the end of March that we would deliver teaching online. We also lowered the fee considerably[7] and the interest was unprecedented. In the 2020 Easter term we nearly doubled enrolments to 460 students[8]. On popular demand we reinstated the Long Vacation courses and enrolled another 120 students. The overall number of students during the April to July period was increased therefore by 130%. This was achieved without any systematic advertising of the courses. The split between undergraduate and postgraduate students remained the same, 50/50.

## 1.2. The staff

In CULP we teach 16 languages and some 70 different courses. In Easter however, enrolment numbers are smaller so in 2020 we offered a dozen languages and 25 courses. While we have 35 teaching staff, in Easter only 17 were scheduled to teach. CULP is normally delivered in blended-learning mode, so all staff are well trained and experienced in designing and producing digital learning materials as well as teaching using a flipped classroom approach. The challenge we suddenly faced, however, was of a completely different order. Based on my interaction with staff in workshops, meetings, and further correspondence with individuals, I can state that all staff accepted with perhaps muted but nonetheless enthusiasm the decision to teach remotely. With some trepidation too, but they did not feel intimidated or inhibited. We quickly came up with an informed and efficient delivery design that relied heavily on the resources and expertise that we already had.

---

7. From £285 to £200 (for students). The main reason for lowering the fees was to attract more students. At the same time, due to the need for additional hardware, software, and training, the cost of delivering the courses was higher.

8. 140 under-graduate and 143 graduate students, 76 staff, and 65 members of the general public.

## 1.3. Technical support

The Language Centre has a dedicated five staff strong technical section. The technical section was able to advise in a timely fashion and offer support for hardware and software issues, procurement as well as necessary training. Such training was delivered initially via real-time Zoom-based workshops and subsequently via asynchronous chat forums and a dedicated Moodle web page containing all relevant information. At the beginning of this crisis, the University Information Service and Teaching and Learning Centre were still finding their way and were not in a position to offer us significant support. The University of Cambridge is collegiate and devolved which makes it harder for any centralised decision or action to be implemented.

## 2. Teaching remotely, online

### 2.1. The decision to teach remotely

On 20 March 2020 the whole of the UK found itself in lockdown. University staff was advised to work from home and since it was mid-term many students decided to leave town and/or not to return to Cambridge. The CULP management agreed that going fully online was the only sensible way forward as the only other alternative seemed to be not teaching at all. The feeling was, however, that the lockdown presented also an opportunity to explore new modes of language teaching delivery. In pedagogical terms, we accepted the situation as a challenge rather than a hindrance. Initially, we were only hoping to attract enough students to be able to run at least some of the courses and gain some valuable experience.

### 2.2. Assumptions underpinning the design of the remote programme

We based the design of the fully remote, online mode of delivery on our previous, very extensive experience of offering blended-learning courses. From its inception in the year 2000, CULP delivered courses that bring together face-to-face teaching and multimedia, and interactive online resources accessible via the Virtual Learning Environment (VLE)[9]. We felt that this long-standing experience of teaching in what is now called a flipped classroom (Bergmann & Sams, 2012; Dunn, 2014) would give our teaching team two clear advantages, as below:

- the availability of digital resources – our VLE already held all or most of the teaching materials in a digital format. This is true for both self-study (homework) as well as classroom teaching resources that are typically accessed via a Smart Board; and

- a sound pedagogical course design approach – our teaching staff were used to designing and delivering courses within a flipped classroom framework.

Our core assumption was that online communication via Zoom would replace face-to-face classroom teaching and be integrated with the VLE (Moodle) into a coherent and pedagogically meaningful teaching and learning platform.

### 2.3. Pedagogical and logistical considerations

In terms of logistics, we were worried that we would not have enough students to be able to run *any* courses. We therefore heavily discounted our fees and hoped to have enough students to run at least some of the courses. The timeframe for preparation was extremely tight and we knew that we might have to compromise and keep things simple, with special reference to teacher training and ongoing technical, logistical, and pedagogical support.

Based on my previous extensive professional experience of teaching remotely, online[10], and in a blended-learning environment at Cambridge, it was clear that we were facing a significant shift and that rather than shovelling teaching

---

9. The VLE was initially CamTools, a local product, and since 2013, Moodle.
10. University of Auckland, New Zealand, 1995-2001.

materials and rebranding activities, we needed to rethink and reinvent our approach to teaching. From the outset, however, I was aware of the magnitude of this task and that the transition had to be approached gradually and managed carefully.

### 2.4. Hardware and software

Teaching staff were now asked to prepare and deliver online teaching from their homes. Not all had dedicated offices or adequate spaces. Schools were closed, so those with small children had the additional problem of childcare that exacerbated the space issue. All staff had networked computers but many, at home, worked on laptops that were not adequate because of the size of the screen[11]. Cameras, microphones, lighting, and seating arrangements represented an issue too. To meet these requirements, The Language Centre's technical section sourced the necessary hardware from our own reserves. We were already in late March or early April when the waiting times for online deliveries was getting longer. Most of this equipment was coming from China, the country that was first hit by the Coronavirus. Since The Language Centre's self-access centre was closed, we borrowed their desktop computers and transported them (using our own, private vehicles) to teachers' homes. We stripped all computers of microphones and cameras, and borrowed more comfortable office chairs and desk lamps. Eventually, we did manage to raise the quality level of the equipment used in the delivery of the courses. Where necessary, and that was in only a couple of cases, we purchased new computers.

By design, all CULP courses make use of the Moodle VLE. This proved to be a significant advantage and the single most important step towards full remote delivery. The next step was to identify the right tool for real-time, audio- and video-communication and the remote delivery of the teaching. Our director of e-learning recommended Zoom. In 2019, the university had already signed a contract with Microsoft and rolled out Teams (MT), a communication and

---

11. A university-wide survey was administered in July and showed that 80% of the university staff worked at home on laptop computers. Laptops feature considerably smaller screens that struggle to accommodate more than 15 little faces in Zoom. They also represent a health risk due to the curved seating posture.

management tool that featured desktop sharing and breakout room facilities but could not display more than six participants on its interface[12]. This posed serious limitations on teaching. Zoom, on the other hand, featured all of these functions and on top of that appeared to be more user friendly and stable. At the time, however, there were security concerns about Zoom. Our technical section was of the view that the Zoom corporation was in the process of addressing these concerns and solving the security issue[13]. Since the university had signed a contract with MT, it was free for us to use, but Zoom required us to purchase the professional licence to have the benefit of using all of its functions. Each teaching staff purchased a monthly subscription and subsequently sent the invoice to the administration for reimbursement.

## 2.5. Initial training and ongoing support

The University Centre for Teaching and Learning[14] provided remote, online teaching training in the form of a series of workshops. These were mostly delivered online, recorded, and subsequently made available from their web pages. They also developed purposeful manuals on teaching and assessment with technology. Support was also sought from training providers external to the university. Apart from these resources being made available later into the crisis (from June typically), their very general approach to teaching left many aspects of our own operation unsupported. Therefore, we decided very early to run language teaching specific workshops and create support groups. The workshops focused on the integration of Zoom and Moodle while the support groups were language, team-based, and looked at specific courses, resources, and teaching styles.

CULP teaching staff are experienced and comfortable in teaching in a blended-learning, flipped classroom mode. Only a very small number of our courses

---

12. https://myteamsday.com/2020/10/02/teams-roadmap-updates/. It has to be said though, by the end of 2020 MS Teams did acquire most of these functionalities.

13. https://www.tomsguide.com/uk/news/zoom-security-privacy-woes

14. https://www.cctl.cam.ac.uk/teaching-2020-21

makes use of a textbook[15] while most of the others rely on bespoke resources designed, produced, and delivered online by our dedicated language centre technical section. Apart from these 'backbone' resources, teachers develop their own teaching materials using a variety of software packages (e.g. PowerPoint, Google Docs, Panopto, audio recorders) and tools (e.g. tablets), to meet the requirements of their individual teaching style and specific groups of learners. The CULP blended-learning environment is defined by the use of the Moodle VLE and, in the classroom, by computer-connected, networked Smart Boards. It must be emphasised at this point that prior to the lockdown, as we just described, most of our teaching resources had already been in digital format. This meant that they were all readily deliverable at a distance, remotely.

Training for the remote, online delivery of the courses started with workshops that looked at the technical properties of Moodle, Zoom, MT, Google Drive, etc. In its regular delivery, CULP already used a range of online services and tools. Students would find course-related information on our CULP webpage, then proceed to enrol via the University Training Booking System – UTBS. They would then receive a link (email) to the university payment system and would attend the course-related resources in Moodle. Just getting to the learning activities implied using four different platforms already! Regular communication would take place via emails that could be generated via UTBS, Moodle, or a personal account. We knew this multitude presented a serious problem and needed solving by unifying the process in one single platform, but March/April 2020 just did not seem quite the right time to tackle this issue. Going completely remote by using a wide range of additional tools would have presented us with additional significant design and training challenges. After the initial technology-driven workshops, we set up an asynchronous technical support forum (Moodle chat room) while we refocused hands-on training on strictly pedagogy-driven issues.

It was of critical importance to conceptually match our previous rich experience and use it to create a new, remote, online teaching platform. Zoom offered

---

15. e.g. Intermediate French and German for Medics.

the possibility to do so as it could be integrated with Moodle to take over the pedagogical functions of the classroom Smart Board (share desktop function).

CULP was one of the rare university units that offered a financial incentive to its teaching staff to undertake the necessary training and to work on the modification of lesson plans and teaching materials. While this financial incentive is certainly not adequate in terms of the many hours this urgent and diverse work entailed, it was certainly understood as an acknowledgement of such work. This sent a strong message to all teaching staff who felt supported by their institution and empowered to face this challenge.

### 2.6. Resources

As we already mentioned, we use just a few paper-based resources (textbooks) in our teaching. The vast majority of the resources were readily available in a digital format. This of course made them readily accessible to our remote students. Some of the teachers did still have pockets of paper-based materials such as photocopies. These were scanned and uploaded into Moodle. The Language Centre holds a vast collection of films and documentaries in DVD format. During the lockdown these were made available to individuals for research purposes only. However, we also have a significant collection of films and documentaries that are readily available online and students were encouraged to make use of those.

### 2.7. The delivery

In the Easter term, we ran 25 courses and delivered remotely/online 1,500 hours of teaching. Our Swahili teacher was left stranded in Zanzibar due to the British Airways cancelling their flights to London. He delivered his lessons from the local primary school that he attended many years prior. The quality of his connection was excellent, and he never had any connectivity or other technical issues[16]. During this period, we only had to postpone two sessions (same day) due to connectivity problems at the outskirts of Cambridge.

---

16. He did complain, though, about the air conditioning being on the weak side!

## 3. Evaluation

### 3.1. Student feedback

CULP features a quality assurance framework that relies, among other tools, on student feedback. Student questionnaires are normally administered online mid-course and at the end of the course. The role of mid-course feedback is to inform in a formative manner teaching staff so they can fine-tune their lesson plans, teaching materials and, if need be, class management patterns. This delivery of CULP had no precedents. To gauge some fairly meaningful data we decided to administer a very slightly modified standard questionnaire that we used (a variation of) over many years. This meant that we had some robust and meaningful historical data for comparison.

Here are some of the most relevant answers compared to the regular 2019-2020 classroom delivery of the course. M/L stands for the first two terms, Michaelmas and Lent. Easter is the third term when teaching was delivered remotely. It must be said that the range of M/L answers we used falls within the range of the historical data. They are not, therefore, extreme in any sense. The number of respondents in the two cohorts was comparable (188/160). Respondents had to circle one answer on the Likert scale where one was strongly disagree, and five strongly agree.

- "The teacher stimulated my interest in the subject": 86% of the M/L and 97% agreed (or strongly agreed) with the statement[17].

- "The teacher was organised and prepared": Given the very short period of time teachers had to be trained to use the remote teaching tools and modify their teaching materials, it came as a surprise that 96% of the respondents thought so (M/L 93%).

---

17. For a full table with all questions and responses see supplementary materials.

- "The course was supported by adequate online resources": 81% thought so in M/L. The remote course saw that percentage skyrocketing to 96%.

- "Exams related to the course learning outcomes": 91% of the remote course students were of that view, up from the M/L's 88%.

- "The teacher used a variety of instructional methods to reach the course objectives": 26% of the remote students agreed and a further 72% strongly agreed (98% in total). In M/L these figures were 34% and 57% (91% in total) respectively.

- One of the most important questions in this survey relates to the students' own perceptions of their attainment (or otherwise). The programme aims at establishing students as independent learners for life and to do so, it is of utmost importance that they feel confident and positive about their own learning. So, in M/L 94% of the students felt they made progress in the course while in the remote course that was the view of 98% of the respondents.

- And finally, 93% of the M/L students thought this was a worthwhile class (4% disagreed) while among the remote students 97% thought so and none disagreed.

The student feedback was extremely positive. However, we need to view it with a pinch of salt. The novelty of the mode of delivery and the severe lockdown influenced significantly and positively student feelings and beliefs. For instance, more Easter students agreed that The Language Centre's website and online information about the courses was adequate. We however, did not alter the web pages in any meaningful way except for adding the new and only most necessary information in relation to the remote/online courses.

This survey, among other information gathered, shows clearly that students are quite open to the idea of remote/online language teaching and learning. More open perhaps, than the teaching staff themselves.

## 3.2. Teacher feedback

The Language Centre features two 'teachers' rooms' in two different buildings. Each of these rooms hold half a dozen workstations connected to printers, scanners, audio-visual tools, and other necessary equipment. The teaching staff, however, always preferred to do most of their lesson preparation work from home. In that sense, the announcement of a lockdown and of the necessity to work and teach from home did not find teachers completely unprepared. Having said that, preparing lessons at home is very different from delivering them from home.

Hardware and software issues were reported and dealt with as per our previous discussion. Some staff reported intermittent but not terminal internet connection issues and were worried about the relevant student connections. It was very quickly made clear to all that any technical problem at the students' end would be theirs to solve. In cases of severe disruption that would impede following the course, such students would be fully reimbursed the fee[18]. This put teachers' minds at ease. Since schools were closed, some teachers had small children running around the house and other family-related distractions. To their great credit, they managed to resolve all of these problems in a friendly, sensible, and positive manner.

In relation to the teaching, teachers highlighted the fatigue element. Suddenly, we all found ourselves with our lesson preparation as well as teaching being performed in front of a computer, as well as all our other professional and social interaction. This was tiring and we addressed the issue by strongly suggesting that all take a ten minute break in between two lessons. Historically, we never used this ten minute break as we all felt it was disruptive and ultimately, time wasted. They also reported a slower pace of lessons. Communication with students with special reference to groups was different. Placing students in breakout rooms is more time consuming when compared to classroom teaching due to the in-built delay. Observing and listening to student performance was

---

18. Although our students were based worldwide, on all five continents, we had none such cases.

also at a somewhat slower pace as a teacher needs to enter a breakout room and interrupt the ongoing dialogue. There were also (mostly) small technical issues to be dealt with such as sharing the desktop, enabling sound, making sure all participants have decent quality of audio and video, etc. This called for a change in lesson plans and a shift of some materials and activities from classroom presentation to self-study and homework. The flipped classroom thus became even more 'flipped'. This was necessary because all our courses are benchmarked against (for instance) the CEFR (Council of Europe, 2020) as is the assessment framework. The ultimate attainment target at the end of the course had, therefore, to stay the same.

Overall, teacher feedback was very positive. This was an edifying and gratifying professional experience. Some teachers, though, voiced preference for teaching face-to-face. Well, the overall consensus was, we can only hope that a day will come when we will be able to, actually, choose the mode of delivery we feel most comfortable with. Until then we will be in full remote, online mode.

### 3.3. Learning outcomes

The courses' assessment frameworks were modified, and the oral component gained in prominence as it was given 50% of the overall mark. Other assessment tools in the courses are online by design: Moodle-based tests, homework, in-class short tests, and a final exam (listening/reading comprehension and writing). The reason for shifting the weight towards the oral component was that this was the only element where we could unequivocally check the identity of the student. Hence the increase in weighing from the standard 30% to 50%.

The retention rate in the 2019/2020 M/L courses was a very healthy 85% while the remote course went up 98%. Only two students dropped out and they both had compelling reasons that they communicated to their teachers and the administration.

The marking schemes and criteria deployed were the same as per the *regular* courses. All teachers reported that their students achieved very satisfactory levels of language attainment and this is documented by the work they produced as well as Zoom recordings of their oral presentations. There was a consensus among teaching staff across all languages and levels that the learning outcomes were comparable to those at the end of the M/L cycle.

## 4. Conclusion

In the academic year 2020/2021, CULP delivers all of its courses remotely/online. Beyond this crisis, I do not see CULP returning to the previous 'normal' but rather diversifying its mode of delivery that will be informed by our experience during the current crisis. I expect that in the future we will be offering blended-learning classroom-based teaching, and remote/online language teaching as well as combinations of the two.

We learnt many lessons in this very short period of time. These relate to hardware and software issues, resources preparation, teacher training, class management, and communication with administration and students. Due to all of these factors, this swift move to remote/online teaching represents an important shift in the ways we communicate and teach. Since we are interested in world/foreign language teaching, this confluence of shifts in communication and teaching patterns is significant. Mobile telephony and networked computers have been with us for over two decades and so have Computer Assisted Language Learning (CALL)[19], blended-learning and, on the margins of mainstream academia, remote/online language learning. However, teaching students skills and knowledge to communicate effectively face-to-face in a foreign country is very different from teaching the same students to communicate effectively and competently remotely and online. During this crisis, we have grown accustomed to communicate with friends, family, and colleagues online. It is hard to see that we are ever going back to the 'old' communication patterns that require face-to-face interaction. This change in communication patterns leads to a change in the

---

19. Also, Technology-Enhanced Language Learning (TELL), Computer-Aided Instruction (CAI), Computer-Aided Language Instruction (CALI), and Computer-Mediated Language Instruction (CMLI).

use and therefore, learning and teaching of foreign languages. This can be said to be a paradigm shift in both the way we live, communicate, and teach.

We, language teaching practitioners and researchers alike, have the opportunity to be active participants and contributors to the development and study of this new language teaching paradigm.

## 5. Supplementary materials

https://research-publishing.box.com/s/ui6gkuhccgw5t3zdp4yt779o15s8btob

## References

Bergmann, J., & Sams, A. (2012). *Flip your classroom: reach every student in every class every day*. International Society for Technology in Education.

Council of Europe (2020). *Common European framework of reference for languages: learning, teaching, assessment*. https://www.coe.int/en/web/common-european-framework-reference-languages

Dunn, J. (2014). *The 6-step guide to flipping your classroom*. http://dailygenius.com/flipped

# 22. Remote online teaching in modern languages in Germany: responses according to audiences and teaching objectives

## Josef Schmied[1]

### Abstract

This chapter reports on the 'Corona teaching' in a department of English studies at a German university of technology. It discusses the general frame in the German university system and in this specific department, faculty and university. It focuses on the responses depending on participants and learning objectives. One larger lecture for 1st year Bachelor of Arts (BA) students used Moodle to teach a traditional knowledge transfer course, the 'History of English language and culture'. One smaller seminar used Big Blue Button (BBB) to teach a more interactive Master of Arts (MA) course on 'Translation theory and technology'. The overall experience was positive for the good students who managed the challenge well, but it was negative for others who were less privileged in their technical equipment or their resilience. Some losses included more social class activities; opportunities included additional learning in the media and digital contexts – possibly invaluable advantages for further developments for modern foreign language specialists in future.

Keywords: COVID-19, online language teaching, modern languages, translation, Moodle lecture, interaction, Germany.

---

1. Chemnitz University of Technology, Chemnitz, Germany; josef.schmied@phil.tu-chemnitz.de; https://orcid.org/0000-0001-8499-3158

**How to cite:** Schmied, J. (2021). Remote online teaching in modern languages in Germany: responses according to audiences and teaching objectives. In N. Radić, A. Atabekova, M. Freddi & J. Schmied (Eds), *The world universities' response to COVID-19: remote online language teaching* (pp. 353-368). Research-publishing.net. https://doi.org/10.14705/rpnet.2021.52.1283

Chapter 22

## 1. The federal and institutional framework

This chapter[2] discusses the experience from the forced online teaching in a modern department of philology at a German university in spring 2020. Although Chemnitz is called a university of technology, like three of the four universities in Saxony, Germany, it has a faculty of humanities with traditional departments like German studies, English studies, media studies, European studies, etc. The teaching in English studies (Anglistik/Amerikanistik in German) is not focused on teacher training for public schools, although many graduates choose this option later (also in the context of teaching refugees and international students that developed in Germany in the last five years). But it offers a wide range of skills useful for today's language service providers in the widest sense. Former students run their own private companies and provide up-to-date response to the departmental teaching from a practical perspective (cf. 3.3 below). Thus, since the introduction of the Bologna system[3] at Chemnitz 15 years ago, the teaching has developed strongly towards digitalisation and intercultural cooperation. This can be seen in 'modern philological' MA seminars like 'project management', where international students are taught German culture in the preparation of a 'Christmas Evening' in December, and German and European students learn about 'Chinese New Year' in February, or 'Translation theory and technology' (which is discussed below). The English Department at Chemnitz had developed such 'modern philological' classes over the years and they were approved and supported by the faculty and university. This 'technological' emphasis was welcome because of the (traditional) name of the university, although the interpretation of the term 'technological' was different in some cases: the university leadership and Saxon Ministry of Education liked to think that it links well with the great German engineering tradition – the department liked the good computer equipment and support by the computer centre. Both sides came together recently in a million-Euro 'collaborative research centre'[4] on 'Hybrid

---

2. This report is based on the experience in my own lectures and seminars and is put in a wider context of discussions with colleagues and friends in similar situations in the Czech Republic, Italy, China, Cameroon, and Rwanda. I wish to thank them all for the collaboration and some suggestions for improvement or clarification of this article.

3. https://ec.europa.eu/education/policies/higher-education/bologna-process-and-european-higher-education-area_en

4. Funding code: SFB1014

Societies: Humans Interacting with Embodied Technologies', which includes a project on lingua franca English interaction of humans and a non-native 'agent'.

From the examples above, it should be absolutely clear that classes in the English studies programme do not aim at learning a language (like in a language centre), but at using the language at an advanced level in modern academic interaction and preparing learners for professional language services afterwards, from creative mediation (translation) and intercultural discourse to media-, discipline-, and reader-/listener-specific writing/presentation, and editing.

This summary shows the background of the classes discussed below: a digital component had been introduced already and seen at least as interesting by the department, faculty, and university as a whole. In this context, the university was hit by 'Corona' in spring 2020. From April onward, all classes had to be held remotely – and this will be done again from October, except on special application. In fact, all university buildings were locked for months and staff were only allowed to meet in small groups (after applying to the Corona task force). All official departmental and faculty meetings were held online via BBB and students and staff were informed regularly about the situation by (usually rector's) circulars[5]. These circulars included links suggesting tools, instruction videos, and online courses for teachers and students. Some recommendations were based on discussions of external and internal task forces; in the end, however, it was colleagues who helped with advice and experience on all levels, departmental and international. Additionally, the federal system in Germany allowed the keen newspaper reader to compare different responses in different universities and disciplines through the collection of relevant newspaper cuttings by the German rectors' conference. Thus, this report is based on the experiences in my own lectures and seminars and is put in a wider context of discussions with international colleagues and colleagues in similar situations. They illustrate concrete experience in different types of classes and may be useful for comparison.

---

5. The first circular, still published on the university webpages in German and English, came on February 6th, the fifth circular introduced the Video Conferencing System BBB on April 1st.

## 2. BA introductory lecture 'History of English language and culture' in Moodle

The first example of 'teaching adaptation' to the Corona situation is from a 1st year/2nd semester BA class, which usually has 60 to 100 listeners, including many international students, not only from the BA English programme, but also from other related areas. Since this is a popular topic combining basic history (from secondary school) and only a few challenging linguistics components (from an introduction in the 1st semester), it attracted a wide range of students, as can be seen from the course description below:

> "[t]his survey lecture shows language in its socio-cultural contexts: its relationship to power and technology, to historical personalities and social groups. It ranges from the Romans to William the Conqueror, from Caxton to Dr Johnson or Noah Webster, from Matthew Arnold to Bill Gates and from the medieval scriptorium to the internet. It provides the background necessary to understand the world-wide forms and functions of English today and tries to draw general conclusions about the socio-cultural factors affecting language (change) in the past and today".

This description shows that in this lecture the learning outcomes and competences (cf. Brendel, Hanke, & Macke, 2019 or Kennedy, Hyland, & Ryan, 2007) were relatively traditional, i.e. a wide spectrum of cultural background knowledge, typical of intercultural language classrooms at advanced level at German universities (cf. Barrett et al., 2014). In the current Common European Framework of Reference (CEFR) illustrative descriptors, they can be described in terms of professional users' 'Exploiting pluricultural repertoires' (German – English, but also British – American – global):

> "[a]t the C levels, this develops into an ability to explain sensitively the background to cultural beliefs, values and practices, interpret and discuss aspects of them, cope with sociolinguistic and pragmatic ambiguity and express reactions constructively with cultural appropriateness" (Council of Europe, 2020, p. 124).

## 2.1. The flipped classroom phase

This learning perspective made it possible immediately before the semester to start with an ad hoc experiment. Students were asked in departmental circulars and online course descriptions to prepare for the class by watching different types of YouTube videos: a professional television film on Old English, a short self-recorded lecture by a German colleague on Old English, a long TV documentary on *The forbidden book – history of the Bible*, and a very short self-made short video on *Why did English become an international language*. Students were warned that each video would require much more time than the weekly lecture and asked to send eight questions and suggested answers in phrases for each film (>500 words). This flipped, or inverted, classroom approach has been discussed for a long time (e.g. Estes, Ingram, & Liu, 2014; Handke & Sperl, 2012) and is discussed again in the current blended learning context, where the discussion after the individual learning phase is online and not in the classroom. Unfortunately, the results of this part were only 'interesting' for the following short online discussion via BBB and not really as 'inspiring' as teacher and tutors had hoped – still, the points given by the tutors were used as extra points in the final assessment.

## 2.2. The Moodle lecture

Although universities in Saxony developed their own 'online education system' several years ago, the lectures for this introduction were put into the same Moodle system as the weekly quizzes and tutorial materials because it allows us to exchange materials with our Italian and Czech colleagues, who use basically the same system. Since teachers at our university tried to adhere to the new European General Data Protection Regulation (GDPR) on data protection and online privacy, which do not allow us to use foreign servers for our data, teachers in Germany were happy when they noticed that many open-source tools were integrated in spring 2020 to their Moodle systems. So, BBB and Etherpad were added for smaller groups in seminars first and Zoom for large lectures later. Most colleagues, it seems, opted for the easiest version of adding sound to their usual power-point presentations and made sure that the audio file was short enough

## Chapter 22

for students limited attention span and small enough for students' to download even with unstable internet connections outside the university campus. This was followed up by regular video office hours and chats or forums – which were hardly used.

### 2.3. The tutorial

In the German university system, some departments and teachers spend a considerable part of their funds on student assistants and tutors. For lectures, teaching materials (such as the YouTube videos mentioned above) are usually checked or even selected by (paid) older students who did well in the class one or two years before. These tutorials are also used to create a less formal atmosphere without the professor where students can speak out and admit when they still have not understood the concepts discussed. Theoretically, this 'understanding' is immediately checked by tutors in weekly quizzes of transfer questions (cf. 2.4), which are the basis of the continuous assessment in the end, as a welcome alternative to the traditional big final test at the end of term.

Unfortunately, the tutorials even lost more students than the lectures because students just attempted the quizzes without using the additional learning opportunities in the tutorials – and tutors were frustrated not only because students did not attend their tutorials but also because they failed even tests that the tutors considered as simple. Many tutors were also not happy that German politicians and university leaders told students that it did not matter if they did not attend online classes and even failed exams – they were guaranteed to have another chance next semester, as their teaching or their exams were not as expected and promised in course descriptions.

### 2.4. The final exam

When it became obvious in June that the university would not go back to the classrooms, online final exams were discussed. It is interesting that in the end, all Safe Exam Browsers (SEB) were considered too easy to cheat in online group exams (e.g. with one system locked by a SEB and another one open used to consult lecture notes or the internet). Thus, teachers had the choice to persuade students to take exams in a special classroom that was equipped according to Corona hygiene regulations or to try online – reassured that they would be given the chance to repeat everything later. The result was – predictably – that almost all students who took the exam online did really well, and those who did not take online teaching seriously failed badly or did not take the exam at all. One positive outcome of the online tests was that Bloom's (1975) taxonomy of higher cognitive skills (application, analysis, evaluation, synthesis) was taken seriously in this open book format (Oxford University, 2020), where the students were expected, or even instructed, to take the relevant passages in the teaching materials as a starting point and transfer and apply this information to new materials (cf. Koksal & Ulum, 2018).

## 2.5. Lessons for future BA lectures

We conclude that this *Introduction to the history of English* is not ideal for online learning if the interactive parts with library visits, small group tutorials, and individual group discussions cannot complement the delivery to hundreds of students online or in a large lecture theatre. Generally, online teaching and exams are an opportunity for the good students to make them even better and a threat for the weaker students who need more personal guidance with time management, note taking, regular revision, and (self-)critical questions. This will have to be achieved in small groups with friendly and trustworthy student tutors if we do not want to lose too many weak students in future.

## 3. MA interactive seminar 'Translation theory and technology' in BBB

The second example of online teaching is from a seminar for MA students on 'Translation theory and technology', which was described as follows (unchanged from the original course catalogue):

## Chapter 22

> "[t]his seminar intends to show that translation today includes important business and technology components. As a business, it is part of a wider range of language services (from language teaching to editing), technologies range from small web-based tools (such as EU databases or Linguee) to the neural networks of DeepL and complex translation memory systems (such as TRADOS). The linguistic focus in this class is on various levels of equivalence (lexical, semantic, pragmatic and textual). Finding this equivalence or making linguistically informed choices between different options is a significant task for translators. We will also consider cultural aspects of translation and explore models and solutions, esp. by discussing whether our Library's English webpages are suitable for international students using English as an international lingua franca and not as a mother tongue".

The seminar also included traditionally a flipped element (cf. 2.1. above) with group work, discussing YouTube lectures by renowned international specialists like Mona Baker (Manchester) or Antony Pym (Tarragona). This element was, of course, maintained this year, except that students were only able to meet in digital break-out rooms and not on campus.

In this class, the learning objectives were more clearly defined than in the lecture above and the interactive component was much more prominent. Despite the traditional name in the German system, the skills taught were based more on the CEFR illustrative descriptors for mediation at C2 level:

> "[c]an mediate effectively and naturally, taking on different roles according to the needs of the people and situation involved, identifying nuances and undercurrents and guiding a sensitive or delicate discussion. Can explain in clear, fluent, well-structured language the way facts and arguments are presented, conveying evaluative aspects and most nuances precisely, and pointing out sociocultural implications" (Council of Europe, 2020, p. 91).

Josef Schmied

## 3.1. Regular meetings via BBB

As this seminar was relatively small (only about 20 students), it was taught using the new online tool, BBB, recommended and supported by links to tuition by the university. Most students used a laptop, but it also worked on modern smartphones. Since this is an international course, students logged in from different parts of Germany (after it became clear that there would be no more classroom teaching, many students did not stay on campus), but also from places as far away as Lebanon, which was not only difficult, but also expensive and showed the commitment of international students. Other international students stayed on campus – and still did not hand in their 'papers' after the class finished in early July or needed an extension until the end of August.

During the weekly meetings, we were joined online by a specialist from the library as a 'customer' (see 3.4. below) and as a resource person because all students were asked to choose texts from the university library web pages and present evidence-based arguments for as many alternative translations as possible. In the first part of the semester, we discussed online how to use free online resources (like DeepL, online dictionaries, online mega corpora, such as the Brigham Young University (BYU) examples below, and parallel texts from library web pages of other universities). They had to be as broad as possible to generate as many as possible alternative versions according to principles of equivalence (Baker, 2018). Finally, students were able to present their preferred options in the shared notes and even take an online vote according to stylistic criteria, especially from a non-native/lingua franca perspective of an international 1st year MA student advanced level (C1 in the CEFR)[6]. This general part was done by individual presentations in BBB and follow-up individual student work with a few online discussions orally (with disciplined use of the microphone) or in writing in the chat. Figure 1 shows an example of a www page presented to encourage students to check possible solutions to critical translation issues. Here we see the entry in the BYU

---

6. Thus the 'translation course' was in fact a user-focused 'stylistics course', since the source text did not have to be a German text from our library, but could also be a text from their 'home' university library in their mother tongue or any other. The only clearly defined variable was the target text user and students were asked to focus on information they considered useful for them, even if it had not been noticed by the institutional customer, i.e. the university librarian.

Chapter 22

databases (Davies, 2010) for *reserve*, which was important in the context of *reserve collection*, i.e. books that are kept in the library only for reference and not given out on loan – an important point for international students, who have to plan their time to work in the library accordingly. Different parts of the BYU entry in Figure 1 support the choice *reserve collection*: the second definition fits well, the academic nature is clear, and the sample sentence on *literature review* is related, but the noun *collection* is not in the collocations list, and the other nouns there are not from the same field either. These parts offer a much wider basis for the discussion of alternatives than traditional bilingual dictionaries and even modern www based tools like Linguee. The discussions on such online resources are basically the same as in the classroom, except that experienced teachers find it easier to read their students' faces in the classroom than online, where technology may (still) require more teacher attention than student reactions.

Figure 1. Screen showing usage features of 'reserve' in the BYU corpora

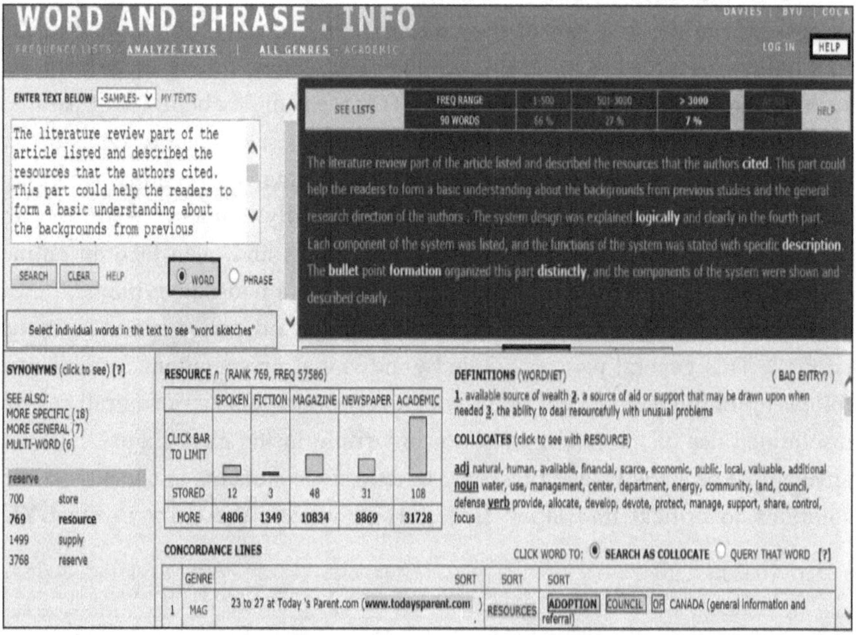

## 3.2. The shared notes

The second part of the BBB meetings consisted mainly of student presentations, where students often (as in normal face-to-face classes) provided far too few choices for crucial passages in the library texts they had chosen to work on and collective brainstorming made available more text alternatives copied into the shared notes.

Figure 2. BBB screen with participants, shared notes, and www work plan

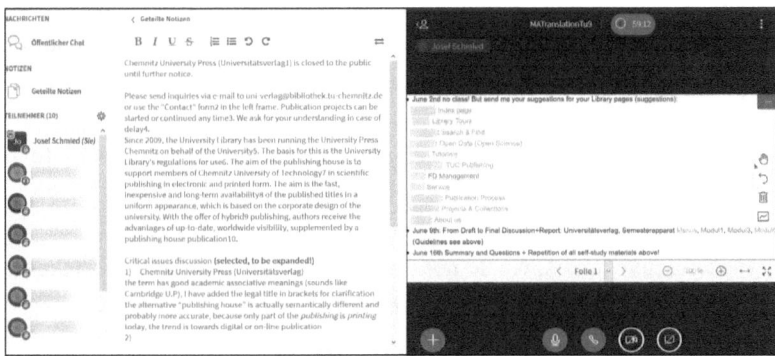

As Figure 2 shows, BBB has the advantage that it provides on one screen the participants list (here anonymised on the left), the shared notes in flexible width in the centre, and, on the right, the work plan from the www course pages or the original www page either in German or the original DeepL translation as a starting point, since some students spoke German only at a B1 level. Such a set up may even be seen as an advantage because it may be more difficult to set up the three parallel perspectives in a traditional classroom (or in Zoom). The notes allow some basic formatting, and everything can be exported and made available in the course cloud or on the course www page later – the same as the recorded version, which is shown by the red button at the top. Figure 2 also shows the disadvantages of BBB shared notes, since much of the original formatting is lost (footnotes, bold for emphasis has to be added just as italics for lexemes/phrases discussed, all important points in student papers later). Unfortunately, all student contributions are 'anonymous', in contrast to the options in Etherpad for instance, where all participants can choose their colour to mark individual contributions, but we also know now from experience that some students prefer it this way.

### 3.3. The social interactive extras

This seminar usually included an (optional) 'excursion' by train (university students enjoy free rides on all public transport in Saxony with their student ID) to a neighbouring town and a translation agency run by a former PhD student, where students learnt three main points in a remarkable demonstration:

- as a professional business, we manage your project and time and submit the final product when it is required;

- as sociable human beings, we can work in a social atmosphere (even in a nice 'villa'), as long as we deliver; and

- as creative artists, we do not translate – we create – and this takes more time and effort than most customers imagine.

This social event (with drinks and snacks provided) had always been considered the highlight of the class, a central contribution to the working atmosphere in the group and a model for student applications for internships/traineeships and even job interviews in their later lives. Unfortunately, these important elements of the seminar could not be replaced; the discussions on professional aspects of translation and language services did not get very far. Interestingly, the agency was not affected by the 'Corona crisis' and worked and delivered as a business throughout the lockdown, which was not as strict in Germany as in other countries. For this class, the interaction with real life business in an important workplace experience was not possible.

### 3.4. The final paper

Although students were given scaffolded, interactive collaboration opportunities in the last few class meetings and the following individual consultations via

BBB, they found it difficult to understand that the 'final translation' was not the main part of this class requirement and only added as an appendix; the main part was the detailed discussion of 'alternative solutions' and the student's well-documented and well-argued final choice for only five to eight different language problems. This involved not only lexemes but also collocations, associations, etc., since this was not an exercise in German-English translation, but rather in advanced English stylistics focusing on media-, institution-, and user-adapted language. The final paper thus was also seen as a formal report to the 'customer', the university library for further reference – and maybe to make library access easier for the translation target group, the next generation of international MA students.

### 3.5. Lessons for future MA seminars

This 'translation' class is a good example for a fruitful blended approach in future: after the first social gathering, where students also divided up into work-groups of different backgrounds and specialisations, most of the presentation discussion could be done online, the real professional touch during the excursion to the translation agency could give the creative thinking a new boost before the final online discussions of alternative solutions and the individual completion of the paper.

## 4. Opportunities and dangers for modern languages

The conclusions drawn from the limited experience presented in this study are based on the current German university system, where the modernisation of the curriculum depends on the department, the technical affordances on the university, and the finances on the state (more southern *Länder* in Germany can usually invest more in higher education). In such relatively stable institutional contexts, professors and students have to remain flexible in times of crisis and make the most of the opportunities while being aware of the dangers they might present.

## 4.1. Towards international exchange and cooperation?

The greatest opportunity of online teaching using world-wide systems (like Moodle, Zoom, or BBB) is the new digital exchange and cooperation. Although international exchange students (at Chemnitz, usually from China, Turkey, Italy, and the Czech Republic) were able and will be able to take part in lectures and seminars, the students' usual interaction with foreign students suffered during the 'Corona restrictions'. The new slogan 'Internationalisation@home' can be expanded in hybrid form: of course, the personal intercultural encounter and cooperation cannot be replaced, yet it can be expanded in digital form. Colleagues who usually send their exchange students can be integrated in digital teaching even before exchange students meet them in person. Students who hesitate to go abroad can at least get a glimpse into 'foreign worlds' by interacting with international students at home and in digital seminars.

## 4.2. Towards commercialisation?

On the 'dangerous' side, the 'Corona experience' demonstrated that online teaching materials for some standard introductory classes (like 'history of English') are easily available on the www today. This may be interpreted by educational economists as an option 'to save' in cases of general survey lectures, which serve wide groups of students in modern English philology according to similar CEFR standards in many similar departments in native and non-native university contexts (cf. Bordet, 2021).

However, the extent to which advanced language learning in a philological department can be moved to remote online mode obviously depends on the specific learning contexts and objectives of the specific course. The limitations of online 'interaction' compared to classroom interaction and even extra-mural activities support the argumentation that blended forms of teaching will be most useful in post-Corona times.

The concrete description of the specific online experience in this contribution can also be seen as a warning against 'easy' commercialisation – 'even in

Germany', where international education and exchange is still highly valued, as this contribution also tried to illustrate.

## 5. General conclusion from Germany

It is clear that the response to the Corona threat does not only depend on technical affordances and the previous training in e-learning for students but also on the psychologies of language teachers and students. For modern philology students who are trained to adapt to new digital developments in a technological world, the experience may not have been as difficult as for others, yet there is no way to avoid crises – we have to learn to cope with them, in language teaching and learning as in other branches of life.

The consensus after the first online semester in Germany seems to be in contrast to many schools: universities were able to cope with the challenges depending on learning objectives and technical affordances. Students learnt to live with uncertainty and risk, which increased their personal resilience. They had to rely on their personal competence in developing digital and learning strategies and in complexity in general. In a small online Deutsche Zentrum für Hochschul- und Wissenschaftsforschung (DZHW) survey (Marczuk, Multrus, & Lörz, 2021), 24,600 students were asked about their experience in *studying in times of the Corona pandemic* and 86% disagreed that 'digital forms were not useable or accessible', whereas 77% agreed that they "missed the personal exchange" – unfortunately, this situation will continue for some time, and students and teachers just have to make the best out of it.

## References

Baker, M. (2018). *In other words. A coursebook on translation.* Routledge.
Barrett, M., Byram, M., Lázár, I., Mompoint-Gaillard, P., & Philippou, S. (2014). *Developing intercultural competence through education.* Council of Europe.
Bloom, B. S. (1975). *Taxonomy of educational objectives. Book 1 cognitive domain.* Longman.

Bordet, G. 2021. eaching online in translation studies: a teacher-researcher's feedback from France. In N. Radić, A. Atabekova, M. Freddi & J. Schmied (Eds), *The world universities' response to COVID-19: remote online language teaching* (pp. 235-248). Research-publishing.net. https://doi.org/10.14705/rpnet.2021.52.1275

Brendel, S., Hanke, U., & Macke, G. (2019). *Kompetenzorientiert lehren an Hochschulen*. Barbara Budrich.

Council of Europe. (2020). *CEFR illustrative descriptors extended version*. https://rm.coe.int/common-european-framework-of-reference-for-languages-learning-teaching/168073ff31

Davies, M. (2010). More than a peephole: using large and diverse online corpora. *International Journal of Corpus Linguistics 15*(3), 412-418. https://doi.org/10.1075/ijcl.15.3.13dav

Estes, M. D., Ingram, R., & Liu, J. C. (2014). A review of flipped classroom research, practice, and technologies. *International HETL Review, 4*(7). https://www.hetl.org/feature-articles/a-review-of-flipped-classroom-research-practice-and-technologies

Handke, J., & Sperl, A. (2012). (Eds). *Das Inverted Classroom Model*. Oldenburg.

Kennedy, D., Hyland, Á., & Ryan, N. (2007). *Writing and using learning outcomes: a practical guide*. University College Cork.

Koksal, D., & Ulum, Ö. G. (2018). Language assessment through Bloom's taxonomy. *Journal of Language and Linguistic Studies, 14*(2), 76-88.

Marczuk, A., Multrus, F., & Lörz, M. (2021). *Die Studiensituation in der Corona-Pandemie. Auswirkungen der Digitalisierung auf die Lern- und Kontaktsituation von Studierenden* (DZHW Brief 01|2021). DZHW. https://doi.org/10.34878/2021.01.dzhw_brief

Oxford University (2020). *Open book exams*. https://www.ox.ac.uk/students/academic/exams/open-book

# Section 5.

# OCEANIA

# 23 "Stay home, be safe, and be kind": University of Auckland's Italian course goes online in a week

## Barbara Martelli[1]

### Abstract

On March 23rd, at the University of Auckland (New Zealand), all lectures were suspended for a week. During this time, both students and staff made a considerable effort to prepare the online delivery of courses. In this chapter we discuss the impact of COVID-19 on the Italian beginners courses offered in Semester 1. With no certainty of when the campus would reopen, and with the well-being of students always considered as a priority, the courses were quickly adapted for distance learning. This change involved multiple aspects and the experience gained, denoted by urgency and flexibility, proving to be a precious resource to face the second semester and, above all, a less predictable and more frightening future; in which not only safety and adaptability, but kindness and mutual respect, should also be the keywords. Designing blended, easily migratable online courses that make use of both technology and up-to-date approaches to language teaching has emerged as a viable strategy for an uncertain future.

Keywords: COVID-19, online language teaching, resources, Italian, New Zealand.

---

1. University of Auckland, Auckland, New Zealand; barbara.martelli@auckland.ac.nz; https://orcid.org/0000-0001-7148-0775

How to cite: Martelli, B. (2021). "Stay home, be safe, and be kind": University of Auckland's Italian course goes online in a week. In N. Radić, A. Atabekova, M. Freddi & J. Schmied (Eds), *The world universities' response to COVID-19: remote online language teaching* (pp. 371-383). Research-publishing.net. https://doi.org/10.14705/rpnet.2021.52.1284

## Chapter 23

## 1. Introduction

In the Faculty of Arts, the School of Cultures, Languages, and Linguistics (CLL) represents the centre for studying European and Asian languages, literatures and cultures, language teaching, linguistics, and translation at the University of Auckland. A variety of Italian language courses are offered for undergraduate, postgraduate, and doctoral students wanting to learn to speak, read, and write Italian from beginner to advanced levels. In particular, the undergraduate language acquisition courses are delivered in three stages (beginners, intermediate, and advanced), divided into two progressive levels (1 and 2), and normally carried out in three years.

## 2. Objectives

In this chapter we will deal with the impact of COVID-19 on Italian beginners courses offered at Stage 1 in Semester 1, between March and July 2020: *Introductory Italian Language* (Italian 100-G) and *Italian Language for Beginners 1* (Italian 106-G). Particular attention will be paid to *Italian 106-G*, as the author of this chapter had personal experience as the tutor[2] of this course, working side by side with the coordinator of Italian language acquisition courses. By adopting a descriptive and participatory perspective, we will discuss how this course was quickly restructured to be completely remotely delivered, what obstacles and strengths have emerged, and what suggestions for the future came to light.

## 3. A different beginning

On March 2nd, 2020, the first semester of the new academic year began at the University of Auckland and, from the very start, it was clear that teaching was not going to be as usual. In fact, just three days earlier, on February 28th, the first case of COVID-19 coronavirus in New Zealand had been reported. The World

---

[2]. At that time, I was a doctoral student in Italian and I worked as a graduate teaching assistant for the Italian language acquisition courses at CLL.

Health Organization had already declared the SARS-CoV-2 outbreak, later renamed COVID-19, as a global health emergency and, on February 3rd, New Zealand had temporarily banned the entry of foreigners from, or those who had travelled through, mainland China. Soon after, anyone who might have been at high risk of exposure had to remain isolated for two weeks. Therefore, although in-class lectures were normally held in the first three weeks of the semester, the impact of COVID-19 had already marked some significant changes on several levels, not least the general climate of precariousness, anxiety, and concern widespread among students and staff, both inside and outside the classroom.

In preparation for the start of the courses, all students were provided briefing information and updates about COVID-19 and its possible impact on their studies. At that time all activities of the University of Auckland were functioning normally as there was no increased risk of contracting the coronavirus from being on campus. However, following the advice of the health authorities, hygiene practices were encouraged and health supplies allocated throughout the campus in order to reduce exposure. Those among students and staff who were feeling unwell or suffering from respiratory infections of any kind and flu-like symptoms were strongly advised to contact a doctor or a health professional immediately and try to isolate themselves from others in the meantime. A health line for counselling was established. Notably the university administration also intensely promoted the practice of kindness, respect, care, and support for each one, without discriminating against those who already wore a facemask or preferred not to come to campus in person anymore. This general emphasis on respect and kindness, as well as the rhetoric of personal and mutual safety are part of the procedures adopted by the New Zealand Government to enforce popular and political consensus to their response to the pandemic.

## 4. Italian beginners courses

The two Italian acquisition courses for beginners available in Semester 1, *Italian 100-G* and *Italian 106-G*, are very similar in terms of curriculum and assessments, but differ in the way they are structured and taught.

Students who attend *Italian 106-G* are expected to attend four contact hours in the classroom; additionally, they need to practise at home by doing activities and homework from the workbook, which serve in preparation for ten weekly online mini-tests. The expectation is that students commit ten hours a week for this course, including class time and personal study. In addition to mini-tests, two in-class group activities, two in-class tests, a final oral exam, and a final written exam count in different percentages towards the final course mark.

*Italian 100-G* is a blended learning course introduced in 2019, after being team-developed during the previous year. It involves a hybrid approach that combines two hours of classroom contact per week and four to five hours of e-learning on the *In Italia con Giacomo app*[3], available online through all fixed and portable digital devices. In this app, Giacomo (an electric Vespa) acts as a travel companion and learning guide. In addition, two or more hours of independent study are required to reach a total of ten hours of study per week.

While the adopted textbook, classroom tests, and final exams are similar to those of *Italian 106-G*, the classroom activities, both marked and unmarked, are designed to meet the need for a differently structured course. Another novelty introduced in 2019 was a virtual café, a space for discussion and sharing among students made available on the Canvas[4] course page. The experience gained in designing and implementing online teaching and learning materials for this blended course proved to be one of the most valuable resources to facilitate and accelerate the transition to full remote teaching of Italian courses for beginners.

Hundred students were enrolled in the Italian beginners course in Semester 1: 29 students in *Italian 106-G*, divided into two streams, and 71 in *Italian 100-G*, divided into four streams. For the first three weeks the course coordinator tutored one stream of *106-G* and three streams of *100-G*, and I was the tutor for the other two streams. Special arrangements had been in place for a small group of students who were unable to attend classes because they could not enter

---

3. In Italia con Giacomo is a digital learning resource of CLL available to students enrolled in Italian 100-G at the URL https://giacomo.arts.auckland.ac.nz/admin/index.php

4. Canvas is the web-based learning management system used by the University of Auckland.

New Zealand or were in temporary isolation as a precaution due to COVID-19. A remote teaching group was thus set up for those students enrolled in *Italian 106-G* (two students) or *Italian 100-G* (four students), as a temporary solution until they could return to class. Regardless of their belonging to one course rather than the other, these students followed the *Italian 100-G* programme, more suitable than the *106-G Italian* programme for online delivery, and their in-class attendance was replaced by the *Giacomo* app. The teaching material was sent via email in pdf form, while all the lectures were recorded daily (voice and computer screen only) and uploaded to the Canvas course page for asynchronous online learning. Students also addressed specific questions and asked for in-depth explanations during the weekly live tutorials exclusively dedicated to them.

## 5. One week to go online

By mid-March, the exponential speed of the spread of the virus in New Zealand began to cause worry, resulting in a series of increasingly restrictive social measures to contain it. On March 19th all indoor gatherings of over 100 people were prohibited and the borders closed to all but New Zealand citizens and permanent residents. On March 21st 2020 the Government introduced a four-tiered alert level system and the Prime Minister announced that New Zealand was at Alert Level 2. At that point, the situation around the campus was extremely precarious, with a very strong feeling in the air that it was not a given that we would meet again in class at the next lesson. Indeed, 48 hours later on March 25th the whole nation went into lockdown and a State of National Emergency was declared, which lasted until June 8th when, having no more active cases of COVID-19, New Zealand returned to Alert Level 1.

Like the other New Zealand tertiary institutions, the university of Auckland was unprepared for this scenario; however, foreseeing a possible change in the COVID-19 alert level and a subsequent campus closure, they had already suspended all teaching for the week of March 23rd-27th. While the pause button was pressed on the lessons, all efforts focused on the preparations and adjustments needed to speed up the process of reaching a full digital teaching and learning mode.

During those 48 hours (and the rest of the week off-campus), the university provided academic staff with the support they needed to be ready for an improvised remote delivery starting Week 4 (March 30th), both via online delivery and with face-to-face sessions. Examples of such support are: video tutorials; live training webinars; workshops for installing and using Zoom[5]; faculty drop-in sessions dedicated to Canvas and other support for remote learning; and university drop-in sessions for remote work issues using a personal device (such as installing a Virtual Private Network (VPN) service[6]).

The transition from face-to-face to full online teaching was swift and substantially completed during this *teaching-free week*, with subsequent improvements derived from the experience gained in the first weeks of online teaching, shared among the CLL language tutors, and enriched with valuable feedback received from students. By Friday, March 27th, we uploaded a fully revised plan for both *Italian 100-G* and *Italian 106-G* onto Canvas, with new dates and deadlines, as all academic activities had been pushed one week back. Secondly, after a successful trial with Zoom, we communicated to the students the video-conferencing links for the Zoom live sessions, which replaced both the contact and office hours. Finally, we established new formats for the group projects assessed, the in-class tests and the oral and written final exams. This rapid shift to online teaching and learning transformed the courses in various respects, such as teaching, didactic materials, assessments, relationships with students, and well-being. We will analyse them more closely in the next paragraphs, referring mainly to *Italian 106-G*.

---

5. Zoom is a cloud-based video conferencing service for which the University of Auckland acquired an institution-wide licence.

6. The VPN service is available to all staff, postgraduate students, and authorised contractors of the University of Auckland. It is needed in order to establish a secure connection to the university network from outside and to access certain resources when working from home, travelling on university business, working from a remote site, or accessing internal university resources not publicly accessible through the internet.

## 6. One teacher, one class

First, we agreed to reassign courses to tutors differently. The course coordinator took over all the streams of *Italian 100-G*, while I was responsible for *Italian 106-G*. With this decision, we aimed to offer an online teaching as consistent as possible through to the end of the semester. Furthermore, while the *100-G* students remained divided into four virtual classrooms, the fewer *106-G* students were merged into a single virtual classroom, which also included the initial remote teaching group.

Beginning with Week 4, all lectures at the University of Auckland were recorded and made available online to meet the needs of those students who might have limited access to high-speed broadband, experience issues with internet connectivity, or face additional challenges related to equipment, study space, and other physical constraints. In our particular case, the small size of the Italian beginners classes allowed us to replace the contact hours in the classroom with hours of live video conference via Zoom. Therefore, we provided distance learning both in real time and asynchronously.

The first challenge was to mitigate the anxiety, both of the instructor and of the students, caused by the transition from face-to-face to digital lessons that could often be disrupted by a number of minor technological issues. Suddenly the public space of the lesson and the private space of the house were intertwined, resulting in a series of frequent and minor inconveniences that in the long run, instead of disturbing the teaching, helped to make lessons homely, friendly, and relaxed. A second challenge was represented by the difficulty in promoting attendance and engagement in the virtual class. Not only was the requirement of minimum class attendance for admission to final exams being waived due to current special circumstances, but the availability of fully recorded and downloadable lessons also increased the number of absent students. Moreover, many of the students, possibly for both logistical and personal reasons, preferred not to turn on the camera and hardly participated if not directly asked to do so. This was a crucial problem, common not only to the other Italian Beginner course but also to the other language courses taught at CLL, heartily discussed in the tutors' online forum, which nevertheless led to different individual solutions and indeed, offers food for thought and research for the future. Our choice was not to push anyone into turning on the video camera but rather to encourage students to feel as comfortable as possible, without renouncing to challenge everyone to be actively involved in class activities. This entailed a considerable effort from the instructor, who often had to engage with face-less nicknames that did not correspond to the names in the class list. There was a risk that only a small group would proactively contribute to the lesson, but, over time, an increased confidence in the new format and a series of ice-breaking group activities enhanced the atmosphere. The breakout rooms, in particular, proved to be a very useful Zoom function, as it allowed to divide the class into small groups to complete specific activities. During these group moments, aimed at strengthening communication and interaction skills, the students lowered their affective filter, feeling relieved of class performance anxiety and encouraged by peer collaboration and mutual correction. By the end of the semester, everyone ended up participating in the lessons at least a little. Thus, the alienating feeling of teaching not only grammar, but also social communication and pragmatics in a new language diminished as Zoom's black boxes and disembodied voices became recognisable, albeit virtual and often invisible, students.

## 7. Digital teaching material

Zoom offers a variety of digital tools that help the teacher digitally replicate much of what happens in a real classroom. For example, in addition to projecting textbook pages and slides via the screen connection tool, it is easy to write and draw on a whiteboard, use a dual monitor, share files, create breakout rooms in which to assign a variable number of students for exercises in pairs, group work, and also oral tests. Following the students' suggestions, the chat tool was also employed more often to communicate particular instructions and solutions to exercises not always made clear by voice.

The textbook (Marin & Magnelli, 2010) adopted in both classes *100-G* and *106-G* was digitised in high quality to be shared by the teacher during the video lessons.

Furthermore, the website of Edilingua publishing house offers much searchable and downloadable content, such as the index and glossary, audio tracks, videos and online activities, educational games and other extra activities, progress tests, and workbook solutions. Some of them are available for free, while others require a code, which is included with the purchase of the hard copy or e-book. Moreover, both instructors and students can find all the workbook exercises, together with a series of resources and tools, on the interactive platform *i-d-e-e*[7].

## 8. Assessment

All assessment tools that count for the final grade had to be quickly adapted to a digital format, via Zoom or Canvas.

*Miniprogetto 1* and *2*, which usually engages students in a collaborative and creative group activity designed for the development of communicative skills in Italian, became instead a written discussion on Canvas. The initial idea of asking the student to record and upload short audio/video was subsequently abandoned due to technical problems[8]. Although the remote assessment of language tasks allowed for less spontaneity than the classroom activity itself and was more exposed to possible plagiarism, it still proved important as an ice-breaking activity and as a stimulus to socialisation, more important than ever now that students were isolated in their own homes and had fewer opportunities for interaction with both the instructor and peers.

The two *in-class tests* were replaced by online quizzes (closed-book), released at a set time, which, as per university guidelines, were available for 24 hours and not timed. On the one hand, the traditional paper version was easily transformed into a quiz on Canvas, which offers numerous options for designing different

---

7. i-d-e-e (italiano digitale edizioni edilingua) is an educational platform created for teachers and students of Italian. It offers a blended learning environment that combines printed material and classroom lessons with different tools and digital learning material available on line.

8. During some trials, recording and uploading video files and sometimes even audio only to the Canvas page often caused the system to freeze, so you had to start over. In anticipation of the page being used by more than 100 users, we have simplified this assessment by asking students to enter only the written dialogue.

types of question, such as multiple choice, true/false, fill-in-the-blank, matching, cloze, essay, text. On the other hand, this format did not guarantee the same reliability as those tests conducted in the classroom and supervised by the tutor, and, overall, it did not seem to be the ideal solution.

The *final oral test* was initially uncertain but, given the excellent digital performance of the students in the Zoom breakout rooms, it was then decided to conduct it in pairs via real-time Zoom sessions. For this occasion only, the students were compelled to have their cameras turned on. This assessment evaluates not only the oral skills achieved in the course but also the ability to converse with a peer in an already experienced communicative situation and, if necessary, to improvise. A good number of students were prepared in this sense and took the exam as if they were in a real class, while the rest memorised a pre-written dialogue, or in some cases, they read it. In one case, with two students based in China, the Zoom connection was so bad that we opted for a group video call on WeChat as a backup plan.

The university decided that there were to be no on-site tests or examinations for the rest of Semester 1, and these were replaced by take-home assessment exercises conducted online, held during the examination period, and open for 24 hours in order to allow for technical challenges or time zone differences. According to these guidelines, the *final written exam* was redesigned as a Canvas quiz that tested the learning outcomes of the course. The 24 hour window also accommodated students who are usually granted additional time to complete a test or examination. For those with disability-related support needs that are not met by additional time alone – as happened for one student of *Italian 106-G* – an alternative solution was found. The final test was problematic in at least two respects. The first was that, despite the numerous announcements and invitations to check the Canvas course pages regularly for important information regarding revised assessment plans, a few students got the date wrong and failed to complete the test within 24 hours. Given the exceptional circumstances, they were still allowed to take the test. The second problem concerned academic integrity, because the online home delivery of the test exposed the risk of academic misconduct, use of online resources, and help received from third parties. Once again, in such a time of uncertainty and challenge for both students and instructors, we decided to value trust, fairness, respect, and responsibility, with the idea of completely redesigning the test in the future.

## 9. Discussion

From the first week of online teaching, we created a stimulating and non-stressful environment through the didactic use of grammar and cultural games, informal suggestions on how to practise the language outside the classroom in a fun way, and several cooperative, not graded, communicative tasks. The function of *ludic language teaching* in reinforcing cognitive, linguistic, social, and emotional skills (Balboni, 2008, p. 40) was not neglected in the virtual space of Zoom. On the contrary, it turned out to be an effective means of socialising remotely, reducing the stress of online performance, and ultimately improving language acquisition.

Awareness of the role of a rich, varied, and stimulating communicative input in promoting and developing competence in a foreign language, guided remote didactic communication not unlike what would have happened in the classroom. The social dynamics of the class group were also monitored and oriented by the instructor, who favoured the creation of exchange networks among the learners and encouraged different types of communication, beyond the sole transmission of information content (Vedovelli, 2002, p. 123).

The courses were delivered online until the end of the semester, which ended on a positive note with the country lifting the lockdown. A final social coffee was organised on June 12th, on the recently reopened campus. So, we were eventually able to see each other in person, wrap up the course, and prepare for the final test with a series of activities that we had not been able to do on Zoom. The final results certainly benefited from the decision of the university to scale up one grade step for all undergraduate and postgraduate final grades as a way to recognise the disruptions caused by COVID-19 to all students' study in

Semester 1. However, they were also a sign that everyone, tutors and students, had committed to getting through the end of such a challenging semester.

## 10. Conclusion

The experience gained during Semester 1 of 2020, marked by both urgency and flexibility, and the effort to make both course content and assignments available online, was not in vain. On the contrary, it proved effective for facing the second half of the academic year, when in-class lessons have alternated with online teaching periods following the changes in COVID-19 alert levels.

Several cues for future reflection and research clearly emerged. Designing blended courses that can be completely transformed into online resources if necessary will certainly be one of the directions to take. Moreover, the possibility of systematically collecting and examining student feedback, as well as the online teaching experiences of other language courses, will provide a more complete critical perspective and provide suggestions for improving the teaching approach.

Although New Zealand has become a global example of an effective response to the pandemic, managing to keep cases of community transmission to almost zero and a very low number of deaths due to COVID-19, the situation remains precarious and worrying. What the sudden and rapid transition to digital teaching and learning taught us is to be flexible and open to new approaches and technology. Above all we learned that cooperation, respect, and kindness are paramount when apprehending a new language and culture in an unpredictable and hostile world.

## 11. Acknowledgements

This chapter is dedicated to language instructors and Information Technology staff of the School of CLL of the University of Auckland.

## References

Balboni, P. (2008). *Fare educazione linguistica: attività didattiche per italiano L1 e L2, lingue straniere e lingue classiche.* UTET Università.

Marin, T., & Magnelli, S. (2010). *The Italian project: an Italian course for English speakers. 1a.: Beginners A1, student's book, workbook and video activities* (2nd ed.). Edilingua.

Vedovelli, M. (2002). *Guida all'italiano per stranieri: la prospettiva del quadro comune europeo per le lingue.* Carocci.

# Author index

**A**
Albuquerque-Costa, Heloísa vii, 125
Amirian, Zahra vii, 167
Atabekova, Anastasia vi, viii, 1, 217
Axelrod, Sarah Luehrman viii, 139

**B**
Belousov, Alexander viii, 217
Bordet, Geneviève viii, 235

**C**
Chen, Yunjie viii, 179
Chodzkienė, Loreta viii, 249
Critchley, Mark ix, 265

**F**
Ferraz, Daniel ix, 125
Freddi, Maria vi, ix, 1, 279

**G**
Gastaldi, María del Valle ix, 111
Ghaffari, Mahbod ix, 295
Grimaldi, Elsa ix, 111

**H**
Heider, Abeer ix, 155

**K**
Kashef, Yasser x, 33
Korostenskienė, Julija x, 249

**M**
Martelli, Barbara x, 371
Mayrink, Mônica Ferreira x, 125
Medvedeva, Olga xi, 249
Mentchen, Silke xi, 307

**N**
Nkemleke, Daniel A. xi, 49

**O**
Oliver del Olmo, Sonia xi, 321
Ope-Davies, Tunde xii, 63

**R**
Radić, Nebojša vi, xii, 1, 337
Rafiei, Adel xii, 167
Ross, Andrew F. xii, 139

**S**
Salem, Heba xii, 79
Schaffner, Sabina vii, xxi
Schmied, Josef vi, xii, 1, 353

**U**
Uwizeyimana, Valentin xii, 95

**Y**
Yastrebov, Oleg xiii, 217

**Z**
Zhang, Li xiii, 179
Zhang, Lianyue xiii, 199
Zheng, Hang xiii, 199

www.ingramcontent.com/pod-product-compliance
Lightning Source LLC
Chambersburg PA
CBHW021133230426
43667CB00005B/101